Climate Change, Disasters and People on the Move

World Trade Institute Advanced Studies

VOLUME 11

The titles published in this series are listed at *brill.com/wtia*

Climate Change, Disasters and People on the Move

Providing Protection under International Law

By

Aylin Yildiz Noorda

TUTA SUB AEGIDE PALLAS · 1683 ·

BRILL
NIJHOFF

LEIDEN | BOSTON

Open access publication of this book has been made possible by the Swiss National Science Foundation.

The Library of Congress Cataloging-in-Publication Data is available online at https://catalog.loc.gov
LC record available at https://lccn.loc.gov/2022914410

Typeface for the Latin, Greek, and Cyrillic scripts: "Brill". See and download: brill.com/brill-typeface.

ISSN 2405-9331
ISBN 978-90-04-52226-8 (hardback)
ISBN 978-90-04-52236-7 (e-book)

This book is printed on acid-free paper and produced in a sustainable manner.

For my mum Ayla and my nieces, Ava, Ivy and Etta

Contents

Acknowledgements

This book is the labour of love of my doctoral studies at the World Trade Institute (WTI), University of Bern. The research was made possible thanks to the generous support of the Swiss National Science Foundation (SNSF), extended to the research project titled 'Framing Environmental Degradation, Human Mobility and Human Development as a Matter of Common Concern' under research grant no. PP00P1163700.

I remain grateful to all who have supported me and inspired me in this journey. In particular, I wholeheartedly thank my research supervisors SNSF Prof. Elisa Fornalé and Dr. Nilüfer Oral. I also thank Prof. Thomas Cottier and Prof. Peter van den Bossche for their continuous support. Through their actions, they showed me what it means to be a caring and responsible scholar and they always went the extra mile to contribute to the development of my career.

My special thanks to the WTI family – the healthy critique provided during annual PhD colloquia by Prof. Manfred Elsig, Prof. Joseph Francois and Prof. Michael Hahn have been key driving forces of my research. I thank the WTI doctoral school, under the guidance of Prof. Doris Oberdabernig and Dr. Octavio Fernandez, for the institutional support. Many thanks to Dr. Rodrigo Polanco, Dr. Iryna Bogdanova, Dr. Zaker Ahmad, Dr. Alexander Beyleveld, Dr. Maria Vasquez Callo-Müller, Marine Roux, Valentino Desilvestro and Umid Yakubkhodjaev for their fellowship. Special thanks to Margrit Vetter, Karin Rosenberg, Sophia Thompson and Pablo Rahul Das for the wonderful administrative support.

I am especially indebted to Dr. Aydin Baris Yildirim – he not only supported me intellectually but has also become my mentor. I owe one of my best friends, Dr. Anqi Wang, a big 'thank you' – since the beginning of my doctoral studies, from gym sessions to hiking in the mountains, she has always been there for me. Special thanks to Prof. Ksenia Polonskaya, Prof. Basil Alexander, Prof. Ezgi Yildiz, Cagla Yazici, Najma Rehouma, Tim Zimmelmann and Prof. Walter Kälin for taking the time to grill me on my work and helping me to become a better scholar. I also thank Murat Hakan Öztürk and Prof. Eberhard Weber, who supported me enormously during my fieldwork research in Fiji.

My heartfelt thanks to my dear family and friends: Ayla Yildiz, Zihni Yildiz, Yavuz Yildiz, Luke Noorda, Mehmet Baysal, Feyzan Baysal, Ece Baysal, Naz Baysal, Ava Bona, Ivy Yildiz, Etta Yildiz, Dr. Nadine Yildiz, Dr. Ronya Özcelik, Dr. Helga Dizdari Hostettler, Dr. Merve Mutlu, Dr. Anil Aksöz, Elvin Yagan, Amalia Mkhitaryan, Barbara Dincer and Janaina Albuquerque. Your unconditional support has been invaluable. I love you all!

Finally, I would like to thank the editorial board of the World Trade Institute Advanced Studies series for their enourmous support and professionalism. I would also like to extend my gratitude to the SNSF for providing the necessary funding to allow for this work to be published open access.

Abbreviations and Acronyms

2030 Agenda	2030 Agenda for Sustainable Development
ARSIWA	Articles on the Responsibility of States for Internationally Wrongful Acts
CBD	Convention on Biological Diversity
CBDR-RC	Common but Differentiated Responsibilities and Respective Capabilities
CEDAW	Convention on the Elimination of Discrimination Against Women
CEDAWCom	Committee on the Elimination of Discrimination Against Women
CESCRCom	Committee on Economic, Social and Cultural Rights
CRC	Convention on the Rights of the Child
CRCom	Committee on the Rights of the Child
CRRF	Comprehensive Refugee Response Framework
CRPD	Convention on the Rights of Persons with Disabilities
CRPDCom	Committee on the Rights of the Persons with Disabilities
COP	Conference of the Parties
ECOSOC	United Nations Economic and Social Council
Excom WIM	Executive Committee of the Warsaw International Mechanism for Loss and Damage under the United Nations Framework Convention on Climate Change
GATS	General Agreement on Trade in Services
GATT	General Agreement on Tariffs and Trade
GHG	Greenhouse Gas
GMG	Global Migration Group
Global Compact for Migration	Global Compact for Safe, Orderly, and Regular Migration
Global Commission	The Global Commission on International Migration
HMDCC	Human mobility in the context of disasters and climate change
HLD	United Nations High-Level Dialogue on International Migration and Development
IASC	Inter-Agency Standing Committee
IAMM	International Agenda for Migration Management
ICRC	International Committee of the Red Cross
ICCPR	International Covenant on Civil and Political Rights

ICESCR	International Covenant on Economic, Social and Cultural Rights
ICRMW	International Convention on the Protection of the Rights of All Migrant Workers and Members of their Families
ICMRWCom	Committee on the Protection of the Rights of All Migrant Workers and Members of their Families
ICJ	International Court of Justice
IDM	International Dialogue on Migration
IDMC	Internal Displacement Monitoring Centre
IDP(s)	Internally Displaced Person(s)
ILA	International Law Association
ILC	International Law Commission
ILO	International Labour Organisation
ILS	International Labour Standards
IPCC	Intergovernmental Panel on Climate Change
IHL	International Humanitarian Law
IHRL	International Human Rights Law
IOM	International Organisation for Migration
ITLOS	International Tribunal of the Law of the Sea
IPCC	Intergovernmental Panel on Climate Change
LDC	Least-Developed Country
MFN	Most-Favoured-Nation
MICIC	Migrants in Countries of Crisis Initiative
NDC(s)	Nationally Determined Commitment(s)
New York Declaration	New York Declaration for Refugees and Migrants
OCHA	United Nations Office for the Coordination of Humanitarian Affairs
OECD	Organisation for Economic Co-operation and Development
OHCHR	Office of the United Nations High Commissioner for Human Rights
OSCE	Organisation for Security and Cooperation in Europe
PACER Plus	Pacific Agreement on Closer Economic Relations Plus
PDD	Platform on Disaster Displacement
PTA	Preferential Trade Agreement
PIF	Pacific Islands Forum
PIS	Pacific Island States
PMDCC	Persons mobile in the context of disasters and climate change
Refugee Convention	Convention Relating to the Status of Refugees
SDG(s)	Sustainable Development Goal(s)

TFD	Task Force on Displacement of the Executive Committee of the Warsaw International Mechanism for Loss and Damage under the United Nations Framework Convention on Climate Change
UDHR	Universal Declaration of Human Rights
UN	United Nations
UNCLOS	United Nations Convention on the Law of the Sea
UNCCD	United Nations Convention to Combat Desertification in Those Countries Experiencing Serious Drought and/or Desertification, Particularly in Africa
UNDRR	United Nations Office for Disaster Risk Reduction
UNEP	United Nations Environment Programme
UNESCO	United Nations Educational, Scientific and Cultural Organisation
UNFCCC	United Nations Framework Convention on Climate Change
UNITAR	United Nations Institute for Training and Research
UNSC	United Nations Security Council
UNGA	United Nations General Assembly
UK	United Kingdom
US	United States of America
USD	United States Dollar
UNHRC	United Nations Human Rights Council
UNHCR	United Nations High Commissioner for Refugees
UNCHR	United Nations Commission on Human Rights
UNHRCom	United Nations Human Rights Committee
UNGA	United Nations General Assembly
UNSC	United Nations Security Council
UPR	Universal Periodic Review
VCLT	Vienna Convention on the Law of Treaties
WIM	Warsaw International Mechanism for Loss and Damage under the United Nations Framework Convention on Climate Change
WTO	World Trade Organisation

Table of Materials

Table of Treaties and Related Instruments

Additional Protocol to the Provisional Arrangement and to the Convention concerning the Status of Refugees coming from Germany (14 September 1939) 198 LNTS 141 (No 4634).

Annex 1B on Movement of Natural Person Supplying Services under the Agreement, General Agreement on Trade in Services 1994 (Marrakesh Agreement Establishing the World Trade Organization), 1869 UNTS 183; 33 ILM 1167 (1994).

Arrangement concerning the Extension to Other Categories of Refugees Certain Measures taken in Favour of Russian and Armenian Refugees (30 June 1928) 89 LNTS 63 (No 2006).

Arrangement relating to the Issue of Identity Certificates to Russian and Armenian Refugees, Supplementing and Amending the Previous Arrangements (12 May 1926) 89 LNTS 47 (No 2004).

Arrangement Relating to the Legal Status of Russian and Armenian Refugees (30 June 1928) 89 LNTS 53 (No 2005).

Arrangement with regard to the Issue of Certificates of Identity to Russian Refugees (5 July 1922) 13 LNTS 238 (No 355).

Agreement concerning the Functions of the Representatives of the League of Nations' High Commissioner for Refugees (30 June 1928) 93 LNTS 377 (No 2126).

Colloquium on the International Protection of Refugees in Central America, Mexico and Panama, Cartagena Declaration on Refugees (22 November 1984) (Cartagena Declaration).

Compact of Free Association Act, Pub. L. No. 99-239, 1985 U.S.C.C.A.N (99 Stat.1770).

Compact of Free Association Amendments Act of 2003, Pub. L. No 108-188, § 331 (a), 117 Stat. 2720, 2781.

Compilation prepared by the Office of the United Nations High Commissioner for Human Rights in accordance with paragraph 15(b) of the annex to Human Rights Council resolution 5/1 and paragraph 5 of the annex to Council resolution 16/21, UN HRC, 18th sess, Working Group on the Universal Periodic Review, UN Doc A/HRC/WG.6/18/VUT/2 (27 January-7 February 2014, adopted 6 November 2013).

Convention against Torture and Other Cruel, Inhuman or Degrading Treatment or Punishment (adopted 10 December 1984, entry into force 16 June 1987) 1465 UNTS 85.

Convention relating to the International Status of Refugees (30 June 1933) 159 LNTS 199 (No 3663).

Convention concerning the Status of Refugees coming from Germany (10 February 1938) 19 LNTS 59 (NO 4461).

Convention on the Elimination of All Forms of Discrimination against Women (adopted 18 December 1976, entry into force 3 September 1981).

Convention on the Rights of the Child (adopted 20 November 1989, entry into force 2 September 1990) 1577 UNTS 3.

General Agreement on Trade in Services 1994 (Marrakesh Agreement Establishing the World Trade Organization, Annex 1B, 1869 UNTS 183; 33 ILM 1167 (1994)).

International Labour Organisation Convention No. 87 concerning Freedom of Association and Protection of the Right to Organise (adopted 9 July 1948, entered into force 4 July 1950) 68 UNTS 17.

International Labour Organisation Convention No. 97 concerning Migration for Employment (Revised) (entered into force 22 January 1952).

International Labour Organisation Convention No. 111 concerning Discrimination (Employment and Occupation) (adopted 25 June 1958, entered into force 15 June 1960) 362 UNTS 31.

International Labour Organisation Convention No. 118 concerning Equality of Treatment (Social Security) (adopted 28 June 1962) 7238 UNTS 940.

International Labour Organisation Convention No 138: Minimum Age Convention (1973).

International Labour Organisation Convention No. 143 concerning Migrant Workers (Supplementary Provisions).

International Labour Organisation Convention No 3: Maternity Protection Convention (1919).

International Labour Organisation Convention No 29: Forced Labour Convention (1930).

International Covenant on Civil and Political Rights (adopted 16 December 1966, entered into force 23 March 1976) 999 UNTS 171.

International Convention for the Protection of All Persons From Enforced Disappearance (adopted 20 December 2006, entered into force 23 December 2010) 2716 UNTS 3.

International Convention on the Elimination of All Forms of Racial Discrimination (adopted 7 March 1966, entry into force 4 January 1969) 660 UNTS 195.

International Covenant on Economic, Social and Cultural Rights (adopted 16 December 1966, entry into force 3 January 1976).

International Convention on Protection of the Rights of All Migrant Workers and Members of Their Families (adopted 18 December 1990, entry into force 1 July 2003).

Maleì Declaration on the Human Dimension of Global Climate Change' (14 November 2007) 1 <www.ciel.org/Publications/Male_Declaration_Nov07.pdf>.

Marrakesh Agreement Establishing the World Trade Organization (adopted 15 April 1994, entered into force 1 January 1995) 1867 UNTS Annex 3.

Organisation of African Unity, Convention Governing the Specific Aspects of Refugee Problems in Africa (10 September 1969) 1001 UNTS 45.

Pacific Agreement on Closer Economic Relations Plus (signed 14 June 2017, entered into force 13 December 2020) <https://pacerplus.org>.

Pacific Islands Forum, Kainaki II Declaration for Urgent Climate Change Now, 50th sess, Forum Communiqué Annex A (13-16 August 2019) <https://www.forumsec.org/wp-content/uploads/2019/08/50th-Pacific-Islands-Forum-Communique.pdf>.

Pacific Islands Forum, Boe Declaration on Regional Security (5 September 2018) <https://www.forumsec.org/2018/09/05/boe-declaration-on-regional-security/> accessed 8 June 2021.

Pacific Islands Forum, Niue Declaration on Climate Change, 39th session, Forum Communiqué Annex B (19-20 August 2008).

Pacific Island Parliamentarians, The Moana Declaration, Outcome Statement of Pacific Parliamentarians for Population and Development (13-15 August 2013).

Plan for the Issue of a Certificate of Identity to Armenian Refugees (31 May 1924) LN Doc CL 72 (a).

Protocol Relating to the Status of Refugees (adopted 31 January 1967, entered into force 4 October 1967) 606 UNTS 267.

Suva Declaration on Climate Change (Issued at the Third Pacific Islands Development Forum Leaders' Summit, 2-4 September 2015, Grand Pacific Hotel, Suva, Fiji) <http://greenbusiness.solutions/wp-content/uploads/2017/08/Suva-declaration-on-climate-change.pdf>.

Tampere Convention on the Provision of Telecommunication Resources for Disaster Mitigation and Relief Operations (adopted 18 June 1998, entered into force 8 January 2005) 2296 UNTS 5.

The Sendai Framework for Disaster Risk Reduction (23 June 2015) UN Doc. A/RES/ 69/283.

The Toledo Initiative on Environmental Refugees and Ecological Restoration, Toledo, Spain (9-10 July 2004).

Treaty on Principles Governing Activities of States in the Exploration and Use of Outer Space, Including the Moon and Other Celestial Bodies (adopted 27 January 1967, entered into force 10 October 1967) 610 UNTS 205.

United Nations Convention to Combat Desertification in those Countries Experiencing Serious Drought and/or Desertification, Particularly in Africa (adopted 14 October 1994, entry into force 26 December 1996) 1954 UNTS 3 (UNCCCD) preamble.

United Nations Convention on the Law of the Sea (adopted 10 December 1982, entered into force 16 November 1994) 1833 UNTS 396.

Universal Declaration of Human Rights (adopted 10 December 1948) UNGA Res 217 A(III) preamble.

United Nations Framework Convention on Climate Change (adopted 9 May 1992, entered into force 21 March 1994) 1771 UNTS 108 <https://treaties.un.org/Pages/ViewDetailsIII.aspx?src=IND&mtdsg_no=XXVII-7&chapter=27&Temp=mtdsg3& clang=_en>.

Vienna Convention on Diplomatic Relations (adopted 18 April 1961, entered into force 24 April 1964) 596 UNTS 261.

Table of Other Primary Legal Sources (All Online Materials Last Accessed 6 April 2022)

AF (Kiribati) [2013] NZIPT 800413 (25 June 2013).

Ahmadou Sadio Diallo (Republic of Guinea v. Democratic Republic of the Congo) (Preliminary Objections) [2007] ICJ Rep 582, 599.

Applicant A v Minister for Immigration and Ethnic Affairs [1997] HCA 4, [1997] 190 CLR 225.

Application of the Convention on the Prevention and Punishment of the Crime of Genocide (The Gambia v. Myanmar) (Provisional Measures) [2020] ICJ (Separate Opinion of Vice-President Xue).

Canada (Attorney General) v Ward [1993] 2 SCR 689.

Case Concerning the Barcelona Traction, Light and Power Company, Limited (Belgium v France) [1970] ICJ.

Case Concerning Gabcikovo-Nagymaros Project (Hungary/Slovakia) Judgment [1997] ICJ Rep. 7, Separate opinion of Vice-President Weeramantry.

Case Concerning Application of the Convention on the Prevention and Punishment of the Crime of Genocide (Croatia v. Serbia) [1996] ICJ Rep 616.

Committee on the Elimination of Discrimination Against Women, Committee on Economic, Social and Cultural Rights, Committee on the Protection of the Rights of All Migrant Workers and Members of their Families, Committee on the Rights of the Child, and Committee on the Rights of Persons with Disabilities, 'Joint Statement on "Human Rights and Climate Change"' (16 September 2019) <https://www.ohchr.org/EN/NewsEvents/Pages/DisplayNews.aspx?NewsID=24998>.

Committee on Economic, Social and Cultural Rights, 'Climate Change and the International Covenant on Economic, Social and Cultural Rights' (Statement, 8 October 2018) <https://www.ohchr.org/en/NewsEvents/Pages/DisplayNews.aspx?NewsID=23691&LangID=E> accessed 29 May 2021.

Communication to the Committee on the Rights of the Child, *In the case of Chiara Sacchi and others v. Argentina, Brazil, France, Germany and Turkey* (23 September 2019) <https://earthjustice.org/sites/default/files/files/2019.09.23-crc-communication-sacchi-et-al-v.-argentina-et-al-redacted.pdf>.

Conference of the Parties to the United Nations Framework Convention on Climate Change, 'Report of the Conference of the Parties on its Twenty-First Session', 21st sess, (29 January 2016) UN Doc FCCC/CP/2015/10/Add. 1 <https://www.un.org/en/development/desa/population>.

Conference of the Parties to the United Nations Framework Convention on Climate Change, 'Report of the Conference of the Parties on its Nineteenth Session' (19th sess, 31 January 2014) UN Doc FCCC/CP/2013/10/Add. 1 <https://unfccc.int/resource/docs/2013/cop19/eng/10a01.pdf>.

Conference of the Parties to the United Nations Framework Convention on Climate Change, Decision 1/CP.16, 'Report of the Conference of the Parties on its sixteenth session, held in Cancun from 29 November to 10 December 2010, Part Two: Action taken by the Conference of the Parties at its sixteenth session' (15 March 2011) UN Doc FCCC/CP/2010/7/Add.1.

Draft Global Pact for the Environment (Preliminary Draft of the Group of Experts, 2017).

ECOSOC, 'Economic, Social and Cultural Rights: Housing and property restitution in the context of return of refugees and internally displaced persons, Final Report of the Special Rapporteur Paulo Sergio Pinheiro, Principles on housing and property restitution for refugees and displaced persons' (28 June 2005) UN Doc E/CN.4/Sub.2/2005/17.

Government of Fiji, Planned Relocation Guidelines, Fiji, Government of Fiji, 2018 <https://www.refworld.org/do cid/5c3c92204.html>.

Government of Fiji, Displacement Guidelines in the Context of Climate Change and Disasters, Fiji, Government of Fiji, 2019.

Guiding Principles on Internal Displacement, (22 July 1998) ADM 1.1, PRL 12.1, PR00/98/109 <https://www.refworld.org/docid/3c3da07f7.html>.

Hedley Byrne & Co. Ltd. v. Heller & Partners Ltd. [1964] A.C. 465, 525.

Horvath v Secretary of State for the Home Department [2000] UKHL 37, [2001] AC 489.

International Labour Conference, Report of the Committee of Experts on the Application of Conventions and Recommendations (articles 19, 22, and 35 of the Constitution), Report III (Part 1B), 101st session 2012, para 776.

International Labour Organisation Recommendation R86: Migration for Employment Recommendation (Revised).

International Labour Organisation Recommendation R151: Migrant Workers Recommendation.

International Labour Organisation, 'Decent work for sustainable development, Director-General's Report I (A)' (2007).

International Labour Organisation Governing Body, '327th report of the Committee on the Freedom of Association' (ILO 2002).

International Labour Organisation, 'ILO Activities for environment and the world of work' (Tripartite Advisory Meeting on Environment and the World of Work, ILO, 2–4 November 1992).

International Law Association, 'International Law and Sea Level Rise, Sydney Conference Report' (2018).

International Law Association, Committee on International Law and Sea Level Rise, Resolution 6/2018.

International Law Association, Committee on International Law and Sea Level Rise, 'Sydney Declaration of Principles on the Protection of Persons Displaced in the context of Sea Level Rise' (2018) Resolution 6/2018.

International Law Commission, Report of the International Law Commission: Sixty Eighth Session (2 May 10 June and 4 July 12 August 2016), UN Doc. A/71/10, 2016 (DAS Report), pp. 13 73, available at <http:/ilegal .un.org/ilc/reports/2016/english/a_71-10.pdf>.

International Law Commission, 'Draft articles on diplomatic protection' (2006) UN Doc A/61/10.

International Law Commission, 'Draft Articles on the Protection of Persons in the Event of Disasters, with Commentaries' (2016) <https://www.refworld .org/docid/5f64dc3c4.html>.

International Law Commission, 'Guiding Principles applicable to unilateral declarations of States capable of creating legal obligations, with commentaries thereto' (2006) UN Doc A/61/10.

International Law Commission, 'Report on the work of the seventieth session' (30 April-1 June and 2 July–10 August 2018) UN Doc A/73/10.

International Law Commission, 'Sea Level Rise in Relation to International Law: First Issues Paper by Bogdan Aurescu and Nilüfer Oral, Co-Chairs of the Study Group on Sea-level Rise in Relation to International Law' (28 February 2020) UN Doc A/CN.4/740.

Ioane Teitiota v. New Zealand (2020) UNHRCom UN Doc CCPR/C/127/D/2928/2016.

LaGrand Case (Germany v United States of America) (Judgment) [2001] ICJ.

Legal Consequences of the Separation of the Chagos Archipelago from Mauritius (Advisory Opinion) [2019] ICJ 169.

L.F.H. Neer and Pauline Neer (USA) v United Mexican States [1926] 4 R.I.A.A. 60.

Matter of Acosta, United States Board of Immigration Appeals (23 November 2010) A-24159781.

Mavrommatis Palestine Concessions (Greece v Great Britain) (Judgement) [1924] PCIJ Series A no 2.

Meeting of the Task Force on Displacement (TFD4) 'Summary' (7-9 September 2020) <https://unfccc.int/sites/default/files/resource/Summary_TFD4_update%20fo r%20Excom%2012.pdf>.

Office of the High Commissioner for Human Rights, 'Report on the Relationship Between Climate Change and Human Rights' UN Doc. A/HRC/10/61, 15 Jan. 2009, 20–41.

Office of the High Commissioner for Human Rights, 'The principle of non-refoulement under international human rights law' <https://www.ohchr.org/Documents/Issues/Migration/GlobalCompactMigration/ThePrincipleNon-RefoulementUnderInternationalHumanRightsLaw.pdf>.

Office of the High Commissioner for Human Rights, 'Views adopted by the Committee under article 5(4) of the Optional Protocol, concerning communication No. 2728/2016' (7 January 2020) ICCPR/C/127/D/2728/2016.

Office of the High Commissioner for Human Rights, 'Views adopted by the Committee under article 5(4) of the Optional Protocol, concerning communication No. 2728/2016' (7 January 2020) ICCPR/C/127/D/2728/2016.

Pacific Small Island Developing States, 'Views on the Possible Security Implications of Climate Change to be included in the report of the Secretary-General to the 64th Session of the United Nations General Assembly' (2009) <https://www.un.org/esa/dsd/resources/res_pdfs/ga-64/cc-inputs/PSIDS_CCIS.pdf>.

Report of the Special Representative of the Secretary-General on Migration (28 December 2016) UN Doc. A/71/728 (Sutherland Report).

Report of the Secretary-General, 'In Safety and dignity: addressing large movements of refugees and migrants' (2016) UN Doc A/70/59.

Republic of the Maldives Ministry of Environment, Energy and Water, 'Report on the First Meeting on Protocol on Environmental Refugees: Recognition of Environmental Refugees in the 1951 Convention and 1967 Protocol Relating to the Status of Refugees' (Male, Maldives, 14–15 August 2006).

Secretariat to the International Convention to Combat Desertification, 'The future strategic framework of the Convention: Draft decision submitted by the Chair of the Committee of the Whole' (14 September 2017) ICCD/COP(13)/L.18 <https://www.unccd.int/sites/default/files/inline-files/ICCD_COP%2813%29_L.18-1716078E_0.pdf> accessed 10 November 2020.

Sixth Committee (Legal) – 75th session, 'Protection of persons in the event of disasters (Agenda Item 89)' (UN, 2020) <https://www.un.org/en/ga/sixth/75/disasters.shtml>.

South West Africa, Ethiopia v South Africa [1961] ICJ Rep 319.

Statement by Sweden on behalf of the Nordic Countries (Denmark, Finland, Iceland, Norway and Sweden) (23 October 2020) <https://www.un.org/en/ga/sixth/75/pdfs/statements/disasters/17mtg_nordic.pdf>.

Statement by Singapore (11 November 2020) <https://www.un.org/en/ga/sixth/75/pdfs/statements/disasters/17mtg_singapore.pdf>.

Statement of the Republic of the Philippines (11 November 2020) <https://www.un.org/en/ga/sixth/75/pdfs/statements/disasters/17mtg_philippines.pdf>.

Statement by Brazil (13 November 2020) <https://www.un.org/en/ga/sixth/75/pdfs/statements/disasters/18mtg_brazil.pdf>.

Statement by Brunei Darussalam (October 2020) <https://www.un.org/en/ga/sixth/75/pdfs/statements/disasters/17mtg_brunei.pdf>.

Statement by Portugal <https://www.un.org/en/ga/sixth/75/pdfs/statements/disasters/17mtg_portugal.pdf>.

Statement by Nigeria (23 October 2020) <https://www.un.org/en/ga/sixth/75/pdfs/statements/disasters/18mtg_nigeria.pdf>.

Statement by Jamaica (23 October 2020) <https://www.un.org/en/ga/sixth/75/pdfs/statements/disasters/17mtg_jamaica.pdf>.

Statement by Tonga (27 October 2020) <https://www.un.org/en/ga/sixth/75/pdfs/statements/disasters/18mtg_tonga.pdf>.

Statement by Japan <https://www.un.org/en/ga/sixth/75/pdfs/statements/disasters/17mtg_japan.pdf>.

Statement by Cuba (11 November 2020) <https://www.un.org/en/ga/sixth/75/pdfs/statements/disasters/17mtg_cuba_e.pdf>.

Statement by Viet Nam <https://www.un.org/en/ga/sixth/75/pdfs/statements/disasters/18mtg_vietnam.pdf>.

Statement by Jamaica (23 October 2020) <https://www.un.org/en/ga/sixth/75/pdfs/statements/disasters/17mtg_jamaica.pdf>.

Statement by Tonga (27 October 2020) <https://www.un.org/en/ga/sixth/75/pdfs/statements/disasters/18mtg_tonga.pdf>.

Statement by Japan <https://www.un.org/en/ga/sixth/75/pdfs/statements/disasters/17mtg_japan.pdf>.

Statement by Cuba (11 November 2020) <https://www.un.org/en/ga/sixth/75/pdfs/statements/disasters/17mtg_cuba_e.pdf>.

Statement by Viet Nam <https://www.un.org/en/ga/sixth/75/pdfs/statements/disasters/18mtg_vietnam.pdf>.

Statement by the United States of America (27 October 2020) <https://www.un.org/en/ga/sixth/75/pdfs/statements/disasters/18mtg_us.pdf>.

Statement by Malaysia (11 November 2020) <https://www.un.org/en/ga/sixth/75/pdfs/statements/disasters/17mtg_malaysia.pdf>.

Statement by Israel (14 October 2020) <https://www.un.org/en/ga/sixth/75/pdfs/statements/disasters/18mtg_israel.pdf>.

Statement by Sierre Leone (11 November 2020) <https://www.un.org/en/ga/sixth/75/pdfs/statements/disasters/17mtg_sierraleone.pdf>.

Statement by Switzerland (11 November 2020) <https://www.un.org/en/ga/sixth/75/pdfs/statements/disasters/17mtg_switzerland.pdf>.

Study Group on the Fragmentation of International Law, Report on the Fragmentation of International Law: Difficulties Arising From the Diversification and Expansion of International Law UN Doc. A/CN.4/L.682 (April 13, 2006) (finalised by Martti Koskenniemi).

Summary prepared by the Office of the United Nations High Commissioner for Human Rights in accordance with paragraph 15(c) of the annex to Human Rights Council resolution 5/1 and paragraph 5 of the annex to Council resolution 16/21 Fiji, UN HRC, 20th sess, Working Group on the Universal Periodic Review, UN Doc A/HRC/WG.6/20/FJI/3 (18 July 2014, adopted 27 October–7 November 2014).

The Nansen Initiative, Agenda for the Protection of Cross-Border Displaced Persons in the Context of Disasters and Climate Change <https://disasterdisplacement.org/wp-content/uploads/2014/08/EN_Protection_Agenda_Volume_I_-low_res.pdf>.

The SS 'Wimbledon', United Kingdom and ors v Germany (Judgment) (1923) PCIJ Series A no 1, ICGJ 235 (PCIJ 1923), 17th August 1923, League of Nations.

United Nations Convention on Combatting Desertification, 'Decision 28/COP.13. The positive role that measures taken under the Convention can play to address desertification/land degradation and drought as one of the drivers that causes migration' (15 September 2017) UN Doc ICCD/COP(13)/21/Add.1.

United Nations Human Rights Council Res 42/21 'Human rights and climate change' (12 July 2019).

United Nations Human Rights Council Res 46/7 'Human rights and the environment' (30 March 2021) UN Doc A/HRC/RES/46/7.

United Nations Human Rights Council Res 38/4 'Human rights and climate change' (5 July 2018) UN Doc A/HRC/RES/38/4.

United Nations Human Rights Council Res 35/20, 'Human Rights and climate change' (22 June 2017) UN Doc A/HRC/RES/35/20.

United Nations Human Rights Council Res 32/33, 'Human rights and climate change' (18 July 2016) UN Doc A/HRC/RES/32/33.

United Nations Human Rights Council Res 29/ 15, 'Human rights and climate change' (22 July 2015) UN Doc A/HRC/RES/29/15.

United Nations Human Rights Council Res 26/27, 'Human rights and climate change' (15 July 2014) UN Doc A/HRC/RES/26/27.

United Nations Human Rights Council Res 18/22, 'Human rights and climate change' (17 October 2011) UN Doc A/HRC/RES/18/22.

United Nations Human Rights Council Res 10/4 'Human rights and climate change' (25 March 2009) UN Doc A/HRC/RES/10/4.

United Nations Human Rights Council Res 7/23, 'Human rights and climate change' (28 March 2008) UN Doc A/HRC/RES/7/23.

United Nations Human Rights Council Res 16/11, 'Human rights and the environment' (12 April 2011) UN Doc A/HRC/RES/16/11.

United Nations Human Rights Council Res 19/10, 'Human rights and the environment' (19 April 2012) UN Doc A/HRC/RES/19/10.

United Nations Human Rights Council Res 25/21, 'Human rights and the environment' (15 April 2014) UN Doc A/HRC/RES/25/21.

United Nations Human Rights Council Res 28/11, 'Human rights and the environment' (7 April 2015) UN Doc A/HRC/RES/28/11.

United Nations Human Rights Council Res 31/8, 'Human rights and the environment' (22 April 2016) UN Doc A/HRC/RES/21/8.

United Nations Human Rights Council Res 34/20, 'Human rights and the environment' (6 April 2017) UN Doc A/HRC/RES/34/20.

United Nations Human Rights Council Res 37/8, 'Human rights and the environment' (9 April 2018) UN Doc A/HRC/RES/37/8.

United Nations Human Rights Council Res 41/15, 'Mandate of the Special Rapporteur on the human rights of internally displaced persons' (19 July 2019) UN Doc A/HRC/RES/41/15.

United Nations Human Rights Council, 'The slow onset effects of climate change and human rights protection for cross-border migrants' (22 March 2018) A/HRC/37/CRP.4.

United Nations Human Rights Council, 'Report of the Special Rapporteur on Human Rights and the Environment on the Issue of Human Rights Obligations relating to the Enjoyment of a Safe, Clean, Healthy and Sustainable Environment' (1 February 2016) UN Doc A/HRC/31/52, para 33.

United Nations Human Rights Council Res 32/33 'Human Rights and climate change' (1 July 2016) UNHRC 32nd Session Agenda item 3.

United Nations Human Rights Council, 'Analytical study on the promotion and protection of the rights of older persons in the context of climate change, Report of the Office of the United Nations High Commissioner for Human Rights' (30 April 2021) UN Doc A/HRC/47/46.

United Nations Human Rights Committee, 'CCPR General Comment No:20 Article 7' (Prohibition of Torture, or other Cruel, Inhuman or Degrading Treatment or Punishment) (10 March 1992) <https://www.refworld.org/docid/453883fb0.html>.

United Nations Human Rights Committee, 'General Comment No. 36, Article 6 (Right to Life)' (3 September 2019) UN Doc CCPR/C/GC/36.

United Nations Human Rights Council Res 7/23, 'Human rights and climate change' (28 March 2008) UN Doc A/HRC/RES/7/23.

United Nations Human Rights Council Res 44/7, 'Human rights and climate change' (16 July 2020) UN Doc A/HRC/RES/44/7.

United Nations General Assembly Res 46/182 (19 December 1991) 78th Plenary Meeting; OCHA, 'What is the cluster approach?' <https://www.humanitarianresponse.info/en/coordination/clusters/what-cluster-approach>.

United Nations General Assembly Res 302 (IV) (1949).

United Nations General Assembly Res 55/215 (2000) GAOR 55th Session.

United Nations General Assembly Res 55/2 (18 September 2000) (Millennium Declaration).

United Nations General Assembly Res 55/235 (30 January 2001).

United Nations General Assembly Res 57/144 (26 February 2003) (Follow-up to the outcome of the Millennium Summit).

United Nations General Assembly Res 73/254 (2018) GAOR 73rd Session.

United Nations General Assembly Res 70/L.34 (22 December 2015).

United Nations General Assembly Res 71/141 'Protection of persons in the event of disasters' (19 December 2016).

United Nations General Assembly Res 71/280 (17 April 2017) UN Doc A/RES/71/280.

United Nations General Assembly Res 70/290 (19 July 2016) GAOR 70th Session.

United Nations General Assembly Res 70/1 Transforming our world: the 2030 Agenda for Sustainable Development (21 October 2015) UN Doc A/RES/70/1, targets 8.7 and 8.8.

United Nations General Assembly, 'Annotated preliminary list of items to be included in the provisional agenda of the seventy-fifth regular session of the General Assembly' (15 June 2020) UN Doc A/75/100, para 89.

United Nations General Assembly, 'Summary record of the 31st meeting' Sixth Committee (31 January 2019) UN Doc A/C.6/73/SR.31.

United Nations General Assembly 'Global Compact on Refugees', Report of the UNHCR (2018) UN Doc A/73/12 (Global Compact on Refugees).

United Nations General Assembly 'Global Compact for Safe, Orderly and Regular Migration' (2019) UN Doc A/RES/73/195 (Global Compact for Migration).

United Nations General Assembly, 'New York Declaration for Refugees and Migrants' (13 September 2016) GAOR 71st Session UN Doc A/71/L.1 (New York Declaration).

United Nations General Assembly, 'Human Rights of Internally Displaced Persons' GAOR 75th Session, Item 72 (b) of the provisional agenda, Promotion and protection of human rights: human rights questions, including alternative approaches for improving the effective enjoyment of human rights and fundamental freedoms, UN Doc A/75/207.

World Trade Organisation Document S/C/W/75; WTO, 'Background note on Mode 4 Measurement' Meeting of the United Nations Technical Subgroup on Movement of Persons -Mode 4 (New York, 22–24 February 2006)<https://unstats.un.org/unsd/tradeserv/TFSITS/TSGMode4/tsg3-feb06/tsg0602-16.pdf>.

World Trade Organisation, 'Presence of Natural Persons (Move 4) Background Note by the Secretariat' (8 December 1998) S/C/W/75.

World Trade Organisation, 'Amendment of the Trade Policy Review Mechanism' (27 July 2017) WT/L/1014.

Introduction

One of the most pressing and complex issues of our time is understanding and addressing the impact of disasters and climate change on human mobility.[1] Simply put, changes in the global climate amplify the risk of disasters, both in their intensity and in their frequency.[2] As air and water temperatures increase, sea levels are rising, precipitation is heavier, droughts and wildfire seasons are longer, storms are supercharged and wind speeds are greater.[3] In this context, people are on the move.[4] This movement is itself arranged along a multiaxial continuum: from internal to cross-border, from temporary to permanent and from planned to unplanned.[5] Recently, the peril that is already evident

1 This book uses 'human mobility' as an umbrella term to refer mainly to three types of movement: migration (which refers generally to voluntary movement), displacement (which refers generally to forced movement), and planned relocation (which describes the settlement of persons in a new location generally by States). See Jane McAdam and others, 'International Law and Sea-Level Rise: Forced Migration and Human Rights' (FNI Report 1/2016), 20; UNFCCC WIM Task Force on Displacement, 'Report of the Task Force on Displacement' (17 September 2018) <https://unfccc.int/sites/default/files/resource/2018_TFD_report_17_Sep.pdf> accessed 6 April 2022, 9.

2 United Nations Office for Disaster Risk Reduction (UNDRR) defines disasters as 'a serious disruption of the functioning of a community or a society at any scale due to hazardous events interacting with conditions of exposure, vulnerability and capacity, leading to one or more of the following: human, material, economic and environmental losses and impacts'. The Intergovernmental Panel on Climate Change (IPCC) defines climate change as a 'change in the state of the climate chat can be identified (e.g., by using statistical tests) by changes in the mean and/or the variability of its properties and that persists for an extended period, typically decades or longer'. See UNDRR, 'Disaster' (UNDRR 2022) <https://www.undrr.org/terminology/disaster> accessed 6 April 2022; IPCC, 'Annex I: Glossary. Global Warming of 1.5°C' (IPCC 2018).

3 UNFCCC WIM Task Force on Displacement and IOM, 'Mapping Human Mobility and Climate Change in Relevant National Policies and Institutional Frameworks' (Activity I.1, 2018); UNHRC, 'The slow onset effects of climate change and human rights protection for cross-border migrants' (22 March 2018) A/HRC/37/CRP.4.; IPCC 'Policymakers' summary of the potential impacts of climate change. Report from Working Group II to IPCC' (1990) 20.

4 IPCC, 'Working Group II Sixth Assessment Report' (IPCC 2022), 1342–1351.

5 In 2020 alone, a series of devastating disasters internally displaced 30.7 million people globally. See IDMC, 'Global Report on Internal Displacement 2021' (IDMC 2021). Furthermore, by 2050, the World Bank Group predicts that three regions in the world, namely the Sub-Saharan Africa, South Asia and Latin America, could see more than 140 million internal climate migrants. The report defines internal climate migration as 'longer-term change of habitual place of residence where slow-onset climate change affects the drivers of movement, on a continuum between voluntary and more forced movement' within countries. See Kumari Rigaud and others, 'Groundswell: Preparing for Internal Climate Migration'

 | DOI:10.1163/9789004522367_002

was echoed by the UN Secretary-General, Antonio Guterres, who underscored that 'unless we are able to defeat climate change, in 2050, the research has forecasted that 300 million people will be flooded by sea water in the world'.[6] According to the World Bank's latest Groundswell report, as many as 216 million people could move within their own countries across six regions of the world due to slow-onset climate change impacts by 2050.[7]

There is an urgent need to act globally in order to prevent future displacement, as well as to simultaneously plan for migration and planned relocation.[8] The UN General Assembly made this point loudly and clearly in 2018, by adopting the Global Compact for Migration and the Global Compact on Refugees, with the former compact incorporating environmental factors as 'drivers of displacement', and the latter as 'drivers which interact with root causes of refugee movement'.[9] This was supported by historic developments in 2021, when the United Nations Child Rights Committee (CRCom) drew attention to the cross-border responsibility of States for harmful impacts of climate change, and the United Nations Human Rights Council (UNHRC) recognised the fundamental right to have a clean, healthy and sustainable environment and created a new Special Rapporteur on the Protection of Human Rights in the Context of Climate Change.[10] In December 2021, during the 26th Conference of the Parties (COP26) to the United Nations Framework Convention on Climate

(World Bank 2018) <https://www.worldbank.org/en/news/infographic/2018/03/19/groundswell---preparing-for-internal-climate-migration> accessed 6 April 2022.

6 'Coal Addiction "Must Be Overcome" to Ease Climate Change, UN Chief Says in Bangkok' (UN News, 2 November 2019) accessed 6 April 2022.

7 Celement Viviane and others, 'Groundswell Part 2: Acting on Climate Migration' (World Bank 2021).

8 US Task Force to the President on the Climate Crisis and Global Migration, 'A Pathway to Protection for People on the Move' (Refugees International 2021); Fachkommission Fluchtursachen (Commission on the Root Causes of Displacement), 'Preventing Crises, Creating Prospects, Protection People' (German Federal Ministry for Economic Cooperation and Development 2021).

9 UNGA 'Global Compact on Refugees', Report of the UNHCR (2018) UN Doc A/73/12 (Global Compact on Refugees); UNGA 'Global Compact for Safe, Orderly and Regular Migration' (2019) UN Doc A/RES/73/195 (Global Compact for Migration).

10 Dr. Ian Fry, who is a dual citizen of Australia and Tuvalu, has been appointed Special Rapporteur. See UNHRC, 'Appointments at the 49th session of the Human Rights Council (28 February to 1 April 2022)' (OHCHR 2022) <https://www.ohchr.org/en/hr-bodies/hrc/sp/hrc49> accessed 6 April 2022. Also see, UNHRC Res 48/13 UN Doc A/HRC/RES/48/13 (2021); UNHRC Res 47/24, 'Human rights and climate change' (14 July 2021) UN Doc A/HRC/47/L.19; CRCom, 'Decision adopted by the Committee under the Optional Protocol to the Convention on the Rights of the Child on a communications procedure, concerning communication No. 104/2019' UN Doc CRC/C/88/D/104/2019.

Change (UNFCCC), States have also reaffirmed under the Glasgow Climate Pact that they should, 'when taking action to address climate change, respect, promote and consider their respective obligations on human rights, the right to health, the rights of indigenous peoples, local communities, migrants, children, persons with disabilities and people in vulnerable situations and the right to development, as well as gender equality, empowerment of women and intergenerational equity'.[11]

Yet, the existing legal infrastructure prioritises fragmented and voluntary approaches, which are heavily dependent on the discretionary power of States in immigration matters.[12] There are two main reasons for this: First, there is a legal gap – in the absence of an international treaty regime concerning human mobility, State obligations are defined under the rubric of different treaty regimes, general principles and customary rules of international law, which only partially address particular aspects of human mobility in the context of disasters and climate change (hereafter 'HMDCC').[13] Second, there is lack of a 'political appetite' – new international cooperative initiatives addressing HMDCC generally do not aim to extend State obligations under international law.[14] This is problematic, because the adverse impacts of disasters and climate change on human mobility can be averted or minimised if concerted actions are prescribed under international law.[15]

---

11 Conference of the Parties to the UNFCCC, 'Glasgow Climate Pact' Decision -/CP.26 (2021).

12 Martin Geiger, 'Migration governance at the global level: Intergovernmental organizations and environmental change-induced migration' in Tim Krieger, Diana Panke and Michael Prepernig, *Environmental Conflicts, Migration and Governance* (Bristol University Press 2020).

13 For instance, see David Hodgkinson and others, '"The Hour When The Ship Comes In": A Convention for Persons Displaced by Climate Change' [2010] 36 Monash University Law Review 1, 69–120.; Frank Biermann and Ingrid Boas, 'Preparing for a Warmer World: Towards a Global Governance System to Protect Climate Refugees' [2010] 10 Global Environmental Politics 1, 60–88.

14 In fact, there is a lack of political appetite in casting climate change as a threat to international peace and security, as evidenced by the draft UN Security Council Resolution, failed to be adopted on 13 December 2021. See International Crisis Group, 'How UN Member States Divided Over Climate Security' (*ICG* 2021). Also see Benoit Mayer and François Crépeau, 'Introduction' in Benoit Mayer and François Crépeau (eds), *Research Handbook on Climate Change, Migration and the Law* (Edward Elgar 2017) 15; Matthew Scott, *Climate Change, Disasters and the Refugee Convention* (Cambridge University Press 2020) 1-8.

15 On averting, minimising, and addressing displacement in the context of climate change, see UNFCCC, 'Report of the Executive Committee of the Warsaw International Mechanism for Loss and Damage associated with Climate Change Impacts' Decision -/CP.24 (2019) <https://unfccc.int/sites/default/files/resource/cp24_auv_ec%20wim.pdf> accessed 6 April 2022.

Against this backdrop, the present volume proposes a holistic and legally binding international response to address HMDCC. The concept of international protection lies at the core of this proposal. Persons in need of international protection are typically entitled to protection against return (*refoulement*) to their country of origin.[16] This book expands on this concept, drawing on the broader literature emphasising the need to prevent future displacement, as well as to facilitate safe, orderly and regular migration in the context of disasters and climate change.[17] Building on this foundation, it advocates for the international protection of persons mobile in the context of disasters and climate change (hereafter 'PMDCC').

In search of a normative framework capable of operationalising the international protection of PMDCC and of attaching specific legal consequences, this book makes use of two theories of international law: (i) community interests and (ii) the common concern of humankind. Both theories narrate the shift in international law from a law of co-existence towards a law of co-operation.[18] They claim that international law does not just serve the interests of individual States, but also protects the interests of humankind.[19] The former theory can generally be understood in terms of multilateral rights and obligations, such as obligations *erga omnes*, which are established and protected in the interest of the 'international community as a whole'.[20] The latter theory adds substance

16 Jane McAdam and Tamara Wood, 'The Concept of "International Protection" in the Global Compacts on Refugees and Migration' [2021] 23 International Journal of Postcolonial Studies 2, 191–206.

17 For instance, see Ezekiel Simperingham, 'State responsibility to prevent climate displacement: The importance of housing, land and property rights' in Dimitra Manou and others, *Climate Change, Migration and Human Rights: Law and Policy Perspectives* (Routledge 2017) 86–98.

18 According to Abi-Saab, when international law is considered as imposing negative obligations on States, then international law is seen as a law of co-existence. A law of co-operation, on the other hand, incorporates positive duties on States to protect. See Georges Abi-Saab, 'Whither the International Community?' [1998] 9 EJIL 2. Wolfrum similarly commented that, '[i]nitially a voluntary act, co-operation has become a legal obligation by virtue of the need to adjust to the existing interdependence of States and by the fact that it was founded upon the common interests of the international community'. See Rüdiger Wolfrum, 'International Law of Cooperation' (Max Planck Encyclopedia 2010) <https://opil.ouplaw.com/view/10.1093/law:epil/9780199231690/law-9780199231690-e1427?prd=EPIL> accessed 6 April 2022.

19 See generally, Antônio Augusto Cançado Trindade, *International Law for Humankind: Towards a New Jus Gentium* (2nd edn, Martinus Nijhoff Publishers 2013).

20 According to Benvenisti and Nolte, 'international community' can be approached in a broad sense, 'for the purpose of exploring the extent to which States owe duties toward those who are affected by their actions and omissions'. Therefore, the relevant international community may extend beyond States and cover 'individuals and groups,

to this approach, by articulating precise obligations to cooperate on the international level and to act to solve global problems.[21]

Framing the international protection of PMDCC under these theories serves two purposes. The first is to supply a forward-looking interpretation of State obligations to address HMDCC, which takes into account the interests and rights of current and future generations. This has the potential to contribute to filling the aforementioned legal gap that persists under international law. The second purpose is to operationalise this interpretation, by identifying precise legal consequences and making observations about their practical utility. This has the potential to shed light on the legal pathways that are already available or can be made available to a wide range of actors – including States, international organisations, civil society, and the general public – which can contribute to tackling the lack of 'political appetite' to engage in concerted efforts.

With these purposes in mind, the first chapter of this study expounds on the need to protect PMDCC at the international level. It begins by characterising HMDCC as a complex problem and international protection as a potential solution. This assertion is supported by analysing the recently adopted Global Compact for Migration and the Global Compact on Refugees, which reinforce the importance of both international protection and the need to address HMDCC on a global scale. The findings resulting from this analysis are then assessed against the examination of the current international legal infrastructure undertaken in the second chapter, leading to a clear understanding of the legal gaps. The third chapter illustrates the legal gaps 'in action' with a case study of the Pacific Island States (PIS). The insights from this case study strengthen the argument that domestic approaches to protection are not enough to effectively address HMDCC.

Building on this foundation, readers are then introduced to the theory of community interests in the fourth chapter, followed by the theory of the common concern of humankind in the fifth chapter. These frameworks provide two separate, although not incompatible, approaches to realising the international

---

whose interests, for various reasons, were not fully considered at the negotiation table or in policymaking bodies'. Eyal Benvenisti and Georg Nolte, 'Introductory Remarks' in Eyal Benvenisti, Georg Nolte and Keren Yalin-mor (eds), *Community Interests across International Law* (Oxford University Press 2018) 5.

21 Thomas Cottier, 'The Principle of Common Concern of Humankind' in Thomas Cottier (ed), *The Prospects of Common Concern of Humankind in International Law* (Cambridge University Press 2021) 3–89. Also see Alexander D. Beyleveld, *Taking a Common Concern Approach to Economic Inequality* (Brill 2022); Lucia Satragno, *Monetary Stability as a Common Concern in International Law* (Brill 2022); Iryna Bogdanova, *Unilateral Sanctions in International Law and the Enforcement of Human Rights* (Brill 2022).

protection of PMDCC. Whilst the former approach envisages an obligation *erga omnes* to protect PMDCC at the international level, the latter conceives of a new treaty regime incorporating novel duties to cooperate and to act.

These analyses feed into the conclusion, which summarises the overall findings of the research, including the conceptual relationships between international protection and HMDCC, on the one hand, and complex problems, community interests and common concerns, on the other. Finally, hypotheses for further research on the topic are briefly explored.

CHAPTER 1

The Need to Provide International Protection to Persons Mobile in the Context of Disasters and Climate Change

This chapter develops the argument that there is a need to provide international protection to PMDCC. It is perhaps no coincidence that this argument rests on a belief that international law is equipped to accomplish this. After all, international law governs the treatment of various categories of persons, including aliens, workers, refugees, stateless persons, persons *hors de combat* and children.[22] In these instances, international law serves the function of providing an international minimum standard for protection – i.e. it provides a minimum set of principles States must respect regardless of their domestic laws.[23] Similarly, when it comes to the international protection of PMDCC, States must agree on a set of principles outlining a minimum standard of treatment, regardless of their domestic laws. In order to unpack these arguments, this chapter begins by characterising HMDCC as a complex planetary and intergenerational problem, and then explores international protection as a potential solution. Finally, to put international protection into context, the chapter examines the commitments of States with respect to HMDCC under the recently adopted Global Compact on Refugees, as well as the Global Compact for Migration.

22 See Walter Kälin and Jörg Künzli, *The Law of International Human Rights Protection* (2nd edn, Oxford University Press 2019) 12–14; Antonio Cassese, *International Law* (2nd edn, Oxford University Press 2005) 375–398; Cançado Trindade (n 19) 515.

23 Hollin Dickerson, 'Minimum standards' (Max Planck Encyclopedia 2010) <https://opil.ouplaw.com/view/10.1093/law:epil/9780199231690/law-9780199231690-e845?prd=EPIL> accessed 6 April 2022. Also see *Ahmadou Sadio Diallo* (*Republic of Guinea v. Democratic Republic of the Congo*) (Preliminary Objections) [2007] ICJ Rep 582, 599 [39]; Rodrigo Polanco, *The Return of Home State to Investor-State Disputes* (Cambridge University Press 2018) 11–22.

1 Human Mobility in the Context of Disasters and Climate Change as a Complex Problem

This section argues that HMDCC is a complex planetary and intergenerational problem. Borrowing from Brunnée, complex planetary and intergenerational problems can be viewed as problem situations, which: (i) emerge from the actions of and interactions between multiple actors; (ii) have multiple, dynamic and interconnected variables; (iii) occur in the conditions of scientific uncertainty and evolving scientific knowledge; (iv) are planetary in scope and intergenerational in their impact.[24] It is possible to think of complex problems as a 'cluster of interrelated problems', which span legal, economic, political, social, environmental, scientific, ethical, demographic and security concerns.[25]

If the first quality of complex problems is unpacked, HMDCC can be framed as emerging from the actions of and interactions between multiple actors. This is connected to the nature of climate change itself. Climate change occurs as a result of human activities influencing the climate and the earth's temperature by, amongst other things, the burning of fossil fuels, cutting down of forests and farming of livestock.[26] This situation calls for costly shifts in the production and consumption processes.[27] States, as well as non-State actors, such as the private sector and consumers, play an important role in bringing this change to today's global economy.[28]

---

24 Jutta Brunnée, 'The Rule of International (Environmental) Law and Complex Problems' in Heike Krieger, Georg Nolte and Andreas Zimmermann, *The International Rule of Law: Rise or Decline?* (Oxford University Press 2019) 211–232.

25 ibid. Also see Jamie Murray, Thomas Webb and Steven Wheatley, *Complexity Theory and Law: Mapping An Emergent Jurisprudence* (Routledge 2019); Julian Webb, 'Law, Ethics and Complexity: Complexity Theory & the Normative Reconstruction of Law' [2005] 52 Cleveland State Law Review 227.

26 IPCC, 'Climate Change 2021: The Physical Science Basis. Contribution of Working Group I to the Sixth Assessment Report of the Intergovernmental Panel on Climate Change' (Cambridge University Press 2021) Chapter 3.

27 See, generally, Zaker Ahmad, *WTO Law and Trade Policy Reform for Low-Carbon Technology Diffusion* (Brill 2021); Aydin Baris Yildirim, *Value Chains and WTO Disputes: Compliance at the dispute settlement mechanism* (Palgrave Macmillan 2020).

28 For instance, see Draft Global Pact for the Environment (Preliminary Draft of the Group of Experts, 2017); World Commission on Environment Law of the International Union for Conversation of Nature, International Council of Environmental Law and International Grouo of Experts for the Pact, 'Note on the United Nations Secretary-General's Report "Gaps in international environmental law and environment-related instruments: towards a global pact for the environment"' (10 December 2018). Also see Jayme Walenta, 'Climate risk assessments and science-based targets: A review of emerging private sector climate action tools' [2019] 11 WIREs Climate Change 2.

As regards the second quality of complex problems, HMDCC has multiple, dynamic and interconnected variables. People are moving in the context of environmental factors and the climate, and there are remarkable early studies documenting these movements.[29] However, climate change is a 'threat multiplier'[30], aggravating stressors people are already experiencing, such as poverty, poor-quality land, poor-quality sanitation, resource scarcity and conflict.[31] Climate change also impacts the intensity and frequency of sudden-onset disasters, such as cyclones, while simultaneously contributing to or causing slow-onset processes, such as sea-level rise.[32] Generally, it is difficult to single out one factor as the only cause of movement, due to these multiple, interconnected variables.[33] What makes the situation even more complex is the fact that these variables are dynamic. While some of the impacts of climate change will be irreversible for millennia, others can be slowed and yet others can be reversed through ambitious mitigation strategies.[34]

This preludes to the third quality of complex problems, which is that they occur in the conditions of scientific uncertainty and evolving scientific knowledge. In order to better map, understand, predict and address HMDCC, there

29 For instance, in his book titled *Laws of Migration* published in 1889, Ravenstein theorised human migration and suggested 'unattractive climate' as one of the causes that 'have produced and still producing currents of migration'. Similarly, Huntington wrote in 1907 that geography appeared to be 'the basis of history in a way that is not generally recognised' and that 'climate changes have been one of the greatest factors in determining the course of human progress'. See Ernst Georg Ravenstein, 'The Laws of Migration' [1889] 52 Journal of the Royal Statistical Society 2, 286; Etienne Piguet, Antoine Pecoud and Paul de Guchteneire (eds), *Migration and Climate Change* (CUP and UNESCO Publishing 2011) 2–3; Ellsworth Huntington, *The Pulse of Asia: A Journey in Central Asia Illustrating the Geographic Basis of History* (Mifflin and Co 1907) 359.

30 In January 2019, the UNSC recognised climate change as a 'threat multiplier' in an open debate, which was tabled by the Dominican Republic. See 'Climate Change Recognized as "Threat Multiplier", UN Security Council Debates Its Impacts on Peace' (UN News 25 January 2019) <https://news.un.org/en/story/2019/01/1031322> accessed 6 April 2022.

31 IDMC, 'No matter of choice: displacement in a changing climate' (Thematic Series, IDMC, 2018); Michael Brzoska, 'Climate Change as a Driver of Security Policy' in Jürgen Scheffran and others, *Climate Change, Human Security and Violent Conflict* (Springer 2012).

32 IPCC (n 26).

33 For instance, the Foresight Report noted that 'it will rarely be possible to distinguish individuals for whom environmental factors are the sole driver of migration'. See the UK Government Office for Science, 'Foresight: Migration and Global Environmental Change' (Final Project Report, London 2011) 9. More recently reiterated in the report: German Cooperation GIZ and PIK, 'Home Lands: Island and Archipelagic States' Policymaking for Human Mobility in the Context of Climate Change' (2020) 22–23. Also see Benoit Mayer, *The Concept of Climate Migration* (Edward Elgar Publishing 2016) 16.

34 IPCC (n 22).

is a need to strengthen joint analyses and the sharing of information.[35] For instance, the UK Government commissioned a Foresight report on 'Migration and Global Environmental Change' to consider the situation over the next 50 years,[36] involving more than 300 experts and 70 background papers. The final report, which was released in 2011, highlighted 'surprising' results: as many people could move internally into areas of environmental risk as migrate from them, while large populations in vulnerable areas may become 'trapped' or choose not to move.[37] This report was particularly important in emphasising that 'planned and facilitated approaches to human migration can ease people out of situations of vulnerability'.[38] In its sixth assessment report, the IPCC similarly assessed the impacts of climate change on four types of movement, namely, adaptive migration, involuntary displacement, organised relocation of populations and immobility.[39] The report emphasised that the diversity in drivers, contexts and outcomes 'make it difficult to offer simple generalisations about the relationship between climate change and migration'.[40] Nevertheless, incredible amount of research undertaken in the last decades suggest a typology of climate-related movement.[41] For instance, the most common form of movement is temporary and/or seasonal internal migration, and there is a growing concern about the future prospects of immobile populations.[42]

Finally, thanks to the evolving scientific knowledge, HMDCC can be described as planetary in scope and intergenerational in its impact. Simply put, no one is immune to the consequences of climate change and disasters. This point was made loud and clear by the IPCC, which stated that the international community must meet the requirements of the Paris Agreement and take further action to control future warming to reduce the future risk of large-scale population displacements.[43] Whether they face flooding, wildfires, drought, desertification or sea-level rise, all countries will need to adapt to a warmer world. Due to the long-term and potentially irreversible effects of

---

35 Global Compact for Migration (n 9), para 18(h). Also, see Susanne Melde, Frank Laczko and Francois Gemenne (eds), 'Making mobility work for adaptation to environmental changes: Results from the MECLEP global research' (IOM 2017).

36 UK Government (n 33) 9.

37 ibid.

38 ibid.

39 IPCC (n 4) 1342–1351.

40 ibid 1349.

41 ibid 1345–1348.

42 ibid.

43 ibid.

climate change, present and future generations will increasingly grapple with the decision of whether or not to move.

2 International Protection as a Solution

Since HMDCC is a complex planetary and intergenerational problem, it can be managed only if all States cooperate in promoting an international minimum standard for the treatment of PMDCC. The author submits that the notion of international protection is well equipped to serve as the basis for a global response. This section begins by expounding on the concept of international protection in international law, before undertaking a conceptualisation of the international protection of PMDCC.

2.1 *The Notion of International Protection in International Law*

One of features of the study and practice of international law that is most taken for granted is the centrality of the idea of 'international protection'. From intellectual property through to human rights, 'international protection' comes to the fore as a concept that provides for an international minimum standard: regardless of domestic laws, international protection in relation to a certain issue designates a global commitment to a standard.

Whilst international protection may relate to the bigger picture of the environment, goods, properties, spaces, objects or animals, the international protection of persons is only concerned with the international minimum standards afforded to individuals and/or specific groups of people.[44]

Historically, customary rules and treaty provisions that aimed to provide a degree of protection to individuals and groups have imposed major limitations on State sovereignty.[45] The initiatives for the creation of these rules and

---

44 For instance, see Sherman Strong Hayden, 'The International Protection of Wild Life: An Examination of Treaties and Other Agreements for the Preservation of Birds and Mammals' (Columbia University Press 2020); Francesco Francioni, 'Public and Private in the International Protection of Global Cultural Goods' [2012] 23 European Journal of International Law 3, 719–730; Malgosia Fitzmaurice, 'International Protection of the Environment' (Volume 293, Collected Courses of the Hague Academy of International Law 2001).

45 James Crawford, *Brownlie's Principles of Public International Law* (9th edn, Oxford University Press 2019) 607–690.

treaties rested on moral, racial, economic, and pragmatic grounds, depending on the type of protection at issue.[46]

For instance, by the mid-nineteenth century, mostly for economic and pragmatic reasons, an international minimum standard for the protection of aliens and their property was advocated.[47] This stood in contrast to national treatments, according to which, in cases of dispute, aliens would need to exhaust local remedies in domestic courts, in line with the applicable domestic laws.[48] The international minimum standard, on the other hand, envisaged alien rights as a specific area of international law, including the right to be free from a denial of justice, the right to have their juridical personality recognised by the receiving State and the right to participate in hearings.[49] Currently, the international minimum standard for the protection of aliens and their property is reflected to some extent in international law, most notably in diplomatic law, which governs the relations between sovereign States, and international economic law, which encompasses the international legal rules on foreign investment and trade.[50]

Another example is the international minimum standard for labour conditions, which can be traced back to the 'social question' – i.e. to the consequences of the growing 'proletarianisation' of the population in industrialised countries as a result of the Industrial Revolution.[51] Under the *laissez-faire*

---

46 For instance, for a debate on the international protection from slavery, see Omar Al Turabi, *Protection from Slavery in the International Legal Order* (Doctoral thesis, University of Bern 2006); Gelien Matthews, *The Other Side of Slave Revolts* (The Society for Caribbean Studies, East Yorkshire 2000). For a private international law perspective on the international protection of adults, see Richard Frimston and others (eds), *International Protection of Adults* (Oxford University Press 2015).

47 Vincent Chetail, *International Migration Law* (Oxford University Press 2019) 61; Dickerson (n 23).

48 Annemarieke Vermeer-Künzli, 'As If: The Legal Fiction in Diplomatic Protection' [2007] 18 EJIL 1, 37–68.

49 Crawford (n 45) 607. Also see *Mavrommatis Palestine Concessions* (*Greece v Great Britain*) (Judgement) [1924] PCIJ Series A no 2; *L.F.H. Neer and Pauline Neer* (*USA*) *v United Mexican States* [1926] 4 R.I.A.A. 60; *LaGrand Case* (*Germany v United States of America*) (Judgment) [2001] ICJ.

50 Andreas Roth, *The Minimum Standard of International Law Applied to Aliens* (Sijthoff, Leiden 1949); Andreas Lowenfeld, *International Economic Law* (2nd edn, Oxford University Press 2002); ILC, 'Draft articles on diplomatic protection' (2006) UN Doc A/61/10; Vienna Convention on Diplomatic Relations (adopted 18 April 1961, entered into force 24 April 1964) 596 UNTS 261.

51 Sandrine Kott, 'ILO: Social Justice in a Global World? A History in Tension' [2019] International Development Policy, 21–39; Jasmien Van Daele, 'The International Labour Organization in Past and Present Research' [2008] 53 International Review of Social History 3.

conception of the State, the free play of forces was guaranteed, which effectively left the workers entirely at their employer's disposal.[52] Workers were in desperate positions: workdays were long (up to seventeen hours), children were employed without restrictions starting from the age of six and women were employed even when pregnant and shortly after childbirth.[53] Demands for social justice kindled the formation of networks during this period, eventually leading to the creation of the ILO and the International Labour Standards (ILS).[54] A century after its creation, the ILO has secured international agreements on important basic international standards, such as the regulation of working hours, maternity protection and the abolition of child labour.[55]

The international protection of refugees has a more recent history, dating back only to the twentieth century.[56] Although the practice of granting asylum has a long heritage, earlier practices generally treated asylum seekers in accordance with national laws concerning aliens.[57] Refugees became a matter of international concern most notably following the end of the First World War, when the dissolution of empires and the rise of nation-states resulted in huge numbers of people forced to seek refuge elsewhere.[58] Concomitantly, the

52 Antony Evelyn Alcock, *History of the International Labour Organisation* (Palgrave Macmillan 1971) 3–11.

53 Van Daele (n 51).

54 See generally, Daniel Maul, *The International Labour Organization: 100 Years of Global Social Policy* (De Gruyter and the ILO 2019); Steve Hughes and Nigel Haworth, *The International Labour Organisation: Coming in from the cold* (Routledge 2011); Albert Thomas, 'The International Labour Organization: Its Origins, Development and Future' [1921] 1 International Labour Review; George N. Barnes, *History of International Labour Office* (London 1926).

55 By 2020, the ILO had adopted 190 Conventions and 206 Recommendations. For instance, see ILO Convention No 3: Maternity Protection Convention (1919); ILO Convention No 29: Forced Labour Convention (1930); ILO Convention No 138: Minimum Age Convention (1973).

56 See in general, Guy S. Goodwin-Gill and Jane McAdam, *The Refugee in International Law* (3rd edn, Oxford University Press 2007).

57 Evan J. Criddle and Evan Fox-Decent, *Fiduciaries of Humanity* (Oxford University Press 2016) chapter 9; Dieter Kugalmann, 'Refugees' (Max Planck Encyclopedia 2010) <https://opil.ouplaw.com/view/10.1093/law:epil/9780199231690/law-9780199231690-e866> accessed 6 April 2022; Khadija Elmadmad, 'Asylum in Islam and Modern Refugee Law' [2008] 277 Refugee Survey Quarterly 2, 51–63.

58 See Randall Lesaffer, 'Peace Treaties and the Formation of International Law' in Bardo Fassbender and Anne Peters (eds), *The Oxford Handbook of the History of International Law* (Oxford Univeristy Press 2012) 71–94.

Bolshevik Revolution led to the plight of some 800,000 Russians, over 600,000 of whom were stripped of their citizenship.[59]

In this context, the League of Nations created a mechanism governing the international protection of persons fleeing across borders. The office of the High Commissioner for Russian Refugees was created in 1921. Under the direction of High Commissioner Fridtjof Nansen[60], this office issued 'Nansen passports' over the course of the following thirteen years, which gave *de jure* stateless persons of Russian, Armenian, Turkish, Assyrian, Assyro-Chaldaean, Syrian, Kurdish and Saar origins international protection.[61] From 1930 until the end of 1938, there was a split mandate over refugees, with their political and legal protection being vested in the League of Nations' Secretary-General and the substantive humanitarian work, especially concerning their resettlement, being entrusted to the Nansen International Office for Refugees.[62] In 1938, the League of Nations established the High Commissioner's Office to oversee all matters relating to the international protection of refugees, which brought an end to the Nansen Office.[63]

During this time, the definition of a refugee (which dictated who was entitled to international protection) was progressively extended. In 1922, it was limited to Russian refugees, before being extended to Armenian refugees in 1924, Turkish, Assyrian, Assyro-Chaldean and assimilated refugees in 1928, and German refugees in 1938.[64]

---

59 Criddle and Fox-Decent (n 57); UNHCR, 'A Special Report: Ending Statelessness Within 10 Years' <https://www.unhcr.org/protection/statelessness/546217229/special-report-ending-statelessness-10-years.html> accessed 6 April 2022.

60 Fridtjof Nansen was a Norwegian scientist, diplomat, and humanitarian, who is a Nobel Peace Prize laureate and a successful polar explorer. It might interest the reader to know that his legacy still continues today with the Nansen Initiative, which was launched in 2012 to build consensus among States about how best to address cross-border displacement in the context of sudden- and slow-onset disasters. See Chapter 2.2.2 of this book.

61 Criddle and Fox-Decent (n 57).

62 ibid.

63 ibid.

64 Arrangement with regard to the Issue of Certificates of Identity to Russian Refugees (5 July 1922) 13 LNTS 238 (No 355); Plan for the Issue of a Certificate of Identity to Armenian Refugees (31 May 1924) LN Doc CL 72 (a); Arrangement relating to the Issue of Identity Certificates to Russian and Armenian Refugees, Supplementing and Amending the Previous Arrangements (12 May 1926) 89 LNTS 47 (No 2004); Arrangement Relating to the Legal Status of Russian and Armenian Refugees (30 June 1928) 89 LNTS 53 (No 2005); Arrangement concerning the Extension to Other Categories of Refugees Certain Measures taken in Favour of Russian and Armenian Refugees (30 June 1928) 89 LNTS 63 (No 2006); Agreement concerning the Functions of the Representatives of the League of Nations' High Commissioner for Refugees (30 June 1928) 93 LNTS 377 (No 2126); Convention relating to the International Status of Refugees (30 June 1933) 159 LNTS 199 (No 3663);

Following the collapse of the League of Nations and in the aftermath of the Second World War, the protection of refugees became the distinct prerogative of a single, specialised UN agency in 1946.[65] This agency was later replaced by the UNHCR and the Refugee Convention was adopted as the primary source of international protection for refugees.[66] The Protocol of 1967 amended the Refugee Convention by removing the temporal and geographical restrictions from the definition of a refugee, in order to cover individuals of all nationalities.[67]

Today, international protection has a specific meaning in international refugee law, which is 'centred on the cardinal principle of *non-refoulement*'.[68] As the UNHCR explains:

> The need for international protection, which concerns all those outside their own country and who are unable to return home because of a serious threat to their life, physical integrity, or freedom as a result of persecution, armed conflict, violence, or serious public disorder, against which their country is unwilling or unable to protect them. Persons in need of international protection are typically entitled to protection against *refoulement*.[69]

By virtue of Article 33 of the Refugee Convention, the prohibition of *non-refoulement* (in other words, non-return) applies to refugees.[70] However, due to the express articulation of the prohibition of *non-refoulement* under international human rights law, today the application of *non-refoulement* extends beyond refugees.[71] Applying the prohibition of *non-refoulement* under

---

Convention concerning the Status of Refugees coming from Germany (10 February 1938) 19 LNTS 59 (No 4461); Additional Protocol to the Provisional Arrangement and to the Convention concerning the Status of Refugees coming from Germany (14 September 1939) 198 LNTS 141 (No 4634).

65 Chetail (n 47) 381–392.

66 In 1949, the UN Relief and Works Agency (UNRWA) was established for the international protection of Palestinian refugees. See UNGA Res 302 (IV) (1949).

67 Protocol Relating to the Status of Refugees (adopted 31 January 1967, entered into force 4 October 1967) 606 UNTS 267.

68 Global Compact on Refugees (n 9), para 5. See Chapter 2.2.1 of this book for a discussion on the principle of *non-refoulement*.

69 UNHCR, 'Migrants in Vulnerable Situations: UNHCR's Perspective' (UNHCR 2017) <https://www.refworld.org/docid/596787174.html> accessed 6 April 2022.

70 Convention Relating to the Status of Refugees (adopted 28 July 1951, entered into force 22 April 1954) 189 UNTS 137 (Refugee Convention) art 33.

71 International Covenant on Civil and Political Rights (adopted 16 December 1966, entered into force 23 March 1976) 999 UNTS 171 (ICCPR); Convention against Torture and Other

international human rights law means examining whether 'in light of the prevailing circumstances and the particular vulnerabilities of those concerned, they can be required to return to their country of origin'.[72] International human rights law thus emphasises that refugees are not the only people who require international protection.[73]

This leads to another type of international protection, namely the international protection of human rights. Since the twentieth century, with the emergence of binding international human rights treaties, human persons now enjoy individual rights under international law.[74] International human rights protection refers to the internationally guaranteed legal entitlements of individuals based on the fundamental characteristics and dignity of the human person, according to which States must respect, protect and fulfil their obligations under international human rights treaties.

More specifically, the 'respect, protect and fulfil' framework gives rise to three legal obligations: the obligation to respect requires States to 'refrain from interfering with or curtailing the enjoyment of human rights'; the obligation to protect requires States to 'protect individuals and groups against human rights

---

Cruel, Inhuman or Degrading Treatment or Punishment (adopted 10 December 1984, entry into force 16 June 1987) 1465 UNTS 85 (CAT); International Convention for the Protection of All Persons From Enforced Disappearance (adopted 20 December 2006, entered into force 23 December 2010) 2716 UNTS 3 (ICPPED).

72 Walter Kälin and Nina Schrepfer, 'Protecting People Crossing Borders in the Context of Climate Change Normative Gaps and Possible Approaches' (UNHCR Legal Protection and Policy Research Series 2012).

73 International human rights law can also be seen as 'expanding' the international protection of refugees. For instance, Puggiani explores the role played by States in translating international protection to refugees and asylum seekers under a human-rights based approach. She argues that the duty of the State is not only to provide protection from persecution, threats, and sustained violence, but must also entail emancipation. She also rests her argument on the difference between the public responsibility to protect and the private desire to assist. See Raffaela Puggioni, *Rethinking International Protection: The Sovereign, the State, the Refugee* (Palgrave Macmillan 2016).

74 The precursors of international human rights law were already challenging the traditional theory that only States and IOs can be subjects of international law. For instance, in the aftermath of the Second World War, the Nuremberg and Tokyo tribunals assumed that individuals possess direct obligations under international law and held them accountable for crimes against humanity, war crimes, and crimes against peace. Going further than these developments, international human rights treaty regimes allow victims of violations to invoke their rights directly at the international level with the creation of the individual complaint and communication procedures. See Cassese (n 22) 375–398; Kälin and Künzli (n 22) 13–17; John Knox, 'Horizontal Human Rights Law' [2008] 102 AJIL 1, 1–47.

abuses'; and the obligation to fulfil means that States 'must take positive action to facilitate the enjoyment of basic human rights'.[75]

Undoubtedly, this is a broad conceptual framework, resting on three generations of rights, as well as several legally binding international treaties.[76] Because it is anchored in an international legal system of rights and corresponding obligations, the 'human-rights-based approach' has been increasingly advocated as a tool to assess norms, including those relating to the international protection of refugees under *non-refoulement*.[77]

To sum up, international protection is an umbrella term used in international law to refer to international minimum standards applicable to a certain issue. Whilst the examples of the international protection of aliens, workers and refugees highlight that international protection can relate to a specific group of individuals, international human rights protection demonstrates that it can also relate to individuals.

---

75 See UN Committee on Economic, Social and Cultural Rights, 'General Comment No 24' (10 August 2017) UN Doc E/C.12/GC/24; OHCHR and Inter-Parliamentary Union, 'Handbook for Parliamentarians' (OHCHR and Inter-Parliamentary Union 2016) 31–38.

76 Three generation of rights are civil and political rights; economic, social and cultural rights; and solidarity or group rights (although this group is contested). The international human rights treaties include: ICCPR (n 71); CAT (n 71); International Convention on the Elimination of All Forms of Racial Discrimination (adopted 7 March 1966, entry into force 4 January 1969) 660 UNTS 195 (ICERD); International Covenant on Economic, Social and Cultural Rights (adopted 16 December 1966, entry into force 3 January 1976) (ICESCR); Convention on the Elimination of All Forms of Discrimination against Women (adopted 18 December 1976, entry into force 3 September 1981) (CEDAW); Convention on the Rights of the Child (adopted 20 November 1989, entry into force 2 September 1990) 1577 UNTS 3 (CRC); International Convention on Protection of the Rights of All Migrant Workers and Members of Their Families (adopted 18 December 1990, entry into force 1 July 2003) (ICRMW); Convention on the Rights of Persons with Disabilities (adopted 13 December 2006, entered into force 3 May 2008) 2515 UNTS 3 (CPRD).

77 For instance, Mazzeschi argues that international human rights standards 'substituted' and 'transformed' the norms on the treatment of aliens. Substitution refers to the expansion of human rights to govern the norms relating to the treatment of aliens. Importantly, in 1985, the UNGA Declaration on the Human Rights of Individuals Who are not Nationals of the Country in which They Live recognised that the UDHR applies to aliens. Transformation refers to the emergence of the individual as an addressee of international law. This meant that foreign nationals were entitled to invoke some of the international primary norms under human rights treaties. See Riccardo Pisillo Mazzeschi, 'The Relationship Between Human Rights and the Rights of Aliens and Immigrants' in Ulrich Fastenrath and others (eds), *From Bilateralism to Community Interest: Essays in Honour of Bruno Simma* (Oxford University Press 2011); David Weissbrodt, *The Human Right to Citizenship* (University of Pennsylvania Press 2015) chapter 1.

2.2 *Conceptualising the International Protection of Persons Mobile in the Context of Disasters and Climate Change*

Drawing on the insights from the previous section concerning the notion of international protection, this section introduces the international minimum standards that should be applicable for the international protection of PMDCC. The author submits that the international protection of PMDCC should aim to: (i) grant protection against return to the country of origin (*non-refoulement*); (ii) prevent future displacement; (iii) facilitate safe, orderly and regular migration in the context of disasters and climate change.

The evident connection between human rights and climate change provides the foundation for justifying the need to grant protection to PMDCC against return to their country of origin.[78] Climate change exacerbates pre-existing inequalities and human rights challenges, 'posing a serious risk to the fundamental rights to life, health, food and an adequate standard of living of individuals and communities across the world'.[79] In 2021, the UNHRC made this point loudly and clearly by recognising the fundamental right to have a clean, healthy and sustainable environment and created a new Special Rapporteur on the Protection of Human Rights in the Context of Climate Change.[80]

As mentioned earlier, under international human rights law, the prohibition of *non-refoulement* extends beyond those recognised as refugees to cover all persons irrespective of the causes of movement.[81] Unfortunately, there is still a need for explicit recognition of the applicability of *non-refoulement* to PMDCC. The main reason for this is that claims based on *non-refoulement* due to the impact of climate change are unlikely to meet the very high threshold of risk to the right to life or inhuman or degrading treatment under international

78 UNEP and Columbia University Sabin Center for Climate Change Law, 'Climate Change and Human Rights' (2015) <https://wedocs.unep.org/bitstream/handle/20.500.11822/9934/Climate-Change-Human-Rights.pdf?sequence=1&isAllowed=y> accessed 6 April 2022.

79 Achim Steiner, 'Foreword' in UNEP, Columbia University Sabin Center for Climate Change Law, 'Cliamte Change and Human Rights' (2015) <https://wedocs.unep.org/bitstream/handle/20.500.11822/9934/Climate-Change-Human-Rights.pdf?sequence=1&isAllowed=y> accessed 6 April 2022.

80 UNHRC (n 10). Also see UNHRC Res 47/24, 'Human rights and climate change' (14 July 2021) UN Doc A/HRC/47/L.19.

81 Basak Cali, Cathryn Costello and Stewart Cunningham, 'Hard Protection through Soft Courts? *Non-refoulement* before the United Nations Treaty Bodies' [2020] 21 German Law Journal 3, 355–384.

human rights law.[82] In order for *non-refoulement* to be applicable under international human rights law, the 'risk [...] must be personal in nature, and cannot be derived merely from the general conditions in the receiving State, except in the most extreme circumstances'.[83] In contrast, because HMDCC is a complex planetary and intergenerational problem, establishing causation of associated harm under the 'traditional model of State responsibility' is problematic.[84] The causes of the movement of persons are not connected to any specific or localised activity, and instead, occur in the context of multiple, dynamic and interconnected variables.

For this reason, an international minimum standard must be agreed upon by States to apply the prohibition of *non-refoulement* to PMDCC. The content of the standard – i.e. the requirements to grant protection against return to the country of origin – can be further fleshed out by States, based on the input of non-State actors, especially the PMDCC themselves.

Furthermore, the international protection of PMDCC must commit States to measures that aim to prevent future displacement. Prevention already plays a key role in the existing, legally non-binding frameworks on displacement.[85] For instance, Principle 5 of the Guiding Principles on Internal Displacement lays out the duty of States to abide by their obligations under international law to prevent and avoid conditions that might lead to displacement in the first place.[86] In the case of HMDCC, prevention must be rooted in ambitious climate mitigation targets, as well as disaster-risk reduction measures.[87] Building on existing voluntary commitments, the international protection of PMDCC

82 This was made particularly evident in the recent decision on the *Ioane Teitiota v New Zealand* case of the UNHRCom. See Chapter 2.2.1 of this book for a further discussion on this topic.

83 *Ioane Teitiota v. New Zealand* (2020) UNHRCom UN Doc CCPR/C/127/D/2928/2016, [9.3] (*Ioane Teitiota*).

84 Vincent Bellinkx and others, 'Addressing Climate Change through International Human Rights Law: From (Extra)Territoriality to Common Concern of Humankind' [2021] 11 Transnational Environmental Law 1, 69–93.

85 For instance, the Task Force on Displacement (TFD) of the UNFCCC refers to 'averting, minimising and addressing' human mobility in the context of climate change. See UNFCCC (n 1).

86 Guiding Principles on Internal Displacement (22 July 1998) ADM 1.1, PRL 12.1, PR00/98/109 <https://www.refworld.org/docid/3c3da07f7.html> accessed 6 April 2022. Also see David Fisher, 'Legal Implementation of Human Rights Obligations to Prevent Displacement Due to Natural Disasters' [2010] 41 Studies in Transnational Legal Policy, 551–590.

87 Simperingham (n 17).

must call for the determination of legally binding measures to prevent future displacement.

Finally, the international protection of PMDCC must emphasise the facilitation of safe, orderly and regular migration. 'Facilitation' means to make something (e.g. an action, a process, etc.) easy or, at least, easier – when applied to migration, it means to make migration easier and lower barriers to mobility.[88] The idea of facilitating the movement of persons as an adaptation strategy to environmental changes represents 'one of the key and novel storylines'.[89] Migration as adaptation can be seen as a strategy to moderate harm, by transforming people's ability to cope with environmental changes.[90] It can also lead to the exploitation of beneficial opportunities, such as seeking employment in an expanded network of labour migration options.[91] Thus, facilitating migration can enable two kinds of adaptation: (i) *in situ*, in which people try to adjust their local systems to adapt to environmental change by relocating internally, and (ii) *ex situ*, in which people look for opportunities across borders, whether temporarily or permanently.[92] In this sense, lowering barriers to mobility can 'emancipate' individuals and improve their living conditions, as well as their enjoyment of human rights.[93]

Taken together, these three pillars represent the international minimum standards that should be applicable in addressing HMDCC. The following chapters refer back to each pillar of the proposed framework, in order to explain the

---

88 Facilitation of migration occurs in the context of freedom of movement, which is a fundamental human right with a long history. Freedom of movement encompasses the rights of individuals to travel and reside within the borders of a State, and to leave any country, including their own, and to return to their own country. However, it is an 'incomplete right' because it is not matched by a State duty of admission. Therefore, it cannot be equated with a right to permanently migrate or a right to enter a country.

89 Giovanni Bettini, 'Climate migration as an adaptation strategy: de-securitizing climate-induced migration or making the unruly governable?' [2014] 2 Critical Studies on Security 2, 180–195.

90 Jurgen Scheffran, Elina Marmer and Papa Sow, 'Migration as a contribution to resilience and innovation in climate adaptation: Social networks and co-development in Northwest Africa' [2012] 33 Applied Geography 119.

91 Maria Lewicka, 'Place attachment: How far have we come in the last 40 years?' [2011] 31:3 Journal of Environmental Psychology; Graeme Hugo and Douglas K. Bardsley, 'Migration and Environmental Change in Asia' in Etienne Piguet and Frank Laczko, *People on the Move in a Changing Climate* (Springer 2014).

92 Ma. Laurice Jamero, 'In-situ adaptation against climate change can enable relocation of impoverished small islands' [2019] 108 Marine Policy 103614, 1–28.

93 Jane McAdam, 'Displacement in the Context of Climate Change and Disasters' in Cathryn Costello, Michelle Foster and Jane McAdam, *The Oxford Handbook of International Refugee Law* (Oxford University Press 2021).

legal gaps and to map out legal pathways for operationalising the international protection of PMDCC.

3 Towards International Protection: The Global Compact on Refugees and the Global Compact for Safe, Orderly and Regular Migration

The UNGA affirmed two historic instruments in 2018. The Global Compact on Refugees was endorsed on 17 December, and is referred to by the UNHCR as 'a unique opportunity to transform the way the world responds to refugee situations'.[94] The Global Compact for Migration was endorsed on 19 December, and is described by the IOM as the first agreement covering 'all dimensions of international migration in a holistic and comprehensive manner'.[95] Both compacts include references to HMDCC and inform the discussion on international protection. This section beings by analysing the notion of a global compact under international law, before moving on to discuss the international protection of PMDCC respectively under the Global Compact on Refugees, and the Global Compact for Migration. It concludes with a discussion of the future implications of these compacts for the development of a framework for the international protection of PMDCC.

3.1 *The Notion of a Global Compact*

The Global Compact on Refugees and the Global Compact for Migration have been viewed as 'opening up a new chapter of law-making in international law'.[96] This alludes to the peculiar space a 'compact' occupies in international relations, which is somewhere between law and politics.[97] This section discusses the emergence of the notion of a global compact in international relations, as well as in refugee situations and international migration. It also analyses the

94 Global Compact on Refugees (n 9).

95 IOM, 'Global Compact for Migration' (*IOM*) <https://www.iom.int/global-compact-migration> accessed 6 April 2022.

96 Peter Hilpold, 'Opening up a new chapter of law-making in international law: The Global Compacts on Migration and for Refugees of 2018' [2021] 26 European Law Journal 3-4, 226–244.

97 Thomas Gammeltoft Hansen, 'The Normative Impact of the Global Compact on Safe, Orderly and Regular Migration' in Marion Panizzon, Elspeth Guild, Isobel Roele and Violeta Moreno-Lax (eds), *What is a Compact? Migrants' Rights and State Responsibilities Regarding the Design of the UN Global Compact for Safe, Orderly and Regular Migration* (Raoul Wallenberg Institute of Human Rights and Humanitarian Law 2017) 7.

legal status of a global compact under international law, with an emphasis on the Global Compact on Refugees and the Global Compact for Migration.

The first global example of a compact in international relations is the launch of the UN Global Compact in 2000 by the UN Secretary-General at the time, Kofi Annan.[98] The UN Global Compact was designed as a voluntary initiative to mainstream ten principles in business activities around the world, in order to promote corporate sustainability in view of the broader sustainability goals of the UN.[99] The continued relevance of the initiative's idea, sustained institutional leadership support and governmental support are some of its 'enabling ingredients'.[100] For over twenty years, the UN Global Compact has been integrating UN issues into the global corporate responsibility movement.[101]

Examining the UN Global Compact, the notion of a global compact can be unpacked within the framework of international relations. First, a compact is not a formal source of international law and is legally non-binding.[102] Compacts can be associated with the wider trends towards the 'informalisation' of sources in international law or the 'softification' of international governance.[103] Second, the term 'compact' was little or never used, which meant

---

98 UNGA Res 55/215 (2000) GAOR 55th Session. See also, UNGA Res 73/254 (2018) GAOR 73rd Session. For more recent activities of the network, see UN Global Compact, '2020 Annual Management Report' (2020) <https://ungc-communications-assets.s3.amazonaws.com/docs/publications/2020-Annual-Management-Report.pdf> accessed 6 April 2022; UN Global Compact, '2017 United Nations Global Compact Progress Report: Business Solutions to Sustainable Development' (2017) <https://d306pr3pise04h.cloudfront.net/docs/publications%2FUN+Impact+Brochure_Concept-FINAL.pdf> accessed 6 April 2022; UN Global Compact, 'Activity Report 2015' (2014) <https://d306pr3pise04h.cloudfront.net/docs/publications%2FUNGC_2015_Activity_Report.pdf> accessed 6 April 2022.

99 Oliver F. Williams, 'UN Global Compact: The Challenge and the Promise' [2004] 14 Business Ethics Quarterly 4, 755–774.

100 Georg Kell, '12 Years Later: Reflections on the Growth of the UN Global Compact' [2012] 52 Business and Society 1, 31–52; George Kell and David Levin, 'The Global Compact Network: An historic experiment in learning and action' [2003] 108 Business and Society Review 2, 151–181.

101 W. Lance Bennett, 'Communicating global activism' [2003] 6 Information, Communication and Society 2, 143–168.

102 In the author's view, it would be interesting to analyse whether a State's commitments under the Global Compact for Migration can be regarded as a binding unilateral declaration under international law. A binding unilateral declaration is made by a State without any requirement for reciprocation or response from another State. Furthermore, it may be related to rights or obligations vis-à-vis the international community at large. For more information on binding unilateral declaration under international law, see ILC, 'Guiding Principles applicable to unilateral declarations of States capable of creating legal obligations, with commentaries thereto' (2006) UN Doc A/61/10.

103 Gammeltoft Hansen (n 97).

that it did not bear the 'baggage of preconception'.[104] Thus, its form and content were shaped freely. By bringing together public and private actors, it has served as a form of 'machinery' to incentivise corporations and States to cooperate on issues about which global consensus is difficult to reach.[105] In this sense, the UN Global Compact sets out common principles and understandings, placing an emphasis on aspects of 'good governance'.[106]

However, the UN Global Compact has significant shortcomings. With vague and flexible principles, no standard of conduct and no monitoring or enforcement mechanisms, the compact fails to hold corporations accountable.[107] Some commentators argue that the compact is used by corporations as an instrument for 'bluewashing', i.e. for wrapping their brand in the blue flag of the UN and using the UN's positive image.[108] In the author's view, the effectiveness of the UN Global Compact is also undermined by the vagueness of the concept of 'sustainability', which lacks a context-specific (or industry-specific) and implementable definition.[109]

---

104 Isobel Roele, 'What are the Forms of UN International Agreements/Understandings and What is Their Legal Effect?' in Marion Panizzon, Elspeth Guild, Isobel Roele and Violeta Moreno-Lax (eds), *What is a Compact? Migrants' Rights and State Responsibilities Regarding the Design of the UN Global Compact for Safe, Orderly and Regular Migration* (Raoul Wallenberg Institute of Human Rights and Humanitarian Law 2017) 11.

105 Panizzon calls this 'issue-linkaging' or 'packaging'. See Marion Panizzon, 'The Global Migration Compact and the Limits of 'Package Deals' for Migration Law and Policy' in Marion Panizzon, Elspeth Guild, Isobel Roele and Violeta Moreno-Lax (eds), *What is a Compact? Migrants' Rights and State Responsibilities Regarding the Design of the UN Global Compact for Safe, Orderly and Regular Migration* (Raoul Wallenberg Institute of Human Rights and Humanitarian Law 2017).

106 Gammeltoft Hansen (n 97).

107 Michael Blowfield and Jedrzej George Frynas, 'Setting New Agendas: Critical Perspectives on Corporate Social Responsibility in the Developing World' [2005] 81 International Affairs 3, 499-513; Michael Blowfield, 'Corporate Social Responsibility: Reinventing the Meaning of Development?' [2005] 81 International Affairs 3, 515–524; Steve Hughes and Rorden Wilkinson, 'The Global Compact: Promoting Corporate Responsibility?' [2001] 10 Environmental Politics 1, 155–159.

108 Kenny Bruno and Joshua Karliner, 'Tangled up in blue' (*Corpwatch*, 1 September 2000) <https://corpwatch.org/article/tangled-blue> accessed 6 April 2022.

109 Sustainable development was defined by the World Commission on Environment and Development in 1987 as 'development that meets the needs of the present without compromising the ability of future generations to meet their own needs'. See World Commission on Environment and Development, 'Our Common Future' (1987). However, what this amounts to with respect to each activity still remains ambiguous. For instance, see Olivier Boiral and others, 'Sustainability rating and moral fictionalism: opening the black box of nonfinancial agencies' [2021] 34 Accounting, Auditing and Accountability Journal 8, 1740–1768; Paul Johnston, Mark Everard, David Santillo and Karl-Henrik

Turning to refugee situations and international migration, the idea of developing two global compacts featured in the report of the UN Secretary-General at the time, Ban Ki-moon.[110] The report was submitted to the UNGA in April 2016 with two purposes.[111] First, it was conceived as a follow-up to the outcome of the Millennium Summit, the Millennium Declaration.[112] The commitments of States in the Millennium Declaration included strengthening international cooperation on 'burden sharing' to 'help' refugees and displaced persons, as well as taking measures to ensure the protection of the human rights of migrants, migrant workers and their families.[113] Second, it aimed to provide background and recommendations to the upcoming high-level plenary meeting on addressing large movements of refugees and migrants, which was to be held in New York in September 2016. The decision to hold a high-level plenary meeting was reached at the end of 2015, mainly triggered by the plight of refugees from Syria and the so-called 'migration crisis'.[114]

The Secretary-General's report reviewed the global trends, the phenomenon of large movements of refugees and migrants, and international cooperation, concluding that:

> In most cases, the actions needed to address the causes of large movements of people across international borders are well-known. New lists of recommendations are not necessary. Instead, mobilization of the political will and the resources to implement the decisions of the international community in the General Assembly, the Security Council and other international forums are needed. Rather than 'preventing' large movements of refugees and migrants, the factors that force refugees and migrants to abandon their homes and communities must be addressed.[115]

Robert, 'Reclaiming the definition of sustainability' [2007] 14 Environmental Science and Pollution Research International 1, 60–66.

110 Report of the Secretary-General, 'In Safety and dignity: addressing large movements of refugees and migrants' (2016) UN Doc A/70/59 (Secretary-General).

111 ibid.

112 UNGA Res 55/2 (18 September 2000) (Millennium Declaration). See also, UNGA Res 55/235 (30 January 2001); UNGA Res 57/144 (26 February 2003) (Follow-up to the outcome of the Millennium Summit).

113 Millennium Declaration (n 112), paras 25 and 26.

114 UNGA Res 70/L.34 (22 December 2015). Also see UNGA Res 70/290 (19 July 2016) GAOR 70th Session.

115 Secretary-General (n 110) para 52.

The report identified three pillars for new global commitments. Pillar 1 involved upholding safety and dignity in large movements of both refugees and migrants, and called upon States to fully implement their legal obligations and previous collective decisions, such as the nine core international human rights treaties, the Paris Agreement on Climate Change and the 2030 Agenda for Sustainable Development.[116] Pillar 2 involved the adoption of a global compact on responsibility-sharing for refugees, which would specifically 'commit Member States to support a comprehensive refugee response whenever a large-scale and potentially prolonged refugee movement occurs'.[117] Pillar 3 called upon the adoption of a global compact for safe, orderly and regular migration, in order to 'elaborate a comprehensive international cooperation framework on migrants and human mobility'.[118]

Five months later, a one-day, high-level plenary meeting of the UNGA to address large movements of refugees and migrants was convened. As a result, the States unanimously adopted the New York Declaration for Refugees and Migrants (New York Declaration).[119] The real significance of the New York Declaration lies in the ambitious and momentous process it initiated: endorsing the entry of IOM into the UN system as a 'related organisation' and launching negotiation and consultation processes for the two new UN Global Compacts.[120]

It was primarily the UNHCR and several European States that pushed for the development of two separate compacts.[121] For the UNHCR, the specific legal regime already in place to protect refugees had to be separated, first, because there was no such regime for international migration and, second, because there was a fear of reopening intergovernmental negotiations on the Refugee Convention, if the commitments for refugees were not drafted under its control.[122] As a result of separating the compacts, the UNHCR was able to lead

116 ibid para 100 and 101.

117 ibid para 68.

118 ibid para 105.

119 UNGA, 'New York Declaration for Refugees and Migrants' (13 September 2016) GAOR 71st Session UN Doc A/71/L.1 (New York Declaration).

120 Chetail (n 47) 325.

121 Diego Badell, 'The EU, migration and contestation: the UN Global Compact for migration, from consensus to dissensus' [2021] Global Affairs, Elizabeth G Ferris and Katharine M Donato, Refugees, *Migration and Global Governance* (Routledge 2020) 1–29, 100–122. Also see Rieko Karatani, 'How history separated refugee and migrant regimes: In search of their institutional origins' [2005] 17 International Journal of Refugee Law 3, 517–541.

122 UNHCR defines a compact as 'an agreement that is not legally binding but that captures, by consensus, political commitments both to principles and to concrete action by Member States'. See UNHCR, 'New York Declaration FAQs' (*UNHCR, February 2018*) <https://www.unhcr.org/584689257> accessed 6 April 2022.

the two-year multi-stakeholder negotiations to develop the Global Compact on Refugees.[123] For European States, having two separate compacts ensured sovereignty over migration and border control.[124]

Apart from the common timeframe for their development, the two compacts remain different.[125] The Global Compact on Refugees is grafted onto a legally binding treaty regime (the Refugee Convention and its Protocol), and it is specific (i.e. it aims to operationalise burden- and responsibility-sharing principles under only four objectives).[126] Therefore, it can be seen as a political declaration of intent.[127] By contrast, the Global Compact for Migration is the first instrument on international migration. It is extensive in scope: organised into twenty-three objectives, it has several aims, including addressing the drivers of migration and protecting the human rights of migrants.[128] It reinstates and reinforces international legal norms relating to migration by drawing on the obligations of States under several sources of international law.[129] This packaging exercise can be seen as a critical step in an ongoing political process, and thus the Global Compact for Migration must not be seen as a final product.[130]

---

123 UNGA Res 71/280 (17 April 2017) UN Doc A/RES/71/280, first preambular paragraph.

124 For instance, UK Prime Minister stressed that 'refugees and economic migrants must be better differentiated [...] [to] ensure that countries had a right to control their borders'. The official declarations are available at <http://www.un.org/press/en/2016/ga11820.doc.htm> accessed 6 April 2022. Also see Chetail (n 47) 328.

125 The Global Compact for Migration was developed as a result of a State-led, UN-assisted discourse. The UNGA President was invited to appoint two country co-facilitators to provide guidance throughout the process, for which he appointed Mexico (Ambassador Juan José Gomez Camacho) and Switzerland (Ambassador Jürg Lauber). The process for the development of the compact was divided into three phases: consultation (April to September 2017), stocktaking (November 2017 to January 2018), and intergovernmental negotiations (February to July 2018). The Global Compact on Refugees was developed in three phases led by the UNHCR: informal thematic discussions (January to November 2017), stocktaking (December 2017), and consultations with Member States and other stakeholders (February to July 2018).

126 Global Compact on Refugees (n 9).

127 Chetail (n 47) 336; Alexander Betts, 'The Global Compact on Refugees: Towards a theory of change?' [2018] 30 International Journal of Refugee Law 4, 623–626.

128 Global Compact for Migration (n 9).

129 ibid.

130 The report of the Special Representative of the Secretary-General on Migration at the time, Peter Sutherland, proposed seeing the Global Compact for Migration as having two functions. First, it 'could bundle agreed norms and principles into a global framework agreement with both binding and non-binding elements'. Second, it could 'identify areas in which States seek to work towards the conclusion of new international norms and treaties'. He used the term 'minilateralism' to describe how small groups of interested States

However, the idea that the Global Compact for Migration could lead to the creation of binding norms concerned States.[131] For instance, the US mission withdrew from the negotiations in December 2017, stating that:

> Compact supporters, recognizing the lack of widespread support for a legally-binding international migration convention, would seek to use the Compact and its outcomes and objectives as a long-term means of building customary international law or so-called "soft law" in the area of migration. The United States is particularly concerned by the novel use of the term "compact" to describe the document. Unlike standard titles for international instruments, "compact" has no settled meaning in international law, but it implies legal obligation. Hence, the Compact is amenable to claims that its commitments are legal obligations or at least evidence of international consensus on universal legal principles. The United States objects to any such claims and holds that neither the Compact nor any commitments by States to implement its objectives create any legal obligations on UN Member States or create new rights or protections for foreign nationals as a matter of conventional or customary international law.[132]

Announcements were made the same year by Hungary, Australia, Austria, the Czech Republic, Slovakia, Israel, Poland and Bulgaria that they would not sign the agreed text.[133] The co-facilitator, Switzerland, decided to hold

---

could work together to develop and implement new ideas that can then be debated, and perhaps be adopted in more formal settings. This mixing of roles of codifying existing rules, on the one hand, and inspiring progressive development, on the other, might be where the true ambition of the compact lies. See Report of the Special Representative of the Secretary-General on Migration, (28 December 2016) UN Doc. A/71/728 (Sutherland Report). Also, Rush perceived the compacts as a 'new model for international lawmaking, one that will shape state behaviour'. See Nayla Rush, 'Avoiding the quicksand of the Global Compact on Refugees' [2018] Center for Immigration Studies.

131 Jeff Crisp, 'Mobilizing political will for refugee protection and solutions: A framework for analysis and action' (World Refugee Council Research Paper 1, 2018); Kelly Currie, 'Explanation of vote in a meeting of the third committee on a UNHCR omnibus resolution' (US Mission to the United Nations, 13 November 2018). Also see Laurens Cerulus and Eline Schaart 'How the UN migration pact got trolled' (*Politico*, 3 January 2019) <politico.eu/article/united-nations-migration-pact-how-got-trolled/> accessed 6 April 2022.

132 US Mission to the UN, 'National Statement of the United States of America on the Adoption of the Global Compact on Safe, Orderly and Regular Migration' (7 December 2018).

133 Espinoza, Hadj-Abdou and Brumat argue that there were four reasons for the opposition to the Global Compact for Migration. First, States with restrictive migration agendas, such as Hungary and the US, viewed approving the Global Compact for Migration as a symbolic

a parliamentary debate on the issue, and has still not adopted the Global Compact for Migration.[134]

This leads to the final difference between the two global compacts – whilst the Global Compact on Refugees was endorsed by a vote of 181 States in favour, the Global Compact for Migration received only 152 votes in favour.[135]

---

act of promoting migration. Second, there was a fear that the compact, even though non-binding now, could amount to common practice or law later. Third, references to human rights, especially with respect to border control, worried some States. Fourth, there was a growing influence of the new far right movements in politics. See Marcia Vera Espinoza, Leila Hadj-Abdou and Leiza Brumat, 'Global Compact for Migration_ what is it and why are countries opposing it?' (*The Conversation*, 7 December 2018) <https:// theconversation.com/global-compact-for-migration-what-is-it-and-why-are-countries-opposing-it-106654> accessed 6 April 2022.

134 On its dispatch dated 3 February 2021, the Federal Council supported the Parliament's assent to the Global Compact for Migration. Importantly, the dispatch states that: 'Unlike the Global Compact on Refugees, the Global Compact for Migration does not address the specific challenges associated with refugees and thus takes account of the need to keep the two categories separate. The objectives set out in the Global Compact are in line with Switzerland's migration policy priorities: secure borders, addressing the root causes of irregular migration and forced displacement, preventing human trafficking, providing assistance and protection on the ground, repatriation and reintegration, and protecting human rights. Safe, orderly and regular migration contributes to the attainment of the Sustainable Development Goals. Parliament's assent to the Global Compact will also enable to Switzerland to participate in and influence discussions on migration at UN level'. See Swiss Federal Council, (Press Release, 3 February 2021) <https://www.admin.ch/gov/en/start/documentation/media-releases/media-releases-federal-council.msg-id-82217.html> accessed 6 April 2022. Also see Vania Nzeyimana and Younes Ahouga, 'The Global Compact for Migration: One Year Later' (*Foraus*, 13 December 2019) <https://www.foraus.ch/posts/the-global-compact-for-migration-one-year-later/> accessed 6 April 2022.

135 The Global Compact on Refugees was endorsed by a vote of 2 against (the US and Hungary), 3 abstentions (Eritrea, Libya and Dominican Republic) and 7 did not vote (North Korea, Israel, Micronesia, Nauru, Poland, Tonga and Turkmenistan). The Global Compact for Migration was endorsed with a vote of 5 against (the US, Hungary, Israel, Czech Republic and Poland), 12 abstentions (Algeria, Australia, Austria, Bulgaria, Chile, Italy, Latvia, Libya, Liechtenstein, Romania, Singapore and Switzerland) and 24 did not vote (Afghanistan, Antigua/Barbuda, Belize, Benin, Botswana, Brunei Darussalam, Democratic People's Republic of Korea, Dominican Republic, Guinea, Kiribati, Kyrgyzstan, Micronesia, Panama, Paraguay, Sao Tome/ Principe, Seychelles, Slovenia, Somalia, Timor-Leste, Tonga, Trinidad/Tobago, Turkmenistan, Ukraine and Vanuatu). See UN News, 'UN affirms "historic" global compact to support world's refugees' (UN News 17 December 2018) <https://news.un.org/en/story/2018/12/1028791> accessed 6 April 2022; UN, 'General Assembly Endorses First-Ever Global Compact on Migration, Urging Cooperation among Member States in Protecting Migrants' (UN 19 December 2018) <https://www.un.org/press/en/2018/ga12113.doc.htm> accessed 6 April 2022.

A common achievement of the two compacts is that international cooperation for refugee situations and international migration has now clearly found its political place in the UN system.[136] Similar to the networking function of the UN Global Compact, the added value of the Global Compact on Refugees and the Global Compact for Migration lies in the institutional frameworks these have created to mobilise political discussions, commitments and actions by bringing together public, civil and private actors.[137]

3.2 *International Protection and the Global Compact on Refugees*

This section discusses the integration of HMDCC and international protection into the Global Compact on Refugees.

In Paragraph 8 of the Global Compact on Refugees, States recognise that:

> [w]hile not in themselves causes of refugee movements, climate, environmental degradation and natural disasters increasingly interact with the drivers of refugee movements. In the first instance, addressing root causes is the responsibility of countries at the origin of refugee movements. However, averting and resolving large refugee situations are also matters of serious concern to the international community as a whole, requiring early efforts to address their drivers and triggers, as well as improved cooperation among political, humanitarian, development and peace actors.[138]

With this statement, the States endorsed the UNHCR's long-standing interpretation of the Refugee Convention, which does not recognise 'climate' or 'environmental' refugees.[139] This paragraph endorses the view that the responsibility to 'address' primarily lies with the State of origin, in other words, the

---

136 Elspeth Guild and Stefanie Grant, 'Migration Governance in the UN: What is the Global Compact and What does it mean?' (2017) Queen Mary School of Law Legal Studies Research Paper No. 252/2017, 15.

137 For a discussion on these institutional frameworks, see Chapter 4.2.3 of this book.

138 Global Compact on Refugees (n 9). This builds on the recognition in the New York Declaration, which recognised that people move in response to the adverse effects of climate change, natural disasters, or other environmental factors. See New York Declaration (n 119) 1.

139 Although, it must be stressed that the UNHCR has 'added value' to the protection of persons in the context of disasters and climate change and has been influential in shaping the international agenda. See Guy S Goodwin-Gill and Jane McAdam, 'UNHCR and Climate Change, Disasters, and Displacement' (UNHCR 2017) <https://www.refworld.org/pdfid/59413c7115.pdf> accessed 6 April 2022. For reasons of the UNHCR's preference against the use of 'climate' or 'environmental' refugees, see Chapter 2.1.1 of this book.

affected State. Furthermore, the paragraph does not mention protection or international protection, instead focusing on 'averting' and 'resolving' large refugee situations, as well as employing early efforts to 'address' their drivers and triggers.

International cooperation for the prevention of the drivers of large refugee situations calls upon the 'international community as a whole' to 'support efforts to alleviate poverty, reduce disaster risks, and provide development assistance to countries of origin, in line with the 2030 Agenda for Sustainable Development and other relevant frameworks'.[140] Although the Global Compact on Refugees references other relevant frameworks in the footnotes, such as the Sendai Framework for Disaster Risk Reduction, the fact that the link with the international climate change regime (such as the UNFCCC or the Paris Agreement) is not clearly articulated represents a missed opportunity.

The role of the international community is further explained in Paragraph 12 of the Global Compact on Refugees, which states that:

> in certain situations, external forced displacement may result from sudden-onset natural disasters and environmental degradation. These situations present complex challenges for affected States, which may seek support from the international community to address them. Support for appropriate responses could build on the operational partnerships between relevant actors, including UNHCR and the International Organization for Migration (IOM), engaging their respective mandates, roles and expertise as appropriate to ensure a coordinated approach.[141]

The only mention of protection when referring to HMDCC is found in Paragraph 63 of the Global Compact on Refugees, which states that:

> where appropriate, stakeholders with relevant mandates and expertise will provide guidance and support for measures to address other protection and humanitarian challenges. This could include measures to assist those forcibly displaced by natural disasters, taking into account national laws and regional instruments as applicable, as well as practices such as temporary protection and humanitarian stay arrangements, where appropriate.[142]

---

140 Global Compact on Refugees (n 9) para 9.
141 Global Compact on Refugees (n 9) para 12.
142 ibid para 63.

At first sight, these paragraphs appear to break little new ground. They merely refer to the practices of stakeholders in supporting affected States when it comes to addressing displacement in the context of disasters and environmental factors. However, a more optimistic reading can show that, despite the apparent pressure exerted on UNHCR by States aiming to keep the compact limited to the Refugee Convention, environmental factors and disasters were ultimately acknowledged.[143] This acknowledgement, in turn, feeds into the implementation of the commitments, which must be done 'in a way which avoids protection gaps and enables all those in need of international protection to find and enjoy it'.[144] Building on this basis, McAdam and Wood argue that using the term refugee as a 'shorthand' for those who require international protection is 'no longer accurate or desirable, and risks arbitrarily privileging the rights of some forced migrants over others'.[145]

Although the text of the compact does not articulate the international protection of PMDCC, the inclusion of HMDCC into the text can be considered as a stepping stone towards recognising 'all those in need of international protection'.[146]

3.3 *International Protection and the Global Compact for Safe, Orderly and Regular Migration*

Through the Global Compact for Migration, States articulated an understanding of HMDCC and placed the compact in the centre of future discussions and actions. This section interprets the relevant sections of the compact in order to discuss these new commitments, and their relationship with the notion of international protection.

Objective 2 of the compact concerns the minimisation of the adverse drivers and structural factors that compel people to leave their country of origin.[147] This objective contains the only thematic cluster in the whole document – under paragraphs (h) to (l), which are dedicated to natural disasters – focused on the adverse effects of climate change and environmental degradation.[148] In

143 McAdam and Wood (n 16) 191–206. Also see Aleinikoff, 'The Unfinished Work of the Global Compact on Refugees' [2018] 30 International Journal of Refugee Law, 611–617.

144 Global Compact on Refugees (n 9) para 61. See also, McAdam and Wood (n 16) 191–206.

145 McAdam and Wood (n 16) 191–206. Also see Hakan G. Sicakkan, 'A Comparative Research Framework for Studying the Global Refugee Compact's Impact on International Protection' (University of Bergen 2021).

146 Global Compact on Refugees (n 9) para 61.

147 Global Compact for Migration (n 9) objective 2. See Elisa Fornalé and Aylin Yildiz, 'GCM Indicators: Objective 2: Minimize the adverse drivers and structural factors that compel people to leave their country of origin' (Refugee Law Initiative 8 August 2019).

148 ibid.

this section, States committed to the following measures: (i) strengthening the joint analysis and sharing of information to better map migration movements; (ii) developing adaptation and resilience strategies to manage sudden-onset and slow-onset natural disasters, the adverse effects of climate change and environmental degradation, taking into account the potential implications for migration; (iii) integrating displacement considerations into disaster preparedness strategies and promoting cooperation; (iv) harmonising and developing approaches and mechanisms at the subregional and regional levels; (v) developing coherent approaches by taking into account State-led consultative processes, such as the Nansen Protection Agenda and the PDD.

Objective 5 concerns the enhancement of the availability and flexibility of pathways for regular migration. This objective is particularly significant for HMDCC for a number of reasons.[149] First, States committed to facilitating regional and cross-regional labour mobility, in accordance with the ILO standards, guidelines and principles and in compliance with international human rights law. Importantly, responding to the needs of migrants in a situation of vulnerability is entrenched as a consideration for such facilitation efforts. Translated into practice, this means that the needs of PMDCC should be taken into account when States negotiate instruments concerning the facilitation of the movement of persons. Examples could include free movement agreements, visa liberalisation and labour mobility cooperation frameworks, as well as free or liberalised movement chapters under PTAs. Second, in paragraph (g), States committed to developing or building on forms of complementary protection based on humanitarian or other considerations for migrants compelled to leave their countries of origin owing to sudden-onset disasters and other precarious situations. Third, in paragraph (h), States committed to cooperating to identify, develop and strengthen solutions for migrants compelled to leave their countries of origin owing to environmental changes. In cases where adaptation in or return to their country of origin is not possible, it is recommended to devise planned relocation and visa options.

Objective 5 is complemented by Objective 18, which commits States to invest in skills development and facilitate the mutual recognition of skills, qualifications and competences. Actions under this objective include concluding bilateral, regional or multilateral mutual recognition agreements or including recognition provisions in other agreements, such as labour mobility or trade agreements.[150]

---

149 Global Compact for Migration (n 9) objective 5.

150 See Fornalé and Yildiz (n 147); Elisa Fornalé, Aylin Yildiz and Federica Cristani, 'Objective 18: Invest in skills development and facilitate mutual recognition of skills, qualifications

The commitments of States to protect the human rights of migrants and to promote their inclusion in host countries can complement these objectives.[151] For instance, under Objective 21, States committed to upholding the prohibition on the collective expulsion and return of migrants when there is a real and foreseeable risk of death, torture or other cruel, inhumane and degrading treatment or punishment, or other irreparable harm, in accordance with international human rights law.[152] McAdam and Wood interpret this as a reference to international protection, arguing that 'the full range of States' international protection obligations remain at the forefront of efforts to implement *both* the Global Compacts'.[153]

Recently, in its decision on the *Ioane Teitiota v New Zealand* case, the UNHRCom referenced the Global Compact for Migration in order to note that both sudden-onset events and slow-onset processes 'can propel cross-border movement of individuals seeking protection from climate change-related harm'.[154] The UNHRCom further confirmed that 'without robust national and international efforts', the effects of climate change may expose individuals to a violation of their rights and trigger the *non-refoulement* obligations of States.[155]

Although the Global Compact for Migration does not articulate the international protection of PMDCC, the inclusion of environmental factors into the compact opens up multiple areas for law and policy-making. The text represents a 'sophisticated' understanding of HMDCC: on the one hand, there is a commitment to strengthening resilience and preventing displacement which will help people stay; on the other hand, pathways for planned and regular migration are encouraged in order to allow people to move out of harm's way.[156] Furthermore, by way of committing to the principle of *non-refoulement*, the implementation of the Global Compact for Migration provides opportunities to discuss the international protection of PMDCC.

---

and competences' in Elspeth Guild and Tugba Basaran (eds), The UN's Global Compact for Safe, Orderly and Regular Migration [2018] Refugee Law Initiative, 51–52.

151 Global Compact for Migration (n 9) objectives 6–8, 13–18 and 22.

152 Global Compact for Migration (n 9) objective 21.

153 McAdam and Wood (n 16) 191–206.

154 *Ioane Teitiota* (n 83).

155 ibid. The relevance of the *non-refoulement* principle under international human rights law and the case of *Ioane Teitiota* are discussed in more detail in Chapter 2.2.1 of this book.

156 Walter Kälin, 'The Migration Compact on Migration: A Ray of Hope for Disaster-Displaced Persons' [2018] 30 IJRL 4, 664.

3.4 *Future Implications*

As the analysis above has demonstrated, although the compacts do not specifically acknowledge the international protection of PMDCC[157], their implementation might provide opportunities to advocate for measures in this direction.[158]

In this sense, the compacts do not adopt the approach proposed by some commentators for creating a legal protection status dedicated to PMDCC.[159] Considering that the Global Compact on Refugees is a political declaration of intent grafted onto the Refugee Convention, it might not have been the right forum to recognise a new international protection status. The Global Compact for Migration, on the other hand, provided a more promising venue: from the beginning, it aspired to be a soft law instrument capable of addressing migration in all its dimensions. However, it failed to deliver on its promise by not recognising the protection needs of PMDCC.[160]

157 Other than the issue of HMDCC, the compacts have been criticised for failing to address four topics: IDPs, large-scale mixed movements, pandemics, and cross-border movements for the purposes of trade, services, investment, and education. See Cecilia Jimenez-Damary, 'Open letter from the Special Rapporteur on the Human Rights of Internally Displaced Persons on the inclusion of IDPs in the Global Compact on Safe, Regular and Orderly Migration, in line with the New York Declaration on Refugees and Migrants' (UN Human Rights Special Procedures, 12 March 2018) <OpenLetterInclusion12March2018.pdf (ohchr.org)> accessed 6 April 2022; Elizabeth E Ferris and Susan F Martin, 'The Global Compacts on Refugees and for Safe, Orderly and Regular Migration: An Introduction to the Special Issue' [2019] 57 International Migration 6, 10; Indranil Chakraborty and Prasenjit, 'COVID-19 outbreak: Migration, effects on society, global environment and prevention' [2020] 728 Science of the Total Environment 138882, 1–7.

158 See Chapter 4.2.3 of this book for a detailed analysis of the follow-up and review mechanisms of the compacts.

159 For proposals of conventions, see Hodgkinson and others (n 13); 'The Toledo Initiative on Environmental Refugees and Ecological Restoration', Toledo, Spain (9–10 July 2004); Dana Zartner Falstrom, 'Stemming the Flow of Environmental Displacement: Creating a Convention to Protect Persons and Preserve the Environment' [2001] 1 Colorado Journal of International Environmental Law and Policy, 1–19.

160 One reason for this could be that the Global Compact for Migration did not want to create 'hierarchies of vulnerability'. Oberoi from OHCHR stated that: 'the global compact on migration should not create hierarchies of vulnerability or distinguish between good migrants and others. The multiplicity of categories meant numerous barriers to claiming rights. In addition, the need for specific protection interventions did not mean that migrants did not have agency. At the same time, migrants in vulnerable situations were entitled to a strengthened duty of care'. See IOM, 'International Dialogue on Migration 2017: Strengthening International Cooperation and Governance of Migration' (18–19 April 2017), 30.

At the crux of these omissions lies the fact that the compacts were negotiated with trade-offs and that they represent a diverse range of interests and aspirations, leading compromises to be made.[161] Both compacts highlight State sovereignty to decide migration and border control policies. Perhaps what makes the compacts 'game-changers' is not what has been left off the agenda, but the fact that, amidst the political storms, international consensus was reached, enabling cooperation on a wide-range of topics related to the human mobility.[162]

4 Conclusion

This chapter has outlined the need to provide international protection to PMDCC. It characterised HMDCC as a complex planetary and intergenerational problem, which (i) emerges from the actions and interactions of multiple actors, (ii) has multiple, dynamic and interconnected variables, (iii) is occuring in the conditions of scientific uncertainty and evolving scientific knowledge, and (iv) is planetary in scope and intergenerational in impact.

In order to address the complex problem of HMDCC, the chapter proposed adopting an international minimum standard to protect PMDCC, which would be founded on three pillars: *non-refoulement*, prevention and facilitation. *Non-refoulement* refers to the granting of protection to PMDCC against return to their country of origin. Prevention refers to taking concrete measures to avoid future displacement. Facilitation refers to lowering barriers to safe, orderly, and regular migration to enable *in situ* and *ex situ* adaptation to climate change and disasters.

161 For instance, Koslowski points out that the compacts significantly expanded international cooperation on border control and international travel. The increased security nexus might impede the ability of asylum seekers to leave their homes and seek refuge elsewhere. See Rey Kowlowski, 'International Travel Security and the Global Compacts on Refugees and Migration' [2019] 57 IOM 6. Furthermore, Hennebry and Petrozziello examine the compacts from a gender perspective, and concluded that 'unless the compacts together can be employed to challenge the existing patriarchal status quo of how individuals on the move are governed, not only will they fail to realize the gender-responsiveness, but they will also fail to achieve "safe" migration for all'. See Jenna L. Hennebry and Allison J. Petrozziello, 'Closing the Gap? Gender and the Global Compacts for Migration and Refugees' [2019] 57 IOM 6, 115–138.

162 Betts states that the basis on which we should judge the compacts must be the difference they make in practice to the lives of migrants, refugees, and other displaced persons. See Betts (n 127) 623–626.

The proposed international minimum standard goes beyond the existing obligations and commitments of States under international law. However, as the discussion on the notion of international protection has shown, persons have been afforded different types of international protection under international law for over a century. Considering the urgency and the complexity of the problem, PMDCC must be protected at the international level in order to save current and succeeding generations from the scourge of climate change.

Finally, in order to compare the proposed international protection with the current commitments of States, the Global Compact on Refugees and the Global Compact for Migration were analysed. The former is a political declaration of intent for burden- and responsibility-sharing with respect to refugees, while the latter is a packaging exercise to reiterate the obligations of States under international law with respect to migrants. Both compacts have significant shortcomings. For instance, they are legally non-binding and they fail to propose an international protection mechanism for PMDCC. Yet, both compacts refer to disasters, the impact of climate change and environmental degradation as drivers of human movement. This demonstrates that States are opening space to discuss HMDCC as a part of international negotiations under the auspices of the UN. The impetus for the international protection of PMDCC as proposed in this chapter is evident.

CHAPTER 2

Mapping the Legal Gaps

This chapter demonstrates that international law does not recognise the international protection of PMDCC.[163] This legal gap persists despite the increasing number of cooperative initiatives aiming to address the complex problem of HMDCC.[164] Furthermore, existing treaties, general principles and customary rules do not provide for the international protection of PMDCC. As a result, this specific case cannot be subsumed under a more general rule of international law.[165] In constructing its argument, this chapter proceeds as follows. First, it examines the relevant international treaty regimes, i.e. the international refugee regime, the international climate change regime, the international desertification regime, the international labour regime, the international trade regime and the international human rights regimes.[166] Second, it analyses the relevant general principles and customary rules in international law concerning *non-refoulement*, displacement and the protection of persons in the event of disasters.[167] Third, it discusses the novel challenge presented by sea-level rise due to anthropogenic climate change and examines the ongoing work of the UN ILC and the ILA to address this issue under international law.[168] The

163 See Mostafa M Naser, *The Emerging Global Consensus on Climate Change and Human Mobility* (Routledge 2021); Sumudu Atapattu, 'Climate change and displacement: protecting "climate refugees" within a framework of justice and human rights' [2020] 11 Journal of Human Rights and the Environment 1, 86–113.

164 For instance, see Chapter 1.3 of this book for an examination of the recently adopted Global Compacts for Migration and on Refugees.

165 Although, as argued in Chapter 4.2 of this book, the international protection of PMDCC as a legal rule can derive from more general principles and rules of international law concerning the basic rights of the human person.

166 On treaty regimes, see Maria Fogdestam Agius, 'Treaty Regimes in International Law' in Maria Fogdestam Agius, *Interaction and Delimitation of International Legal Orders* (Brill 2015) 28–55; Study Group on the Fragmentation of International Law, Report on the Fragmentation of International Law: Difficulties Arising From the Diversification and Expansion of International Law UN Doc. A/CN.4/L.682 (April 13, 2006) (finalised by Martti Koskenniemi).

167 Kälin and Schrepfer (n 72).

168 ILC, 'Sea Level Rise in Relation to International Law: First Issues Paper by Bogdan Aurescu and Nilüfer Oral, Co-Chairs of the Study Group on Sea-level Rise in Relation to International Law' (28 February 2020) UN Doc A/CN.4/740; ILC, 'Report on the work of the seventieth session' (30 April-1 June and 2 July-10 August 2018) UN Doc A/73/10, 326; ILA, International Law and Sea Level Rise, Sydney Conference Report (2018). Also see ILA, Committee on International Law and Sea Level Rise, Resolution 6/2018.

chapter concludes by highlighting that the international protection of PMDCC has the potential to fill the legal gap by defining the responsibilities of rights-holders and the obligations of duty-bearers.[169]

1 Relevant International Treaty Regimes

From the mid-seventeenth century's little ice age[170] to the 'Dust Bowl' of the 1930s[171] and the 1986 Chernobyl nuclear disaster[172], people have been driven to move by environmental factors. Yet, an international treaty regime that addresses the protection needs of persons mobile due to environmental factors has never been created.[173] Since the 1980s, studies looking into the human movement–environment nexus have blossomed.[174] The IPCC's

169 For a discussion on the concept of duty-bearers, see Wouter Vandenhole, 'Obligations and responsibility in a plural and diverse duty-bearer human rights regime' in Wouter Vandenhole (ed), *Challenging Territoriality in Human Rights Law* (Routledge 2015).

170 Goeffrey Parker, *Global Crisis: War, Climate Change and Catastrophe in the Seventeenth Century* (Yale Univeristy Press 2013).

171 Myron Gutmann and others, 'Two Population-Environment Regimes in the Great Plains of the United States, 1930–1990' [2006] 27 Population and Environment 2, 191–225.

172 Marco Armiero and Richard Tucker (eds), *Environmental History of Modern Migrations* (Routledge 2017); William Yardley, 'Alaskan Town Seeks Lifeline amid Climate Change' (The New York Times 2007) <https://www.nytimes.com/2007/05/27/world/americas/27iht-27alaska.5880856.html> accessed 6 April 2022.

173 In fact, there was a large disregard of environmental factors from migration studies during most of the 20th century. Since the 1980s, there has been a 'rebirth' of the migration-environment nexus. Piguet and others identified four main trends to explain this disregard in literature. First, a powerful Western-centric idea claimed that technological progress would decrease the influence of nature on human life and hence, on migration. Second, environment-based explanations of migration were rejected to the benefit of socio-cultural approaches or Marxist/economist perspectives. Third, the rise of economic paradigm in migration theory meant that economic factors were given most of the central role to explain human movement. Finally, forced migration was premised on strong political factors according to the idea that States are making refugees, which failed to include the role of our environment. See Piguet, Pecoud and Guchteneire (n 29) 3–4. See also, Etienne Piguet, "From Primitive Migration" to "Climate Refugees": The Curious Fate of the Natural Environment in Migration Studies' [2012] 103:1 Annals of the Association of American Geographers 148.

174 The discussions evolved through two polarised camps. The first camp, the so-called 'alarmists' or 'maximalists', 'extract[ed] the environmental variable from a cluster of causes and proclaim[ed] the associated out-migration to be the direct result of environmental degradation'. They also viewed the human movement-environment nexus as a potential source of conflict and security threat that could be caused by 'flocks' of 'environmental refugees'. The second camp, the so-called 'sceptics' or 'minimalists', started from

acknowledgement in 1990 that '[t]he gravest effects of climate change may be those on human migration as millions are displaced by shoreline erosion, coastal flooding and severe drought' was a particular catalyst for further studies.[175] Acknowledging that the issue is too complex and that the danger of oversimplifying is too great, scholars have landed on a 'general consensus', which calls for developing comprehensive approaches.[176] The existing treaty regimes

---

the premise of the complexity of the migration-environment nexus. They criticised the 'alarmist' predictions for, amongst others, failing to account for the capacity of people to adapt to the adverse impacts of environmental changes. For alarmist viewpoints, see Jodi Jacobson, 'Environmental Refugees: A Yardstick of Habitability' [1988] Worldwatch Paper No: 86; Norman Myers and Jennifer Kent, 'Environmental Exodus: An Emergent Crisis in the Global Arena' [1995] Climate Institute. Also see Norman Myers and Jennifer Kent (ed), *The New Atlas of Planet Management* (University of California Press 2005); Arthur Westing, 'The Environmental Component of Comprehensive Security' (Sage 1989) 129–134. Ashok Swain, 'Environmental Migration and Conflict Dynamics: Focus on Developing Regions' [1996] 17 Third World Quarterly 5; Thomas Homer-Dixon, 'On the Threshold: Environmental Changes as Causes of Acute Conflict' [1991] 16 International Security 2, 76–116.; Angela Oels, From Securitization of Climate Change to Climatization of the Security Field (Springer 2012) 199; Wolfgang Kempf, 'A sea of environmental refugees? Oceania in an age of climate change' in Elfriede Hermann, Karin Klenke and Michael Dickhardt (eds), *Form, Macht, Differenz: Motive und Felder ethnologischen Forschens* (Göttingen: Göttingen University Press 2009). For the minimalist viewpoints, see UK Government (n 33) 27–28; Bettini, 'Climate Barbarians at the Gate? A critique of apocalyptic narratives on climate refugees' [2013] 45 Geoforum, 63–64; Alexander Betts, 'Survival Migration: A New Protection Framework' in Alynna Lyon and others (eds), *Global Governance: A Review of Multilateralism and International Organizations* (Brill Nijhoff 2020); Emily Wilkinson and others, 'Climate-induced migration and displacement: closing the policy gap' (ODI 2016); March Helbling, 'Attitudes towards climate change migrants' [2020] 160 Climatic Change, 89–102.

175 IPCC, 'First Assessment Report' (WMO 1990), para 5.10.10.

176 McAdam summed up the 'general consensus among migration scholars' as follows: '(a) climate change-related movement is a multi-causal phenomenon; most movement will be within countries rather than across borders; (b) climate-change related movement is likely to take different forms, and will require a variety of responses at the local, national, regional and international levels; (c) migration is a rational adaptation strategy to climate change processes, and should be supported as such; most people do not want to leave their homes, and sometimes the most vulnerable will not be able to move; (d) there is a need to strengthen legal, policy, institutional and administrative frameworks; planning and policy must be underpinned by a strong scientific and empirical basis; (e) policy needs to be proactive, not just remedial; (f) there is a need to strengthen operational and technical capacities, including through further funding; there must be sufficient budgetary support for long-term planning; (k) affected populations should be included in decision-making through participatory processes; (1) comprehensive approaches are needed-for example, migration management should be linked with other policy objectives, including climate change adaptation, disaster risk reduction, humanitarian responses and sustainable development; (m) multi-stakeholder partnerships, involving public and private

have served as important vehicles to explore and promote comprehensiveness.[177] This section examines how the international refugee regime, international climate change regime, international desertification regime, international labour regime, international trade regime and international human rights regimes have shaped and been shaped by the need to address HMDCC.

1.1 *International Refugee Regime*

The international refugee regime outlines the rights, obligations and responsibilities that States have towards asylum-seekers and refugees, as well as offering opportunities for cooperation on responsibility- and burden-sharing.[178] The regime centres around the Refugee Convention of 1951 and its Protocol of 1967 as the main legal sources, as well as the UNHCR as the primary agency.[179] This section discusses whether the purpose of the refugee regime – that is, ensuring that refugees receive access to international protection – may be utilised to provide international protection to PMDCC.

According to the Refugee Convention, there are five grounds to be granted the status of a refugee, namely the applicant's race, religion, nationality, membership of a particular social group or political opinion. Environmental factors, such as climate change or disasters, are not included.[180]

Nevertheless, whether PMDCC could be recognised as 'refugees' has been intensively debated.[181] Some of the earliest mentions are found in Vogt in 1948, who used the notion of an 'ecological refugee'[182], and Brown in 1970s, who

---

service actors, need to be developed; and (n) all responses should be underpinned by basic human rights principles'. See Jane McAdam, *Climate Change, Forced Migration and International Law* (Oxford University Press 2012) 235–236.

177 Koko Warner, 'Global environmental change and migration: Governance challenges' [2010] 20 Global Environmental Change 3, 402–413.

178 Alexander Betts, 'The Refugee Regime Complex' [2010] 29 Refugee Survey Quarterly 1, 12–37.

179 ibid.

180 For instance, see *Matter of Acosta*, A-24159781, United States Board of Immigration Appeals, 23 November 2010; *AF (Kiribati)* [2013] NZIPT 800413 (25 June 2013); *Ioane Teitiota* (n 83); Jane McAdam, 'The Emerging New Zealand Jurisprudence on Climate Change, Disasters and Displacement' [2015] 3(1) Migration Studies 131; Scott (n 14).

181 In the author's view, the adoption of the Global Compact for Refugees settled this debate and States have endorsed the view that environmental factors alone are not grounds to qualify for a refugee protection. See Chapter 1.3.2 of this book for a more detailed discussion.

182 'Ecological refugee' was used in the report of the Worldwatch Institute, which is a Washington-based non-governmental organisation, established by environmentalist Lester Brown in 1974. The early projects of the organisation analysed the potential links between migration and environmental disruptions.

advanced the concept of an 'environmental refugee'.[183] The term 'environmental refugee' was 'officially' popularised by El-Hinnawi in his UNEP report entitled *Environmental Refugees* in 1985.[184]

El-Hinnawi's report was particularly powerful in drawing attention to the potentially devastating impacts of unchecked development and pollution on 'forced migration'.[185] He used the factor of 'environmental disruption' as a qualifier which referred to 'any physical, chemical, and/or biological changes in the ecosystem (or resource base) that render it, temporarily or permanently, unsuitable to support human life'.[186] He defined environmental refugees as 'people who have been forced to leave their traditional habitat, temporarily or permanently, because of a marked environmental disruption (natural and/or triggered by people) that jeopardised their existence and/or seriously affected the quality of their life'.[187] He distinguished between three types of environmental refugees: (i) those who are temporarily displaced because of environmental stress, such as floods, earthquakes and other natural disasters; (ii) those who are permanently displaced and must be resettled in a new area as a consequence of human intervention, such as dam construction; (iii) those who have migrated within their own country due to the severe deterioration of their environment and who no longer have the resources necessary to meet their basic needs.[188] Although his work was criticised for being too broad and impractical, it has paved the way for studies to examine HMDCC in the coming decades.[189]

Shortly afterwards, in 1989, the UNHCR's Executive Committee mandated that the organisation look at the issue of the international protection of

183 Lester Russell Brown, Patricia McGrath and Bruce Stokes, 'Twenty Two Dimensions of the Population Problem' [1976] Worldwatch Institute, 7–82.

184 Essam El Hinnawi, 'Environmental Refugees' [1985] 2 UNEP, 1–41.

185 Høeg, E. & Tulloch, C. D, 'Sinking strangers: Media representations of climate refugees on the BBC and Al Jazeera' [2013] 43 Journal of Communication Inquiry 3, 225–248; David Keane, 'Environmental causes and consequences of migration: A search for the meaning of "environmental refugees"' [2004] 16 Georgetown Environmental Law Review, 209–223.

186 El Hinnawi (n 184) 466; Diane Bates, 'Environmental Refugees? Classifying Human Migrations Caused by Environmental Change' [2002] 23 Population and Environment 5, 465–477.

187 El Hinnawi (n 184) 466.

188 ibid.

189 Astri Suhrke and Annamaria Vinsentin, 'The Environmental Refugee: A New Approach' 1991; Francois Gemenne, *Environmental Changes and Migration Flows: Normative Frameworks and Policy Responses* (PhD thesis, Institut d'Etudes Politiques de Paris and Université de Liége 2009).

'environmentally displaced persons'.[190] Their report, entitled *Solutions and Protection*, observed that natural and ecological disasters (as well as extreme poverty) are causes of migration and uprootedness that could 'contribute to flows of persons across borders'.[191]

Although the UNHCR's report did not use the term 'refugees' to describe environmentally displaced persons, the popularisation of 'environmental refugees' resonated well with popular discourse.[192] For instance, the Carteret Islanders in Papua New Guinea were relocated within their country largely due to sea-level rise and were characterised in popular media as 'the world's first environmental refugees'.[193] To quote Dina Ioanesco, the head of the Migration, Environment and Climate Change Division of the IOM, the 'image of "climate refugees" resonates metaphorically to all as it mirrors the current images we see of those escaping wars and conflicts. With the threat of climate change we imagine millions becoming refugees in the future'.[194]

Concomitantly, the term 'climate refugees' received support from governments. In 2006, the government of the Maldives convened an international conference to discuss the protection and resettlement of 'climate refugees' and proposed the amendment of the Refugee Convention.[195] For a small island nation threatened by rising sea levels, the availability of a clear international legal status that provides international protection and resettlement options was a matter of national security.[196] Similarly, in the run-up to the UNFCCC

---

190 UNHCR ExCom, 'Report of the Working Group on Solutions and Protection to the Forty-second Session of the Executive Committee of the High Commissioner's Programme' (12 August 1991) UN Doc EC/SCP/64, paragraph 8.

191 ibid.

192 Bettini (n 163) 63. See Steven Saphore, 'Why Canada needs to think about accepting climate change refugees' (CBC, 21 May 2021) <https://www.cbc.ca/news/science/what-on-earth-trees-climate-refugees-1.6034396> accessed 6 April 2022.

193 Sanjay Gupta, 'Pacific swallowing remote island Chain' (CNN, 2007) <http://edition.cnn.com/CNN/Programs/anderson.cooper.360/blog/2007/07/pacific-swallowing-remote-island-chain.html> accessed 6 April 2022.

194 Dina Ionesco, 'Let's Talk About Climate Migrants, Not Climate Refugees' (UN Sustainable Development Goals Blog 2019) <https://www.un.org/sustainabledevelopment/blog/2019/06/lets-talk-about-climate-migrants-not-climate-refugees/> accessed 6 April 2022.

195 See Republic of the Maldives Ministry of Environment, Energy and Water, 'Report on the First Meeting on Protocol on Environmental Refugees: Recognition of Environmental Refugees in the 1951 Convention and 1967 Protocol Relating to the Status of Refugees' (Male, Maldives, 14–15 August 2006) mentioned in Frank Biermann and Ingrid Boas, 'Protecting Climate Refugees: The Case for a Global Protocol' [2008] 50 Environment: Science and Policy for Sustainable Development 6, 8–17.

196 See 'Maleì Declaration on the Human Dimension of Global Climate Change' (14 November 2007) 1 <www.ciel.org/Publications/ Male_Declaration_Nov07.pdf> accessed 6 April 2022.

conference of 2009, the Bangladeshi finance minister stated that the Refugee Convention could be revised to protect 'climate refugees', since the Convention has been 'through other revisions, so this should be possible'.[197]

However, the call for the recognition of 'environmental/climate refugees' has also faced a strong backlash.[198] These arguments can be grouped together under three headings. The first group of objections relates to a textual interpretation of the definition of a refugee under the Refugee Convention.[199] Commentators argue that environmental factors are not recognised as one of the five grounds for refugee protection.[200] Furthermore, they claim that the definition of a refugee fundamentally concerns individuals, whereas environmental factors are indiscriminate and do not target persons based on grounds recognised in the Convention.[201] An individualised determination of the status of a refugee would be ill-suited to mass-displacement scenarios induced by environmental changes, such as in the case of displacement of a community due to a cyclone.[202] Moreover, commentators point out that the refugee definition is forward-looking, meaning that it is limited to persons who have already fled their own country due to risks of civil or political discrimination.[203] By

---

197 See Harriet Grant, James Randerson and John Vidal, 'UK Should Open Borders to Climate Refugees, Says Bangladeshi Minister' (The Guardian, 4 December 2009) <http://www.guardian.co.uk/environment/ 2009/nov/30/rich-west-climate-change/print> accessed 6 April 2022.

198 See, for instance, Tanja Dreher and others, 'Climate Refugees or Migrants? Contesting Media Frames on Climate Justice in the Pacific' [2014] 9 Environmental Communication 1, 1–19; Daniel Faber and others, 'Give me Shelter from the Storm: Framing the Climate Refugee Crisis in the Context of Neoliberal Capitalism' [2017] 28 Capitalism Nature Socialism 3, 1–17.

199 See Benoit Mayer and Francois Crépeau (eds), *Research Handbook on Climate Change, Migration and the Law* (Edward Elgar 2017); Kate Pincock and Alexander Betts, *The Global Governed? Refugees as Providers of Protection and Assistance* (CUP 2020). For instance, see *Matter of Acosta* (n 180); Ioane Teitiota (n 83); McAdam (n 176) 131; Scott (n 14).

200 UNHCR, 'Legal considerations regarding claims for international protection made in the context of the adverse effects of climate change and disasters' (1 October 2020) <https://www.refworld.org/pdfid/5f75f2734.pdf> accessed 6 April 2022; Adrienne Anderson, Michelle Foster, Hélène Lambert and Jane McAdam, 'Imminence in refugee and human rights law: a misplaced notion for international protection' [2019] 68 ICLQ 1, 111–140.

201 Brian Opeskin, Richard Perruchoud, Jillyanne Redpath-Cross, *Foundations of International Migration Law* (Cambridge University Press 2012) 178. Also see *Horvath v Secretary of State for the Home Department* [2000] UKHL 37, [2001] AC 489; *Applicant A v Minister for Immigration and Ethnic Affairs* [1997] *HCA 4,* [1997] *190 CLR 225; Canada (Attorney General) v Ward* [1993] 2 SCR 689.

202 McAdam (n 176) 186.

203 Sarah M. Munoz, 'Environmental Mobility in a Polarized World: Questioning the Pertinence of the "Climate Refugee" Label for Pacific Islanders' [2021] Journal of

contrast, most HMDCC occurs internally.[204] Since the status of a refugee entails forced movement across borders, this may prevent from addressing the needs of the majority of PMDCC due to a rigid category.[205]

The second group of objections relates to the phenomenon of HMDCC. According to some commentators, even if the definition of a refugee under the Refugee Convention were to be amended to include environmental factors, it would be difficult to successfully invoke this justification before domestic authorities.[206] This is due to the multi-causal nature of HMDCC, which makes it very difficult to prove that environmental factors are the sole cause of the forced movement.[207] Furthermore, commentators highlight that a well-founded fear of being persecuted by one's own government is required for the determination of refugee status.[208] It is more often the case that those who move due to environmental factors are not facing the risk of persecution by their own government on the basis of environmental factors.[209] Antonio Guterres, who was the UN High Commissioner for Refugees at the time, reinforced this view:

> As the refugee definition only applies to those who have crossed an international border, the difficulties in characterizing climate change as 'persecution', and the indiscriminate nature of its impacts, it does not

International Migration and Integration; Pincock and Betts (n 199); Mayer and Crépeau (eds) (n 199).

204 Caroline Zickgraf, 'Climate change, slow onset events and human mobility: reviewing the evidence' [2021] 50 Current Opinion in Environmental Sustainability, 21–30; UK Government (n 33).

205 McAdam (n 176) 186.

206 Kelly Buchanan, 'New Zealand: 'Climate change refugee' case overview' [2013] Global Legal Research Center; Ingrid Boas and others, 'Climate migration myths' [2019] 9 Nature Climate Change, 901-903.

207 Etienne Piguet, 'From "primitive migration" to "climate refugees": The curious fate of the natural environment in migration studies' [2013] 103 Annals of the Association of American Geographers 1, 148–162.

208 Andrew Baldwin, Christiane Fröhlich and Delf Rothe, 'From climate migration to anthropocene mobilities: Shifting the debate' [2018] 14 Mobilities *3*, 289–297; Jane McAdam, 'Swimming Against the Tide: Why a Climate Change Displacement Treaty is Not the Answer' in Mary Crock (ed), *Refugees and Rights* (Routledge 2015).

209 In the case of *A and Another* before the High Court of Australia, Dawson J reflected this view: 'By including in its operative provisions the requirement that a refugee fear persecution, the Convention limits its humanitarian scope and does not afford universal protection to asylum seekers. No matter how devastating may be the epidemic, natural disaster or famine, a person fleeing them is not a refugee within the terms of the Convention'. *Applicant A* (n 201).

expressly cover those fleeing a natural disaster or slow-onset degradation in living conditions owing to the environment.[210]

The third group of objections question the morality and the politics of recognising 'environmental/climate refugees'.[211] What are the moral reasons for privileging environmental refugees over other forced migrants, such as those fleeing poverty, famine or a pandemic (e.g. COVID-19)? Furthermore, the UNHCR has rejected the recognition of an environmental refugee status, in large part because it lacks the resources to address their needs.[212] The lack of political appetite to formally extend international refugee protection has also been pointed out.[213] According to the commentators who make this argument, migration is a field largely left to sovereign decisions, with political trends in favour of tightening border controls.[214] This has led to a stream of proposals shifting the focus from the notion of an 'environmental refugee' to more modest and non-binding initiatives incorporating terms such as 'cross-border displaced persons in the context of disasters and climate change'.[215] Finally, some studies show that people affected by environmental changes reject being referred to as refugees and opt for local terminologies.[216] A case study from Papua New Guinea, for instance, shows that 'someone who wanders from

210 UN High Commissioner for Refugees Antonio Guterres, 'Migration, Displacement and Planned Relocation' (31 December 2012) <https://www.unhcr.org/news/editorial/2012/12/55535d6a9/migration-displacement-planned-relocation.html?query=2050> accessed 6 April 2022.

211 McAdam (n 176) 187.

212 John Podesta, 'The Climate crisis, Migration and Refugees' (Report Brooklings, 25 July 2019) <https://www.brookings.edu/research/the-climate-crisis-migration-and-refugees/> accessed 6 April 2022.

213 Mayer and Crépeau (eds) (n 199) 15. Also see Scott (n 14) 1–8.

214 Mayer and Crépeau (eds) (n 199) 15.

215 Nansen Initiative, Agenda for the Protection of Cross-Border Displaced Persons in the Context of Disasters and Climate Change adopts this terminology. The Nansen Initiative, Agenda for the Protection of Cross-Border Displaced Persons in the Context of Disasters and Climate Change, <https://disasterdisplacement.org/wp-content/uploads/2014/08/EN_Protection_Agenda_Volume_I_-low_res.pdf> accessed 6 April 2022.

216 See, for instance, Johannes Luetz and Peni Hausia Havea, 'We're not Refugees, We'll Stay Here Until We Die! Climate Change Adaptation and Migration Experiences Gather From the Tulun and Nissan Atolls of Bougainville, Papua New Guinea' in Leal Filho (ed), *Climate Change Impacts and Adaptation Strategies for Coastal Communities: Climate Change Management* (Springer 2018); Jane McAdam, 'Refusing "refugee" in the Pacific: (de)constructing climate-induced displacement in international law' in Etienne Piguet, Antoine Pecoud and Paul de Guchteneire (eds), *Migration and Climate Change* (CUP and UNESCO Publishing 2011).

place to place' (*tripman/tripmeri*' in the local language) was amongst the preferred terms, as it conveys flexibility and is 'not a sealed identity' contrary to the identity of a refugee.[217]

An exception has arisen in practice, however, with the so-called 'nexus dynamics'. According to the UNHCR, situations of nexus dynamics arise when the refugee criteria interact with disasters or adverse effects of climate change.[218] One example is when a government uses the context of a disaster as a pretext for persecutory acts against certain groups.[219] Another is conflict due to resource constraints, in which environmental changes act as a potential driver of refugee movement.[220] Reliance on such nexus dynamics is very limited and depends on the determination by relevant national authorities. However, such persons could be granted refugee status.[221]

Moreover, there could be situations in which regional instruments extend the refugee protection safeguarded under the Refugee Convention. The Convention governing the Specific Aspects of Refugee Problems in Africa of 1969,[222] adopted by the Organisation of African Unity, and the Cartagena Declaration on Refugees of 1984,[223] adopted by the Colloquium on the International Protection of Refugees in Latin America, Mexico and Panama, are a case in point. These instruments extend refugee protection to persons

217 Luetz and Havea (n 217) 14.

218 UNHCR, 'Climate change and disaster displacement' <https://www.unhcr.org/climate-change-and-disasters.html> accessed 6 April 2022.

219 For instance, see the case of Haitians being persecuted after Cyclone Dorian hit the Bahamas in October 2019. Nisha Stickles and Hannah Jiang, 'Haitian migrants, homeless from Hurricane Dorian, could now be deported from the Bahamas' (Business Insider, 21 October 2019) <https://www.businessinsider.com/haitian-hurricane-dorian-evacuees-pushed-out-of-bahamas-2019-10?r=US&IR=T> accessed 6 April 2022. Also see Walter Kälin and Jane McAdam, 'Environmental displacement' in Yann Aguila and Jorge E. Vinuales (eds), *A Global Pact for Environment* (C-EENRG 2019) 159–166.

220 Tim Krieger, Diana Panke and Michael Pregernig (eds), *Environmental Conflicts, Migration and Governance* (Bristol University Press 2020); UNICEF United Kingdom, 'No Place to Call Home: Protecting Children's Rights When the Changing Climate Forces Them to Flee' (UNICEF United Kingdom 2017); UNHCR, 'Legal Considerations on Refugee Protection for People Fleeing Conflict and Famine Affected Countries' (UNHCR 2017).

221 For a case study of Italy, see Elisa Fornalé, 'Floating Rights in Times of Environmental Challenges' in Cataldi and others (eds), *Migration and Fundamental Rights: the Way Forward* (Napoli: Editoriale Scientifica 2019).

222 Organization of African Unity, Convention Governing the Specific Aspects of Refugee Problems in Africa (10 September 1969) 1001 UNTS 45 (OAU Convention).

223 Colloquium on the International Protection of Refugees in Central America, Mexico and Panama, Cartagena Declaration on Refugees (22 November 1984) (Cartagena Declaration).

fleeing 'events seriously disturbing public order'.[224] Examples include the responses of Brazil and Mexico, primarily during 2010–2012, to the cross-border movement of Haitians following the 2010 earthquake, in the context of insecurity, violence and human rights violations in Haiti, as well as Kenya's and Ethiopia's responses, primarily during 2011–2012, to the cross-border movement of Somalis in the context of drought, food insecurity, famine, conflict and violence.[225] These experiences show that international refugee law may form part of a toolbox of options, alongside other legal and policy options available to States, for providing international protection.[226] One presumption is that if severe environmental changes cause a breakdown of public order, then refugee protection might be applicable.[227]

As this section has discussed, the international refugee regime currently does not recognise environmental factors as a ground for refugee protection. Three main reasons were highlighted to explain this, namely reasons deriving from a textual interpretation of the definition of a refugee under the Refugee Convention, from the multi-causal nature of the phenomenon of HMDCC and from the moral and political considerations of recognising a new refugee protection status. Despite these arguments, international refugee protection remains relevant for HMDCC to the extent that there might be a situation of 'nexus dynamics' or in cases where regional refugee instruments might be used to extend protection.

1.2 *International Climate Change Regime*

The climate change regime clusters around the institutions formed and the treaties negotiated under the auspices of the UNFCCC.[228] Especially since the

224 OAU Convention (n 222) Article 1(2); Cartagena Declaration (n 223) N.220, Paragraph III(3). See Federica Cristani, Elisa Fornalé and Sandra Lavenex, 'Environmental Migration Governance at the Regional Level' in Tim Krieger, Diana Panke and Michael Pregernig (eds), *Environmental Conflicts, Migration and Governance* (Bristol University Press 2020).

225 Sanjula Weerasinghe, 'In Harm's Way: International protection in the context of nexus dynamics between conflict or violence and disaster or climate change' (UNHCR 2018) <https://www.unhcr.org/5c1ba88d4.pdf> accessed 6 April 2022.

226 James Hathaway, *The Law of Refugee Status* (Butterworths 1991) at pages 92–94; James Hathaway, 'Food Deprivation: A Basis for Refugee Status?' [2014] 81 Soc Res 327; Vikram Kolmannskog, 'Climate Change, Environmental Displacement and International Law' [2012] 24 J Int Dev 1071.

227 States in Central and South America have recognised Haitians applying for asylum following the 2010 earthquake as refugees under the Cartagena Declaration definition. For more information, see McAdam and others (n1) para 88.

228 Robert O. Keohane and David G. Victor, 'The Regime Complex for Climate Change' [2011] 9 Perspectives on Politics 1, 7–23; Daniel Bodansky, 'The History of the Global Climate

IPCC's recognition of the climate change–human mobility nexus in its first report in 1990, HMDCC has been increasingly studied by actors engaging in climate change governance.[229] In order to build on these efforts, the Executive Committee of the UNFCCC Warsaw International Mechanism for Loss and Damage (Excom WIM) established the Task Force on Displacement (TFD) in 2015 with the aim of developing recommendations to 'avert, minimize and address displacement related to the adverse impacts of climate change'.[230] This section discusses the cooperative work undertaken by the TFD and its role in contributing to the creation of a protection mechanism for PMDCC.

In 2013, the UNFCCC WIM was established with a mandate to enhance 'knowledge and understanding of comprehensive risk management approaches' and 'action and support, including finance, technology and capacity-building', as well as to strengthen the 'dialogue, coordination, coherence and synergies among relevant stakeholders' for loss and damage, amongst other things.[231] Two years later, the Excom WIM was mandated to create the TFD.[232] Currently comprising fourteen members, the TFD represents perspectives from the fields of development, adaptation, human mobility, humanitarianism, civil society, least-developed countries, and loss and damage.[233] Their recommendations to 'avert, minimize and address displacement related to the adverse impacts of climate change' were delivered in 2018 during the 24th Conference of the Parties (COP24), and were 'welcomed' by the COP.[234]

Change Regime' in Urs Luterbacher and Detlef F. Sprinz, *International Relations and Global Climate Change* (Massachusetts Institute of Technology 2001) 23–40.

229 In its sixth assessment report, the Working Group II of the IPCC assessed the impacts of climate change on adaptive migration, involuntary displacement, organised relocation of populations from sites highly exposed to climatic hazards, and immobility. It has built a typology, supported by real-life examples. See IPCC (n 4), 1342–1351.

230 Conference of the Parties to the United Nations Framework Convention on Climate Change, Report of the Conference of the Parties on its Twenty-First Session, 21st sess, (29 January 2016) UN Doc FCCC/CP/2015/10/Add. 1 <https://www.un.org/en/development/desa/population> accessed 6 April 2022.

231 Conference of the Parties to the United Nations Framework Convention on Climate Change, 'Report of the Conference of the Parties on its Nineteenth Session' (19th sess, 31 January 2014) UN Doc FCCC/CP/2013/10/Add. 1 <https://unfccc.int/resource/docs/2013/cop19/eng/10a01.pdf> accessed 6 April 2022.

232 Conference of the Parties to the United Nations Framework Convention on Climate Change, 'Report of the Conference of the Parties on its Twenty-First Session' (21st sess, 29 January 2016) UN Doc FCCC/CP/2015/10/Add. 1.

233 These members are representatives from the UNDP, UNHCR, IOM, ILO, Advisory Group on Climate Change and Human Mobility, IFRC, PDD, UNFCCC NGO constituency group 'Youth NGOs', UNFCCC Adaptation Committee, UNFCCC LDCs Expert Group, and ExCom of WIM. See Task Force on Displacement (n 1).

234 Decision 10/CP.24 FCCC/CP/2018/10/Add.1; UNFCCC (n 15).

The non-binding recommendations made by the TFD include: formulating laws, policies and strategies at all levels (including the community, national, regional and international levels) that reflect the importance of integrated approaches to averting, minimising and addressing displacement related to the adverse impact of climate change, as well as in the broader context of human mobility; enhancing research and data collection to better map human mobility related to the adverse impacts of climate change; and integrating human mobility challenges and opportunities into both national planning processes and the relevant policy agendas.[235]

Protection is explicitly referred to as part of the recommendation to continue developing and sharing good practices.[236] Here, the TFD 'encourages' the protection of affected individuals and communities within existing national laws, as well as international protocols and conventions, where applicable.[237] It falls short of explicitly laying out a conceptual framework for protecting the PMDCC at the international level.

Nonetheless, the TFD plays a pivotal role in providing the foundations for achieving international consensus on addressing HMDCC for three main reasons. First, TFD's work has contributed to 'displacement riskification', i.e. the construction of displacement in terms of the risks associated with displacement in the context of climate change.[238] 'Riskification' allows for the inclusion of new concerns and assessments of adverse symptoms of climate change on human mobility, including food security, water security, sea-level rise, civil conflict and coastal degradation.[239] This paves the way for the conceptualisation of integrated approaches to addressing HMDCC, and calls for the use of relevant treaty regimes, as well as non-binding legal instruments, in accordance with international human rights law.[240]

---

235 The examples given for relevant policy agendas are: the Sendai Framework, SDGs, World Humanitarian Summit, the GFMD, and the Global Compacts on Migration and Refugees. See UNFCCC (n 15) para 47 (d).

236 ibid para 51 (iii) (c).

237 ibid.

238 However, as Odeyemi notes, this aspect is not being incorporated in TFD's reports to the COP. See Christo Odeyemi, 'UNFCCC's posture on displacement riskification: Conceptual suggestions' [2021] 10 Progress in Disaster Science.

239 ibid. Also see Malin Mobjörk and others, 'Climate-related security risks: towards an integrated approach' (Stockholm International Peace Research Institute, Stockholm 2016).

240 For instance, the TFD paid attention to not replicating the work of the UN Network on Migration under the Global Compact for Migration. See 'Meeting of the Task Force on Displacement (TFD4) Summary' (7–9 September 2020) <https://unfccc.int/sites/default/files/resource/Summary_TFD4_update%20for%20Excom%2012.pdf> accessed 6 April 2022.

Second, the TFD has been an important forum for conducting advocacy for the preparation and dissemination of reports and policy recommendations on HMDCC.[241] For instance, the TFD technical members were recently encouraged by the co-chair of the UN ILC Study Group on Sea-level Rise in Relation to International Law, Patricia Galvao-Teles, to provide input to the report on the protection of persons affected by sea-level rise.[242] Another example is how the role of the TFD in disseminating the recently concluded report by the UN Special Rapporteur on the Human Rights of IDPs, Cecilia Jimenez-Damary, was affirmed in a recent discussion.[243]

Third, according to its new mandate, the TFD is charged with helping Excom WIM in guiding the implementation of the recommendations.[244] The 2019–2021 Plan of Action of the TFD, referred to as 'phase 2', focuses on the themes of national and subnational policy and practice, international and regional policy, data and assessment, and framing and linkages.[245] The TFD is supposed to prepare factsheets providing an annual overview of global disaster displacement, as well as developing user-friendly knowledge products bearing on nexus situations (climate change/disaster and conflict/violence).[246] Technical issues, such as understanding how to access finance for averting, minimising, and addressing displacement associated with climate change, are also envisaged in the plan of action.[247] By deciding on concrete steps for implementing its recommendations, the TFD advances the engagement of various actors in order to strengthen the global response.

241 Atapattu (n 163) 86–113; Benoit Mayer, 'Migration in the UNFCCC workstream on loss and damage: an assessment of alternative framings and conceivable responses' [2017] 6 Transnational Environmental Law 1, 107–129.

242 TFD (n 240).

243 The report examines internal displacement in the context of the slow-onset adverse effects of climate change. See UNGA, 'Human Rights of Internally Displaced Persons' GAOR 75th Session, Item 72 (b) of the provisional agenda, Promotion and protection of human rights: human rights questions, including alternative approaches for improving the effective enjoyment of human rights and fundamental freedoms, UN Doc A/75/207.

244 UNFCCC, 'Report of the Executive Committee for the Warsaw International Mechanism for Loss and Damage associated with Climate Change Impacts' (15 February 2019) UNFCCC/SB/2019/5/Add.1 <https://unfccc.int/sites/default/files/resource/sb2019_05_add1.pdf> accessed 6 April 2022.

245 UNFCCC (n 15).

246 ibid.

247 UNFCCC, 'Plan of Action' <https://unfccc.int/process-and-meetings/bodies/constituted-bodies/executive-committee-of-the-warsaw-international-mechanism-for-loss-and-damage-wim-excom/task-force-on-displacem ent/documents#eq-2> accessed 6 April 2022.

Yet, the powers of the cooperative mechanism remain weak: its recommendations are legally non-binding on the States Parties to the UNFCCC, and hence there is no accountability or enforcement mechanism beyond the voluntary implementation process.[248] It is up to each State to decide how to approach the issue of averting, minimising and addressing displacement in the context of climate change. Therefore, the international climate change regime does not offer international protection to PMDCC.

1.3 *International Desertification Regime*

The UNCCD is the bedrock of the desertification regime, which aims to reverse land degradation trends and improve living conditions, by encouraging international cooperation and partnership for effective action at all levels.[249] In its preamble, Parties to the UNCCD accept that desertification is an 'urgent concern of the international community', and acknowledged the significant impacts of desertification and drought on 'important social problems … arising from migration, displacement of persons and demographic dynamics'.[250] This section discusses the integration of human mobility considerations into the desertification regime.[251]

Adopted in 1994, the UNCCD includes legally binding commitments by States to protect various matters, including land and water resources, local and traditional knowledge, intellectual property rights, and cattle.[252] Yet, the protection of persons mobile in the context of desertification is not envisaged in the treaty. Instead, States are encouraged to 'take into account, where relevant,

248 The UNFCCC has 197 parties, including all UN Member States. See United Nations Framework Convention on Climate Change (adopted 9 May 1992, entered into force 21 March 1994) 1771 UNTS 108 <https://treaties.un.org/Pages/ViewDetailsIII.aspx?src=IND&mtdsg_no=XXVII-7&chapter=27&Temp=mtdsg3&clang=_en> accessed 6 April 2022.

249 Pierre Marc Johnson, Karel Mayrand and Marc Paquin, 'The United Nations Convention to Combat Desertification in Global Sustainable Development Governance' in Pierre March Johnson, Karel Mayrand and Marc Paquin (eds), *Governing Global Desertification: Linking Environmental Degradation, Poverty and Participation* (Routledge 2016) 1–10.

250 United Nations Convention to Combat Desertification in those Countries Experiencing Serious Drought and/or Desertification, Particularly in Africa (adopted 14 October 1994, entry into force 26 December 1996) 1954 UNTS 3 (UNCCCD) preamble.

251 Luca Salvati, 'Economic Causes and Consequences of Desertification' [2021] Oxford Research Encyclopedia of Environmental Science; Michelle Leighton, 'Desertification and Migration' in in Pierre March Johnson, Karel Mayrand and Marc Paquin (eds), *Governing Global Desertification: Linking Environmental Degradation, Poverty and Participation* (Routledge 2016) 43–58.

252 UNCCD (n 250) Article 6(d), Article 8(3)(e), Article 4(2) (d), Article 16 (g), and Article 18(1) (e).

the relationship between poverty, migration caused by environmental factors, and desertification'.[253]

This commitment is supported by regional implementation annexes.[254] For instance, the regional implementation annex for Africa (Annex 1) encourages the taking into consideration of 'the difficult socio-economic conditions … which induce internal, regional and international migrations'.[255] Annex 1 further states that the national action programmes (NAPs) of African countries shall include measures to improve the economic environment with a view to eradicating poverty by 'defining and applying population and migration policies to reduce population pressure on land'.[256] In addition, the subregional programmes shall focus on 'early warning systems and joint planning for mitigating the effects of drought, including measures to address the problems resulting from environmentally induced migrations'.[257]

Beyond the letter of the UNCCD, the Conference of the Parties (COP) of the UNCCD and related conferences have been pushing for more detailed understandings of linkages between desertification and human mobility.[258] Already in 1994, the UNCCD secretariat and the government of Spain organised an international symposium on desertification and migration, which concluded that the 'freedom of people to stay at home, on their land and in their own culture, deserves to be supported by the international community'.[259] During COP7, held in Nairobi in 2005, Morocco 'urged parties to be proactive in their response to the impact of desertification on migration'.[260] That same year, the 3rd Committee for the Review of the Implementation of the UNCCD (CRIC3) conducted a plenary discussion on the impact of land degradation and desertification on migration and conflict.[261] During the discussion, it was

---

253 ibid, Article 17 (1) (e).

254 See UNCCD (n 250) Annex II, Article 2; Annex III, Article 2(c).

255 ibid Annex I, Article 3 (e).

256 ibid article 8 (a).

257 ibid article 11 (f).

258 Andreas Rechkemmer, 'Societal Impacts of Desertification: Migration and Environmental Refugees?' in Hans Günter Brauch and others (eds), *Facing Global Environmental Change* (Springer 2009) 151–158.

259 United Nations Convention to Combat Desertification Committee for the Review of the Implementation of the Convention, 'Overview of Panel Discussions and Global Interactive Dialogues During the Third Session of the Committee for the Review of the Implementation of the Convention' (Third Session, 2–11 May 2005) <https://www.unccd.int/sites/default/files/sessions/documents/ICCD_CRIC3_MISC.2/misc2eng.pdf> accessed 6 April 2022.

260 IISD, 'CCD COP-7 Highlights' (Earth Negotiations Bulletin, Vol 4 No 183, 25 October 2005).

261 CRIC was was established by COP as a subsidiary body to the COP to assist it in regularly reviewing the implementation of the UNCCD. See Decision 1/COP.5, 'Additional

suggested that NAPs should facilitate necessary linkages between migration and desertification.[262]

Importantly, in 2017, COP13 adopted a decision to produce a study on the 'role that measures taken under the Convention can play to address desertification/land degradation and drought as one of the drivers that causes migration'.[263] The UNCCD secretariat published its report in 2019, which it prepared together with the IOM.[264] The report is particularly impressive for drawing attention to the 'complex nexus' of migration, on the one hand, and desertification, land degradation and drought (DLDD), on the other.[265] Beyond the conceptualisation exercise, the report consists of a collection of good practices, followed by policy review and recommendations.[266] The recommendations to the States Parties to the UNCCD are clustered under three headings: (i) prioritising community-focused sustainable land management and restoration efforts; (ii) harnessing migration policy and practice; (iii) maximising synergies across policy areas.[267]

Under its 2018–2030 Strategic Framework, the UNCCD is expected to continue to work towards improving the living conditions of affected populations, which consists of 'substantially' reducing 'migration forced by desertification and land degradation'.[268] Despite the long-standing awareness and interest of the desertification regime on human mobility, current efforts are non-binding

---

procedures or institutional mechanisms to assist in the review of hte implementation of the Convention' ICCD/COP (5)/11/Add.1 <https://www.unccd.int/sites/default/files/sessions/documents/2019-08/1COP5_0.pdf> accessed 6 April 2022.

262 United Nations Convention to Combat Desertification Committee for the Review of the Implementation of the Convention, 'Overview of Panel Discussions and Global Interactive Dialogues During the Third Session of the Committee for the Review of the Implementation of the Convention' (Third Session, 2–11 May 2005) <https://www.unccd.int/sites/default/files/sessions/documents/ICCD_CRIC3_MISC.2/misc2eng.pdf> accessed 6 April 2022.

263 UNCCCD, 'Decision 28/COP.13. The positive role that measures taken under the Convention can play to address desertification/land degradation and drought as one of the drivers that causes migration' (15 September 2017) UN Doc ICCD/COP(13)/21/Add.1.

264 IOM and UNCCD, 'Addressing the Land Degradation – Migration Nexus: the Role of the UNCCD' (1 August 2019).

265 ibid.

266 ibid.

267 Ibid.

268 This is Strategic Objective 2, Expected Impact 2.4. See ICCD, 'The future strategic framework of the Convention: Draft decision submitted by the Chair of the Committee of the Whole' (14 September 2017) ICCD/COP(13)/L.18 <https://www.unccd.int/sites/default/files/inline-files/ICCD_COP%2813%29_L.18-1716078E_0.pdf> accessed 6 April 2022.

in nature and do not prescribe a universal response to addressing the international protection of PMDCC.

1.4 *International Labour Regime*

The international labour regime encompasses the large body of the ILO's binding conventions and non-binding recommendations, which are collectively referred to as the International Labour Standards (ILS).[269] Access to decent work and social justice in the context of environmental changes has been a key policy framework of the ILO.[270] It has worked with governments, employers and unions on the transition to a low-carbon economy for years, as a result of which it established the Green Jobs Programme in 2008 and adopted the guidelines for a just transition towards environmentally sustainable economies and societies for all in 2015.[271] The ILO's focus on labour migration in the context of environmental changes is relatively new.[272] Here, the main stance of the ILO has been that, if conducted in line with the ILS, migration has the capacity to be an effective adaptive strategy to environmental changes.[273] This section begins by discussing the protection of migrant workers under the ILS, before turning to examine the ILO's work on promoting migration as an adaptive strategy to environmental changes.

Today, around 60% of all migrants are migrant workers.[274] Demographic projections for the next forty years suggest that international labour migration will become an increasingly important factor in sustaining the productivity of national economies.[275] Under targets 8.7 and 8.8 of the 2030 Agenda,

---

269 ICRMW is discussed under the international human rights regimes in Chapter 1.1.6.

270 ILO, 'ILO Activities for environment and the world of work' (Tripartite Advisory Meeting on Environment and the World of Work, ILO, 2–4 November 1992). ILO, 'Decent work for sustainable development, Director-General's Report I (A)' (2007); ILO, "Decent work for sustainable development – the challenge of climate change' (Governing Body Working Party on the Social Dimension of Globalization, 2007).

271 ILO, 'Working in a changing climate: The Green Initiative: Report of the Director General to the International Labour Conference', 106th Session (ILO, 2017); ILO, 'Guidelines for a Just Transition Towards Environmentally Sustainable Economies and Societies for All' (ILO, 2015).

272 ILO, 'The Global Crisis: Causes, Responses and Challenges' (ILO, 2011). See Sophia Kagan, Meredith Byrne, and Michelle Leighton, 'Organizational Perspectives from the ILO' in Benoit Mayer and Francois Crépeau (eds), *Research Handbook on Climate Change, Migration and the Law* (Edward Elgar 2017).

273 See Kagan, Byrne and Leighton (n 272).

274 ILO, *Global Estimates on International Migrant Workers – Results and Methodology* (ILO 2015).

275 Ryszard Cholewinski, 'International Labour Migration' in Brian Opeskin and others (eds), *Foundations of International Migration Law* (Cambridge University Press 2012).

States echoed the importance of migration for the world of work and called for the eradication of forced labour and the protection of the rights of migrant workers.[276]

The ILO has repeatedly confirmed that 'all international labour standards apply to migrant workers, unless otherwise stated'.[277] As early as 1919, 'the protection of the interests of workers when employed in countries other than their own' was enshrined in the Preamble to the ILO's Constitution.[278] The ILO has further emphasised that:

> [the] human rights of all migrant workers, regardless of their status, should be promoted and protected. In particular, all migrant workers should benefit from the principles and rights in the 1998 ILO Declaration on Fundamental Principles and Rights at Work and its Follow-up, which are reflected in the eight fundamental ILO Conventions, and the relevant United Nations human rights Conventions.[279]

The international protection of migrant workers is expressed within the framework of the ILS in three ways.[280] First, the ILS is applied to workers irrespective of their nationality and legal status, unless otherwise specified.[281] Second, legally binding conventions have been adopted which are specifically tailored for the protection of migrant workers.[282] Finally, non-binding instruments

276 UNGA Res 70/1 Transforming our world: the 2030 Agenda for Sustainable Development (21 October 2015) UN Doc A/RES/70/1, targets 8.7 and 8.8.

277 ILO, multilateral framework on labour migration: Non-binding principles and guidelines for a rights-based approach to labour migration. 2006. Geneva. Paragraph 9(a).

278 Constitution of the ILO (1 April 1919) <https://www.refworld.org/docid/3ddb5391a.htm> accessed 6 April 2022.

279 ILO, *Multilateral framework on labour migration: Non-binding principles and guidelines for a rights-based approach to labour migration* (ILO Geneva, 2008) para 8.

280 The ILO defines migrant workers as 'all international migrants who are currently employed or unemployed and seeking employment in their present country of residence'. See ILO, *Global Estimates on International Migrant Workers – Results and Methodology* (ILO 2015).

281 Philip Alston, 'Core labour standards and the transformation of the international labour rights regime' [2004] 15 EJIL 3, 457–521.

282 See, in general, Aziz Choudry, *Just Work?: Migrant Workers' Struggles Today* (Pluto Press 2016); Michael Hasenau, 'Part I: The Genesis of the Convention: ILO Standards on Migrant Workers: The Fundamentals of the UN Convention and Their Genesis' [1991] 25 International Migration Review 4, 687–697.

have been developed relating to the enhancement of the protection of migrant workers.[283]

Of relevance are ILO Conventions No. 87 on the Freedom of Association and Protection of the Right to Organize, No. 111 on Discrimination (Employment and Occupation) and No. 118 on Equality of Treatment (Social Security).[284]

Convention No. 87 provides that workers and employers shall have the right to establish and join organisations of their own choosing without previous authorisation.[285] The Committee on Freedom of Association has stated that with the exception of Art. 9 concerning armed forces and the police, Convention No. 87 applies to all workers, including migrant workers.[286] Whether employed on a permanent basis, for a fixed term or as a contract employee, all workers should have the right to establish and join organisations of their own choosing.[287]

Similarly, Convention No. 111 has been interpreted by the Committee of Experts on the Application of Conventions and Recommendations as applicable to all migrant workers, including those in an irregular situation.[288] Everyone is entitled to protection from discrimination in the form of any distinction, exclusion or preference in employment and occupation made on the basis of sex, race, religion, political opinion and social origin.[289] Migrant workers are particularly vulnerable to prejudices and differences in treatment in the labour market, and therefore the ILO members party to Convention No. 111 are obliged to actively work to combat discrimination.[290]

---

283 See ILO, 'ILO's International Legal Framework on Labour Migration' <https://www.ilo.org/africa/areas-of-work/labour-migration/relevant-standards/lang--en/index.htm> accessed 6 April 2022.

284 ILO Convention No. 87 concerning Freedom of Association and Protection of the Right to Organise (adopted 9 July 1948, entered into force 4 July 1950) 68 UNTS 17; ILO Convention No. 111 concerning Discrimination (Employment and Occupation) (adopted 25 June 1958, entered into force 15 June 1960) 362 UNTS 31; ILO Convention No. 118 concerning Equality of Treatment (Social Security) (adopted 28 June 1962) 7238 UNTS 940.

285 ILO Convention No. 87 concerning Freedom of Association and Protection of the Right to Organise (adopted 9 July 1948, entered into force 4 July 1950) 68 UNTS 17, article 2.

286 ILO Governing Body, '327th report of the Committee on the Freedom of Association' (ILO 2002).

287 ILO, 'Freedom of Association: Digest of decisions and principles of the Freedom of Association Committee of the Governing Body of the ILO' (Fifth (revised) edition 2006), para 214.

288 International Labour Conference, Report of the Committee of Experts on the Application of Conventions and Recommendations (articles 19, 22, and 35 of the Constitution), Report III (Part 1B), 101st session 2012, para 778.

289 ILO Convention No. 111 (n 284) art 1(1).

290 ibid art 2. International Labour Conference (n 288) para 776.

Furthermore, Convention No. 118 ensures the equality of treatment of nationals and non-nationals in social security rights, based on the principle of reciprocity.[291] Each State party to Convention No. 118 may accept the obligations in respect of any or more branches of social security and extend equal treatment to the citizens of other party States.[292]

In addition, the legislative body of the ILO has adopted two Conventions which specifically relate to the protection of migrant workers, namely, No. 97 on Migration for Employment and No. 143 on Migrant Workers (Supplementary Provisions).[293] Both conventions are complemented by non-binding Recommendations, namely No. 86 and No. 151 respectively.[294]

Convention No. 97 entered into force on 22 January 1951 and has been ratified by 50 States.[295] It applies to migrants regularly admitted for employment and covers all stages of the migration process.[296] It does not afford protection to irregular migrant workers. Based on the principle of non-discrimination, it articulates the equal treatment of lawfully residing migrant workers with national workers with respect to matters such as hours of work, family allowances, social security and trade union membership.[297] Recommendation No. 86 complements the convention, aiming to 'facilitate the international distribution of manpower and in particular the movement of manpower from countries which have a surplus of manpower to those countries that have a deficiency'.[298] In the annex, it includes a Model Agreement on Temporary and Permanent Migration for Employment, including Migration of Refugees and Displaced Persons.[299] The annex aims to provide a template for bilateral labour agreements between States, and the addition of specific provisions tailored

291 ILO Convention No. 118 (n 284) article 3(1).

292 ibid article 2.

293 ILO Convention No. 97 concerning Migration for Employment (Revised) (entered into force 22 January 1952); ILO Convention No. 143 concerning Migrant Workers (Supplementary Provisions).

294 ILO Recommendation R86: Migration for Employment Recommendation (Revised); ILO Recommendation R151: Migrant Workers Recommendation.

295 ILO, 'Ratifications of C097 – Migration for Employment Convention (Revised), 1949 <https://www.ilo.org/dyn/normlex/en/f?p=NORMLEXPUB:11300:0::NO::P11300_INSTRUMENT_ID:312242> accessed 6 April 2022.

296 ILO Convention No. 97 (n 293) article 11(1).

297 ibid article 6(1).

298 ibid article 4. ILO Recommendation R86: Migration for Employment Recommendation (Revised).

299 ibid.

towards refugees and displaced persons facilitates the taking of measures with a view to accelerating and simplifying formalities.[300]

Convention No. 143 is broader in scope, as it applies to all migrant workers, including irregular migrant workers. It entered into force on 9 December 1978 and has been ratified by only 25 States.[301] It consists of two parts, which address migration under abusive conditions and equality in opportunity and treatment.[302] Adopted at a time when the international community was paying particular attention to migration-related abuses, such as the smuggling of migrant workers, the convention 'underscores the need for inter-state cooperation and collaborative measures to prevent this phenomenon'.[303] Recommendation No. 151 complements the convention and focuses especially on the formulation and application of national social policies which enable migrant workers and their families to share the advantages enjoyed by nationals.[304]

Furthermore, the ILO has developed non-binding instruments relating to the enhancement of the protection of migrant workers. In 2006, it published the 'Multilateral Framework on Labour Migration: Non-binding principles and guidelines for a rights-based approach to labour migration'.[305] The framework was developed following the establishment of the World Commission on the Social Dimension of Globalisation in 2002, which noted that the 'absence of a multilateral framework to govern cross-border movements had given rise to a number of collateral problems in the exploitation of migrant workers, growth in irregular migration, rise in trafficking of human beings, and brain drain from developing countries'.[306] Two years later, a resolution aiming at a fair deal for migrant workers in the global economy was adopted by the International Labour Conference, which called for an ILO Plan of Action on

300 ibid.

301 ILO, 'Ratifications of C143 – Migrant Workers (Supplementary Provisions) Convention' <https://www.ilo.org/dyn/normlex/en/f?p=NORMLEXPUB:11300:0::NO:11300:P11300_INSTRUMENT_ID:312288:NO> accessed 6 April 2022.

302 ILO Convention No. 143 (n 293).

303 Cholewinski (n 75) 258. Also see Ryszard Cholewinski, *International Migration Law: Developing Paradigms and Key Challenges* (TMC Asser Press 2007).

304 ILO, 'Ratifications of C097 – Migration for Employment Convention (Revised), 1949 <https://www.ilo.org/dyn/normlex/en/f?p=NORMLEXPUB:11300:0::NO::P11300_INSTRUMENT_ID:312242> accessed 6 April 2022.

305 ILO, 'Multilateral Framework on Labour Migration: Non-binding Principles and Guidelines for a Rights-Based Approach to Labour Migration' (ILO 2006) <https://www.ilo.org/wcmsp5/groups/public/---ed_protect/---protrav/---migrant/documents/publication/wcms_178672.pdf> accessed 6 April 2022.

306 ibid.

Labour Migration.[307] The framework represents the 'centrepiece' of the plan of action, by addressing, amongst other things, the protection of migrant workers, the expansion of international cooperation, decent work for all and governance of migration.[308]

It is also possible to locate the rights of migrant workers within the Decent Work Agenda of the ILO, launched in 1999. It is made up of four elements (job creation, rights at work, social protection and social dialogue) and two cross-cutting principles (gender equality and non-discrimination).[309] It aims to ensure human-oriented development in the globalisation of working life and works together with the SDGs.[310] Under the Decent Work Programmes, the ILO has given special emphasis to the rights of vulnerable groups of workers, including the migrant workers.[311] For instance, the ILO Asia Region implemented a decent work programme during the period 2006–2015, which focused on five priority objectives, one of which was the protection of migrant workers.[312]

However, the role of the ILO in protecting the rights of migrant workers suffers from significant limitations. Conventions No. 97 and No. 143 have a very low rate of ratification (51 and 26 ratifications respectively).[313] Furthermore, the non-binding Multilateral Framework on Labour Migration 'clearly recognizes the sovereign right of all nations to determine their own migration policies'.[314] The Decent Work Agenda and its implementation programmes are also tied to country participation. This legal reality aids the 'protection gap' for migrant workers at the international level, with particular consequences on

307 ibid.

308 ibid.

309 ILO, Decent Work Agenda (1998). Also see Vicente Silva, 'The ILO and the future of work: The politics of global labour policy' [2021] Global Social Policy.

310 Gillian MacNaughton and Diane F. Frey, 'Decent Work, Human Rights and the Sustainable Development Goals' [2016] 47 Georgetown Journal of International Law, 607–664.

311 ILO, *Working on a warmer planet: The effect of heat stress on productivity and decent work* (ILO 2009). See Jorma Rantanen, Franklin Muchiri and Suvi Lehtinen, 'Decent Work, ILO's Response to the Globalization of Working Life: Basic Concepts and Global Implementation with Special Reference to Occupational Health' [2020] International Journal of Environmental Research and Public Health.

312 ILO, 'Statistical Report of the Decent Work Decade 2006–15: Asia-Pacific and the Arab States' (ILO 2016).

313 ILO, 'Ratifications of C143 – Migrant Workers (Supplementary Provisions) Convention' <https://www.ilo.org/dyn/normlex/en/f?p=NORMLEXPUB:11300:0::NO:11300:P11300_INSTRUMENT_ID:312288:NO> accessed 6 April 2022.

314 ILO, 'Multilateral Framework on Labour Migration: Non-binding Principles and Guidelines for a Rights-Based Approach to Labour Migration' (ILO 2006) <https://www.ilo.org/wcmsp5/groups/public/---ed_protect/---protrav/---migrant/documents/publication/wcms_178672.pdf> accessed 6 April 2022.

the vulnerable groups of migrant workers, such as female domestic workers, and temporary and irregular labour migrants.[315]

It is in this context that the ILO started to work on the labour migration–environmental change nexus.[316] Using migration as an adaptation strategy has been a focal point of the ILO's advocacy.[317] In 2013, the ILO launched a three-year project with UNESCAP and UNDP to explore more fully migration as a resilience strategy to climate change by leading the development of a technical-capacity-building project in the Pacific region.[318] The ILO's technical support in this project was based on the understanding that if international migration channels were not expanded for the citizens of the Pacific Island States, a significant proportion of the population could be 'trapped' by the worsening living conditions in the context of environmental changes.[319] This project played a role in the development of national labour migration policies in Kiribati and Tuvalu, and worked with access to permanent and temporary skilled pathways in countries, such as Australia and New Zealand.[320]

The meaning and application of migration as adaptation is open to interpretation.[321] Generally, it stands for a strategy to cope with environmental

---

315 Piyasiri Wickramasekara, 'Globalisation, International Labour Migration and Rights of Migrant Workers' [2009] 29 Third World Quarterly 7, 1247–1264; Elisa Fornalé, 'Regional migration governance and social protection of migrant workers' in Oreste Foppiani, Oana Scarlatescu, *Family, Separation, and Migration: An Evolution-Involution of the Global Refugee Crisis. Population, Family and Society* (Peter Lang 2018) 107–120.

316 UNESCAP and ILO, 'Climate Change and Migration Issues in the Pacific' (ILO 2014); ILO, 'The employment impact of climate change adaptation: Input Document for the G20 Climate Sustainability Working Group' (ILO 2018); ILO, 'Future of Work for Climate Resilience in the Pacific Islands' (ILO 2019); ILO, 'Working on a Warmer Planet: The impact of heat stress on labour productivity and decent work' (ILO 2019).

317 Andrew Baldwin and Elisa Fornalé, 'Adaptive Migration: Pluralising the debate on climate change and migration' [2017] 183:4 The Geographical Journal, 323.

318 The Pacific Climate Change and Migration Project <https://www.unescap.org/subregional-office/pacific/pacific-climate-change-and-migration-project> accessed 6 April 2022. See also, UN University Institute for Environment and Human Security, 'Factsheet: Climate Change and migration in the Pacific: Links, attitudes and future scenarios in Nauru, Tuvalu and Kiribati' <http://i.unu.edu/media/ehs.unu.edu/news/11747/RZ_Pacific_EHS_ESCAP_151201.pdf> accessed 6 April 2022.

319 ILO, 'Enhancing the Capacity of Pacific Island Countries to Address the Impacts of Climate Change to Migration' (1 June 2013–1 June 2015) <https://www.ilo.org/global/topics/labour-migration/projects/WCMS_226212/lang--en/index.htm> accessed 6 April 2022.

320 UN, 'Climate Change and Migration Issues in the Pacific' (2014) <https://www.unescap.org/sites/default/files/Climate-Change-and-Migration-Issues-in-the-Pacific.pdf> accessed 6 April 2022.

321 The notion of migration as an adaptive mechanism has a long pedigree, with origins in evolutionary biology and environmental determinism. For Charles Darwin, adaptation

changes, which potentially reduces the burden of the environment on the sending household.[322] It can be reactive, concurrent or anticipatory on a temporal scale, and take place autonomously or in a planned way.[323] Against the dominant conceptualisations of vulnerable populations as passive victims, migration as adaptation emerges to stress the resilience of people in adapting.[324]

According to the ILO, labour migration can diversify household income and reduce resource pressure on vulnerable populations, eventually providing opportunities for moving away from affected areas 'in a less destabilizing process than mass relocation'.[325] The ILO has been advocating for practices that will reduce the cost of movement, eliminate exploitative and expensive recruitment procedures, identify sectors with likely labour shortages, expand opportunities to internationally recognised qualifications and enhance vocational trainings.[326] In its World Employment Social Outlook 2018 report, the ILO emphasised that '[s]ocial protection systems are the first line of defence against the negative impact on incomes of climate change and environmental degradation'.[327] Facilitating mobility ensures the portability of social protection, and 'thus increase the options available to poor and vulnerable households to improve their adaptive capacity'.[328]

---

meant the organic modification of species to better fit and flourish in their environment. Progressing in social sciences, especially in anthropology and archeology, the term adaptation became associated with how cultures or societies were able to respond to or cope with changes in their socio-economic systems. Human history shows that migration has been a part of this coping mechanism through, for instance, circular migration, nomadic pastoralism and transhumance. See UK Climate Change and Migration Coalition, 'Climate Outreach and Information Network. Migration as Adaptation: exploring mobility as a coping strategy for climate change' <http://climatemigration.org.uk/wp-content/uploads/2014/02/migration_adaptation_climate.pdf> accessed 6 April 2022; Scheffran, Marmer and Sow (n xo).

322 Frank Laczko and Etienne Piguet, 'Regional Perspectives on Migration, the Environment and Climate Change' in Etienne Piguet and Frank Laczko (eds), *People on the Move in a Changing Climate: Global Migration Issues* (Global Migration Issues, Vol. 2, Springer 2014) 16.

323 ibid.

324 Laurie Parsons and Jonas Ostergaard Nielsen, 'The Subjective Climate Migrant: Climate Perceptions, Their Determinants, and Relationship to Migration in Cambodia' [2020] 111 Annals of the American Association of Geographers, 971–988; Etienne Piguet, 'Linking climate change, environmental degradation, and migration: a methodological overview' [2010] WIREs Climate Change, 517–524; Caroline Zickgraf, 'Keeping people in place: political factors of (im)mobility and climate change' [2019] 8 Social Sciences 8, 228.

325 See Kagan, Byrne, and Leighton (n 272) 330.

326 ibid.

327 ILO, 'World Employment Social Outlook 2018' (2018).

328 ibid.

As this section has discussed, the foreground of the ILO's advocacy has been that, when governed in accordance to ILS, labour migration can be an important adaptive response for people facing slow onset environmental changes or disasters.[329] The protection of the rights of migrant workers is an essential part of ensuring that there is 'well-managed' and 'rights-based' labour mobility within the context of environmental changes.[330] Unfortunately, the two legally binding conventions from the ILO that directly address the rights of migrant workers (Conventions No. 97 and No. 143) have a very low rate of ratification (51 and 26 ratifications respectively). Other relevant ILO instruments, such as the Decent Work Agenda, remain non-binding. Thus, the international labour regime does not impose a legally binding obligation upon States to guarantee the facilitation of labour mobility as an adaptation strategy, whilst protecting the rights of migrant workers.

1.5 *International Trade Regime*

The main legal instruments of the international trade regime are the WTO Agreements and preferential trade agreements (PTAS).[331] Trade agreements can be important tools to facilitate the mobility of persons, especially in the context of disasters and climate change.[332] This section discusses the relevance of WTO law and PTAS, in order to address the protection gap concerning PMDCC.[333]

Within the international trade regime, the WTO is the only intergovernmental organisation dealing with rules of trade between States.[334] Founded in 1995 with the Marrakesh Agreement, the WTO currently has 164 members, including

329 Elisa Fornalé, 'The Future Role of Labor Mobility Mechanisms in the Context of Environmental Degradation: Building or Crumbling Adaptation Strategies?' in Elisa Fornalé and Sophia Kagan, 'Climate Change and Human Mobility in the Pacific Region: Plans, Policies and Lessons Learned' (KNOMAD Working Paper 31, 2017) <https://www.knomad.org/sites/default/files/2017-12/KNOMAD_WP31_Climate%20Change%20and%20 Human%20Mobility%20in%20the%20Pacific%20Region.pdf> accessed 6 April 2022.

330 ILO, 'Climate change, displacement and labour migration' <https://www.ilo.org/global/topics/labour-migration/climate-change/green-jobs/lang--en/index.htm> accessed 6 April 2022.

331 Peter Van den Bossche and Werner Zdouc, *The Law and Policy of the World Trade Organization* (Cambridge University Press, 4th edn, 2017).

332 Thomas Cottier and Anirudh Shingal, 'Migration, Trade and Investment: Towards a New Common Concern' [2021] 55 Journal of World Trade 1, 51–76.

333 Fornalé (n 329).

334 Thomas Cottier (ed), *The Challenge of WTO Law: Collected Essays* (The Blissett Group 2007).

the US, China, Russia and the EU countries.[335] The complete set of WTO rules consists of about 30 agreements and commitments, running to some 30,000 pages, which address trade in three areas: goods, services and intellectual property. The General Agreement on Tariffs and Services (GATS) is the binding framework governing the rules on trade in services applicable to all WTO Members.[336] 'Mode 4' of the GATS represents the binding commitments of the WTO Member States for the movement of natural persons in order to supply services.[337]

Having entered into force in 1995, the GATS mainly aims to progressively liberalise trade in services, to encourage economic growth and development and to increase the participation of developing countries in the global trade in services.[338] The GATS was born in a context in which services were increasingly being recognised as a distinct economic category.[339] Today, trade in services represents a rapidly evolving sector of trade.[340] In 2017, trade in services accounted for 65% of the world's GDP,[341] and it makes up about 29.7% of the EU's GDP.[342]

Under the GATS, there are four possible 'modes' of supplying services.[343] The so-called 'Mode 4' is the movement of natural persons for the purpose of supplying services, sometimes referred to as 'services mobility'.[344] Services

335 WTO, 'Members and Observers' <https://www.wto.org/english/thewto_e/whatis_e/tif_e/org6_e.htm> accessed 6 April 2022. Also see Thomas Cottier, 'Preparing for Structural Reform in the WTO' [2007] 10 Journal of International Economic Law 3, 497–508.

336 General Agreement on Trade in Services 1994 (Marrakesh Agreement Establishing the World Trade Organization, Annex 1B, 1869 UNTS 183; 33 ILM 1167 (1994)).

337 Marion Panizzon, 'A Ménage à Trois? GATS Mode 4, EPAs, and Bilateral Migration Agreements' [2010] 44 Journal of World Trade 6, 1207–1252.

338 Van den Bossche and Zdouc (n 331) 54–65.

339 William J Drake and Kalypso Nicolaidis, 'Ideas, Interests and Institutionalisation: Trade in Services and the Uruguay Round' [1992] 46 International Organisation 1, 37–100.

340 Ingo Borchert and others, 'The Evolution of Services Trade Policy Since the Great Recession' (World Bank Group, Policy Research Working Paper 9265, June 2020).

341 World Bank, 'Services, value added (% of GDP)' <https://data.worldbank.org/indicator/NV.SRV.TOTL.ZS> accessed 6 April 2022.

342 World Bank, 'Trade in services (% of GDP) – European Union' <https://data.worldbank.org/indicator/BG.GSR.NFSV.GD.ZS?locations=EU> accessed 6 April 2022.

343 Laure Ritchie Dawson, 'Labour Mobility and the WTO: The Limits of GATS Mode 4' [2012] 51 International Migration 1, 1–23.

344 WTO Document S/C/W/75; WTO, 'Background note on GATS Mode 4 Measurement' Meeting of the United Nations Technical Subgroup on Movement of Persons -Mode 4 (New York, 22 – 24 February 2006) <https://unstats.un.org/unsd/tradeserv/TFSITS/TSGMode4/tsg3-feb06/tsg0602-16.pdf> accessed 6 April 2022.

mobility is usually considered as a subset of labour mobility.[345] Article I.2(d) of the GATS defines this mode as 'the supply of a service [...] by a service supplier of one Member, through presence of natural persons of a Member in the territory of another Member'.[346]

The GATS Annex on Movement of Natural Persons Supplying Services under the Agreement further elaborates on this definition by providing two categories.[347] The first category contains 'natural persons who are service suppliers of a Member', which covers self-employed and independent service suppliers who obtain their remuneration directly from customers.[348] The second category contains 'natural persons of a Member who are employed by a service supplier of a Member'.[349] The mainstream interpretation of the second category is that it covers foreigners working as independent suppliers on a contractual basis to companies in the host country, instead of being directly employed by such companies.[350] Within this definition and scope, binding commitments to liberalise the movement of service suppliers are made by the WTO Members.

Whether GATS Mode 4 can be viewed as promoting the facilitation of the movement of persons requires critical reflection.[351] On the one hand, Mode 4 commitments multilaterally open the national services markets for natural persons.[352] States are free to make commitments, and their commitments can even reach beyond the scope of the GATS.[353] For instance, Jacobsson observes that the US quota for highly skilled persons in specialty occupations (the

345 Marion Panizzon, Gottfried Zürcher and Elisa Fornalé, 'Introduction: Conceptualising a Pluralist Framework for Labour Migration' in Marion Panizzon, Gottfried Zürcher and Elisa Fornalé (eds), *The Palgrave Handbook of International Labour Migration: Law and Policy Perspectives* (Palgrave 2015) 1–14.

346 GATS (n 336) article 1(2).

347 ibid.

348 OECD, World Bank and IOM, 'A Quick Guide to the GATS and Mode 4' (Geneva, Palais des nations, 12–14 November 2003) <https://www.iom.int/sites/default/files/jahia/webdav/site/myjahiasite/shared/shared/mainsite/microsites/IDM/workshops/Trade_2004_04051004/related%20docs/quick_guide.pdf> accessed 6 April 2022.

349 WTO, 'Presence of Natural Persons (Move 4) Background Note by the Secretariat'(8 December 1998) S/C/W/75.

350 Jürgen Bast, 'Commentary on the Annex on Movement of Natural Persons Supplying Services Under the Agreement' in Rüdiger Wolfrum, Peter Tobias Stoll and Clemens Feinäugle (eds), *WTO – Trade in Services* (Martinus Nijhoff 2008) 573–595.

351 Chetail (n 47) 95–97.

352 Rupa Chanda, 'Movement of Natural Persons and the GATS' [2001] 24 The World Economy 5, 631–654.

353 Antonia Carzaniga, 'The GATS, Mode 4, and Pattern of Commitments' in Aaditya Mattoo and Antonia Carzaniga (eds), Moving People to Deliver Services (The World Bank/OUP 2003) 21–26.

so-called H-1B visa) provides for the possibility of an employment relationship in the host State, which is an expansion to the mainstream interpretation of the second category of services mobility.[354]

In practice, however, Mode 4 remains an 'underused channel for liberalising temporary mobility',[355] for two main reasons.[356] First, its role is limited to service-supplying persons from WTO Member States.[357] In other words, the citizens of non-WTO member countries cannot take advantage of the commitments listed. This limits the relevance, importance and effectiveness of GATS Mode 4.

Furthermore, Mode 4 commitments are very few in number, with remittances totalling less than 6% of total trade in services.[358] This has often been related to the Most-Favoured-Nation (MFN) clause of WTO law, which requires a country to provide any concessions, privileges or immunities granted to one nation in a trade agreement to all other WTO member countries.[359] This obligation may discourage WTO members from liberalising the temporary movement of service suppliers in the first place.[360]

Moreover, the content of the few commitments that exist have significant shortcomings.[361] The commitments are usually limited to a specific period of time, even though the GATS does not set any temporal limits.[362]

---

354 Johanna Jacobsson, 'GATS Mode 4 and Labour Mobility: The Significance of Employment Market Access' in Marion Panizzon, Gottfried Zürcher and Elisa Fornalé (eds), *The Palgrave Handbook of International Labour Migration: Law and Policy Perspectives* (Palgrave 2015) 61–95; Johanna Jacobsson, 'Liberalisation of Service Mobility in the EU's International Trade Agreements: As External as it Gets' [2013] 15 European Journal of Migration and Law 3, 245–261.

355 Panizzon (n 337) 1221.

356 Natasha Ward, 'Facilitating temporary movement' in Rahel Kunz, Sandra Lavenex and Marion Panizzon, *Multilayered Migration Governance: The Promise of Partnership* (Routledge 2012).

357 Steve Charnovitz, 'Trade Law Norms on International Migration' in T Alexander Aleinikoff and Vincent Chetail (eds), *Migration and International Legal Norms* (TMC Asser Press 2003) 252.

358 Philip Martin, 'Low-Skilled Labour Migration and Free Trade Agreements' in Marion Panizzon, Gottfried Zürcher and Elisa Fornalé (eds), *The Palgrave Handbook of International Labour Migration: Law and Policy Perspectives* (Palgrave 2015) 205–230.

359 Anqi Wang, *The Interpretation and Application of the Most-Favoured-Nation Clause in Investment Arbitration* (Brill 2022); Tomer Broude, 'Most-Favoured Nation Principle, Equal Protection, and Migration Policy' [2010] 24 Georgetown Immigration Law Journal 3, 553–564.

360 Panizzon (n 337) 1221.

361 Joel P Trachtman, *The International Law of Economic Migration: Toward the Fourth Freedom* (WE Upjohn Institute for Employment Research 2009) 115–127.

362 Jacobsson (n 354) 245–261.

The commitments also have a 'high-skill bias', which is to the disadvantage of developing and least-developed countries that have a surplus of low-skilled labour.[363] Most commitments are also 'unbound', meaning that there is no opening or only a partial opening, mostly for intra-corporate transfers and business visitors.[364] Therefore, although an important framework which limits national sovereignty over the admission of foreigners, WTO GATS Mode 4 'encroaches' into the field of migration only insofar as 'people's movement across State borders is necessary to carry out the trade that it regulates'.[365] It does not require States to open their labour markets nor does it require States to lift visa or work permit application procedures. It is well established that persons seeking access to the employment market in the host member, as well as measures regarding citizenship, residence or employment on a permanent basis do not concern the GATS.[366]

Since 2001, there have been several attempts to expand the GATS Mode 4 commitments of States.[367] During the Doha round of negotiations of the WTO, Members discussed the expansion of the classes of workers covered under the commitments, as well as the abandonment of the economic-needs test, which gives wide discretion to States on who to admit.[368] Some States insisted on addressing issues of 'social dumping' through trade provisions observing minimum working rights; however this issue was kept apart from the multilateral trade negotiations.[369] Any new or improved commitments for services mobility have not been achieved. With the WTO itself currently being in 'crisis' and facing existential challenges, expressions of improved community-wide interests on this matter have yet to be seen.

Due to these significant limitations of WTO GATS Mode 4, the role of PTAS in facilitating the movement of persons has been gaining importance.[370] PTAS

---

363 Panizzon (n 337).

364 ibid.

365 Jacobsson (n 354).

366 GATS (n 336).

367 OECD, World Bank and IOM, 'A Quick Guide to the GATS and Mode 4' (Geneva, Palais des nations, 12–14 November 2003) <https://www.iom.int/sites/default/files/jahia/webdav/site/myjahiasite/shared/shared/mainsite/microsites/IDM/workshops/Trade_2004_04051004/related%20docs/quick_guide.pdf> accessed 6 April 2022.

368 ibid.

369 UNHRC, 'Report of the Special Rapporteur on the human rights of migrants on the impact of bilateral and multilateral trade agreements on the human rights of migrants' (4 May 2016) A/HRC/32/40.

370 Sandra Lavenex, 'Regional migration governence – building block of global initiatives?' [2019] 45 Journal of Ethnic and Migration Studies 8, 1275–1293; Kamaal R Zaidi, 'Harmonizing Trade Liberalization and Migration Policy through Shared Responsibility: A

are regional or cross-continental trading blocs that give preferential access to certain products from the participating countries, usually by reducing tariffs.[371] They allow for the establishment of arrangements through which one WTO Member State can grant more favourable trade conditions to other parties of the arrangement and not to the rest of the WTO members, therefore representing an important exception to the MFN clause.[372]

There are at least 20 major multilateral PTAs and several hundred bilateral ones.[373] PTAs proliferated with the rise of regional trading blocs; approximately 120 countries currently participate in regional arrangements that include free movement provisions.[374] The Economic Community of West African States (ECOWAS), the Common Market for Eastern and Southern Africa (COMESA), the East Africa Community (EAC), the Southern Africa Development Community (SADC) and the Economic Community of Central African States (ECCAS) serve as prominent examples from Africa. The Association of South East Asian Nations (ASEAN) and the Asia-Pacific Economic Cooperation (APEC) are examples from the Asia-Pacific region. Finally, the Common Market of the South (MERCOSUR), the Caribbean Community (CARICOM) and the Organisation of Eastern Caribbean States (OECS) represent examples from Latin America and the Caribbean.[375]

PTAs can regulate the movement of persons by replicating the GATS Mode 4 modalities or by including additional commitments.[376] The growing interconnectedness between trade and migration, which were traditionally two separate fields, can be viewed within the context of globalisation.[377] With increasing global trade, there was a desire to liberalise economies and to

Comparison of the Impact of Bilateral Trade Agreements and the GATS in Germany and Canada' [2010] 37 Syracuse Journal of International Law 267.

371 Antonia Carnaziga, 'A Warmer Welcome? Access of Natural Persons under PTAs' in J Marchetti and M Roy (eds), *Opening Markets for Trade in Services: Countries and Sectors in Bilateral and WTO Negotiations* (Cambridge University Press 2008) 474–502.

372 GATS (n 336) paragraphs 4 to 10 of Article XXIV, Article XXVIII bis.

373 WTO, 'Database on Preferential Trade Arrangements' <http://ptadb.wto.org/?lang=1> accessed 6 April 2022.

374 Vincent Chetail, 'The Transnational Movement of Persons under General International Law – Mapping the Customary Law Foundations of International Migration Law' in Vincent Chetail and Céline Bauloz (eds), *Research Handbook on International Law and Migration* (2014) 1–72.

375 ibid.

376 Sonja Nita, 'Free Movement of People within Regional Integration Processes: A Comparative View' in Sonja Nita and others, *Migration, Free Movement and Regional Integration* (UNESCO Publishing and UNU Institute on Comparative Regional Integration Studies 2017).

377 UNHRC (n 369).

facilitate the mobility of labour.[378] According to this account, migrants were viewed as 'factors of production' and 'commoditised'.[379] Although there are still significant barriers to free movement, PTAs have increasingly been addressing migration governance mechanisms, such as visa requirements, asylum request procedures and WTO GATS Mode 4 commitments.[380]

A general observation suggests that PTAs between developed and developing countries are limited to the GATS Mode 4 commitments or highly skilled workers.[381] However, PTAs between only developed countries or only developing countries can incorporate more openness.[382] For instance, both the EU and the CARICOM give preferential access to persons beyond the GATS Mode 4 commitments.[383] The EU has the principle of the free movement of persons.[384] CARICOM allows for the free movement of skills and labour.[385] In contrast, the Pacific Agreement on Closer Economic Relations Plus (PACER Plus), which is a PTA signed by Australia, New Zealand and nine Pacific island countries, merely replicates the GATS Mode 4 commitments.[386]

PTAs can be viewed as expanding 'the repertoire of measures and actions, often with a view to bypassing regulatory and discretionary hurdles created by immigration authorities'.[387] They can grant indefinite stays and facilitate permanent resettlement, ease access to foreign labour markets through the mutual recognition of skills schemes, waive work permit requirements and waive travel document requirements in cases where documents have been lost or damaged.[388] The rights and benefits might be extended unevenly, according to the categories of people on the move, such as migrant workers, students, refugees and business people.[389]

---

378 ibid.

379 ibid.

380 ibid.

381 Martin (n 358) 226.

382 Rupa Chanda, 'Mobility of Less-Skilled Workers under Bilateral Agreements: Lessons for the GATS' [2009] 43 Journal of World Trade 3, 479–506.

383 L Alan Winters, 'The Temporary Movement of Workers to Provide Services' in Aaditya Mattoo and Antonia Carzaniga (eds), *Moving People to Deliver Services* (The World Bank/OUP 2003) 480–540.

384 Sergio Carrera, 'What does free movement mean in theory and practice in an enlarged EU?' [2005] 11 European Law Journal 6, 699–721.

385 Amy Francis, 'Free Movement Agreements & Climate-Induced Migration: A Caribbean Case Study' [2019] 1 Columbia Law School, 1–28. Also see German Cooperation GIZ and PIK (n 33).

386 See Chapter 3.2.2 of this book for a discussion on PACER Plus in more detail.

387 Panizzon, Zürcher and Fornalé (n 345) 11.

388 Nita (n 376).

389 ibid.

However, as the Special Rapporteur on the Human Rights of Migrants at the time, François Crépeau, observed, 'while trade liberalization has led to economic growth and social welfare generally, such progress has sometimes come at the expense of the human rights of migrants'.[390] In his report on the impact of bilateral and multilateral trade agreements on the human rights of migrants, the Special Rapporteur drew attention to the reality that although trade is not inherently negative, 'the power imbalances, protectionism and national interests that influence the global economy have resulted in trade systems that exacerbate the precariousness of low-wage migrant workers and directly and systematically infringe upon their human rights'.[391] The recommendations advanced by the Special Rapporteur included making explicit references to international human rights and labour instruments in all new and renegotiated trade agreements, developing a global mobility framework in consultation with IOs, trade unions and civil society, and ensuring that trade and mobility agreements do not erode existing social and mobility protections granted through commitments in other agreements.[392]

Against this backdrop, the relevance of GATS Mode 4 commitments of WTO Member States, as well as PTAs, for addressing HMDCC may be discussed. Elisa Fornalé, for instance, argues that international migration and environmental vulnerability may influence new multilateral instruments, regional economic migration opportunities, and bilateral schemes.[393] She holds that,

> advancing a holistic approach that includes climate justice, human rights, and development is increasingly desirable to develop adequate measures to protect people affected by or at risk of being affected by the impact of climate changes. The main challenge to identifying cross-border mobility as an adaptation strategy is how to link this option to binding obligations, such as bilateral or regional agreements, by incorporating moral and justice responsibilities to improve the lives of affected populations and allowing for full respect for the human rights of vulnerable populations.[394]

A case in point is the Caribbean Islands region, where there are regional PTAs that can provide legal pathways to people fleeing their homes in the context

390 UNHRC (n 369).
391 ibid.
392 ibid.
393 ibid.
394 ibid.

of disasters and climate change.[395] Regional free-movement agreements empower people in the Caribbean Islands to make short cross-border trips to take up employment when a disaster hits, to send remittances back home and to help rebuild, as well as to enhance their skills and exchange knowledge.[396]

As this section has demonstrated, the international trade regime provides significant legal tools to advance a 'holistic' approach to the international protection of PMDCC. Services mobility under WTO GATS Mode 4, as well as the facilitation of different types of mobility under PTAs, can enhance people's capacities to respond to the impact of disasters and climate change. However, as this section has pointed out, WTO GATS Mode 4 remains 'underused'. Similarly, the facilitation of the movement of persons under PTAs shows limitations, especially if the PTA is signed between developing and developed countries. Any proposed international protection for PMDCC needs to pay attention to both the strengths and the weaknesses of the international trade regime.

1.6 *International Human Rights Regimes*

The UN Charter and the UDHR are the pillars of the international human rights regimes, which the OHCHR was established in order to promote.[397] Furthermore, nine core international human rights treaties, and one optional protocol, have been adopted by States in order to respect, protect and fulfil a set of interrelated and indivisible civil, political, economic, social and cultural rights.[398] Ten treaty bodies, i.e. committees of independent experts, were established to monitor the implementation of these sources.[399] This section discusses the roles of the OHCHR and the treaty bodies in providing international protection for PMDCC.

Although no explicit right to climate and disaster protection is enshrined in international human rights treaties, the OHCHR has recognised that climate

395 Francis (n 385).

396 ibid; Annita Montoute, Debbie Mohammed and Jo Francis, 'Prospects and Challenges for Civil Society and Climate Change Engagement in the Caribbean: The Case of Trinidad and Tobago' 47 Caribbean Studies 2; Leon Sealey-Huggins, '1.5°C to stay alive': climate change, imperialism and justice for the Caribbean' [2017] 38 Third World Quarterly 11, 2444–2463.

397 Universal Declaration of Human Rights (adopted 10 December 1948) UNGA Res 217 A(III) preamble; Declaration by the United Nations (adopted 1 January 1942) <https://www.un.org/fr/sections/history-united-nations-charter/1942-declaration-united-nations/index.html> accessed 6 April 2022; UNGA Res 48/141 (7 January 1994) GAOR 48th Session Agenda item 114(b).

398 ICERD (n 76); ICCPR (n 71); ICESCR (n 76); CEDAW (n 76); CAT (n 71); CRC (n 76); ICRMW (n 76); ICPPED (n 71); CPRD (n 76).

399 Kälin and Künzli (n 22) 15.

change and disasters pose significant risks to the full enjoyment of human rights, including the rights protected under the ICCPR (e.g. the right to life, the right to be free from inhuman and degrading treatment, the right to culture, the right to self-determination), the ICESCR (e.g. the right to health, the right to adequate housing), and the CRC (e.g. the rights to life, survival and development, the right to family relations and to not be separated from one's parents against one's will).[400]

The OHCHR's work on disasters and climate change have primarily been aimed at highlighting the essential obligations and responsibilities of States.[401] It has been discharging this vision by carrying out studies and discussions with a view to the adoption of resolutions by the UNHRC.[402]

The first resolution addressing climate change and human rights was adopted in 2008 by the UNHRC, which acknowledged, amongst other things, the relevance of the right to development and to have access to water, as well as the needs of present and future generations.[403] Subsequent resolutions addressed several matters related to protection in the context of climate change, including the disproportionate impact of climate change on persons with disabilities, as well as older persons.[404] These resolutions play a pivotal

400 ICESCRCom, 'Climate Change and the International Covenant on Economic, Social and Cultural Rights' (Statement, 8 October 2018) <https://www.ohchr.org/en/NewsEvents/Pages/DisplayNews.aspx? NewsID=23691&LangID=E> accessed 6 April 2022; Office of the High Commissioner for Human Rights (OHCHR), 'Report on the Relationship Between Climate Change and Human Rights' UN Doc. A/HRC/10/61, 15 Jan. 2009, 20–41; UNHRC Res 32/33 'Human Rights and climate change' (1 July 2016) UNHRC 32nd Session Agenda item 3.

401 OHCHR, 'Key Messages on Human Rights and Climate Change' <https://www.ohchr.org/Documents/Issues/ClimateChange/KeyMessages_on_HR_CC.pdf> accessed 6 April 2022.

402 See UNHRC 'Analytical study on the promotion and protection of the rights of older persons in the context of climate change, Report of the Office of the United Nations High Commissioner for Human Rights' (30 April 2021) UN Doc A/HRC/47/46. Also see John Knox, 'Linking Human Rights and Climate Change at the United Nations' [2009] 33 Harvard Environmental Law Review 2, 477.

403 UNHRC Res 7/23, 'Human rights and climate change' (28 March 2008) UN Doc A/HRC/RES/7/23.

404 UNHRC Res 44/7, 'Human rights and climate change' (16 July 2020) UN Doc A/HRC/RES/44/7; UNHRC 42/21 'Human rights and climate change' (12 July 2019). Also see UNHRC Res 46/7 'Human rights and the environment' (30 March 2021) UN Doc A/HRC/RES/46/7; UNHRC Res 38/4 'Human rights and climate change' (5 July 2018) UN Doc A/HRC/RES/38/4; UNHRC Res 35/20, 'Human Rights and climate change' (22 June 2017) UN Doc A/HRC/RES/35/20; UNHRC Res 32/33, 'Human rights and climate change' (18 July 2016) UN Doc A/HRC/RES/32/33, UNHRC Res 29/ 15, 'Human rights and climate change' (22 July 2015) UN Doc A/HRC/RES/29/15; UNHRC Res 26/27, 'Human rights and climate change' (15 July 2014) UN Doc A/HRC/RES/26/27; UNHRC Res 18/22, 'Human rights and climate change'

role in the international climate change regime. For instance, the first mention of human rights in the context of the UNFCCC was made with a reference to UNHRC Resolution 10/4.[405]

Treaty bodies also play a significant role in interpreting the obligations of States in the context of disasters and climate change.[406] In September 2019, five treaty bodies – CEDAWCom, CESCRCom, CRMWCom, CRCom and CRPDCom – published a joint statement on human rights and climate change.[407] The statement urged all States to 'take into consideration their human rights obligations as they review their climate commitments'.[408] It added that human rights mechanisms have an important role to play in 'ensuring that States avoid taking measures that could accelerate climate change, and that they dedicate the maximum available resources to the adoption of measures aimed at mitigating climate change'.[409] Here, the joint statement focused on the role of preventing future foreseeable harm to the effective enjoyment

(17 October 2011) UN Doc A/HRC/RES/18/22; UNHRC Res 10/4 'Human rights and climate change' (25 March 2009) UN Doc A/HRC/RES/10/4; UNHRC Res 7/23, 'Human rights and climate change' (28 March 2008) UN Doc A/HRC/RES/7/23. See also, UNHRC Res 16/11, 'Human rights and the environment' (12 April 2011) UN Doc A/HRC/RES/16/11; UNHRC Res 19/10, 'Human rights and the environment' (19 April 2012) UN Doc A/HRC/RES/19/10; UNHRC Res 25/21, 'Human rights and the environment' (15 April 2014) UN Doc A/HRC/RES/25/21; UNHRC Res 28/11, 'Human rights and the environment' (7 April 2015) UN Doc A/HRC/RES/28/11; UNHRC Res 31/8, 'Human rights and the environment' (22 April 2016) UN Doc A/HRC/RES/21/8; UNHRC Res 34/20, 'Human rights and the environment' (6 April 2017) UN Doc A/HRC/RES/34/20; UNHRC Res 37/8, 'Human rights and the environment' (9 April 2018) UN Doc A/HRC/RES/37/8.

405 Conference of the Parties to the UNFCC, Decision 1/CP.16, 'Report of the Conference of the Parties on its sixteenth session, held in Cancun from 29 November to 10 December 2010, Part Two: Action taken by the Conference of the Parties at its sixteenth session' (15 March 2011) UN Doc FCCC/CP/2010/7/Add.1. Also see UNFCCC, 'Integrating human rights at the UNFCCC' <https://www.ohchr.org/EN/Issues/HRAndClimateChange/Pages/UNFCCC.aspx> accessed 6 April 2022.

406 Valentina Carraro, 'Promoting Compliance with Human Rights: The Performance of the United Nations' Universal Periodic Review and Treaty Bodies' [2019] 63 International Studies Quarterly 4, 1079–1093; Marc Limon, 'Human Rights and Climate Change: Constructing a Case for Political Action' [2009] 33 Harvard Environmental Law Review 2, 439–476.

407 Committee on the Elimination of Discrimination Against Women, Committee on Economic, Social and Cultural Rights, Committee on the Protection of the Rights of All Migrant Workers and Members of their Families, Committee on the Rights of the Child, and Committee on the Rights of Persons with Disabilities, 'Joint Statement on "Human Rights and Climate Change"' (16 September 2019) <https://www.ohchr.org/EN/NewsEvents/Pages/DisplayNews.aspx?NewsID=24998> accessed 6 April 2022.

408 ibid.

409 ibid.

of human rights by combating climate change.[410] The statement clearly articulated that '[f]ailure to take measures to prevent foreseeable human rights harm caused by climate change, or to regulate activities contributing to such harm, could constitute a violation of States' human rights obligations'.[411]

The statement also highlighted that the risk of harm from climate change is particularly high 'for those segments of the population already marginalised or in vulnerable situations or that, due to discrimination and pre-existing inequalities, have limited access to decision-making or resources, such as women, children, persons with disabilities, indigenous peoples and persons living in rural areas'.[412] In response, the five treaty bodies recommended seeing persons in vulnerable situations not as victims, but as 'agents of change'.[413] One important consequence of this approach is that it guarantees the participation of 'essential partners in the local, national and international efforts to tackle climate change'.[414] In this regard, States have a positive duty to mandate human rights due diligence and 'protect and defend effectively the rights of environmental human rights defenders, including women, indigenous and child environmental defenders'.[415]

Another consequence of the recognition of 'agents of change' is how it translates into the field of migration. As the treaty bodies state:

> 5. Migrant workers and members of their families are forced to migrate because their States of origin cannot ensure the enjoyment of adequate living conditions, due to the increase in hydrometeorological disasters, evacuations of areas at high risk of disasters, environmental degradation and slow-moving disasters, the disappearance of small island states due to rising sea levels, and even the occurrence of conflicts over access to resources. Migration is a normal human adaptation strategy in the face of the effects of climate change and natural disasters, as well as the only option for entire communities and has to be addressed by the United Nations and the States as a new cause of emerging migration and internal displacement.
>
> 6. In that regard, States must address the effects of climate change, environmental degradation and natural disasters as drivers of migration

410 ibid.
411 ibid.
412 ibid.
413 ibid.
414 ibid.
415 ibid.

> and ensure that such factors do not hinder the enjoyment of the human rights of migrants and their families. In addition, States should offer complementary protection mechanisms and temporary protection or stay arrangements for migrant workers displaced across international borders in the context of climate change or disasters and who cannot return to their countries.[416]

In their future of work, the treaty bodies committed to keep under review the impacts of climate change and disasters on the rights holders protected under their respective treaties.[417] A great example is the landmark *Sacchi et al.* decision on the CRCom in 2021, where 16 children from various nationalities submitted communication under the Third Optional Protocol of the UNCRC, requesting the CRCom to determine that climate change represents a children's rights crisis.[418] The petitioners argued that their rights to life and health, the priorisation of a child's best interests, and the cultural rights of the petitioners from indigenous communities were being violated by the respondent States – namely, Argentina, Brazil, France, Germany and Turkey – due to their disregard of the measures needed to prevent and mitigate climate change.[419]

Although the CRCom found that the communication was inadmissible because the petitioners had not exhausted domestic remedies in the respondent countries, it noted that 'climate change has an adverse effect on the enjoyment of rights by individuals both within and beyond the territory of the State

416 ibid. Migrant workers and members of their families are protected under the ICRMW. ICRMW is one of the nine core international human rights instruments and is the longest with 93 articles. The overall aim is to recognise that all migrant workers, regardless of, for instance, nationality, age, marital status, and political opinion, are entitled as human beings to the enjoyment of fundamental rights in the entirety of the migration process. An important limitation of ICRMW is its low rate of ratification. As of May 2020, it has been ratified by 55 States. See Carla Edelenbos, 'Committee on Migrant Workers and implementation of the ICRMW' in Ryszard Cholewinski, Paul de Guchteneire and Antoine Pécoud (UNESCO 2009) 100–122.

417 Committee on the Elimination of Discrimination Against Women, Committee on Economic, Social and Cultural Rights, Committee on the Protection of the Rights of All Migrant Workers and Members of their Families, Committee on the Rights of the Child, and Committee on the Rights of Persons with Disabilities, 'Joint Statement on "Human Rights and Climate Change"' (16 September 2019) <https://www.ohchr.org/EN/NewsEvents/Pages/DisplayNews.aspx?NewsID=24998> accessed 6 April 2022.

418 Communication to the Committee on the Rights of the Child, In the case of Chiara Sacchi and others v. Argentina, Brazil, France, Germany and Turkey (23 September 2019) <https://earthjustice.org/sites/default/files/files/2019.09.23-crc-communication-sacchi-et-al-v.-argentina-et-al-redacted.pdf> accessed 6 April 2022.

419 ibid.

party' and concluded that 'the State party has effective control over the sources of emissions that contribute to causing reasonably foreseeable harm to children outside its territory'.[420] This is a historic ruling on the harmful effects of climate change on children's rights, as a State party can be held responsible for the adverse impacts of its carbon emissions on the rights of children both within and outside its territory.[421] In June 2021, the CRCom decided to draft a general comment on children's rights and the environment with a special focus on climate change, with a view to completion in 2023.[422] This general comment will undoubtedly bring more clarity on the interpretation and application of the CRC to the climate crisis.

As this section has demonstrated, the OHCHR and the treaty bodies play an important role in interpreting the binding obligations of States under international human rights treaties in relation to disasters and climate change. Human rights are central to enabling the creation of a meaningful international protection mechanism for PMDCC.[423] Knowing this, the civil society and Indigenous People's organisations have called for the creation of a UN Special Rapporteur on Human Rights and Climate Change since 2010.[424] In 2021, the UNHRC recognised for the first time that having a clean, healthy and sustainable environment is a fundamental right and created a new Special Rapporteur on the Protection of Human Rights in the Context of Climate Change.[425] Such a new mandate has the potential to further build on the work of John Knox, the Special Rapporteur on Human Rights and the Environment at the time, who

420 CRCom (n 10).

421 OHCHR, 'UN Child Rights Committee rules that countries bear cross-border responsibility for harmful impact of climate change' (11 October 2021) <https://www.ohchr.org/EN/NewsEvents/Pages/DisplayNews.aspx?NewsID=27644&LangID=E> accessed 6 April 2022.

422 Child Rights Environment, 'General Comment No. 26' <https://childrightsenvironment.org/about/> accessed 6 April 2022.

423 Bellinkx and others (n 84).

424 Clémence Billard Schachter and Francesca Mingrone, 'A UN Special Rapporteur on Human Rights & Climate Change? Regional Perspectives' (Centre for International Environmental Law, January 2021) <https://www.ciel.org/wp-content/uploads/2021/02/UNSR-Report_English_2-5.pdf> accessed 6 April 2022. Also see 'An Open Letter by Global Civil Society and Indigenous Peoples for the Establishment of a new UN Special Rapporteur on Human Rights and Climate Change, To the States Members and Observers of the United Nations Human Rights Council' (2021) <https://franciscansinternational.org/fileadmin/media/2021/UN_Sessions/HRC47/Open_Letter_SRCC_HRC47.pdf> accessed 6 April 2022.

425 UNHRC (n 10). Also see UNHRC (n 80).

identified 'the obligation to protect against the infringement of human rights by climate change' in 2016.[426]

2 Relevant International Rules and Principles

This section examines the principle of *non-refoulement* under international law, the protection of displaced persons and the protection of persons in the event of disaster. The analysis critically engages with, first, the substance of these rules and principles and, second, the procedural mechanisms created for their promotion and enforcement, in order to flesh out the legal gap in the international protection of PMDCC.

2.1 *Non-refoulement*

The principle of *non-refoulement* (non-return) prohibits States from transferring or removing a person from a place of safety within their jurisdiction or under their effective control to a place where there is a risk that they may face a qualifying type of harm.[427] Notably expressed under the Refugee Convention, *non-refoulement* has reached beyond the sphere of refugee law to offer broader protection with the express articulation of the prohibition under international human rights law.[428] Currently, the prohibition of *non-refoulement* applies to all persons on the move at all times, irrespective of migration status or the

426 UNHRC, 'Report of the Special Rapporteur on Human Rights and the Environment on the Issue of Human Rights Obligations relating to the Enjoyment of a Safe, Clean, Healthy and Sustainable Environment' (1 February 2016) UN Doc A/HRC/31/52, para 33.

427 It is also debated whether *non-refoulement* amounts to a peremptory norm (*jus cogens*) under international law. See Chetail (n 47) 197; Sir Elihu Lauterpacht and Daniel Bethlehem, 'The Scope and Content of the Principle of Non-Refoulement' in Erika Feller, Volker Türk and Frances Nicholson (eds), *Refugee Protection in International Law: UNHCR's Global Consultations on International Protection* (Cambridge University Press 2003) 252; Jean Allain, 'The jus cogens nature of non-refoulement' [2001] 13 International Journal of Refugee Law 4, 533–558; Robert L Newmark, 'Non-Refoulement Run Afoul: The Questionable Legality of Extraterritorial Repatriation Programs' [1993] 71 Washington University Law Review 3; UNHCR, 'Advisory Opinion on the Extraterritorial Application of Non-Refoulement Obligations under the 1951 Convention relating to the Status of Refugees and its 1967 Protocol' <https://www.unhcr.org/4d9486929.pdf> accessed 6 April 2022.

428 Refugee Convention (n 70); ICCPR (n 71); CAT (n 71); ICPPED (n 71); The Declaration on Territorial Asylum 1967; the American Convention on Human Rights 1969.

reasons for movement.[429] This section discusses the nature and application of the prohibition of *non-refoulement* to provide international protection for PMDCC.

Section 1, Article 33 of the Refugee Convention formulates the prohibition of *non-refoulement* as follows:

> No Contracting State shall expel or return ('refouler') a refugee in any manner whatsoever to the frontiers of territories where his life or freedom would be threatened on account of his race, religion, nationality, membership of a particular social group or political opinion.[430]

This prohibition serves the purpose of protecting the interests and rights of asylum seekers, as well as receiving States and third States. Asylum seekers are protected under the prohibition of *non-refoulement* from being sent back to a place where they are likely to face harm.[431] Receiving States are protected under Section 2 of Article 33 of the Refugee Convention, which allows States to return the asylum seeker if the person 'constitutes a danger to the community' of the receiving State or if there are 'reasonable grounds' for regarding them as a 'danger to the security' of the receiving State.[432] Finally, the principle of *non-refoulement* is a significant safeguard against unilateral measures to 'dump' refugees in another country, which protects the interests of third States.[433]

With the expression of the prohibition of *non-refoulement* under international human rights agreements, most notably the CAT and the ICCPR, *non-refoulement* is now formulated as a guarantee 'that no one should be returned to a country where they would face torture, cruel, inhuman or degrading treatment or punishment and other irreparable harm'.[434] The UNHRCom

429 OHCHR, 'The principle of non-refoulement under international human rights law' <https://www.ohchr.org/Documents/Issues/Migration/GlobalCompactMigration/ThePrincipleNon-RefoulementUnderInternationalHumanRightsLaw.pdf> accessed 6 April 2022.

430 Refugee Convention (n 70).

431 Human Rights Committee, General Comment No. 31, para 12; CRC, General Comment No. 6, para 27 (see also para 84); CAT, General Comment No. 4 (2017) on the implementation of article 3 of the Convention in the context of article 22. para. 13.

432 Refugee Convention (n 70) art 33.

433 Tally Kritzman-Amir, 'Community Interests in Migration and Refugee Law' in Eyal Benvenisti, Georg Nolte and Keren Yalin-mor (eds), *Community Interests across International Law* (Oxford University Press 2018) 351.

434 OHCHR (n 429). Cornelis Wouters, 'International Refugee and Human Rights Law: Partners in Ensuring International Protection and Asylum' in Scott Sheeran and Nigel Rodley (eds), *Routledge Handbook of International Human Rights Law* (Routledge 2013) 231–243.

underscored in its General Comment No. 20 that 'States Parties must not expose individuals to the danger of torture or cruel, inhuman or degrading treatment or punishment upon return to another country by way of their extradition, expulsion or refoulement'.[435]

The prohibition of *non-refoulement* under international human rights law broadens the protection guaranteed under international refugee law in at least two ways. First, the obligations under human rights law directly bind States, unlike the application of international refugee law, where States enjoy a degree of latitude in implementing their obligations by establishing and deciding domestic asylum procedures and outcomes.[436] Second, under international human rights law, the principle operates without personal scoping restrictions, which can be contrasted with the five qualifying grounds for persecution under the Refugee Convention.[437] The obligation of a State not to return a migrant therefore might be engaged irrespective of the causes of movement under international human rights law.[438]

A communication by Ioane Teitiota provided a special opportunity for the UNHRCom to interpret the applicability of the prohibition of *non-refoulement* to HMDCC.[439] Teitiota is an I-Kiribati citizen who was deported from New Zealand along with his wife and children.[440] In his communication to the UNHRCom, he argued that New Zealand violated his right to life by rejecting his asylum application.[441] He argued that the severe impact of climate change

---

435 UNHRCom, 'CCPR General Comment No:20 Article 7 (Prohibition of Torture, or other Cruel, Inhuman or Degrading Treatment or Punishment) (10 March 1992) <https://www.refworld.org/docid/453883fb0.html> accessed 6 April 2022.

436 Chetail (n 47) 198.

437 Vincent Chetail, 'Are Refugee Rights Human Rights? An Unorthodox Questioning on the Relations between International Refugee law and International Human Rights Law' in R Rubio-Marin (ed), *Human Rights and Immigration* (Collected Courses of the Academy of European Law, Oxford University Press 2014) 36–37.

438 Cali, Costello and Cunningham (n 81) 355–384.

439 *Ioane Teitiota* (n 83).

440 ibid.

441 The Immigration and Protection Tribunal in New Zealand undertook an analysis in line with the view that 'while in many cases the effects of environmental change and natural disasters will not bring affected persons within the scope of the Refugee Convention, no hard and fast rules or presumptions of non-applicability exist. Care must be taken to examine the particular features of the case'. The Tribunal interpreted the right to life under the ICCPR as involving a positive obligation of the State to fulfil this right 'by taking programmatic steps to provide for the basic necessities of life'. Their conclusion was that Teitiota 'could not point to any act or omission by the Government of Kiribati that might indicate a risk that he would be arbitrarily deprived of his life within the scope of Article 6 of the Covenant'. His appeals to the High Court, the Court of Appeal, and the Supreme Court of New Zealand were denied on the ground that if he returned to Kiribati, he would

in Kiribati triggered the *non-refoulement* obligation of New Zealand not to send him back to Kiribati.[442]

There were two grounds substantiating his complaint with regards to the situation in Kiribati: first, the scarcity of habitable space, which has in turn caused violent land disputes that endanger his life; second, environmental degradation, including saltwater contamination of the freshwater supply.[443] He claimed that:

> the effects of climate change and sea level rise forced him to migrate from the island of Tarawa in the Republic of Kiribati to New Zealand. The situation in Tarawa has become increasingly unstable and precarious due to sea level rise caused by global warming. Fresh water has become scarce because of saltwater contamination and overcrowding on Tarawa. Attempts to combat sea level rise have largely been ineffective. Inhabitable land on Tarawa has eroded, resulting in a housing crisis and land disputes that have caused numerous fatalities. Kiribati has thus become an untenable and violent environment for the author and his family.[444]

Against this backdrop, the UNHRCom recalled that the right to life 'includes the right of individuals to enjoy a life with dignity and to be free from acts or omissions that would cause their unnatural or premature death'.[445] It accepted that sea-level rise is 'likely' to render Kiribati uninhabitable.[446] Yet, 'the timeframe of 10 to 15 years' could 'allow for intervening acts' by Kiribati, 'with the assistance of the international community, to take affirmative measures to protect and, where necessary, relocate its population'.[447] Kiribati 'was taking adaptive measures to reduce existing vulnerabilities and build resilience to

---

not face serious harm, even though the Supreme Court stated that environmental degradation from climate change and other natural disasters could 'create pathways into the Refugee Convention or other protected person jurisdiction'. See *Ioane Teitiota* (n 83).

442 Jane McAdam, 'Protecting People Displaced by the Impacts of Climate Change: The UN Human Rights Committee and the Principle of non-refoulement' [2020] 114 AJIL 718; Simon Behrman and Avidan Kent, 'The Teitiota case and the limitations of the human rights framework' [2020] 75 QIL, 25–39.

443 *Ioane Teitiota* (n 83) para 3.

444 ibid para 2.1.

445 See UNHRCom, 'General Comment No. 36, Article 6 (Right to Life)' (3 September 2019) UN Doc CCPR/C/GC/36.

446 *Ioane Teitiota* (n 83) para 9.12.

447 ibid.

climate change-related harms'.[448] Therefore, although 'severe environmental degradation can adversely affect an individual's well-being and lead to a violation of the right to life', the *non-refoulement* obligation of New Zealand in this particular case was not triggered.[449] As a result, the UNHRCom concluded that Teitiota's removal to Kiribati did not violate his right to life under Article 6 of the ICCPR.[450]

There were essentially two reasons why the appeal to human rights protection failed in this case.[451] First, the UNHRCom held that the danger faced was not specific enough to Teitiota and that climate change was indiscriminate in its effects on all inhabitants of Kiribati.[452] Second, and relatedly, if a claim of *non-refoulement* is based on general conditions, then the applicant must provide 'substantial grounds for believing that there is a real risk of irreparable harm' to the enjoyment of a protected right.[453]

The dissenting opinion of Duncan Laki Muhumuza criticised the insistence on demonstrating a greater risk of harm than the general population.[454] As he put it, 'New Zealand's action is more like forcing a drowning person back into a sinking vessel, with the "justification" that after all, there are other voyagers on board'.[455]

The Vasilka Sancin's individual opinion similarly criticised the majority opinion, and stated that the onus should have been on New Zealand to show that Teitiota and his family in fact enjoy access to 'safe drinking water' in Kiribati, in order to comply with New Zealand's positive duty to protect life from risks arising from known natural hazards.[456] Instead, Teitiota was expected to substantiate his claim that he did not have access to 'potable water'.[457]

Commentators also pointed out the relevance of the prohibition of inhumane and degrading treatment under Article 7 of the ICCPR, which the UNHRCom did not directly address – largely due to the fact that the communication was filed under Article 6 of the ICCPR, which protects the right to life.[458] According to this line of argument, in cases where an applicant can

448 ibid.
449 ibid.
450 ibid.
451 Behrman and Kent (n 442) 25–39.
452 ibid.
453 ibid.
454 *Ioane Teitiota* (n 83), dissenting opinion of Duncan Laki Muhumuza.
455 ibid.
456 *Ioane Teitiota* (n 83), individual opinion of Vasilka Sancin.
457 ibid.
458 McAdam (n 176); Eugénie Delval, 'From the UN Human Rights Committee to European Courts: Which protection for climate-induced displaced persons under European Law?'

substantiate the real risk of inhumane and degrading treatment due to the impacts of climate change, the obligation to not return might be triggered.[459]

In the author's view, the *Teitiota* decision demonstrates that the international protection of PMDCC that is proposed in this book needs to expressly state the application of the principle of *non-refoulement*. In the absence of a clear articulation to this effect, a protection gap simply emerges. As this section has demonstrated, the interpretation of the right to life under Article 6 of the ICCPR was not able to afford protection to Teitiota and his family from being returned to Kiribati.

2.2 *Protection in the Event of Displacement*

Internal displacement has been an issue at the international level for a considerable time, with various IOs and other actors providing relief to people who flee their homes to escape conflict, violence and disaster.[460] Recently, there

(EU Migration and Asylum Law and Policy Blog, 8 April 2020) <https://eumigrationlawblog.eu/from-the-u-n-human-rights-committee-to-european-courts-which-protection-for-climate-induced-displaced-persons-under-european-law/> accessed 6 April 2022.

459 For instance, Caskey argues that if an applicant can substantiate the real risk of increased land salinization forcing them to leave their residence, or of rising temperatures to force their retreat from an area, then the prohibition of non-refoulement under Article 7 of the ICCPR arises. Christopher Caskey, 'Non-Refoulement and Environmental Degradation: Examining the Entry Points and Improving Access to Protection' (Global Migration Research Paper No 26, 2020) Global Migration Centre, Graduate Institute of International and Development Studies.

460 Why the international community should be concerned with the treatment of IDPs is a legitimate question. Cohen argues that there were a combination of factors to form an international response to protect the IDPs. First, there has been a growth of the number of IDPs, from 1.2 million in 1982 to an estimated 20 million in 1995 and it was realised that internal displacement can undermine national, as well as regional and international security. Second, towards the end of the Cold War era, there was a change in the notion of sovereignty, towards a framing of 'sovereignty as responsibility', which was later developed into the doctrine of responsibility to protect (R2P). R2P relates to the failure of a State in fulfilling its responsibilities towards its own citizens, in which case the protection falls within the responsibility of the international community. A similar principle is applicable to the protection of IDPs. Governments have the primary responsibility to protect their displaced populations, and in the failure to discharge that responsibility, the international community has the right to engage. A third reason is the 'particular vulnerability' of IDPs. IDPs experience problems as a result of their displacement, including lack of shelter, access to services, formal documents and political rights; loss of property and access to livelihoods; discrimination because of being displaced; and challenges relating to return and integration. The particular vulnerabilities IDPs face can be contrasted with other internal migrants, who move voluntarily within the borders of their countries, and hence do not summon international protection. See Roberta Cohen, 'Nowhere to Run, No Place to Hide' [2002] 58 Bulletin of the Atomic Scientists 6, 36–45. Also see Khalid Koser,

has been a growing recognition that many refugees and cross-border displaced persons were internally displaced before crossing an international border.[461] This has motivated the establishment of initiatives to address cross-border displacement, including in the context of disasters and climate change.[462] This section discusses the relevant non-binding international instruments on internal and cross-border displacement, as well as the cooperative mechanisms set up to provide protection.[463] It argues that these instruments and mechanisms provide the basis for the international protection of PMDCC.[464]

In 1992, at the request of the UNCHR, Francis Deng compiled the international standards relevant to the protection of internally displaced persons (IDPs) under the non-binding Guiding Principles on Internal Displacement.[465] The Guiding Principles on Internal Displacement describe IDPs as follows:

> persons or groups of persons who have been forced or obliged to flee or to leave their homes or places of habitual residence, in particular as a result of or in order to avoid the effects of armed conflict, situations of generalized violence, violations of human rights or natural or human-made disasters, and who have not crossed an internationally recognized State border.[466]

'Internally Displaced Persons' in Alexander Betts (ed), *Global Migration Governance* (Oxford University Press 2011).

461 IDMC, 'The Invisible Majority: The Displacement Continuum' (IDMC Thematic Series, November 2017) <https://www.internal-displacement.org/sites/default/files/inline-files/20171113-idmc-intro-cross-border-thematic-series_1.pdf> accessed 6 April 2022.

462 Julia Toscano, 'Climate Change Displacement and Forced Migration: An International Crisis' [2015] 6 Arizona Journal of Environmental Law and Policy 1, 460–487.

463 Jane McAdam, 'From the Nansen Initiative to the Platform on Disaster Displacement: Shaping International Approaches to Climate Change, Disasters and Displacement' [2016] 39 University of New South Wales Law Journal 4, 1518–1546.

464 See Vikram Kolmannskog and Lisetta Trebbi, 'Climate change, natural disasters and displacement: a multi-track approach to filling the protection gap' [2010] 92 ICRC 879, 713–730.

465 Convinced of the need to address 'gray areas' and protection gaps, a new international mechanism was created to address the human rights of IDPs. In 2004, Walter Kälin was appointed as the first Representative on the Human Rights of IDPs, a function which was taken up by Chaloka Beyani in 2010 and Cecilia Jimenez-Damary in 2016. See UNHRC Res 41/15, 'Mandate of the Special Rapporteur on the human rights of internally displaced persons' (19 July 2019) UN Doc A/HRC/RES/41/15.

466 Guiding Principles on Internal Displacement (22 July 1998) ADM 1.1, PRL 12.1, PR00/98/109 <https://www.refworld.org/docid/3c3da07f7.html> accessed 6 April 2022.

This definition is broad with respect to the causes of movement.[467] It not only refers to natural or human-made disasters, but also to violations of human rights.[468] This definition thus covers people who are evacuated or who flee from their homes to escape the impacts of disasters and climate change, as well as people who are forced to flee in the aftermath of a disaster.[469]

IDPs are internationally protected under the cluster approach, which was established by the UNGA as a part of the Humanitarian Reform Agenda in 2005.[470] Under the cluster approach, the responsibility for the protection of IDPs in the context of disasters is shared by the UNHCR, OHCHR and UNICEF, under the Global Protection Cluster (GPC).[471] The 2020–2024 Strategic

---

467 The African Union Convention for the Protection and Assistance of Internally Displaced in Africa (the Kampala Convention) is the only regional binding instrument that has adopted this definition. Complementing the general obligations of States on the protection of IDPs, the Kampala Convention also includes the obligation to take measures to protect and assist persons who have been internally displaced due to natural or human made disasters. See Francis Deng and Romola Adeola, 'The Normative Influence of the UN Guiding Principles on the Kampala Convention in the Protection of Internally Displaced Persons in Africa' [2021] 65 Journal of African Law, 59–72.

468 Alexandra Bilak and Avigail Shai, 'Internal Displacement Beyond 2018: The Road Ahead' [2018] 59 Forced Migration Review, 49–52; Walter Kälin, 'The Guiding Principles on Internal Displacement as international minimum standard and protection tool' [2005] 24 Refugee Survey Quarterly 3, 27–36.

469 McAdam and others (n 1).

470 The cluster approach emerged following the serious deficiencies in the international response mechanism to humanitarian crises, as a result of which people falling under the mandate of certain international organisations had benefited from assistance (e.g. children under UNICEF, or refugees under UNHCR), whereas others, especially the IDPs, received *ad hoc* and unpredictable assistance. Whilst the cluster approach is not limited to IDPs, one of the biggest motivations for the new system was to fill the 'protection gap' experienced by IDPs. At the international level, the cluster approach aims to 'strengthen the system-wide preparedness and technical capacity to respond to humanitarian emergencies, and provide clear leadership and accountability in the main areas of humanitarian response'. At the national level, it aims to 'strengthen partnerships, and the predictability and accountability of international humanitarian action, by improving prioritization and clearly defining the roles and responsibilities of humanitarian organizations'. The Inter-Agency Standing Committee (IASC) designates the 'sectors' of humanitarian action and appoints both UN and non-UN humanitarian organisations as sector leaders. There are currently eleven clusters, which complement the food (solely led by WFP) and refugee sectors (solely led by UNHCR). See IASC, 'Guidance Note on Using the Cluster Approach to Strengthen Humanitarian Response' (24 November 2006); UNGA Res 46/182 (19 December 1991) 78th Plenary Meeting; OCHA, 'What is the cluster approach?' <https://www.humanitarianresponse.info/en/coordination/clusters/what-cluster-approach> accessed 6 April 2022.

471 GPC's work is guided by the IASC Policy on Protection in Humanitarian Action and the ICRC Professional Standards for Protection Work. See Global Protection Cluster

Framework of GPC particularly stresses climate change and disasters as triggers of internal displacement, committing to more effective coordination in all operations.[472]

However, the GPC's role with respect to 'climate-related disaster response' and 'climate preparedness' is a work in progress.[473] For instance, in order to unpack its role, the GPC organised a consultation event in 2020, with the suggestions including advocating for 'climate refugees', incorporating climate change as a key focus, identifying different protection concerns and coordinating 'all actors worldwide' by creating a platform.[474]

Concomitantly, two international cooperative initiatives have been established to address the protection needs of IDPs, including in the context of disasters. Spearheaded by UNHCR, UN OCHA and the Special Rapporteur on the Human Rights of IDPs, the GP20 Plan of Action was launched in 2018.[475] The plan particularly aims to advance 'prevention', 'protection' and 'solutions' for IDPs, by focusing on the prevention of the conditions that cause displacement, improving the lives of people already displaced and encouraging more inclusive, coherent and strategic action among stakeholders engaged with and affected by internal displacement 'no matter the cause'.[476]

Working Group, 'Handbook for the Protection of Internally Displaced Persons' (31 March 2010) <https://www.unhcr.org/protection/idps/4c2355229/handbook-protection-internally-displaced-persons.html?query=internally%20displaced%20persons> accessed 6 April 2022.

472 Protection is defined as 'all activities aimed at obtaining full respect for the rights of the individual in accordance with the letter and the spirit of the relevant bodies of law, including International Humanitarian Law and International Refugee Law'. See Global Protection Cluster, 'Protection in a Climate of Change: Strategic Framework 2020–2024' (2020) <https://www.globalprotectioncluster.org/wp-content/uploads/GPC-Strategic-Framework_digital_version-1.pdf> accessed 6 April 2022.

473 GPC, 'Consultation event report, Climate Preparedness and Community-based Protection' <https://www.globalprotectioncluster.org/wp-content/uploads/PHAP_Climate-preparedness-and-community-based-protection-Consultation-event-report-1.pdf> accessed 6 April 2022.

474 ibid.

475 The plan of action focuses on four priorities: engaging IDPs in decision-making processes that affect them; promoting, developing and implementing national frameworks to prevent and address internal displacement; enhancing the quality of data and analysis on internal displacement; and addressing protracted displacement while driving solutions for IDPs. See GPC, 'GP20 Plan of Action for Advancing Prevention, Protection and Solutions for Internally Displaced People' <https://www.globalprotectioncluster.org/_assets/files/unhcr-gp20-plan_of_action-a5-scren.pdf> accessed 6 April 2022.

476 ibid.

In 2019, the UN Secretary-General Antonio Guterres established the High-Level Panel on Internal Displacement to 'find concrete solutions to internal displacement and alleviating the impact on millions of affected people'.[477] Amongst other things, disasters and the adverse effects of climate change have been chosen as focus areas of the panel.[478] The final output of the panel is intended to be a report consisting of 'concrete and practical recommendations' to UN Member States, the UN system and other relevant stakeholders, which can provide an important basis for the establishment of a legal rule on the international protection of PMDCC.[479]

Turning to cross-border displacement, an important State-led consultative process was launched by Switzerland and Norway in 2012.[480] Named after Fridtjof Nansen, the first High Commissioner for Refugees, the Nansen Initiative aimed to address the challenges of cross-border displacement in the context of disasters and climate change.[481] After a round of discussions and consultations in Central America, South Asia, the Greater Horn of Africa and the Pacific, the Agenda for the Protection of Cross-Border Displaced Persons in the Context of Climate Change (Protection Agenda) was established and endorsed by 109 governmental delegations at a global intergovernmental meeting in 2015.[482]

The Protection Agenda comprises three parts and three annexes.[483] The parts concern (i) protecting cross-border disaster-displaced persons, (ii)

---

477 UN, 'UN Secretary-General's Statement announcing the establishment of a High-Level Panel on Internal Displacement' (23 October 2019, New York) <https://www.un.org/internal-displacement-panel/news/23-october-2019-secretary-generals-statement-announcing-establishment-high-level-panel-internal> accessed 6 April 2022.

478 UN, 'Terms of Reference: High-Level Panel on Internal Displacement' <https://www.un.org/internal-displacement-panel/sites/www.un.org.internal-displacement-panel/files/tor_of_the_panel.pdf> accessed 6 April 2022; UN, 'Consultation in Asia concludes with recommendations on disaster displacement for UN High-Level Panel' (19 November 2020) <https://www.un.org/internal-displacement-panel/content/consultation-asia-concludes-recommendations-disaster-displacement-un-high-level-panel> accessed 6 April 2022; UN, 'Pacific governments call for urgent action on disaster displacement in light of the climate crisis' (11 February 2011) .

479 UN, 'Terms of Reference: High-Level Panel on Internal Displacement' <https://www.un.org/internal-displacement-panel/sites/www.un.org.internal-displacement-panel/files/tor_of_the_panel.pdf> accessed 6 April 2022.

480 The Nansen Initiative (n 215).

481 Francois Gemenne and Pauline Brücker, 'From the Guiding Principles on Internal Displacement to the Nansen Initiative: What the Governance of Environmental Migration Can Learn From the Governance of Internal Displacement' [2015] 27 International Journal of Refugee Law 2, 245–263.

482 The Nansen Initiative (n 215).

483 ibid.

managing disaster displacement risk in the country of origin and (iii) establishing priority areas for future action.[484] The annexes concern the regional dynamics of disaster-related human mobility, effective practices for cross-border disaster-displacement and disaster displacement references in international, (sub-)regional and bilateral agreements, declarations and policies, as well as the conclusions of regional consultations.[485]

The Protection Agenda stresses that the 'current and emerging realities call for increased preparedness, solidarity and cooperation by States, (sub-) regional organisations and the international community to prevent, avoid, and respond to disaster displacement and its causes'.[486] This is transposed into application via the priority areas for future action, which call for, amongst other things, collecting data, strengthening the management of disaster displacement risk in the country of origin and enhancing the use of humanitarian protection measures.[487]

---

484 ibid.

485 ibid.

486 ibid.

487 Humanitarian protection measures are especially a tool to provide international protection to cross-border displaced persons in the context of disasters and climate change. These can generally be in two forms: a State can admit cross-border disaster-displaced persons into its territory and allow such persons to stay at least temporarily, or a State can refrain from returning non-citizens to a disaster affected country who were already present in the receiving country when the disaster occurred. An example is the US Temporary Protected Status (TPS), which since 1990 has been offering humanitarian protection to hundreds of thousands of non-citizens who are unable to return to their countries of origin. TPS functions as a 'blanket' form of relief, and grants all nationals of particular countries work authorisation and protection against deportation. The Department of Homeland Security chooses to award TPS to a particular country after analysing the situation, which could be based on armed conflicts, epidemics, and other extraordinary and temporary conditions. TPS has also covered situations of environmental disasters. For instance, after the devastating effects of Hurricane Mitch in 1999, citizens of Honduras and Nicaragua have been protected under the TPS, and have been holding this status for more than 20 years. Furthermore, States can adopt measures to manage displacement risks within their borders, which would have the effect of addressing the root causes of cross-border disaster-displacement. In this sense, the Protection Agenda promotes the use of planned relocation as a preventative or responsive measure to the risk of displacement. See Alice Edwards, 'Temporary Protection, Derogation and the 1951 Refugee Convention' [2012] 13 Melbourne Journal of International Law,1–40; Claire Bergeron, 'Temporary Protected Status after 25 Years: Addressing the Challenge of Long-Term Temporary Residents and Strengthening a Centerpiece of US Humanitarian Protection' [2018] 2 Journal on Migration and Human Security 1, 22–43.2; Meltem Ineli-Ciger and Achilles Skorda, 'Temporary Protection' (Max Planck Encyclopedia 2019) <https://opil.ouplaw.com/view/10.1093/law-epil/9780199231690/law-9780199231690-e2200> accessed 6 April 2022.

As a follow-up to the Nansen Initiative, Platform on Disaster Displacement (PDD) was formed in 2016.[488] PDD aims to implement the Protection Agenda by promoting measures, bringing together partners, facilitating regional efforts and framing key messages.[489]

According to its strategy for 2019–2022, the PDD will continue to actively participate in international platforms concerning climate change, disaster risk reduction and human rights.[490] In particular, the Protection Agenda and the work of the PDD have been recognised by States in the recently adopted Global Compact for Migration.[491] PDD aims to be involved in the follow-up and implementation of the Global Compacts for Migration and on Refugees, deepening the interaction between international migration and refugee regimes with environmental factors.[492]

It must be noted, however, that the PDD's work – similar to the Protection Agenda – does not aim to expand States' legal obligations under international law.[493] In this sense, the work of the PDD, and the Protection Agenda itself, can be interpreted as promoting current best practices, instead of normatively challenging them in order to raise them up to a higher degree of legal obligation.[494]

As this section has demonstrated, internal and cross-border displacement in the context of disasters and climate change are addressed to an extent under

488 McAdam (n 176) 1518–1546.

489 Structurally, the work of the PDD is directed by the Steering Group, which has 18 members, including the EU. The Steering Group is led by the Chair and the Vice Chair which are subject to a one and a half year term. On 3 December 2020, Fiji took over the chairmanship and France became the Vice-Chair. See PDD <https://disasterdisplacement.org/> accessed 6 April 2022.

490 PDD, 'PDD Strategy 2019–2022' <https://disasterdisplacement.org/wp-content/uploads/2019/06/26062019-PDD-Strategy-2019-2022-FINAL_to_post_on_website.pdf> accessed 6 April 2022. OHCHR, 'Addressing human rights protection gaps in the context of migration and displacement of persons across international borders resulting from the adverse effects of climate change and supporting the adaptation and mitigation plans of developing countries to bridge the protection gaps - Report of the United Nations High Commissioner for Human Rights' (23 April 2018) UN Doc A/HRC/38/21. Also see OHCHR, 'The Slow onset effects of climate change and human rights protection for cross-border migrants' (22 March 2018) UN Doc A/HRC/37/CRP.4.

491 Global Compact for Migration (n 9) objective 2.

492 ibid.

493 The Nansen Initiative (n 215) 7.

494 Chien-yu Liu, 'Disaster Displacement in Humanitarian and Development Contexts' in Veronica Fynn Bruey and Steven W. Bender, Deadly Voyages: Migrant Journeys across the Globe (The Rowman and Littlefield Publishing Group Inc 2020).

non-binding instruments and cooperative mechanisms.[495] However, these remain largely voluntary, and thus fail to create a legally binding, universal response.

2.3 *Protection in the Event of Disasters*

Influenced largely by the challenges raised by the 2004 tsunami affecting the Indian Ocean, the ILC decided in 2007 to include in its programme of work the topic 'Protection of Persons in the Event of Disasters'.[496] On the basis of eight reports submitted by the Special Rapporteur Eduardo Valencia-Ospina, as well as the comments provided by States and other relevant actors, the ILC adopted the final text of the Draft Articles on the Protection of Persons in the Event of Disasters (Draft Articles) in 2016.[497] The ILC's Draft Articles in this area represent a significant step towards the development of legislation.[498] Since 2020,

495 Other non-binding legal tools that complement the mentioned instruments include, the 2005 Pinheiro Principles on Housing and Property Restitution for Refugees and Displaced Persons, the 2010 Handbook for the Protection of Internally Displaced Persons, and the 2014 Mend Guide: Comprehensive Guide for Planning Mass Evacuations in Natural Disasters. See ECOSOC, 'Economic, Social and Cultural Rights: Housing and property restitution in the context of return of refugees and internally displaced persons, Final Report of the Special Rapporteur Paulo Sergio Pinheiro, Principles on housing and property restitution for refugees and displaced persons' (28 June 2005) UN Doc E/CN.4/Sub.2/2005/17; Global Protection Cluster Working Group, 'Handbook for the Protection of Internally Displaced Persons' (31 March 2010); Global Camp Coordination and Camp Management Cluster, 'The MEND Guide: Comprehensive Guide for Planning Mass Evacuations in Natural Disasters' (31 December 2014).

496 The international legal architecture pertaining to the prevention and response to 'disasters' is characterised by a 'pot pourri' of binding and non-binding instruments. See Craig Allan and Therese O'Donnell, 'A Call to Alms? Natural Disasters, R2P, Duties of Cooperation and Unchartered Consequences' [2012] 17 Journal of Conflict and Security Law 3, 345; UNGA Res 69/283, 'The Sendai Framework for Disaster Risk Reduction' (23 June 2015) UN Doc. A/RES/69/283; Convention on Assistance in the Case of a Nuclear Accident or Radiological Emergency (adopted 26 September 1986, entered into force 26 February 1987) 1457 UNTS 134; Tampere Convention on the Provision of Telecommunication Resources for Disaster Mitigation and Relief Operations (adopted 18 June 1998, entered into force 8 January 2005) 2296 UNTS 5.

497 The Special Rapporteur preferred to define disasters as 'a calamitous event or series of events resulting in widespread loss of life, great human suffering and distress, mass displacement, or large-scale material or environmental damage, thereby seriously disrupting the functioning of society'. Although the scope extends to human-made disasters, the commentary clarifies that mere situations of political and economic crisis would not be covered. See ILC, 'Report of the International Law Commission: Sixty Eighth Session' (2 May 10 June and 4 July 12 August 2016), UN Doc. A/71/10, 2016 (DAS Report) 13 73.

498 Previous initiatives addressing this issue include the IASC Operational Guidelines on the Protection of Persons in the Context of Natural Disasters, which were developed with

the UNGA has, drawing on the recommendation of the ILC, been elaborating a convention on the basis of the Draft Articles.[499] This section discusses the content of the Draft Articles and the elaboration by the UNGA of a convention on the protection of persons in the event of disasters.

It is important to clarify that the Draft Articles do not provide an international framework for the protection of PMDCC. Although, by virtue of the principle of non-discrimination, the Draft Articles apply to all persons in the event of a disaster, regardless of their nationality, the aim is not to address the admission, stay and return of non-citizens.[500] Instead, the Draft Articles aim to 'facilitate the adequate and effective response to disasters, and reduction of the risks of disasters, so as to meet the essential needs of the persons concerned, with full respect for their rights'.[501]

With this purpose, the Draft Articles, consisting of a preamble and 18 draft articles, are designed to reflect two dimensions.[502] The vertical/human dimension acknowledges human dignity, human rights and humanitarian principles as reminders of the existing positive and negative obligations of States in disaster scenarios.[503] The horizontal dimension, on the other hand, mainly addresses the legal relations among the affected States and assisting actors.[504] The primary role of the affected State in ensuring the protection of persons

---

the support of the Brookings-Bern Project on Internal Displacement. See IASC, 'IASC Operational Guidelines on the Protection of Persons in Situations of Natural Disasters' (The Brookings – Bern Project on Internal Displacement, January 2011) <https://interagencystandingcommittee.org/system/files/legacy_files/Operational_guidelines_nd.pdf> accessed 6 April 2022.

499 UNGA, 'Annotated preliminary list of items to be included in the provisional agenda of the seventy-fifth regular session of the General Assembly' (15 June 2020) UN Doc A/75/100, para 89; UNGA, 'Summary record of the 31st meeting' Sixth Committee (31 January 2019) UN Doc A/C.6/73/SR.31; UNGA Res 71/141 'Protection of persons in the event of disasters' (19 December 2016).

500 ILC, 'Draft Articles on the Protection of Persons in the Event of Disasters, with Commentaries' (2016) <https://www.refworld.org/docid/5f64dc3c4.html> accessed 6 April 2022, Draft Article 6(6).

501 ILC, 'Draft articles on the protection of persons in the event of disasters' (2016) UN Doc A/71/10, draft Article 2.

502 ibid para. 48.

503 Bartolini argues that the vertical dimension is reflected in Articles 4–6 (human dignity, human rights, humanitarian principles), and the horizontal dimension in Articles 7–17 (including disaster risk reduction, and relief/recovery phases) of the Draft Articles. See Giulio Bartolini, 'A Universal Treaty for Disasters: Remarks on International Law Commission's Draft Articles on the Protection of Persons in the Event of Disasters' [2019] 99 International Review of the Red Cross 906, 1103–1138.

504 ibid.

and the provision of disaster relief assistance is balanced with the duties to cooperate and to seek external assistance.[505]

The UNGA has taken note of the Draft Articles, and invited governments to submit comments for the elaboration of a binding convention.[506] In November 2020, a lively debate took place at the Sixth Committee of the UNGA on this issue.[507] Several delegations supported the elaboration of an international convention on the basis of the Draft Articles, due to reasons such as the significance of the topic, the need to facilitate international cooperation in this area, the need to contribute to reaching SDG 13 and the way in which the Draft Articles are progressively developing international law governing disaster response.[508]

Climate change played a role in the statements of several delegations who showed support for the elaboration of a convention.[509] For instance, Jamaica emphasised the increased frequency and severity of naturally occurring disasters and the growing impact of climate change on vulnerable States.[510] Tonga,

505 ILC (n 501), draft articles 7 and 11.

506 Twenty four delegations submitted statements during the seveny-third session of the UNGA. See UNGA, 'Summary record of the 31st meeting' Sixth Committee (31 January 2019) UN Doc A/C.6/73/SR.31; UNGA Res 71/141 'Protection of persons in the event of disasters' (19 December 2016).

507 Sixth Committee (Legal) – 75th session, 'Protection of persons in the event of disasters (Agenda Item 89)' (UN, 2020) <https://www.un.org/en/ga/sixth/75/disasters.shtml> accessed 6 April 2022.

508 See Statement by Sweden on behalf of the Nordic Countries (Denmark, Finland, Iceland, Norway and Sweden) (23 October 2020) <https://www.un.org/en/ga/sixth/75/pdfs/statements/disasters/17mtg_nordic.pdf>; Statement by Singapore (11 November 2020) <https://www.un.org/en/ga/sixth/75/pdfs/statements/disasters/17mtg_singapore.pdf>; Statement of the Republic of the Philippines (11 November 2020) <https://www.un.org/en/ga/sixth/75/pdfs/statements/disasters/17mtg_philippines.pdf>; Statement by Brunei Darussalam (October 2020) <https://www.un.org/en/ga/sixth/75/pdfs/statements/disasters/17mtg_brunei.pdf>; Statement by Portugal <https://www.un.org/en/ga/sixth/75/pdfs/statements/disasters/17mtg_portugal.pdf>; Statement by Nigeria (23 October 2020) <https://www.un.org/en/ga/sixth/75/pdfs/statements/disasters/18mtg_nigeria.pdf>.

509 Statement by Jamaica (23 October 2020) <https://www.un.org/en/ga/sixth/75/pdfs/statements/disasters/17mtg_jamaica.pdf> accessed 6 April 2022; Statement by Tonga (27 October 2020) <https://www.un.org/en/ga/sixth/75/pdfs/statements/disasters/18mtg_tonga.pdf> accessed 6 April 2022; Statement by Japan <https://www.un.org/en/ga/sixth/75/pdfs/statements/disasters/17mtg_japan.pdf> accessed 6 April 2022; Statement by Cuba (11 November 2020) <https://www.un.org/en/ga/sixth/75/pdfs/statements/disasters/17mtg_cuba_e.pdf> accessed 6 April 2022; Statement by Viet Nam <https://www.un.org/en/ga/sixth/75/pdfs/statements/disasters/18mtg_vietnam.pdf> accessed 6 April 2022.

510 Statement by Jamaica (23 October 2020) <https://www.un.org/en/ga/sixth/75/pdfs/statements/disasters/17mtg_jamaica.pdf> accessed 6 April 2022.

Japan, Cuba and Viet Nam similarly addressed the relationship between disasters and climate change.[511] Furthermore, Brazil noted that it views mass displacement as one of the consequences of 'major disasters', and shared its involvement at the PDD.[512]

Several delegations expressed the view that the topic could be best addressed through guidelines and practical cooperation or found the elaboration of a convention premature.[513] Malaysia, for instance, was of the view that the elements of the Draft Articles that 'seek to develop or create new duties or obligations would, for the time being, seem to be more appropriately pursued as best practice principles or guidelines'.[514] Malaysia justified its position based on the existing body of international, regional and domestic law, and considered the ILC's work to be 'most valuable where it assists States to understand and implement their prevailing obligations'.[515] Furthermore, Israel held that 'undertaking to engage in a protection mission should not be considered in terms of legal rights and duties', and called for the Draft Articles to remain as guidelines or guiding principles.[516] Similarly, the US expressed its position that this issue was best approached through the provision of practical guidance and cooperation.[517]

511 Statement by Tonga (27 October 2020) <https://www.un.org/en/ga/sixth/75/pdfs/statements/disasters/18mtg_tonga.pdf> accessed 6 April 2022; Statement by Japan <https://www.un.org/en/ga/sixth/75/pdfs/statements/disasters/17mtg_japan.pdf> accessed 6 April 2022; Statement by Cuba (11 November 2020) <https://www.un.org/en/ga/sixth/75/pdfs/statements/disasters/17mtg_cuba_e.pdf> accessed 6 April 2022; Statement by Viet Nam <https://www.un.org/en/ga/sixth/75/pdfs/statements/disasters/18mtg_vietnam.pdf> accessed 6 April 2022.

512 Statement by Brazil (13 November 2020) <https://www.un.org/en/ga/sixth/75/pdfs/statements/disasters/18mtg_brazil.pdf> accessed 6 April 2022.

513 Statement by the United States of America (27 October 2020) <https://www.un.org/en/ga/sixth/75/pdfs/statements/disasters/18mtg_us.pdf> accessed 6 April 2022; Statement of Malaysia (11 November 2020) <https://www.un.org/en/ga/sixth/75/pdfs/statements/disasters/17mtg_malaysia.pdf> accessed 6 April 2022; Statement by Israel (14 October 2020) <https://www.un.org/en/ga/sixth/75/pdfs/statements/disasters/18mtg_israel.pdf> accessed 6 April 2022.

514 Statement of Malaysia (11 November 2020) <https://www.un.org/en/ga/sixth/75/pdfs/statements/disasters/17mtg_malaysia.pdf> accessed 6 April 2022.

515 Statement of Malaysia (11 November 2020) <https://www.un.org/en/ga/sixth/75/pdfs/statements/disasters/17mtg_malaysia.pdf> accessed 6 April 2022.

516 Statement by Israel (14 October 2020) <https://www.un.org/en/ga/sixth/75/pdfs/statements/disasters/18mtg_israel.pdf> accessed 6 April 2022.

517 Statement by the United States of America (27 October 2020) <https://www.un.org/en/ga/sixth/75/pdfs/statements/disasters/18mtg_us.pdf> accessed 6 April 2022.

Several delegations, while welcoming the Draft Articles, commented on the need to further elaborate on their scope, content and application.[518] Brazil and Bangladesh, for instance, pushed for a clear distinction between natural and human-made disasters, with Brazil pointing to the challenges involved in addressing both in a single instrument.[519]

Although the conclusion of a treaty is favoured especially by the project's Special Rapporteur and the UN Secretary-General, the willingness of States to participate in this formal venture has yet to be demonstrated.[520] The issue will be discussed during the 76th session of the UNGA, which is scheduled to open on 14 September 2021.[521] A treaty on this topic would represent a milestone in clarifying the legal rights and obligations of affected States, affected persons, as well as assisting States and other assisting actors.[522] However, as the Draft Articles currently stand, the international protection of PMDCC is not addressed. Therefore, the proposed international protection of PMDCC could build on the Draft Articles and their ongoing elaboration at the UNGA.

---

518 Statement by Switzerland (11 November 2020) <https://www.un.org/en/ga/sixth/75/pdfs/statements/disasters/17mtg_switzerland.pdf> accessed 6 April 2022; Statement by Sierre Leone (11 November 2020) <https://www.un.org/en/ga/sixth/75/pdfs/statements/disasters/17mtg_sierraleone.pdf> accessed 6 April 2022; Statement by Egypt (11 November 2020) <https://www.un.org/en/ga/sixth/75/pdfs/statements/disasters/17mtg_egypt.pdf> accessed 6 April 2022; Statement by Italy (23 October 2020) <https://www.un.org/en/ga/sixth/75/pdfs/statements/disasters/17mtg_italy.pdf> accessed 6 April 2022; Statement by Thailand (23 October 2020) <https://www.un.org/en/ga/sixth/75/pdfs/statements/disasters/17mtg_thailand.pdf> accessed 6 April 2022; Statement by Iran (13 November 2020) <https://www.un.org/en/ga/sixth/75/pdfs/statements/disasters/18mtg_iran.pdf> accessed 6 April 2022. Statement by Bangladesh (11 November 2020) <https://www.un.org/en/ga/sixth/75/pdfs/statements/disasters/17mtg_bangladesh.pdf> accessed 6 April 2022. Also see full text of written comments received individually from Turkey, Japan, Italy, El Salvador, Cuba and Colombia, <https://www.un.org/en/ga/sixth/75/disasters.shtml> accessed 6 April 2022.

519 Statement by Brazil (13 November 2020) <https://www.un.org/en/ga/sixth/75/pdfs/statements/disasters/18mtg_brazil.pdf> accessed 6 April 2022.

520 UNGA 'Protection of persons in the event of disasters – Report of the Secretary-General' (21 July 2020) GAOR 75th Session, Item 89 on the provisional agenda UN Doc A/75/214.

521 UNGA, Sixth Committee (Legal) – 75th session, 'Protection of persons in the event of disasters (Agenda Item 89)' (UN, 2020) <https://www.un.org/en/ga/sixth/75/disasters.shtml> accessed 6 April 2022.

522 Dire Tladi, 'The International Law Commission's Draft Articles on the Protection of Persons in the Event of Disasters: Codification, Progressive Development or Creation of Law from Thin Air?' [2017] 16 Chinese Journal of International Law 425; Therese O'Donnell, 'Vulnerability and the International Law Commission's Draft Articles on the Protection of Persons in the Event of Disasters' [2019] 68:3 ICLQ 573.

3 A Novel Challenge: Sea-Level Rise and International Law

Sea-level rise prompts many novel legal challenges in international law.[523] One question relates to statehood: what are the legal implications should the territory and population of a State disappear?[524] Another question relates to the law of the sea: how does the inundation of low-lying coastal areas and of islands impact their baselines and maritime zones?[525] Yet another question concerns forced migration and human rights: what protection do persons directly impacted by sea-level rise enjoy?[526] This section discusses the ongoing work by the ILA and the UN ILC to address the impact of sea-level rise under international law, as well as the prospects of the international protection of PMDCC.

The IPCC identified two primary contributors to sea-level rise: (i) the expansion of the ocean as it warms and (ii) the transfer of water currently stored on land to the ocean, particularly from land ice (glaciers and ice sheets).[527] The warming of our oceans and melting of ice are a central part of the Earth's response to increasing GHG concentrations.[528] The rate of sea-level rise during the 21st century is projected to be faster than during the 20th century.[529] Whereas low-emission scenarios show a very likely rise of at least 0.3 metres above 2000 levels by 2100, highest-emission scenarios show a 2.5 metres rise by the same year.[530] Perhaps the most unsettling fact yet is that even if GHG concentrations are stabilised, the sea level will continue to rise for centuries.[531]

Although more than 70 States are or are likely to be directly affected by sea-level rise, it is unarguable that small island states stand on the frontline.[532]

523 McAdam and others (n 1); Davor Vidas, 'Sea-level Rise and International Law: At the Convergence of Two Epochs' [2014] 4 Climate Law 1, 70–84; Nilüfer Oral, 'International Law as an Adaptation Measure to Sea-level Rise and Its Impacts on Islands and Offshore Features' [2009] 34 The International Journal of Marine and Coastal Law 3.

524 ILC (n 168), 326.

525 ibid.

526 ibid.

527 IPCC, 'Special Report on the Ocean and Cryosphere in a Changing Climate' (2019); IPCC, 'Sea Level Change' in Climate Change 2013: The Physical Science Basis. Contribution of Working Group 1 to the Fifth Assessment Report of the Intergovernmental Panel on Climate Change (Cambridge University Press 2013) <https://www.ipcc.ch/site/assets/uploads/2018/02/WG1AR5_Chapter13_FINAL.pdf> accessed 6 April 2022.

528 ibid.

529 ibid.

530 ibid.

531 ibid. Also see IPCC (n 4).

532 ILC (n 168).

There is an impending threat of the displacement of people due to loss of territory, as well as to water and food security.[533] In the case of low-lying island countries, sea-level rise might render some islands uninhabitable or might cause significant loss of territory, eventually leading the entire country to be inundated.[534]

The ILA and the UN ILC have been working to address these issues.[535] The ILA Committee on International Law and Sea Level Rise (ILA Committee) was established in 2012, following the report of the ILA Committee on Baselines under International Law of the Sea which acknowledged that sea-level rise was an issue that extended beyond baselines and the law of the sea.[536] The newly established committee decided to examine the issue from three perspectives: (i) the law of the sea, (ii) forced migration and human rights, and (iii) issues of statehood and international security.[537]

---

533 Curt Storlazzi and others, 'Most atolls will be uninhabitable by the mid-21st century because of sea-level rise exacerbating wave-driven flooding' [2018] 4 Science Advances 4; E Bird and V Prescott, 'Rising global sea levels and national maritime claims' [1989] 1 Marine Policy Reports 3, 1–20.; Derek William Bowett, 'The legal regime of islands in international law' [1979] Oceana Publications.

534 Alfred Soons, 'The Effects of a Rising Sea Level on Maritime Limits and Boundaries' [1990] 37 Netherlands International LR 207; Geoffrey Lean, 'Disappearing World: Global Warming Claims Tropical Island' (Independent, 24 December 2006); Ann Powers and Christopher Stucko, 'Introducing the Law of the Sea and the Legal Implications of Rising Sea Levels' in Michael B. Gerrard and Gregory E. Wannier, *Threatened Island Nations: Legal Implications of Rising Seas and a Changing Climate* (Cambridge University Press 2013).

535 There were previous attempts to address this issue. For instance, in 2005, the UN Sub-commission on the Promotion and Protection of Human Rights adopted a resolution, which called on the Commission of Human Rights to appoint a Special Rapporteur to prepare 'a comprehensive study on the legal implications of the disappearance of States and other territories for environmental reasons, including their implications for the human rights of their residents', but this study has not occurred. See UN Commission on Human Rights, 'The legal implications of disappearance of States and other territories for environmental reasons, including the implications for the human rights of their residents, with particular reference to the rights of indigenous peoples' (Report on the 61st session, 14 March – 22 April 2005) E/CN.4/DEC/2005/112.

536 See International Law Association Committee on Baselines under the International Law of the Sea, Final Report (2012), Sofia Conference, 30 <http://ilareporter.org.au/wpcontent/uploads/2015/07/Source-1-Baselines-Final-Report-Sofia-2012.pdf> accessed 6 April 2022. This report stated that 'the existing law of normal baseline applies in situations of significant coastal change caused by both territorial gain and territorial loss. Coastal states may protect and preserve territory through physical reinforcement, but not through the legal fiction of a charted line that is unrepresentative of the actual low-water line'. Also see ILA (n 168).

537 Davor Vidas, David Freestone and Jane McAdam, 'International Law and Sea Level Rise: The New ILA Committee' [2019] Brill Research Perspectives in International Law.

Following two interim reports, the ILA Committee adopted the Sydney Declaration of Principles on the Protection of Persons Displaced in the Context of Sea Level Rise (Sydney Declaration) in 2018.[538] The Sydney Declaration constitutes a key international document which outlines nine relevant international law principles.[539] The first four principles relate to the general duties of States, including the primary duty and responsibility of States to protect and assist affected persons; the duty to respect the human rights of affected persons; the duty to take positive action; and the duty to cooperate.[540] The duty of States to take positive action includes reducing disaster risk and adapting to the adverse effects of climate change, preventing displacement of persons, and protecting and assisting persons in the event of displacement.[541]

The remaining five principles specifically refer to human mobility in the context of sea-level rise, with an emphasis on the evacuation, planned relocations, migration, and internal and cross-border displacement of affected persons.[542] Here, the Sydney Declaration declares that States 'should' take several measures.[543] For instance, in Principle 7, the ILA Committee supports the facilitation of migration as an adaptation strategy, expressing the view that States 'should' recognise temporary, circular or permanent migration, review existing domestic laws – as well as bilateral and regional migration arrangements – and consider new laws and agreements, in accordance with applicable international human rights law and international labour law.[544]

According to Principle 9, States 'should' admit persons displaced across borders in the context of disasters linked to sea-level rise, if the persons are 'personally and seriously at risk of, or already affected by, a disaster, or if their State of origin is unable to protect and assisted them due to the disaster (even if temporarily)'.[545] Furthermore, States 'should' not return persons 'to territories where they face a serious risk to their life or safety or serious hardship, in particular due to the fact that they cannot access necessary humanitarian assistance or protection'.[546]

538 ILA (n 168).
539 ibid.
540 ibid.
541 ibid.
542 ibid.
543 ibid.
544 ibid.
545 ibid.
546 This can be compared with the test determined by UNHRCom in its decision on the *Ioane Teitiota v New Zealand* case. See Chapter 2.2.1 of this book for a detailed discussion.

The ILA Committee's work on the particular aspects of statehood and other relevant issues in relation to sea-level rise is currently underway, which will shed some light on the progressive development of international law in this area.

The UN ILC, for its part, decided to include the topic 'sea-level rise in international law' in its programme of work for 2019, establishing an open-ended Study Group on the topic, to be co-chaired on a rotating basis by ILC members Nilüfer Oral, Patricia Galvão Teles, Bogdan Aurescu, Yacouba Cissé and Juan José Ruda Santolaria.[547] The proposal by the FSM for the inclusion of this topic on the long-term programme of the ILC was highly influential in prompting the ILC to consider this topic.[548]

The Study Group aims to look at the legal implications of sea-level rise, with respect to three main areas: the law of the sea, statehood and the protection of the persons affected.[549] It will not examine causation, responsibility, liability or the protection of the environment and climate change per se.[550] The outcome will be a final report of the Study Group, accompanied by a set of conclusions on its work.[551] The Study Group aims to perform 'a mapping exercise of the legal questions raised by sea-level rise and its interrelated issues … This effort could contribute to the endeavors of the international community to respond to these issues and to assist States in developing practicable solutions in order to respond effectively to the issues prompted by sea-level rise'.[552]

The first issues paper published by the Study Group, prepared by Bogdan Aurescu and Nilüfer Oral, was released in 2020 and examined the issues relating to the law of the sea.[553] Governments, as well as other relevant actors, contributed to this process.[554] Moving forward, the Study Group Members Juan José Ruda Santolaria and Patricia Galvão Teles will focus on issues related to

547 ILC (n 168).

548 ibid para 15. For the proposal of the FSM, see Document ILC (LXX)/LT/INFORMAL/1 of 31 January 2018 (on file with the Codification Division).

549 ILC (n 168).

550 ibid.

551 ILC (n 168) para 26.

552 ibid para 18.

553 ibid.

554 For instance, see Information by Pacific Islands Forum (30 December 2019) <https://legal.un.org/ilc/sessions/72/pdfs/english/slr_pif.pdf> accessed 6 April 2022. Also see UNGA, 'Report of the International Law Commission on the work of its seventy-second session (2020). Topical summary of the discussion held in the Sixth Committee of the General Assembly during its seventy-fifth session, prepared by the Secretariat' (3 February 2021) International Law Commission 72nd Session (Geneva, 26 April-4 June and 5 July-6 August 2021) UN Doc A/CN.4/734/Add.1.

statehood, as well as the protection of persons affected by sea-level rise in 2021.[555]

In the author's view, both the Sydney Declaration and the future work of the ILC on the protection of persons affected by sea-level rise represent highly important foundations for a legal rule on the international protection of PMDCC. As this section has discussed, the ILA Committee has compiled significant principles for the protection of persons displaced in the context of sea-level rise. The UN ILC Study Group is currently undertaking its mapping exercise on the protection of persons affected. These collaborative exercises demonstrate that there is an urgent and undeniable need to address the legal gap in the international protection of PMDCC.

4 Conclusion

This chapter has dealt with the legal gap that persists in international law when it comes to the international protection of PMDCC. It has examined the relevant international treaty regimes (i.e. the refugee regime, the climate change regime, the desertification regime, the labour regime, trade regime and the human rights regimes), the relevant international rules and principles (i.e. the principle of *non-refoulement*, protection in the event of displacement and protection in the event of disasters), and the novel challenge brought by sea-level rise in international law.

The analysis has shown that the evolution of international cooperation to address HMDCC has been dramatic, resulting largely from new non-binding instruments (such as reports, guidelines, resolutions and agendas) and developments in practice (such as the Teitiota decision of the UNHRCom or the implementation of the Protection Agenda).

Second, the actors in relevant treaty regimes have retained their distinctive identities and studied the issue of HMDCC from their own perspectives and mandates. The formation of the TFD under the international climate change regime has contributed to breaking down this 'silo approach'.[556] Multidisciplinary and multi-stakeholder approaches are particularly important for

555 ILC (n 168) para 225.

556 Karen Sudmeier-Rieux and others, 'Introduction: Exploring Linkages Between Disaster Risk Reduction, Climate Change Adaptation, Migration and Sustainable Development' in Karen Sudmeier-Rieux and Others (eds), *Identifying Emerging Issues in Disaster Risk Reduction, Migration, Climate Change and Sustainable Development* (Springer 2017).

understanding the complex problem posed by HMDCC and creating a global response.

Third, despite the considerable interest in and awareness of the need to address HMDCC, there is no legally binding obligation to protect PMDCC at the international level. Means and methods of accountability should be made available to create a global response and provide international protection to PMDCC.[557]

557 On effectiveness of international legal norms, see Daniel Thürer, *International Humanitarian Law: Theory, Practice, Context* (Hague Academy of International Law 2011) 154–160.

CHAPTER 3

Legal Gaps in Action – Insights from the Pacific Island States

This chapter sketches the regional implications of the legal gap in the international protection of PMDCC by undertaking a case study of the Pacific Island States (PIS).[558] The adverse impact of climate change and disasters have long been articulated as an 'existential threat' for the PIS,[559] which have often been framed as 'sites of future catastrophic forced migration'.[560] Yet, as this chapter demonstrates, the PIS have not established a regional response for the regional protection of PMDCC.[561] This seriously reinforces the legal gap that exists under international law and hinders efforts to prevent and address the adverse impact of climate change and disasters on human mobility.[562] In order to develop its argument, this chapter first sets the scene by discussing the impact of climate change and disasters on the region. Then, it explores HMDCC in the region, first, by comparing the available pathways for inter- and intra-regional movement, and second, by examining the recently adopted regional trade agreement, i.e. the Pacific Agreement on Closer Economic Relations Plus (PACER Plus), in order to discuss the prospects of a regional approach to

558 The Pacific Island States (PIS) consist of 22 countries and territories; of which 12 are independent states, 2 are self-governing territories, and 8 are dependent territories. The independent states are Fiji, Samoa, Nauru, Tonga, Papua New Guinea (PNG), Solomon Islands, Tuvalu, Kiribati, Vanuatu, Federated States of Micronesia (FSM), Republic of the Marshall Islands (RMI), and Palau. The self-governing territories are Cook Islands, and Niue, which are in free association with New Zealand. The dependent territories are French Polynesia, New Caledonia, Wallis and Futuna, Commonwealth of the Northern Mariana Islands, Pitcairn Islands, and Tokelau.

559 UN Secretary-General, 'Secretary-General's remarks on Climate Change [as delivered]' (10 September 2018) <https://www.un.org/sg/en/content/sg/statement/2018-09-10/secretary-generals-remarks-climate-change-delivered> accessed 6 April 2022; Asian Development Bank, 'An Existential Threat: How Climate Change is Impacting the Atoll Countries' (9 December 2019) <https://www.adb.org/news/videos/existential-threat-how-climate-change-impacting-atoll-countries> accessed 6 April 2022.

560 Jon Barnett and Celia McMichael, 'The effects of climate change on the geography and timing of human mobility' 39 Population and Environment, 339–356.

561 Eberhard Weber, 'Envisioning South-South relations in the fields of environmental change and migration in the Pacific Islands – past, present and futures' [2015] 2 Bandung: Journal of the Global South 6.

562 Laczko and Piguet (n 322) 1–20.

human mobility. Finally, the chapter examines planned relocation as a policy tool that provides domestic protection to PMDCC. It begins by tracing the notion of planned relocation historically, before examining the planned relocation policies of Vanuatu and Fiji.

1 Setting the Scene

Geographically fragmented and sea-locked, the PIS stretch over a large area of ocean covering 30 million km^2, almost the size of the African continent.[563] The total population of the region is estimated to be 10 million, with about 6.9 million people living in Papua New Guinea (PNG) and about 900,000 people living in Fiji.[564]

The fifth assessment report of the IPCC concluded with high confidence that there was a 'risk of death, injury, ill-health, or disrupted livelihoods' in small island states and low-lying coastal zones 'due to storm surges, coastal flooding, and sea-level rise'.[565] Acknowledging the similarities in the challenges they face, the PIS have been forming or joining negotiation blocs and advocacy groups, in order to demand international action on climate mitigation, adaptation, and loss and damage.[566]

Within the UN system, the PIS are part of the Small Island Developing States (SIDS), which represent a group of developing small island countries facing similar sustainable development challenges.[567] Growing out of the need to

563 Neil L. Andrew and others, 'Coastal proximity of populations in 22 Pacific Island Countries and Territories' [2019] 14 Plos One 9; Stephen Levine, *Pacific Ways: Government and Politics in the Pacific Islands* (Victoria University Press 2016); Hoe Ee Khor, Roger P. Kronenberg and Patrizia Tumbarello (eds), *Resilience and Growth in the Small States of the Pacific* (IMF 2016).

564 The Nansen Initiative, 'Human Mobility, Natural Disasters and Climate Change in the Pacific' (Background Paper, 21–24 May 2013) <https://disasterdisplacement.org/wp-content/uploads/2015/03/BP_Human_BP_Mobility_Natural_Disasters_and_Climate_Change_in_the_Pacific.pdf> accessed 6 April 2022.

565 IPCC, 'Summary for Policymakers' in Ottmar Edenhofer and others, *Climate Change 2014: Mitigation of Climate Change. Contribution of the Working Group III to the Fifth Assessment Report of the Intergovernmental Panel on Climate Change* (Cambridge University Press 2014) 13.

566 See Greg Fry and Sandra Tarte, *The New Pacific Diplomacy* (ANU Press 2015).

567 The SIDS was first recognised as a distinct group of developing countries at the United Nations Conference on Environment and Development in June 1992. The Barbados Programme of Action was developed in 1994 to assist the SIDS in their sustainable development efforts. An important framework launched by the SIDS in 2014 is the Accelerated Modalities of Action (SAMOA Pathway) which sets out the sustainable development

raise funds for climate change adaptation and mitigation projects, eleven PIS formed the Pacific Small Island Developing States (PSIDS) with the specific aim of representing their collective voice during major UN negotiations and processes, including the SDGs.[568] Several PIS are also active members of the Alliance of Small Island Developing States (AOSIS),[569] the Climate Vulnerable Forum,[570] the Climate Action Pacific Partnership[571] and the Coalition of Low Lying Atoll Nations on the issue of Climate Change.[572] These ties have

---

priorities of islands. SAMOA Pathway has 18 priority areas, which are: sustained and sustainable, inclusive and equitable economic growth and decent work for all; climate change; sustainable energy; disaster risk reduction; oceans and seas; food security and nutrition; water and sanitation; sustainable transport; sustainable consumption and production; management of chemicals and water, including hazardous waste; health and NCDs; gender equality and women's empowerment; social development; biodiversity; invasive alien species; means of implementation, including partnerships; SIDS priorities for the post-2015 development agenda; monitoring and accountability. See UN-OHRLLS, 'SIDS Accelarated Modalities of Action Pathway' <http://prdrse4all.spc.int/sites/default/files/samoa-pathway.pdf> accessed 6 April 2022.

568 PSIDS grew out of a need to raise funds for climate change adaptation and mitigation projects, and in time has gained impetus to promote the common interests of its members. Its members are Fiji, RMI, FSM, Nauru, Palau, Samoa, Solomon Islands, Tonga, Tuvalu, Vanuatu, and PNG. See PSIDS, 'Views on the Possible Security Implications of Climate Change to be included in the report of the Secretary-General to the 64th Session of the United Nations General Assembly' (2009) <https://www.un.org/esa/dsd/resources/res_pdfs/ga-64/cc-inputs/PSIDS_CCIS.pdf> accessed 6 April 2022.

569 Alliance of Small Island Developing States (AOSIS) has 44 members and 5 observers. From PIS, all twelve independent countries, and two self-governing territories are members. Additionally, American Samoa and Guam are observers. See Espen Ronneberg, 'Small Islands and the Big Issue: Climate Change and the Role of the Alliance of Small Island States' in Cinnamon Pinon Carlarne, Kevin R. Gray and Richard Tarasofsky, The Oxford Handbook of International Climate Change Law (Oxford University Press 2016) 761–790.

570 Climate Vulnerable Forum has 48 members in total. Fiji, RMI, Palau, PNG, Samoa, Tuvalu, and Vanuatu are members from the PIS. For a recent statement of the forum, see Climate Vulnerable Forum, 'Climate Change and Human Rights' (Joint Statement, 46th Session of the Human Rights Council, 09 March 2021) <https://thecvf.org/our-voice/statements/chair/46th-hrc-session-joint-statement-on-climate-change-and-human-rights/> accessed 6 April 2022.

571 Climate Action Pacific Partnership was established in 2017 to form a coalition of Pacific stakeholders to exchange ideas and provide inputs to the UNFCCC process. See Climate Action Pacific Partnership, 'Background to the Climate Action Pacific Partnership' (2017) <https://cop23.com.fj/wp-content/uploads/2019/03/CAPP_III_CAPP_backgroud.pdf> accessed 6 April 2022.

572 Kiribati, Tuvalu, RMI, Tokelau, and the Maldives are members of the Coalition of Low Lying Atoll Nations on the issue of Climate Change, which aims to voice the position of the frontline nations to climate change in a unified voice. See SPREP, 'Atoll nations make a collective stand for their right to remain in their islands in the face of climate change'

inevitably led to an exciting development in 2021, when the current chairs of AOSIS, namely, Tuvalu and Antigua and Barbuda, established the 'Commission of Small Island Developing States on Climate Change and International Law'.[573] Importantly, the founding members authorised this Commission to request an advisory opinion from ITLOS concerning climate change, sea-level rise, protection of the marine environment and international responsibilities.[574]

The Fijian Presidency of the UNFCCC COP23 in 2017 was especially significant for small island nations.[575] Fiji intended to advocate for the climate-related vulnerabilities of SIDS and to ensure that the completed version of the Paris Agreement Work Programme (also called the Paris Rulebook) at the next COP included priorities, such as increased pledges for climate adaptation and addressing loss and damage.[576] Such priorities were to be achieved in the Fijian 'Bula Spirit' of friendliness, inclusiveness and solidarity.[577] Fiji launched two important initiatives with this aim: a 'Grand Coalition' of nations, regions, cities, towns, civil society, labour, the private sector, women, youth and communities for climate action, and the Talanoa Dialogue for Climate Ambition, which operationalised the Facilitative Dialogue mandated at COP21, to share ideas, skills and experiences through storytelling.[578] COP23 marked itself as an

---

(12 December 2019) <https://reliefweb.int/report/kiribati/atoll-nations-make-collective-stand-their-right-remain-their-islands-face-climate> accessed 6 April 2022.

573 David Freestone, Richard Barnes and Payam Akhavan, 'Agreement for the Establishment of the Commission of Small Island States on Climate Change and International Law' [2022] International Journal of Marine and Coastal Law; Simona Marinescu, 'COP26: Major polluting countries face legal action from small island states over rising sea levels' (UNSDG 2021) <https://unsdg.un.org/latest/blog/cop26-major-polluting-countries-face-legal-action-small-island-states-over-rising-sea> accessed 6 April 2022.

574 For the appointed fourteen legal experts, see COSIS on Climate Change and International Law, 'Committee of Legal Experts' (Twitter 2022) <https://twitter.com/cosis_ccil/status/1495555277453934594> accessed 6 April 2022.

575 George Carter, 'Pacific Island States and 30 Years of Global Climate Change Negotiations' in Carola Klöck and others (eds), *Coalitions in the Climate Change Negotiations* (Routledge 2021).

576 Lisa Benjamin, Adelle Thomas, Rueanna Haynes, 'An 'Islands' COP'? Loss and Damage at COP23' [2018] 27 Review of European, Comparative and International Environmental Law 3, 332–340.

577 Wolfgang Obergassel and others, 'The calm before the storm: an assessment of the 23rd Climate Change Conference (COP 23) in Bonn' [2018] 30 Environmental Law and Management, 104–113.

578 Luis Mundaca and others, 'The global expansion of climate mitigation policy interventions, the Talanoa Dialogue and the role of behavioural insights' [2019] 1 Environmental Research Communications 6; Rosemary Lyster, 'The idea of (Climate) Justice, neoliberalism and the Talanoa Dialogue' [2019] Journal of Human Rights and the Environment, 35–61; Feja Lesniewska and Linda Siegele, 'The Talanoa Dialogue: A Crucible to Spur

'Islands' COP', with the rotating Presidency being held by a small island nation for the first time.[579]

In spite of collective efforts at the international level on climate action, the PIS lack a regional integration body similar to the European Union, the African Union or the Caribbean Community.[580] Instead, several political fora provide space for regional and sub-regional cooperation, such as the Pacific Islands Forum (PIF),[581] Pacific Islands Development Forum (PIDF),[582], the Melanesian Spearhead Group (MSG),[583] and the Polynesian Leaders Group (PLG).[584] There are also several regional technical organisations, such as the Secretariat of the Pacific Community (SPC)[585] and the Secretariat of the Pacific Regional Programme (SPREP).[586]

In the absence of legally binding regional responses, declarations have been used to reflect consensus. The PIF adopted one of the earliest regional declarations on climate change, the so-called Niue Declaration, in 2008.[587] The Niue Declaration encouraged PIF members to 'increase their technical and financial support for climate change action on adaptation, mitigation

Ambitious Global Climate Action to Stay Within the 1.5°C Limit' [2018] 12 Carbon and Climate Law Review 1, 41–49.

579 Benjamin, Thomas and Haynes (n 576) 3.

580 Lavenex (n 370) 1275–1293.

581 Founded in 1971, PIF has 18 members, which are Australia, New Zealand, Cook Islands, FSM, Fiji, French Polynesia, Kiribati, Nauru, New Caledonia, Niue, Palau, PNG, RMI, Samoa, Solomon Islands, Tonga, Tuvalu, and Vanuatu.

582 PIDF members are Fiji, FSM, Kiribati, Nauru, Marshall Islands, Palau, Solomon Islands, Timor-Leste, Tokelau, Tonga, Tuvalu, and Vanuatu.

583 MSG members are Fiji, PNG, Solomon Islands, Vanuatu, and the Kanak and Socialist National Liberation Front of New Caledonia. Indonesia is recognised as an associate member.

584 PLG members are the leaders of American Samoa, the Cook Islands, French Polynesia, Niue, Samoa, Tonga, Tokelau, Tuvalu, and Wallis and Futuna.

585 For the recent strategic plan of the SPC, see Pacific Community, 'Pacific Community Strategic Plan 2016–2020' (2015) <https://spccfpstore1.blob.core.windows.net/digitallibrary-docs/files/d0/d0efd0a7e8a3e94dc7ae8024fd0ad099.pdf?sv=2015-12-11&sr=b&sig=uCJXrg3%2BN1%2BSNtgigVaznh1cN2AN9jbYUs0Zwdey1y0%3D&se=2021-12-04T14%3A22%3A39Z&sp=r&rscc=public%2C%20max-age%3D864000%2C%20max-stale%3D86400&rsct=application%2Fpdf&rscd=inline%3B%20filename%3D%22Pacific_Community_Strategic_Plan_20162020.pdf%22> accessed 6 April 2022.

586 For the recent strategic plan of SPREP, see SPREP, 'Strategic Plan 2017–2026' (2015) <https://www.sprep.org/attachments/Publications/Corporate_Documents/strategic-plan-2017-2026.pdf> accessed 6 April 2022.

587 Pacific Islands Forum, Niue Declaration on Climate Change, 39th session, Forum Communiqué Annex B (19–20 August 2008).

and if necessary, relocation'.[588] Currently, this pledge finds its place within the greater framework of the 2050 Strategy for the Blue Pacific Continent of the PIF.[589] This strategy aims to build a strong and resilient Pacific region by ensuring social, cultural, environmental and economic integrity.[590] Although it is expected to be finalised in 2021, some of the challenges the strategy will address include: ongoing vulnerabilities to environmental, climate change, disaster risk and economic shocks; continued dependency on aid and external financing; low levels of economic growth; stubborn levels of poverty and rising inequalities; and structural constraints, such as distance from markets.[591]

Another important regional declaration is the Moana Declaration, which was released by the Pacific Island Parliamentarians in 2013 on the occasion of the 6th Asia Pacific Population Conference.[592] The Moana Declaration includes the commitment to 'address the cross-cutting nature of population issues, vulnerability to climate change, globalisation and environmental degradation', as well as to 'apply a human-rights based approach to the issues of internally displaced persons, refugees and asylum seekers in the Pacific'.[593]

In 2015, the Suva Declaration on Climate Change was endorsed during the 3rd Summit of the PIDF.[594] Its demands include: that 'loss and damage [...] be anchored as a standalone element that is separate and distinct from adaptation in the Paris Agreement'; 'a special provision in the Paris Agreement to fast-track urgent action required to assist the most vulnerable countries that are already experiencing existential threats from climate change'; and that 'adaptation measures for Pacific Small Island Developing States [...] be 100% grant financed'.[595]

---

588 ibid.

589 Pacific Islands Forum, '2050 Strategy Blue Pacific Continent' <https://www.forumsec.org/2050strategy/> accessed 6 April 2022.

590 ibid.

591 ibid.

592 Pacific Island Parliamentarians included Fiji, Cook Islands, Nauru, Kiribati, Niue, Samoa, Tonga, Vanuatu, Solomon Islands, PNG and the FSM. See Moana Declaration (Outcome Statement of Pacific Parliamentarians for Population and Development, 13–15 August 2013) <https://www.icpdtaskforce.org/resources/PACIFICCONFERENCEOFPARLIAMENTARIANSFORADVOCACYONICPDBEYOND2014OutcomeStatement.pdf> accessed 6 April 2022.

593 ibid.

594 Suva Declaration on Climate Change (Issued at the Third Pacific Islands Development Forum Leaders' Summit, 2–4 September 2015, Grand Pacific Hotel, Suva, Fiji) <http://greenbusiness.solutions/wp-content/uploads/2017/08/Suva-declaration-on-climate-change.pdf> accessed 6 April 2022.

595 This ambitious declaration is in line with the vision of the organisation. PIDF is a Fiji-led regional forum that has been evolving since 2010, following the suspension of Fiji

In 2019, two important regional declarations were adopted. The PIDF adopted the Nadi Bay Declaration on the Climate Change Crisis in the Pacific.[596] This declaration '[s]trongly support[s] the need for a UN Resolution to establish a Legal Framework to protect the rights of people displaced by climate change that impedes access to basic rights to life, water, food, and housing for many millions of people around the world'.[597] Shortly afterwards, the Kainaki II Declaration for Urgent Climate Change Now was issued by the PIF.[598] This declaration builds on the Boe Declaration on Regional Security, which identified climate change as the single greatest threat facing the region.[599] The Kainaki II Declaration raises the bar and acknowledges a 'climate change crisis'.[600] It references 'achieving net zero carbon by 2050' twice, and mentions a 'just transition from fossil fuels'.[601] It also calls on the international community to meet their climate finance commitments to jointly mobilise USD 100 billion per year by 2020, in response to which the UK has announced it will double its contribution to the Green Climate Fund.[602]

As this section has discussed, the PIS face major challenges due to the impact of climate change and disasters.[603] As one commentator maintains,

---

from PIF after the *coup d'état* which lead the Bainimarama government to assume power. It advances the Pacific Island nations' 'shared interests and common concerns around sustainable development' by 'renewing special cultural bonds and regional kinships' to the exclusion of Australia and New Zealand. However, it is important to note that regardless of pioneering this project, Fiji is currently an active member of PIF, which includes Australia and New Zealand. See Litia Mawi, 'Fiji's Emerging Brand of Pacific Diplomacy: A Fiji government perspective' in Greg Fry and Sandra Tarte, *The New Pacific Diplomacy* (ANU Press 2015) 101–110; Makereta Komai, 'Fiji's Foreign Policy and the New Pacific Diplomacy' in Greg Fry and Sandra Tarte, *The New Pacific Diplomacy* (ANU Press 2015) 111–124.

596 Pacific Islands Development Forum, Nadi Bay Declaration on the Climate Change Crisis in the Pacific (29–30 July 2019) <https://www.documentcloud.org/documents/6226356-Nadi-Bay-Declaration-on-Climate-Crisis-2019.html> accessed 6 April 2022.

597 ibid.

598 Pacific Islands Forum, Kainaki II Declaration for Urgent Climate Change Now, 50th sess, Forum Communiqué Annex A (13–16 August 2019) <https://www.forumsec.org/wp-content/uploads/2019/08/50th-Pacific-Islands-Forum-Communique.pdf> accessed 6 April 2022.

599 Pacific Islands Forum, Boe Declaration on Regional Security (5 September 2018) <https://www.forumsec.org/2018/09/05/boe-declaration-on-regional-security/> accessed 6 April 2022.

600 Pacific Islands Forum (n 598).

601 ibid.

602 ibid.

603 Jon Barnett, 'Adapting to Climate Change in Pacific Island Countries: The Problem of Uncertainty' [2001] 29 World Development 6, 977–993.

'[t]he fate of the Pacific island nations ultimately depends less on how much they speak than on who is listening and whether those listeners take action. Unfortunately, the most important listeners have proven tone deaf'.[604] The failed attempt of Palau and the Marshall Islands to galvanise the necessary support at the UNGA in order to seek an advisory opinion from the ICJ on whether countries have a legal responsibility to ensure that any activities on their territory that emit GHG do not harm other States is a case in point.[605]

2 Human Mobility in the Context of Disasters and Climate Change in the Region

Although the PIS stand at the frontline of climate change and disasters, there are a wide range of available legal pathways for inter- and intra-regional mobility.[606] One of the reasons for this differentiation is the lack of a regional approach to human mobility.[607] In order to unpack the nuances between different PIS, this section first compares the available legal pathways for movement and then analyses the prospects for a regional approach to human mobility by focusing on PACER Plus, which includes a chapter on the movement of natural persons and a side-arrangement on labour mobility.[608]

2.1 *Comparing the Pathways for Inter- and Intra-regional Movement*

When comparing the available legal pathways for mobility in the region, it is possible to divide the eleven independent PIS into four groups.[609]

---

604 Betzalel Newman, 'Sunk Coast Fallacy: How Island Nations Should Approach Climate Diplomacy' (Council on Foreign Relations, 7 August 2019).

605 Benjamin Norman Forbes, 'AOSIS v The World: A Blueprint for the First International Multi-Party Climate Change Case' [2021] 8 Groningen Journal of International Law 2; Daniel Bodansky, 'The Role of the International Court of Justice in Addressing Climate Change: Some Preliminary Reflections' [2017] 49 Arizona State Law Journal 689–712.

606 Fornalé (n 329).

607 Eberhard Weber, 'Trade agreements, labour mobility and climate change in the Pacific Islands' [2017] 17 Regional Environmental Change, 1089–1101.

608 Alisi Kautoke-Holani, 'Labour Mobility in the PACER Plus' [2018] 5 Asia and the Pacific Policy Studies 1, 90–101.

609 This section does not discuss the mobility options available for self-governing territories and dependent territories in the Pacific region. This is majorly because persons from these territories are entitled to New Zealander, Australian, (US) American, French or British citizenships, depending on the territory. See World Bank, 'Pacific Possible. Long-term Economic Opportunities and Challenges for Pacific Island Countries' (2017) <https://documents1.worldbank.org/curated/en/168951503668157320/pdf/ACS22308-PUBLIC-P154324-ADD-SERIES-PPFullReportFINALscreen.pdf> accessed 6 April 2022.

The first group consists of the RMI, FSM and Palau, which have 'open access' to the US,[610] as provided for under the Compacts of Free Association between the US, FSM, RMI, and Palau.[611] Under the UN trusteeship system, FSM, RMI and Palau were administered by the US, and the Compacts were signed as an extension to the trusteeship agreement 'to promote the development of the people of the Trust Territory toward self-government or independence as appropriate to the particular circumstances of the Trust Territory and its peoples and the freely expressed wishes of the peoples concerned'.[612] Under the Compacts, the US has certain types of duties relating to assistance for and the security and defence of the island nations.[613]

The Compacts also include immigration provisions, which give the citizens of the FSM, RMI and Palau the right to enter, work and live in the US with some restrictions, such as on voting rights.[614] One of the most salient limitations is the lack of financial support for affected persons to make use of the compact immigration provisions, the legal provisions on the denial of admission on health-related grounds and the inherently uncertain status of the migrants under the compact (for instance, the compacts are unilaterally terminable by any party).[615] In contrast to the GATS Mode 4 and PTAs, the Compact facilitates the movement of persons in the context of decolonisation.[616] It is important to note, however, that considering the nuclear testing carried out on a massive scale by the US in the region during the years of the trusteeship, the Compact has been viewed as an 'arrangement for strategic denial'.[617]

The second group consists of Fiji, Samoa and Tonga, which have 'high mobility', through historical ties as well as bilateral agreements providing limited

610 Kevin Morris, 'Navigating the Compact of Free Association: Three Decades of Supervised Self-Governance' [2019] 41 University of Hawaii Law Review 2, 388–440.

611 Compact of Free Association Act, Pub. L. No. 99–239, 1985 U.S.C.C.A.N (99 Stat.1770); Compact of Free Association Amendments Act of 2003, Pub. L. No 108–188, § 331 (a), 117 Stat. 2720, 2781; see also Act of Nov. 14, 1986, Pub. L. No. 99–658, § 312, 100 Stat. 3672, 3695.

612 Donald R. Shuster, 'The Republic of Palau and its Compacts, 1995–2009' [2009] 44 The Journal of Pacific History 3, 325–332.

613 Robert A. Underwood, 'The amended U.S. Compacts of Free Association with the Federates States of Micronesia and the Republic of the Marshall Islands: less free, more compact' (East-West Center Working Papers, September 2003).

614 Briana Dema, 'Sea level Rise and the Freely Associated States: Addressing Environmental Migration under the Compacts of Free Association' [2012] 37 Columbia Journal of Environmental Law, 177–204.

615 ibid.

616 Jon Hinck, 'The Republic of Palau and the United States: Self-Determination Becomes the Price of Free Association' [1990] 78 California Law Review, 915–972.

617 Morris (n 610) 388–440.

access to New Zealand.[618] For instance, New Zealand offers the Pacific Access Category (PAC), which grants permanent residency visas through a ballot to 250 Fijian citizens, 250 Tongan citizens, 75 Tuvaluan citizens and 75 I-Kiribati citizens.[619] Furthermore, due to its previous colonial ties, New Zealand offers the Samoan Quota Resident Visa to 1,100 Samoan citizens per year, which grants indefinite leave to live, work and study in New Zealand.[620]

The third group consists of PNG, Solomon Islands and Vanuatu, which have 'low mobility' due to severely restricted external labour market access.[621] Although these countries participate in several temporary labour mobility programmes offered by New Zealand and Australia, their citizens are not eligible for PAC.[622] Nonetheless, these countries (along with other PIS) participate in four important temporary labour mobility programmes, which can be mentioned here.[623] First, since 2012, the MSG skills movement scheme has allowed 400 people from each member State (i.e. PNG, Solomon Islands, Vanuatu and Fiji) to work in another MSG country temporarily.[624] Second, New Zealand's Recognised Seasonal Employer Scheme (RSE), which was launched in 2007, allows workers from nine participating PIS to be recruited for a maximum of 7 months (in the case of the Tuvaluans and Kiribati, a maximum of 9 months).[625] Third, the Australian Seasonal Worker Programme (SWP), which was launched as a pilot programme in 2008, assists Australian employers in the

618 World Bank (n 609).

619 New Zealand Government, 'Information about Pacific Access Category Visa' <https://www.immigration.govt.nz/new-zealand-visas/apply-for-a-visa/about-visa/pacific-access-category-resident-visa> accessed 6 April 2022.

620 New Zealand Government, 'Information about Samoan Quota Resident Visa' <https://www.immigration.govt.nz/new-zealand-visas/apply-for-a-visa/about-visa/samoan-quota-scheme-resident-visa> accessed 6 April 2022.

621 World Bank (n 609).

622 Richard Bredford, Charlotte Bredford, Janet Wall and Margaret Young, 'Managed Temporary Labour Migration of Pacific Islanders to Australia and New Zealand in the Early Twenty-first Century' [2017] 48 Australian Geographer 1, 37–57.

623 Yvonne Underhill-Sem and Evelyn Marsters, 'Labour Mobility in the Pacific: A Systematic Literature Review of Development Impacts' [2017] New Zealand Institute for Pacific Research.

624 MSG, 'Melanesian Spearhead Group Secretariat' <https://www.msgsec.info/msg-skills-movement-scheme/> accessed 6 April 2022; Carmen Voigt-Graf, 'Melanesians on the Move' (Development Policy Centre, 2 February 2015) <http://devpolicy.org/wp-content/uploads/wp-post-to-pdf-enhanced-cache/1/melanesians-on-the-move-20150202.pdf> accessed 6 April 2022.

625 New Zealand Government, 'Recognised Seasonal Employer (RSE) Scheme Research' <https://www.immigration.govt.nz/about-us/research-and-statistics/research-reports/recognised-seasonal-employer-rse-scheme> accessed 6 April 2022.

agriculture sector nationwide and the accommodation sector in selected locations to provide access to workers from nine participating PIS for a maximum period of nine months.[626] Fourth, Australia's Pacific Labour Scheme (PLS) was launched in 2018, to 'step up' Australia's engagement in the Pacific.[627] The PLS is open to all sectors of employment, and provides access to low- and semi-skilled workers from ten participating countries (nine PIS plus Timor-Leste) for a maximum period of three years.[628]

The fourth group consists of Kiribati and Tuvalu, which are two low-lying atoll nations that have been severely impacted by climate change, but lack open labour market access.[629] Although I-Kiribati and Tuvaluan citizens are eligible to participate in PAC, as well as RSE, SWP and PLS, they face competition from the larger PIS included in these schemes.[630] As two low-lying atoll nations, Kiribati and Tuvalu are particularly vulnerable to the impact of sea-level rise.[631] Compounded with the fact that these countries also do not have 'advantages', such as deposits of natural resources or substantial tourism revenue, some commentators argue that the citizens of these countries should be given preferential access to labour markets.[632]

---

626 Australian Government, 'Seasonal Worker Programme' <https://www.dese.gov.au/seasonal-worker-programme> accessed 6 April 2022. See Richard Curtain and Stephen Howes, 'Governance of the Seasonal Worker Programme in Australia and sending countries' (Development Policy Centre, 8 December 2020) <https://apo.org.au/sites/default/files/resource-files/2020-12/apo-nid309985.pdf> accessed 6 April 2022.

627 Australian Government, '2017 Foreign Policy White Paper' <https://www.dfat.gov.au/publications/minisite/2017-foreign-policy-white-paper/fpwhitepaper/pdf/2017-foreign-policy-white-paper.pdf> accessed 6 April 2022; Australian Government, 'Pacific Labour Mobility' <https://www.dfat.gov.au/geo/pacific/engagement/pacific-labour-mobility> accessed 6 April 2022.

628 John Connell and Kirstie Petrou, 'Pacific Labour Mobility: Towards a future research agenda' (University of Sydney, 2019)> http://pacificlabour.siteindev.com.au/wordpress-content-dir/uploads/2019/10/Pacific-Labour-Mobility-Towards-a-future-research-agenda.pdf> accessed 6 April 2022.

629 World Bank (n 609).

630 Carmen Voigt-Graf and Sophia Kagan, 'Migration and labour mobility from Kiribati' (Australian National University, Development Policy Centre Discussion Paper 56, Marc 2017).

631 J.A Church and others, '2013: Sea Level Change' in IPCC, *Climate Change 2013: The Physical Science Basis. Contribution of Working Group I to the Fifth Assessment Report of the Intergovernmental Panel on Climate Change* (Cambridge University Press 2012).

632 Sophia Kagan, 'Making the case for preferential access to labour markets for Kiribati and Tuvalu migrants' (Development Policy Blog, 20 January 2015) <https://devpolicy.org/making-the-case-for-preferential-access-to-labour-markets-for-kiribati-and-tuvalu-migrants-20140120/> accessed 6 April 2022; Roy Smith and Karen E. McNamara, 'Future migrations from Tuvalu and Kiribati: exploring government, civil society and donor perceptions'

This section has demonstrated that the citizens of the PIS benefit from different inter- and intra-regional pathways for movement. There are several reasons for this situation, such as colonial history, in the case of the Samoan Quota Resident Visa, and sub-regionalism, in the case of the MSG skills movement scheme.[633] These pathways contribute to defining the adaptive capacities of individuals and communities in the context of disasters and climate change.[634]

2.2 *The Prospects for a 'Regional' Approach to Human Mobility: PACER Plus, Free Movement and Labour Mobility*

PACER Plus is a regional PTA which was opened for signature on 14 June 2017 and entered into force on 13 December 2020.[635] Australia, New Zealand and six PIS (i.e. Samoa, Kiribati, Tonga, Solomon Islands, Niue and Cook Islands) are Parties to the Agreement.[636] Additional members – namely, Nauru, Tuvalu and Vanuatu – have signed, but not yet ratified it.[637] Although not the first PTA of the region, PACER Plus is particularly important, because it consists of a chapter on the movement of natural persons and a separate arrangement on labour mobility. This section examines the role of PACER Plus in enhancing the development of a 'regional' approach to HMDCC.

As discussed earlier, trade agreements can be important tools for facilitating the mobility of persons, especially in the context of disasters and climate change.[638] In this context, PACER Plus builds on the original PACER, which was ratified in 2001 as a framework agreement for gradual trade and economic integration.[639] However, PACER is not the front-runner for addressing human

---

[2015] 7 Climate and Development 1, 47–59; Roy Smith, 'Should they stay or should they go? A discourse analysis of factors influencing relocation decisions among the outer islands of Tuvalu and Kiribati' [2013] 1 Journal of New Zealand and Pacific Studies 1, 23–39.

633 For a discussion on sub-regionalism, see Tess Newton Cain, 'The Renaissance of the Melanesian Spearhead Group' in Greg Fry and Sandra Tarte, *The New Pacific Diplomacy* (ANU Press 2016) 151–160.

634 François Gemenne and Julia Blocher, 'How can migration support adaptation? Different options to test the migration-adaptation nexus' (IOM Working Paper Series No.1/2016) <https://publications.iom.int/system/files/pdf/working_paper_series_1.pdf>.

635 PACER Plus (signed 14 June 2017, entered into force 13 December 2020) <https://pacerplus.org> accessed 6 April 2022.

636 See PACER Plus, 'Countries Involved' <https://pacerplus.org> accessed 6 April 2022.

637 ibid.

638 See Chapter 2.1.5 of this book.

639 PACER Plus also replaced the South Pacific Regional Trade and Economic Cooperation Agreement (SPARTECA). See Cheryl Carmichael, 'SPARTECA, PICTA, and the WTO: How the Pacific Island States are Impacted by Free Trade Agreements' (PhD thesis, University of Prince Edward Island, December 2019) <https://islandscholar.ca/islandora/object/ir%3A23072/datastream/PDF/view> accessed 6 April 2022. Also see Jane Kelsey, 'A

mobility in the region. It was only in 2012, with the adoption of the Pacific Island Countries Trade Agreement – Agreement in Services (PICTA TIS), that some PIS discussed the prospects of a regional arrangement for human mobility.[640] This was done via the inclusion of a provision for the preparation of a Temporary Movement of Natural Persons (TMNP) Protocol as a part of PICTA TIS.[641] It is yet to be seen whether the TMNP Protocol will be prepared.

In the absence of a regional approach to human mobility, trade negotiations for PACER Plus provided a significant opportunity to promote policy cooperation in this area.[642] One of the critical demands made by the negotiating PIS on Australia and New Zealand was greater labour mobility for their workers in the latter countries.[643] However, it is hard to argue that PACER Plus achieved this.[644] On the one hand, a chapter on the movement of natural persons was included in the text of the PTA. On the other hand, the content of this chapter is a simple reproduction of the WTO GATS Mode 4 Commitments of the States Parties. Thus, preferential treatment for services mobility amongst the member states was not implemented.

Similarly, the arrangement on labour mobility does not liberalise labour market access. Instead, Australia, New Zealand and twelve PIS have reached several 'understandings'.[645] At the core of these understandings lies the establishment of the Pacific Labour Mobility Annual Meeting (PLMAM). The PLMAM is a mechanism for advancing cooperation and review progress on the

People's Guide to PACER' (Pacific Network on Globalisation, August 2004) <http://aftinet.org.au/cms/sites/default/files/APeoplesGuidetoPACER.pdf> accessed 6 April 2022.

640 PICTA TIS was signed by ten PIS: namely, the Cook Islands, FSM, Kiribati, Nauru, Samoa, Solomon Islands, Tonga, Tuvalu, Vanuatu, RMI.

641 Wadan Narsey, 'PICTA, PACER and EPAs: weaknesses in Pacific island countries' trade policies' (Pacific Economic Bulletin, 19 (3), 2004, Asia Pacific Press) <https://openresearch-repository.anu.edu.au/bitstream/1885/157729/1/193_picta.pdf> accessed 6 April 2022.

642 Kautoke-Holani (n 608) 90–101.

643 Pacific Network on Globalisation, 'PACER-Plus Labour Mobility Analysis : Unbound promises and an annual meeting' (February 2020) <https://www.bilaterals.org/IMG/pdf/p+_arrangement_on_labour_mobility_analysis.pdf> accessed 6 April 2022.

644 For a critical evaluation of PACER Plus, see Adam Wolfenden, 'Pacer Plus: the case against' (Development Policy Blog, 25 November 2020) <https://devpolicy.org/pacer-plus-the-case-against-20201125-2> accessed 6 April 2022.

645 These twelve PIS are: Cook Islands, FSM, Kiribati, Nauru, Niue, Palau, RMI, Samoa, Solomon Islands, Tonga, Tuvalu and Vanuatu. See Arrangement on Labour Mobility <https://www.dfat.gov.au/sites/default/files/arrangement-on-labour-mobility.pdf> accessed 6 April 2022.

key objectives of the arrangement, including the enhancement of the existing labour mobility schemes and the facilitation of other forms of temporary labour mobility, technical and vocational education and training, as well as the recognition of qualifications and the registration of occupations.[646]

Interestingly, during the meeting of the PLMAM in 2019, the participants considered the scope and options for a Labour Mobility Secretariat, which could be formed either as a part of the PACER Plus implementation unit, as a standalone secretariat or as a secretariat housed in the PIFS.[647] Participants expressed a range of views and debated the allocation of resources for such a body.[648] In June 2021, the ministerial representatives' meeting of the Parties to PACER Plus 'welcomed' the decision to host the Labour Mobility Secretariat in the PACER Plus implementation unit.[649] However, it remains unclear as of yet what functions this new secretariat will perform.[650]

In conclusion, although PACER Plus might be viewed as a stepping stone in the direction of discussing a regional approach to human mobility, the current commitments do not open up market access or come closer to creating free movement. As discussed earlier, PTAs can provide legal pathways to people fleeing their homes in the context of disasters and climate change.[651] For instance, regional free-movement agreements empower people of the Caribbean Islands to make short cross-border trips to take up employment when a disaster hits, to send remittances back home and to help rebuild, as well as to enhance their skills and exchange knowledge.[652] As they are highly vulnerable to the impact of disasters and climate change and as they lack international protection, the citizens of the PIS could benefit from regional approaches to facilitating movement.

646 ibid.

647 Pacific Labour Mobility Annual Meeting, Outcome Statement (7–9 October 2019) <https://www.mfat.govt.nz/assets/Aid-Prog-docs/Partnerships/PLMAM-2019-Outcome-Statement.pdf> accessed 6 April 2022.

648 ibid.

649 PACER Plus Communiqué (30 June 2021) PP.MIN.003/C/FINAL <https://storage.googleapis.com/pacer-plus/PP.MIN.003.C.FINAL_Adopted_2JULY.pdf> accessed 6 April 2022.

650 Richard Curtain, 'Is PLMAM fit for purpose?' (Development Policy Blog, 21 October 2019) <https://devpolicy.org/is-plmam-fit-for-purpose-20191021> accessed 6 April 2022.

651 See Chapter 2.1.5 of this book.

652 Francis (n 385); Montoute, Mohammed and Francis (n 396) 2; Sealey-Huggins (n 396) 2444–2463.

3 Learning from the Domestic Approaches to Protection

Given the lack of a regional approach to HMDCC, the prospect of an inquiry into domestic approaches to protecting PMDCC remains highly relevant. Recently, Vanuatu and Fiji have become one of the first countries to launch domestic frameworks on displacement and the planned relocation of communities in the context of environmental changes.[653] This development followed the increasing calls at the international and regional levels to identify adaptation strategies to slow- or sudden-onset environmental events and to take action in cases where land is no longer habitable.[654] On the one hand, planned relocation serves as an adaptative measure to climate change, which can be used as a protective tool that aims to reduce the risk of harm and discharge the duty of States' to uphold human rights.[655] On the other hand, it must be adopted as a measure of last resort, with careful safeguards being applied at each stage, since a failure to do so can have long-term ramifications for individual and collective civil, political, economic and cultural rights.[656] This section will first discuss the notion of planned relocation, before analysing the policies of Vanuatu and Fiji.

3.1 *The Notion of Planned Relocation and the Pacific Island States*

In the last few decades, increasing attention has been directed at developing policy and legal frameworks to address planned relocation in the context of climate change and disasters, as well as neighbouring concepts, such as evacuation, displacement and resettlement. Generally, significant differences can

---

653 Dalila Gharbaoui, 'Climate change, planned relocation and land governance in the Pacific region' (PhD thesis, Université de Liége, 24 May 2021) <https://orbi.uliege.be/handle/2268/242334> accessed 6 April 2022.

654 Elizabeth Ferris and Sanjula Weerasinghe, 'Promoting Human Security: Planned Relocation as a Protection Tool in a Time of Climate Change' [2020] 8 Journal on Migration and Human Security 2, 134–149.

655 Melanie Pill, 'Planned Relocation from the Impacts of Climate Change in Small Island Developing States: the Intersection Between Adaptation and Loss and Damage' in Walter Leal Filho, *Managing Climate Change Adaptation in the Pacific Region* (Springer, 2020) 129–150.

656 See, eg, Task Force on Displacement (n 1). See, eg, Pacific Community (SPC), Secretariat of the Pacific Regional Environment Programme (SPREP), Pacific Islands Forum Secretariat (PIFS), United Nations Development Programme (UNDP), United Nations Office for Disaster Risk Reduction (UNISDR) & University of the South Pacific (USP), 'Framework for Resilient Development in the Pacific: An Integrated Approach to Address Climate Change and Disaster Risk Management 2017–2030' (2016) <http://gsd.spc.int/frdp/assets/FRDP_2016_Resilient_Dev_pacific.pdf> accessed 6 April 2022.

be identified between these concepts. Evacuation means 'the rapid movement of persons away from the immediate threat or impact of a disaster to a place of shelter, in order to secure their security, safety and well-being'.[657] Displacement is 'the movement within a State and/or across international borders of persons who are forced or obliged to leave their homes or places of habitual residence due to sudden-onset natural hazards and/or slower, cumulative pressures occurring in the context of sea level rise'.[658] Planned relocation differs from these two concepts, and can be defined as 'a planned process in which persons voluntarily move or are forced to move away from their homes or places of temporary residence, are settled in a new location within their own or another State, and are provided with the conditions for rebuilding their lives'.[659] Resettlement, by contrast, is a bit harder to distinguish conceptually from relocation, which might be the reason why policy makers and legislators often find themselves using the terms interchangeably.[660] In the context of international refugee law, resettlement has a defined legal meaning, which is the 'selection and transfer of refugees from a State in which they have sought protection to a third State which has agreed to admit them – as refugees – with permanent residence status'.[661] However, it is reasonable to use 'resettlement' synonymously with 'relocation' and 'planned relocation' outside of the context of refugees, in the sense of a policy or legal response adopted by authorities to address the effects of climate and environmental changes.[662]

A quest to trace the origins of resettlement and planned relocation reveals the long history of how these concepts have been carved into legal tools. Studying their development from the 18th century onwards, McAdam argues that the seeds of the idea of transferring populations from high-density

657 ILA (n 168) 3.

658 ibid.

659 ibid.

660 See, eg, Government of Vanuatu, National Policy on Climate Change and Disaster-Induced Displacement, Vanuatu, Government of Vanuatu, 2018 <https://perma.cc/3R75-K3JN> accessed 6 April 2022; Government of Fiji, Planned Relocation Guidelines, Fiji, Government of Fiji, 2018 <https://www.refworld.org/do cid/5c3c92204.html> accessed 6 April 2022.

661 United Nations High Commissioner for Refugees (UNHCR), *UNHCR Resettlement Handbook* (Geneva, UNHCR, 2011) <https://www.unhcr.org/46f7c0ee2.pdf> accessed 6 April 2022.

662 It must be noted that resettlement can also refer to relocations in the context of development projects. See Jeanette Schade, 'Climate Change and Planned Relocation: Risks and a Proposal for Safeguards' in Thomas Faist and Jeanette Schade (eds), *Disentangling Migration and Climate Change: Methodologies, Political Discourses and Human Rights* (Netherlands, Springer 2013) 185.

'danger zones' to low-density areas had been planted as a pre-emptive solution to many crises over the centuries.[663] These challenges included: responding to anticipated human overpopulation, overcoming resource scarcity (especially in the context of colonisation), solving displacement and refugee problems, and redistributing ethnic minorities so as to concentrate them in particular territories.[664] By the 20th century, resettlement and relocation had evolved from individual intellectual deliberations to internationalised concepts requiring international cooperation, to the extent that, during a conference by the International Labour Organisation in 1938, the proposal to create a permanent international committee on cross-border resettlement was briefly entertained.[665] More recently, environmental destruction and degradation due to development-based projects has rekindled the debate on the implications of evictions, displacement, relocation and resettlement.[666] The construction of dams and airports, as well as mining and nuclear-testing activities, have been and continue to be examples of the forced relocation of communities.[667]

Perspectives from the distant and recent past reiterate that the planned relocation of communities is not a new concept.[668] On the contrary, it has been utilised as a political and legal instrument in a plethora of contexts, alongside its neighbouring concept resettlement. It would be pertinent to ask why, despite its long history, international law has lagged behind in creating a framework to address planned relocation.

An international framework on planned relocation would undoubtedly use analogies with the past as a 'diagnostic and predictive tool',[669] serving

---

663 Jane McAdam, 'Relocation and resettlement from colonisation to climate change: the perennial solution to danger zones' [2015] 3 London Review of International Law 1, 95.

664 ibid 94–120.

665 ibid 96.

666 Asia-Pacific Network for Global Change Research (APN), 'Community Relocation as an Option for Adaptation to the Effects of Climate Change and Climate Variability in Pacific Island Countries' (Suva, APN, 2005) <https://www.sprep.org/att/irc/ecopies/pacific_region/643.pdf> accessed 6 April 2022.

667 See Stuart Kirsch, 'Lost Worlds: Environmental Disaster, "Culture Loss, and the Law"' [2001] 42 Current Anthropology 2, 167–198; Brooke Wilmsen and Michael Webber, 'What can we learn from the practice of development-force displacement and resettlement for organised resettlements in response to climate change?' [2015] 58 Geoforum 1, 76–85.

668 See Ronald W. Perry and Michael K. Lindell, 'Principles for Managing Community Relocation as a Hazard Mitigation Measure' [1997] 5 Journal of Contingencies and Crisis Management 1, 49–59.

669 Thomas Birk, 'Relocation of reef and atoll island communities as an adaptation to climate change: learning from experience in Solomon Islands' in Kirsten Hastrup and Karen Fog Olwig (eds), Climate Change and Human Mobility: Challenges to Social Sciences (Cambridge University Press 2012) 99.

to emphasise the difficulties inherent in the governance and implementation of planned relocation, from landlessness, homelessness and food insecurity through to marginalisation, social disarticulation and morbidity.[670] Furthermore, it would also build on the theoretical basis offered by international human rights instruments, even though none of these documents address the unique and complex social, economic and political crises communities face due to climate-induced displacement.[671]

Starting with the decision, referred to as the Cancun Adaptation Framework adopted during COP16 to the UNFCCC, the international community gradually identified the potential interlinkages between climate change and the movement of people.[672] Within this preliminary framework the emphasis was on the identification of adaptative measures and initiatives aiming to reduce the vulnerability of natural and human systems against actual or expected effects of climate change.[673] Against this background, the concerns over the effects of climate change on human migration and displacement were addressed as matters for cooperation, rather than for liability or compensation, and planned relocation was suggested as a possible adaptation strategy.[674] In cases where habitation on land is no longer possible and the population in question lacks the resources for planned migration, government-assisted relocation was put forward as a solution.[675]

The establishment of the UNFCCC WIM breathed new life into planned relocation within the framework the climate change regime. WIM was created in 2013, with a mandate to enhance 'knowledge and understanding of comprehensive risk management approaches' and 'action and support, including finance, technology and capacity-building' as well as to strengthen 'dialogue, coordination, coherence and synergies among relevant stakeholders' for loss

670 Schade (n 662) 109.

671 Robin Bronen, 'Climate-induced Community Relocations: Creating an Adaptive Governance Framework Based in Human Rights Doctrine' [2011] 35 N.Y.U. Review of Law & Social Change 2, 394–395.

672 United Nations Conference of the Parties to the United Nations Framework Convention on Climate Change (UNFCCC), Report of the Conference of the Parties on its Sixteenth Session, UN Doc FCCC/CP/2010/7/Add. 1, 15 March 2011, para. 14(f).

673 Intergovernmental Panel on Climate Change (IPCC), 'Definition of Terms Used Within the DCC Pages, Glossary A', IPCC Data Distribution Centre <https://www.ipcc-data.org/guidelines/pages/glossary/glossary_a.html> accessed 6 April 2022.

674 Koko Warner, 'Human Migration and Displacement in the Context of Adaptation to Climate Change: the Cancun Adaptation Framework and Potential for Future Action' [2012] 30 Government and Policy 6, 1066.

675 Eli Keene, 'Resources for Relocation: In Search of a Coherent Federal Policy on Resettling Climate-Vulnerable Communities' [2018] 48 Texas Environmental Law Journal 1, 119–142.

and damage, amongst others.[676] Two years later, the TFD was established within the WIM in the same vein, in order to 'develop recommendations' to 'avert, minimise and address displacement related to the adverse impacts of climate change'.[677] Its recommendations were delivered during the COP in 2018, and include: facilitating and initiating planned relocation as an option of last resort and transposing international tools aimed at protecting the human rights of the concerned population to the regional and national levels.[678]

Whether in the context of colonialism, disasters or climate change, the PIS have experience with planned relocation. Historically, at least three planned cross-border relocations were carried out during the colonial period and at least three more were contemplated.[679] In the context of climate change, Campbell and others have identified 37 relocations due to natural hazards and disasters in the region.[680] Reflecting on these past relocation experiences is a crucial part of informing the development of the current frameworks.[681] Building on this idea, the representatives and experts at the regional consultations of the Nansen Initiative stressed that the participation of the relocating community was as crucial as the participation of the community inhabiting the lands to which the relocation occurs.[682] This is particularly true in relation to the customary land laws prominent in the Pacific region, which generally apply to most of the lands in the PIS. Contrary to freehold lands, customary lands have significant restrictions on permanent alienation.[683] Therefore, a community

676 Conference of the Parties to the United Nations Framework Convention on Climate Change, 'Report of the Conference of the Parties on its Nineteenth Session' (19th sess, 31 January 2014) UN Doc FCCC/CP/2013/10/Add. 1 <https://unfccc.int/resource/docs/2013/cop19/eng/10a01.pdf> accessed 6 April 2022.

677 Task Force on Displacement (n 1).

678 ibid.

679 Jane McAdam, 'Historical Cross-Border Relocations in the Pacific: Lessons for Planned Relocations in the Context of Climate Change' [2014] 49 Journal of Pacific History, 301.

680 Asia-Pacific Network for Global Change Research, 'Community Relocation as an Option for Adaptation to the Effects of Climate Change and Climate Variability in the Pacific Island Countries' (2015) <https://www.apn-gcr.org/resources/files/original/48ce301c4d1fi a8ffc7d4c5e8da32b15.pdf> accessed 6 April 2022.

681 The Nansen Initiative, 'Human Mobility, Natural Disasters and Climate Change in the Pacific: Summary of Conclusions, Nansen Initiative Pacific Regional Consultation' (Outcome Report, Cook Islands, 21–24 May 2013) <https://disasterdisplacement.org/wp-content/uploads/2014/08/OR_Human_Mobility_Natural_Disasters_and_Climate_Change_in_the_Pacific.pdf> accessed 6 April 2022.

682 ibid.

683 The notion of customary land dates back to British colonial times, according to which such lands could not be permanently alienated. In certain British colonies and protectorates, the common law rule on the ultimate ownership of all the land in the country by the King was not applied. Instead, legislation provided that the King owned only the land

relocating outside of the boundary of its customary lands into another community's lands might have to seek consent according to traditional customs.[684]

Regionally, the incorporation of planned relocation into national policy and legal frameworks has been emphasised in several key documents. For instance, the Niue Declaration, adopted in 2008, includes a commitment to encouraging an increase in 'technical and financial support for climate change action on adaptation, mitigation and, if necessary, relocation' was adopted in 2008 by sixteen PIS, together with Australia and New Zealand.[685]

The Moana Declaration, which was adopted in 2013, emphasised 'a human rights-based approach to the issues of internally displaced persons, refugees and asylum seekers in the Pacific'.[686]

Two recent regional declarations, namely, the Nadi Bay Declaration on the Climate Change Crisis in the Pacific[687] and the Kainaki II Declaration for Urgent Climate Change Now,[688] reiterate that forced migration and displacement will remain an essential part of the climate change crisis.

Furthermore, the Framework for Resilient Development in the Pacific: An Integrated Approach to Address Climate Change and Disaster Risk Management 2017–2030 was adopted as 'voluntary guidelines for the Pacific Islands region'.[689] The Framework advises the national and subnational governments and administrations to 'integrate human mobility aspects, where appropriate, [...] through targeted national policies and actions, including relocation [...]'.[690]

---

that was not owned by the indigenous people. To read more about the application of this rule in Fiji, please refer to Jennifer Corrin-Care and Donald Edgar Paterson, *Introduction to South Pacific Law* (Cavendish, Routledge 2017) 317–318.

684 The Nansen Initiative (n 681).

685 Pacific Islands Forum (n 587).

686 Pacific Island Parliamentarians, The Moana Declaration, Outcome Statement of Pacific Parliamentarians for Population and Development (13–15 August 2013), recommendation 3.

687 Pacific Islands Development Forum, Nadi Bay Declaration on the Climate Change Crisis in the Pacific (29–30 July 2019) <https://www.documentcloud.org/documents/6226356-Nadi-Bay-Declaration-on-Climate-Crisis-2019.html> accessed 6 April 2022.

688 Pacific Islands Forum (n 598).

689 SPC, SPREP, PIFS, UNDP, UNISDR & USP, Framework for Resilient Development in the Pacific: An Integrated Approach to Address Climate Change and Disaster Risk Management 2017–2030.

690 Goal 1 of the Framework for Resilient Development recommends 'strengthened integrated adaptation and risk reduction to enhance resilience to climate change and disasters'.

With time, these regional documents began to influence national frameworks addressing climate change and natural disasters.[691] Vanuatu and Fiji are the first countries in the Pacific region to specifically dedicate frameworks to planned relocation.[692] Although there exist no binding commitments on liability and compensation, planned relocation projects are gradually establishing a sufficient foundation to become eligible for funding from donors as an adaptation strategy to climate change.[693] This has the potential to motivate governments, especially those heavily impacted by climate change, to place the creation of legal frameworks on planned relocation on their agenda. Other interested stakeholders can also potentially be motivated, such as international and regional organisations and the civil society, which can take up the cause of preventing climate-induced displacement through planned relocation.[694]

In conclusion, it is possible to view planned relocation in the context of disasters and climate change as a protective measure that aims to prevent future harm by moving people out of harm's way.[695] It is also a powerful tool that provides a solution to 'allow displaced people to rebuild lives when a disaster or future risks associated with disasters, environmental degradation, or adverse effects of climate change threaten human security at origin or render places of origin unfit for habitation'.[696]

---

691 Koko Warner and others, 'National Adaptation Plans and Human Mobility' [2015] 49 Forced Migration Review.

692 Carol Farbotko and Celia McMichael, 'Voluntary immobility and existential security in a changing climate in the Pacific' [2019] 60 Asia Pacific Viewpoint 2, 148–162; Jessie Connell and Sabira Coelho, 'Planned relocation in Asia and the Pacific' [2018] Forced Migration Review, 46–49.

693 Seizing the opportunity, Fiji launched the first fund titled Climate Change Relocation and Displaced Peoples Trust Fund for Communities and Infrastructure. The aim is to receive international support for planned relocation projects. For more information about the launch, see World's First-Ever Relocation Trust Fund for People Displaced by Climate Change for People Displaced by Climate Change Launched by Fijian Prime Minister, <https://www.fiji.gov.fj/Media-Centre/News/WORLD%E2%80%99S-FIRST-%E2%80%93EVER-RELOCATION-TRUST-FUND-FOR-PEOP> accessed 6 April 2022. To read the Act of Parliament, see Government of Fiji, Climate Relocation of Communities Trust Fund Act 2019, <https://laws.gov.fj/Acts/DisplayAct/2562> accessed 6 April 2022.

694 Daniel Lund, 'Navigating slow-onset risks through foresight and flexibility in Fiji: emerging recommendations for the planned relocation of climate-vulnerable communities' [2021] 50 Current Opinion in Environmental Sustainability, 12–20.

695 Ferris and Weerasinghe (n 654) 137–138.

696 ibid.

3.2 *Planned Relocation Policy of Vanuatu*

Vanuatu has launched its National Policy on Climate Change and Disaster-induced Displacement (National Policy) in September 2018.[697] Before discussing the National Policy as a protection tool, this section first gives some background information about Vanuatu.

Vanuatu is a Small Island Developing State under the UN system, with a population of 282,000 people scattered over 80 islands.[698] It is considered to be one of the world's most vulnerable countries to natural hazards, ranking as the most at-risk in 2016.[699] It incurs an average of USD 48,000 million a year in losses due to natural hazards, corresponding to 6.6% of its GDP.[700] These losses reached an astronomical figure of USD 450 million, representing approximately 64% of the country's GDP, in March 2015 when the Category 5 Tropical Cyclone Pam struck Vanuatu.[701] A combination of factors explain its vulnerability, including its high exposure to disaster events, the increasing intensity and frequency of extreme weather events due to the impact of climate change, and the effects of developmental challenges.[702]

While the reasons for internal migration and displacement in Vanuatu are complex, sudden- and slow-onset disasters create additional pressure for people to become mobile.[703] For instance, increased volcanic activity in the Ambae Island started a process of evacuation in 2017, which was eventually finalised when the entire population of the island comprising around 11,000 people was relocated to the neighbouring islands of Maewo and Santo.[704] Tropical Cyclone Pam, on the other hand, impacted an estimated 188,000

697 Government of Vanuatu (n 660).

698 UN Data, *Vanuatu* (2019) <http://data.un.org/en/iso/vu.html> accessed 6 April 2022.

699 Bündnis Entwicklung Hilft and United Nations University Institute for Environment and Human Security (UNU-EHS), 'World Risk Report 2016' <https://reliefweb.int/sites/reliefweb.int/files/resources/WorldRiskReport2016_small.pdf> accessed 6 April 2022.

700 Global Facility for Disaster Reduction and Recovery (GFFDR), 'Vanuatu' (2019) <https://www.gfdrr.org/en/vanuatu> accessed 6 April 2022.

701 ibid.

702 Government of Vanuatu (n 660).

703 Siobhan McDonnell, 'The importance of attention to customary tenure solutions: slow onset risks and the limits of Vanuatu's climate change and resettlement policy' [2021] 50 Current Opinion in Environmental Sustainability, 281–288.

704 International Federation of Red Cross and Red Crescent Societies (IFRC), 'Emergency Plan of Action Final Report, Vanuatu: Ambae Volcanic Eruption 2018' (IFRC, 2019) <https://reliefweb.int/sites/reliefweb.int/files/resources/MDRVU00502dfr%20%281%29.pdf> accessed 6 April 2022.

people, of whom more than 65,000 were recorded as internally displaced.[705] A case study of the Mataso island community members shows that the islands struck by Cyclone Pam had to endure periods as long as six days without any assistance from the government, in situations without adequate shelter and with little food.[706] Environmental degradation, tsunamis, flooding, sea-level rise and drought have also been identified as triggers of temporary and permanent displacement.[707]

Addressing internal displacement has presented challenges for the government of Vanuatu, particularly since there was a lack of clarity about which government agency was resonsible.[708] Although the communities in need of assistance tended to approach the area councils, in addition to provincial and municipal governments, the procedures to be followed by these agencies and the contact points at the national level were not well defined.[709] As a result, responses were adopted on an ad hoc and fragmented basis, with communities receiving support and assistance from different agencies in their various mandates and capacities. In 2016, the Vanuatu Climate Change and Disaster Risk Reduction Policy had called for the 'development of a national policy on resettlement and internal displacement',[710] which was fulfilled with the adoption of the National Policy.[711] The National Policy was developed with the technical support of the IOM, funded by the IOM Development Fund.[712] It aims to 'help guide emergency and development planners to work together with the Government of Vanuatu to address the needs of all communities affected by displacement'.[713] Its development is stated to have followed a 'conflict-sensitive approach' and to have incorporated the views of 'many different stakeholders'

705 Pacific Community (SPC), 'Tropical Cyclone Pam Lessons Learned Workshop Report' (Suva, SPC 2015) <http://www.spc.int/sites/default/files/wordpresscontent/wp-content/uploads/2016/12/TC-Pam-Lessons-Learned-Report.pdf> accessed 6 April 2022.

706 Margaretha Wewerinke-Singh and Tess Van Geelen, 'Protection of Climate Displaced Persons under International Law: A Case Study from Mataso Island, Vanuatu' [2018] 19 Melbourne Journal of International Law 1, 18.

707 Government of Vanuatu (n 660) 11.

708 ibid 14.

709 ibid 15.

710 Government of the Republic of Vanuatu, 'Vanuatu Climate Change and Disaster Risk Reduction Policy 2016–2030', section 7.6.6.

711 The adoption of the National Policy, as well as the establishment of the National Advisory Board on Climate Change and Disaster Risk Reduction and the formulation of a disaster and climate change committee in every province to help communities are commended in the UPR outcome report.

712 Government of the Republic of Vanuatu (n 660) 8.

713 ibid 7.

as a result of 'wide-ranging' consultations with communities affected by displacement, and government and non-government agencies at the national, provincial and local levels.[714]

The National Policy proposes twelve strategic priority areas for action, which are divided into systems-level and sectoral-level interventions. Systems-level interventions relate to the following areas: institutions and governance; safeguards and protection; evidence, information and monitoring; and capacity-building, training and resources. Sectoral-level interventions relate to: safety and security; land, housing, planning and environment; health and well-being; education; infrastructure and connectivity; agriculture, food security and livelihoods; traditional knowledge, culture and documentation; and, finally, access to justice and public participation. Furthermore, there are 'cross-cutting priorities' including disaster risk reduction, climate change adaptation, community participation, gender responsiveness, partnerships, social inclusion, and safe and well-managed migration, which aim to underpin the twelve strategic priority areas.[715]

The scope of the National Policy encompasses five broad groups of people, which are categorised as internally displaced people, people at risk of displacement and/or relocation, people living in informal or peri-urban settlements, internal migrants and other communities directly or indirectly impacted by displacement.[716] Regardless of this categorisation, the National Policy specifically states that it does not aim to discriminate against affected communities on the basis of the cause of displacement.[717] A broad concept of disaster which includes natural and human-made crises is therefore preferred. Furthermore, a spectrum of effects, from evictions to planned relocation, are covered.

The National Policy envisages a mainstreaming process into existing and future government policies and legislation, annual plans, work programmes, and sector plans and policies. The development of two instruments has been committed to for further implementation: a comprehensive Implementation Plan and Monitoring and Evaluation Framework, which will outline the specific roles and responsibilities of different government agencies and partners, and the Standard Operating Procedures, which will oversee emergency response, return and reintegration, evictions and planned relocation.[718]

714 ibid 8.

715 ibid.

716 ibid 19.

717 ibid 7.

718 ibid Annex E.

One of the guiding principles envisaged in the National Policy is the protection of human rights and dignity. Domestically, Chapter 2 of the Constitution of the Republic of Vanuatu (Constitution of Vanuatu) governs fundamental rights and duties. The freedom of movement, the protection of property, the right to security and the freedom of expression are amongst the range of rights guaranteed under the Constitution of Vanuatu. The duties of the persons include safeguarding the nation's wealth, resources and environment in the interests of both the present generation and future generations, cooperating fully with others in the interests of interdependence and solidarity, and contributing to the attainment of national objectives.[719]

Furthermore, under Chapter 12 of the Constitution of Vanuatu, all land in the Republic of Vanuatu belongs to the indigenous custom owners and their descendants.[720] Accordingly, the rules of custom form the basis of ownership and use of land. Customary land inheritance is predominantly patrilineal, meaning men are generally land owners.[721] Article 81 of the Constitution of Vanuatu vests the Government with the power to buy land from custom owners and transfer ownership of it to indigenous citizens or indigenous communities from over-populated islands.[722] This power could represent the basis for the voluntary relocation of persons or communities from overpopulated islands. However, planned relocation for other reasons may require the consent of custom land owners for access, use and (if applicable) ownership of land. Therefore, the community subject to planned relocation in the context of climate change and disasters must be assisted in exercising their right to adequate housing and land in conformity with the customary rules of Vanuatu.

According to the most recent UPR report, Vanuatu has taken positive steps to improve the human rights situation since its last review, which was concluded in 2014. It formed a national implementation plan for the recommendations contained in the previous UPR, becoming the first PIS to take such a step.[723] As a result, it has enacted various laws on the protection of rights, including laws on health, education and access to information.[724] Furthermore, Vanuatu

719 Constitution of the Republic of Vanuatu arts. 7(d), (f), (g).

720 ibid Chapter 12.

721 Allens Linklaters LLP, Housing, Land and Property Law in Vanuatu, International Federation of Red Cross and Red Crescent Societies and Australian Red Cross (2017) <https://www.sheltercluster.org/sites/default/files/docs/vanuatu_disaster_law_hlp_mapping.pdf> accessed 6 April 2022.

722 Constitution of the Republic of Vanuatu art. 81.

723 UNHRC, Report of the Working Group on the Universal Periodic Review Vanuatu, 41st sess, Agenda Item 6, UN Doc A/HRC/41/10 (24 June-12 July 2019, adopted 5 April 2019).

724 ibid.

graduated from the status of least developed country in 2020, which, as the UN Secretary-General Antonio Guterres noted, happened 'despite the setbacks it has suffered from the ever-worsening impacts of climate change and natural disasters, as well as the economic devastation caused by the COVID-19 pandemic, on tourism, trade and remittances'.[725]

One of the most important topics in relation to which serious human rights concerns were raised is the rights of women. Currently, none of the 52 elected members of the Parliament of Vanuatu are women.[726] How Vanuatu's patriarchal and customary structures impinge on the struggle of women to achieve full equality in all aspects of social and political life has long been discussed.[727] Participation in decision-making at all levels is especially noted as being restricted by the violence women face.[728] This can have serious implications for the planned relocation of communities. From the perspective of community-based rights, the transparent and inclusive participation of the community in the process may not be achieved if women are left out. From the perspective of the satisfaction of individual human rights, women are entitled to the enjoyment of their rights without fear. Ensuring that women are included and can actively participate in the planning, decision-making and implementation processes of planned relocation is crucial. In this regard, the UPR outcome report recommends that Vanuatu include women in the National Advisory Board on Climate Change and Disaster Risk Reduction to ensure the effective participation in the planning, decision-making and implementation processes of the National Policy.[729] The National Policy itself adopts gender equity and responsiveness as a guiding principle.[730] It is important to be vigilant of the

725 United Nations Office of the High Representative for the Least Developed Countries, Landlocked Developing Countries and Small Island Developing States, 'Vanuatu Graduates from Least Developed Country Status' <https://www.un.org/ohrlls/news/vanuatu-graduates-least-developed-country-status> accessed 6 April 2022.

726 See, generally, UN CEDAW, Concluding observations on the combined fourth and fifth periodic reports of Vanuatu, 63rd sess, Committee on the Elimination of Discrimination Against Women, UN Doc CEDAW/C/VUT/CO/4-5 (9 March 2016).

727 See, generally, Compilation prepared by the Office of the United Nations High Commissioner for Human Rights in accordance with paragraph 15(b) of the annex to Human Rights Council resolution 5/1 and paragraph 5 of the annex to Council resolution 16/21, UN HRC, 18th sess, Working Group on the Universal Periodic Review, UN Doc A/HRC/WG.6/18/VUT/2 (27 January-7 February 2014, adopted 6 November 2013).

728 UN CEDAW (n 726).

729 UN HRC (n 723) para 90.17.

730 The National Policy explains the guiding principle of gender equity and responsiveness as: 'planning for durable solutions must be responsive to the different risks and needs of all people, including women, men, children. All people must be included in durable

activities of the newly established Ministry of Climate Change and the Gender and Protection Cluster, which aims to work towards gender and protection issues in the context of disasters and climate change.[731]

3.3 *Planned Relocation Policy of Fiji*

Fiji has adopted its Planned Relocation Guidelines in 2018 and Displacement Guidelines (together referred to as 'Guidelines') in December 2019.[732] This section first introduces Fiji and then analyses the Guidelines.

Fiji is located in the Pacific Ocean over a total geographical area of 18,272 km^2.[733] It has a population of approximately 900,000 people living on over 332 mountainous and volcanic islands.[734] Approximately 90% of the people live in three urban centres situated on the coast.[735] Cyclones, storm surges, coastal erosion, floods and sea level rise are among some of the known risks facing the human settlements in these centres.[736] Rural communities along the coast are similarly vulnerable to sea-level rise, cyclones and storm surges.[737] Furthermore, thousands of people live in low-lying outer islands of Fiji, which are "difficult and expensive to protect against sea level rise and storm surges, calling into question their viability over the long term".[738] Thus, human settlements in Fiji are vulnerable to the impact of climate change.[739]

In 2006, Vunidogoloa village, which is situated on the coast of Fiji's second-largest island, known as Vanua Levu, approached the Fijian government for

---

solutions planning and have equal opportunities to lead community-driven recovery processes'.

731 ibid.

732 Government of Fiji (n 660). Government of Fiji, Displacement Guidelines in the Context of Climate Change and Disasters, Fiji, Government of Fiji, 2019 <https://www.pacificclimatechange.net/sites/default/files/documents/Displacement%20Guidelines.%20In%20the%20context%20of%20climate%20change%20and%20disasters.pdf> accessed 6 April 2022.

733 United Nations Office of the High Representative for the Least Developed Countries, Landlocked Developing States and Small Island Developing States (UN-OHRLLS), 'About SIDS' (2019) <http://unohrlls.org/about-sids/> accessed 6 April 2022.

734 ibid.

735 Government of Fiji, 'National Adaptation Plan' (2018) <https://www4.unfccc.int/ sites/NAPC/Documents/Parties/National%20Adaptation%20Plan_Fiji.pdf> accessed 6 April 2022.

736 ibid.

737 ibid.

738 ibid.

739 ibid.

relocation assistance.[740] Coastal erosion, flooding and sea level rise were the predominant reasons for this appeal.[741] The community was 'trapped' by the high tide caused by the rising sea level and heavy rains.[742] The process of relocation took around seven years and was finalised in 2014.[743] As a result, the community moved two kilometres inland to approximately 30 new houses within its own customary land boundaries, thus making this process the first government-assisted relocation in Fiji.[744] The total cost of the project was FJD 978,228 (approx. USD 472,789).[745]

The relocation of Vunidogoloa village took place in a legal vacuum – in the absence of any domestic laws or policies directly addressing and planning relocation processes. The relocation of Narikoso village, which is situated on Fiji's fourth-largest island, Kadavu, was the second government-assisted relocation in Fiji.[746] A National Relocation Taskforce Team was formed to support this relocation.[747] A national consultation for the development of a national framework thus began in 2015. Shortly afterwards, the Fijian Ministry of Economy took over the process to develop the Planned Relocation Guideline.[748] Affected communities, households and individuals are specifically referred to as having been consulted during the formulation stage.[749] This composition is stated to

740 Karen McNamara and HeleneJacot Des Comboes, 'Planning for Community Relocations Due to Climate Change in Fiji' [2015] 6 International Journal of Disaster Risk Science, 315.

741 ibid.

742 Clothilde Tronquet, 'From Vunidogoloa to Kenani: An Insight into Successful Relocation' [2015] The State of Environmental Migration Review.

743 United Nations Office for the Coordination of Humanitarian Affairs (UNOCHA), Fiji: Building resilience in the face of climate change (2014) <https://www.unocha.org/story/fiji-building-resilience-face-climate-change> accessed 6 April 2022.

744 ibid.

745 Celia McMichael, Carol Farbotko and Karen E. McNamara, 'Climate-Migration Responses in the Pacific Region' in Cecilia Menjivar, Marie Ruiz, and Immanuel Ness (eds), *The Oxford Handbook of Migration Crises* (Oxford University Press 2019) 297–314.

746 Georgetown University, United Nations High Commissioner for Refugees (UNHCR) and International Organisation for Migration (IOM), 'A Toolbox: Planning Relocations to Protect People from Disasters and Environmental Change' (2017) <https://www.refworld.org/pdfid/596f15774.pdf> accessed 6 April 2022.

747 ibid.

748 Both the Planned Relocation and Disaster Guidelines were established with the support of the German Corporation for International Cooperation GmbHv (Deutsche Gesellschaft für Internationale Zusammenarbeit GmbH, also known as GIZ, the German development agency). The GIZ has been helping fifteen governments in the Pacific in various ways to adapt to climate change. GIZ, 'Adapting to climate change: a new start in Fiji' (2017) <https://www.giz.de/en/mediacenter/57948.html> accessed 6 April 2022.

749 Government of the Republic of Fiji (n 660).

be 'inclusive' and 'gender responsive', one that serves to enhance 'the involvement and collaboration of all range of stakeholders'.[750]

The Planned Relocation Guideline is structured in two parts. The first part gives an overview and includes the definition of planned relocation, as well as its main pillars and principles. Accordingly, planned relocation is 'understood as a solution-oriented measure, involving the State, in which a community (as distinct from an individual/household) is physically moved to another location and resettled permanently there'.[751] The principles listed in the Guideline are applicable to all stages and consist of: a human-centred approach (i.e. the application of anthropocentric management concerns of environmental resources); a livelihood-based approach (i.e. addressing the specific adaptation needs of communities and households on the move); a human-rights based approach (i.e. upholding the rights of individuals to meaningful and transparent engagement throughout the planned relocation process); a preemptive approach (i.e. ensuring potential humanitarian crises are avoided); and a regional approach (i.e. bringing domestic policies in line with existing regional norms).[752]

The second part of the Planned Relocation Guideline concerns the three stages of planned relocation, which are: the pre-planned relocation process, the in-planned relocation process and the post-planned relocation process.[753] For each stage, there is specific guidance tailored towards government stakeholders and 'other stakeholders', which are defined as 'non-State actors'.[754] The clear designation of the roles attributed to State and non-State actors is a lesson learnt from the relocation of Vunidogoloa village.[755] The coordination amongst various stakeholders who contributed to the process in Vunidogoloa was heavily criticised, since problems such as the reduplication of the same task by different actors arose.[756] The Planned Relocation Guideline conditions the disclosure of a 'transparent participation plan' as early as possible in order to engage all stakeholders in a collaborated and efficient cooperation.[757]

750 ibid.

751 ibid 7.

752 ibid 9.

753 ibid 11–15.

754 ibid.

755 Dhrishna Charan, Manpreet Kaur and Priyatma Singh, 'Customary Land and Climate Change Induced Relocation – A Case Study of Vunidogoloa Village, Vanua Levu, Fiji' in Leal Filho (ed), *Climate Change Adaptation in Pacific Countries* (Springer 2017) 19–33.

756 Annah E. Piggott-McKellar and others, 'Moving People in a Changing Climate: Lessons from Two Case Studies in Fiji' [2019] 8 Social Sciences 5, 133.

757 Government of the Republic of Fiji (n 660) 13.

The Disaster Guideline was launched with the aim of providing complementary support to the existing Fijian legal and policy framework, especially the Planned Relocation Guideline.[758] Distinct from the Planned Relocation Guideline, it is not a State-led process and aims to 'reduce the vulnerabilities associated with displacement and consider durable solutions to prevent and minimise the drivers of displacement'.[759] Therefore, it outlines 'all preventive measures'[760]. With a view to protecting individuals and communities from and during displacement, and to provide durable solutions in the aftermath, the Displacement Guideline adopts five key principles: a human-centred approach, a human rights–based approach, a livelihood-based approach, a capacity building approach and equity approach. By admitting that its primary obligations to provide protection to the people at risk or affected by displacement, the Fijian government further designated the roles of stakeholders, and the rights of individuals, households and communities in line with international instruments.

So far, Fiji has identified 81 communities for potential relocation,[761] of which 42 have been recommended for relocation.[762]

The Planned Relocation Guideline states that when implementing a planned relocation process in Fiji, 'addressing human rights aspects is unavoidable in all three stages of movement'.[763] The same emphasis is present in the Displacement Guideline. Therefore, ensuring that the planned relocation is sustainable in all phases of movement is tied to the safeguards deriving from community-based rights and individual human rights. An analysis of the human rights situation in Fiji might indicate some of the problems that are currently emerging and could become an issue in the future.

The situation regarding the rule of law in Fiji represents an initial point of inquiry. With a history of four coups d'état since independence from colonial rule in 1970, Fiji is rated as a 'hybrid regime',[764] in which strict limitations on

---

758 Government of Fiji (n 732).

759 ibid 1.

760 ibid 4.

761 Government of the Republic of Fiji, 'Second National Communication to the United Nations Framework Convention on Climate Change' (2013) <https://unfccc.int/resource/docs/natc/fjinc2.pdf> accessed 6 April 2022.

762 Government of the Republic of Fiji, 'A Green Growth Framework of Fiji' (2014), <https://pafpnet.spc.int/pafpnet/attachments/article/475/GREEN%20GROWTH%20FRAMEWORK.PDF> accessed 6 April 2022.

763 Government of the Republic of Fiji (n 660).

764 This is according to the Democracy Index compiled by the Economist Intelligence Unit (EIU), which classifies 165 countries as one of the four classifications (i.e. full democracies, flawed democracies, hybrid regimes or authoritarian regimes), based on five

any legal challenges to the actions and decisions of the Fijian government allegedly exist.[765] Fiji's previous UPR Report, which was finalised in 2014, remained very critical of the law-making process, which was observed to take the form of decrees 'passed at short notice and without public debate or scrutiny'.[766] The Constitution of the Republic of Fiji (Constitution of Fiji) is stated to prevent any legal challenges against decrees, and as a result there is 'allegedly no legal method of challenging actions and decisions of the Government'.[767] Interference in the work of the judiciary by the Attorney General,[768] the lack of independence and credibility of law enforcement bodies, particularly with the militarisation of the police force,[769] and repressive policies towards the media[770] were further mentioned in the previous UPR report. The new UPR highlights ongoing incidents of torture and ill-treatment,[771] as well as the intensification of restrictions on freedom of expression, assembly and association.[772]

A critical reading of the Bill of Rights in Fiji, which is found in Sections 6 to 45, Chapter 2 of the Constitution, can inform the discussion.[773] The Fijian Bill of Rights binds 'the legislative, executive and judicial branches of government at all levels, and every person performing the functions of any public office'.[774] Relevant rights enshrined in the Constitution include: the right to education (Section 31), the right to economic participation (Section 32), the right to housing and sanitation (Section 35), the right to adequate food and water (Section 36), the right to health (Section 38), the right to a clean and

categories: electoral process and pluralism; civil liberties; the functioning of government; political participation and political culture. More information about Fiji's profile is available at <http://country.eiu.com/fiji> accessed 6 April 2022.

765 Summary prepared by the Office of the United Nations High Commissioner for Human Rights in accordance with paragraph 15(c) of the annex to Human Rights Council resolution 5/1 and paragraph 5 of the annex to Council resolution 16/21 Fiji, UN HRC, 20th sess, Working Group on the Universal Periodic Review, UN Doc A/HRC/WG.6/20/FJI/3 (18 July 2014, adopted 27 October-7 November 2014).

766 ibid 3.

767 ibid.

768 ibid 25.

769 ibid 28.

770 ibid 32.

771 Compilation on Fiji, Report of the Office of the United Nations High Commissioner for Human Rights, UN HRC, 24th sess, Working Group on the Universal Periodic Review, UN Doc A/HRC/WG.6/34/FJI/2 (22 August 2019, adopted 4–15 November 2019), para 35.

772 ibid.

773 Constitution of the Republic of Fiji (2013) <https://www.constituteproject.org/constitution/Fiji_2013.pdf?lang=en> accessed 6 April 2022, chapter 2.

774 ibid section 6(1).

healthy environment (Section 40), childrens' rights (Section 41) and the rights of people with disabilities (Section 42). However, these rights may be limited under states of emergency,[775] as well as according to the specific conditions stipulated in each respective section. The previous UPR report observed that the Bill of Rights is comprehensive but weak, due to severe limitations on many rights, including the 'claw-back clause' according to which the Fijian government would simply need to show that a limitation is 'reasonable'.[776] The new UPR report conveys similar worries, with recommendations to repeal the Bill of Rights on the grounds that it limits guaranteed rights.[777]

The freedom of movement and residence is protected under Section 21 of the Constitution of Fiji, which includes the right to move freely throughout Fiji and the right to leave Fiji.[778] According to Section 21(6)(f), this right can be restricted in order to regulate, control or prohibit 'the entry of persons on to land or property owned or occupied by others'.[779] This provision must be read in conjunction with rules on land and property ownership. Section 28 of the Constitution specifically addresses the ownership and protection of the iTaukei, Rotuman and Banaban customary lands, three indigenous communities of Fiji.[780] An important exception to the prohibition of the permanent alienation of such lands is State acquisition for 'a public purpose' under Section 27.[781] It is important to note that the State is required to revert to the customary owners 'if the land is no longer required by the State'.[782] Protection of freehold land ownership, as well as other rights and interests in land (such as leases), is stipulated under Section 29.

Customary land in Fiji corresponds to 87% of the overall land.[783] So far, the relocation in Fiji has largely taken place within the boundaries of the community's customary land.[784] How a community could permanently relocate outside of its own customary land into the customary land of another community

775 ibid section 43.
776 UNHRC (n 765) para 5.
777 Compilation on Fiji, Report of the Office of the United Nations High Commissioner for Human Rights, UN HRC, para 32.
778 Constitution of the Republic of Fiji (n 773), section 21(3).
779 ibid section 21(6)(f).
780 ibid section 38.
781 ibid section 38.
782 ibid sections 28(2), 28(4) and 28(6).
783 UNHRC (n 772) para 108.
784 Amanda Bertana, 'The role of power in community participation: Relocation as climate change adaptation in Fiji' [2020] 38 Environment and Planning: Politics and Space 5, 902-919.

is a question that might create a need to seek alternative solutions, such as the purchase of freehold estates.[785] Demarcation problems in relation to the customary lands of communities surface during the implementation of disaster risk reduction and climate adaptation projects, meaning that planned relocation might face similar difficulties.[786]

Furthermore, the planned relocation of Vunidogoloa village revealed serious problems with gender awareness.[787] For instance, the newly constructed homes had no separate space for women, not even a separate kitchen, which exposed women to the risk of invasion of their privacy and bodily integrity.[788] The National Gender Policy was released by the Ministry in 2014, which commits to, amongst other things, the promotion of gender-aware policies on climate change and disaster relief.[789] Yet, in its recent report, CEDAWCom provided recommendations to Fiji on a plurality of issues, including ensuring that women participate in the drafting of plans and strategies for disaster preparedness, as well as protecting rural women from land grabbing.[790]

4 Conclusion

This chapter presented a case study of the PIS, as a means of examining the regional responses to HMDCC given the absence of an international protection mechanism for PMDCC. The analysis has demonstrated that, as a region highly vulnerable to the effects of disasters and climate change, the PIS have been advocating for rigorous climate action at the international level. However, this call for action has not resulted in the creation of a regional approach to

785 Carol Farbotko and others, 'Relocation planning must address voluntary immobility' (Nature, 13 July 2020) <https://www.nature.com/articles/s41558-020-0829-6> accessed 6 April 2022.

786 Marilyn E. Lashley, 'Strange Bedfellows? Customary Systems of Communal Land Tenure and Indigenous Land Rights in New Zealand, Fiji, and Australia' [2011] 34 Pacific Studies 2.

787 Andreas Kopf, Michael Fink and Eberhard Weber, 'Gender Vulnerability to Climate Change and Natural Hazards: The Case of Tropical Cyclone Winston, Fiji' in Sara N. Amin, Danielle Watson, and Christian Girard, Mapping Security in the Pacific: A Focus on Context, Gender and Organisational Culture (Routledge 2020).

788 Amanda Rae Bertana, 'Environmentally induced migration in Fiji' (PhD thesis, University of Utah, May 2018) <https://www.proquest.com/docview/2306288585?pq-origsite=gscholar&fromopenview=true> accessed 6 April 2022.

789 Ministry for Social Welfare, Women and Poverty Alleviation, 'Fiji National Gender Policy' (2014), section 5.15(1).

790 UN CEDAW, Concluding observations on the fifth periodic report of Fiji, paras 49(g) and 50(e).

HMDCC. In fact, citizens of the PIS benefit from different inter- and intra-regional pathways for migration.

Recently, with the adoption of PACER Plus, a more visible step in the direction of discussing a regional approach to human mobility was taken. Although PACER Plus includes a chapter on the movement of natural persons, and a separate arrangement on labour mobility, the current commitments of States Parties do not liberate market access or come closer to creating free movement in the region. Perhaps with the establishment of a Labour Mobility Secretariat in the PACER Plus implementation unit, as well as through PLMAM, new commitments can be made in the near future.

Noting the lack of a regional response to addressing HMDCC, this chapter concluded by examining domestic approaches. The notion of planned relocation as a protection tool was discussed by examining its specific uses in Vanuatu and Fiji. Analyses have shown that planned relocation can prevent future harm by moving people out of harm's way. However, it must be used as a measure of last resort, and a human rights–based approach must be embedded throughout all stages of planned relocation. A failure to do so might result in long-term ramifications for individual and collective civil, political, economic and cultural rights.

As planned relocation finds expressions in national frameworks, it is gradually acquiring a sufficient foundation to become eligible for funding from donors as an adaptation strategy in relation to climate change. Fiji's recently launched climate change relocation fund is a case in point.[791] This provides further evidence for alternative domestic solutions to protecting PMDCC, in the absence of an international or regional response.

791 See World's First-Ever Relocation Trust Fund for People Displaced by Climate Change for People Displaced by Climate Change Launched by Fijian Prime Minister, <https://www.fiji.gov.fj/Media-Centre/News/WORLD%E2%80%99S-FIRST-%E2%80%93EVER-RELOCATION-TRUST-FUND-FOR-PEOP> accessed 6 April 2022. To read the Act of Parliament, see Government of Fiji, Climate Relocation of Communities Trust Fund Act 2019, <https://laws.gov.fj/Acts/DisplayAct/2562> accessed 6 April 2022.

CHAPTER 4

The International Protection of Persons Mobile in the Context of Disasters and Climate Change as a Community Interest

This chapter develops the argument that the international protection of PMDCC can be framed as a community interest and gives rise to an obligation *erga omnes*.[792] Obligations *erga omnes* exist for a State towards the international community.[793] Generally, this means that all other States are entitled to claim that the obligation should be complied with in any given circumstances.[794] This concept did not spring into existence overnight, but has a long trajectory of development.[795] Essentially, the theory of community interests provides for its legal rationale.[796] Thus, the starting point for discussing the international protection of PMDCC as an obligation *erga omnes* is the examination of the theory of community interests in international law. After laying down the necessary theoretical foundations, this chapter applies them to demonstrate how the international protection of PMDCC as an obligation *erga omnes* can affect the modalities of enforcing international law. In particular, in order to enforce this obligation, it proposes pathways that make use of the existing procedural aspects of international law and the follow-up and review mechanisms of the Global Compact on Refugees and the Global Compact for Migration. The chapter concludes with a critical evaluation of this approach and whether it can succeed in filling the legal gap and address the institutional shortcomings in order to provide adequate international protection for PMDCC.

792 'Community interests' and 'common interests' are used interchangeably throughout this book.

793 *Case Concerning the Barcelona Traction, Light and Power Company, Limited (Belgium v France)* [1970] ICJ, para 33 and 34.

794 Giorgio Gaja, *The Protection of General Interests in the International Community* (364 Recueil des cours de l'Académie de Droit International, Leiden:Nijhoff 2011) 97.

795 As Lord Devlin once said, 'new categories in the law do not spring into existence overnight'. See *Hedley Byrne & Co. Ltd. v. Heller & Partners Ltd.* [1964] A.C. 465, 525, per Lord Devlin.

796 Isabel Feichtner, 'Community Interest' (Max Planck Encyclopedia 2007) <https://opil.ouplaw.com/view/10.1093/law:epil/9780199231690/law-9780199231690-e1677?prd=EPIL> accessed 6 April 2022.

1 The Theory of Community Interests in International Law

The notion of community interests does not have a settled or uniform definition in international law. Generally, it refers to instances in international law in which States transcend the reciprocal exchange of benefits and go beyond the delimitation of sovereign spheres of influence.[797] Community interests can generally be attributed to multilateral rights and obligations, established and protected in the interest of 'the international community as a whole'.[798] Despite their elusive nature, community interests seem to be reflected in legal concepts, such as obligations *erga omnes*.[799] This section begins by discussing the origins and content of the notion of community interests, before undertaking a closer examination of one of its legal effects, namely obligations *erga omnes*.

1.1 *Revival and Content*

From the very beginning of modern public law, the idea that the international legal order recognises a global society and nurtures community-wide obligations was discussed.[800] Unfortunately, during the nineteenth century, this idea was overthrown by the Westphalian approach to international law, which conceived of it as essentially based on more or less specific inter-State consent.[801] In 1945, the UN Charter laid the foundations for a paradigm shift by

---

797 ibid.

798 James Crawford, *Multilateral Rights and Obligations in International Law* (319 Recueil des cours de l'Académie de Droit International, Leiden: Nijhoff 2006).

799 Others include obligations *jus cogens*. See Christian J. Tams and Alessandra Asteriti, 'Erga Omnes, Jus Cogens and Their Impact on the Law of State Responsibility' in Malcolm D. Evans and Panos Koutrakos (eds), *The International Responsibility of the European Union* (Cambridge University Press 2013).

800 For instance, Wolfrum observes that M. Tullius Cicero and Hugo Grotius qualified pirates as *hostes gentium*, which represents one of the earliest examples of a community interest. See Rüdiger Wolfrum, 'Identifying Community Interests in International Law: Common Spaces and Beyond' in Eyal Benvenisti, Georg Nolte and Keren Yalin-mor (eds), *Community Interests across International Law* (Oxford University Press 2018) 19.

801 It is important to note that there were international judges who put forward different views. For instance, Judge Jessup had stated that '[i]nternational law has long recognised that States may have legal interests in matters which do not affect their financial, economic, or other "material", or, say, "physical" or "tangible" interests'. In specific situations 'State [therefore have] a legal interest in the general observance of the rules of international law'. ICJ Reports 1962, 425. Mentioned in Christian Tams, *Enforcing Obligations Erga Omnes in International Law* (Cambridge University Press 2004) 51. Also see The SS 'Wimbledon', *United Kingdom and ors v Germany*, Judgment, (1923) PCIJ Series A no 1, ICGJ 235 (PCIJ 1923), 17th August 1923, League of Nations.

proclaiming the promotion of universal respect for, and observance of, human rights and fundamental freedoms for all.[802] This section examines the revival of community interests in the twentieth century, with a particular focus on the doctrinal discussion.

Simma undertook one of the earliest systematic analyses of community interests in 1994.[803] He examined the works of a range of scholars, judges and other actors, who 'succeeded in building up a feeling of worldwide "togetherness" which cares little about legal niceties and the sovereignty-sensitivities of Governments'.[804] His main assertion was that the traditional structures and processes of international law were based upon a 'bilateralist grounding', which had 'legal and moral deficiencies', and that the notion of community interests was being developed in order to 'mature' international law into 'a much more socially conscious legal order'.[805]

He interpreted bilateralism in the sense of an 'every-man-for-himself' doctrine.[806] This meant that bilateralism 'ran' international legal obligations, responsibilities and enforcement between States, and that it was up to each State to protect its own rights or to renounce claims to its rights.[807] Third States or non-State actors had no possibility to intervene and invoke responsibility.[808] Borrowing from Weil, Simma observed that the legal and moral deficiencies of this system were that:

> [it] left it to Governments to will and act internationally in ways that they would be morally restrained from willing and acting internally,

802 However, it must be noted that it is unclear whether the founders intended to profoundly change the parameters of traditional international law. See Karl Zemanek, 'New Trends in the Enforcement of Erga Omnes Obligations' [2000] Max Planck Yearbook of United Nations Law.

803 Bruno Simma dedicated his general course at The Hague Academy of International Law to the topic 'From Bilateralism to Community Interests in International Law'. His scholarly work has been a source of inspiration. During his career, he served as an ICJ judge, as well as a member of the UN ILC and ECOSOC. See Bruno Simma, *From Bilateralism to Community Interest in International Law* (250 Recueil des cours de l'Académie de Droit International, Leiden: Nijhoff 1994).

804 ibid para 6.

805 ibid.

806 Simma mentions Prosper Weil's conception of relative normativity of international law, which provides an instance of every-man-for-himself doctrine. See Prosper Weil, 'Towards Relative Normativity in International Law?' [1983] American Journal of International Law 77.

807 Simma (n 803) para 2.

808 ibid.

> murdering human beings in the million in war, tolerating oppression and starvation and disease and poverty, human cruelty and suffering, human misery and human indignity, of kinds, and on a scale, that they could not tolerate within their internal societies.[809]

The 'antithesis' of bilateralism was the 'assertion of community interests in the development of international law in a different direction, as it were'.[810] Simma provided a tentative definition of community interests, which 'perceive[d] it as a consensus according to which respect for certain fundamental values is not to be left to the free disposition of States or *inter se* but is recognised and sanctioned by international law as a matter of concern to all States'.[811] He explained and exemplified this definition through a rigorous analysis of the posited legal norms (and, where applicable, judicial interpretations of such norms) about international peace and security, solidarity between developed and developing countries, the protection of the environment, the concept of the common heritage of humankind and the international concern with human rights.[812] As these instances showed, the existence of community interests does not derive from scientific abstraction, but rather flows from the recognition of concrete problems.[813]

Simma approached the self-interests of States as something different from community interests.[814] Although certain issues, such as the protection of the environment, might show an overlap, others were 'far detached from individual State interests', such as, in his opinion, the universal protection of human

809 ibid para 5.
810 ibid.
811 ibid para 6.
812 ibid.
813 ibid.
814 Although Besson supported the claim that States are not inherently self-interested, and observed that bilateral and multilateral treaties between States often protect community interests. According to her, a properly understood approach to State consent and sovereignty can actually contribute to the legitimate identification and protection of community interests, and effectively promote community interests domestically and abroad. She approached State consent as a democratic condition/exception to the legitimacy of international law, and reinforced a democratic institutional design that can translate domestic community interests to the global level. Similarly, State sovereignty reflects legitimate spheres of political self-determination about community interests, even more so when these States are democratic, according to Besson. See Samantha Besson, 'Community Interests in International Law: Whose Interests Are They and How Should We Best Identify Them?' in Eyal Benvenisti, Georg Nolte and Keren Yalin-mor (eds), *Community Interests across International Law* (Oxford University Press 2018) 47–49.

rights.[815] Hence, he defined the international community as 'a community that comprises not only States, but in the last instance all human beings' and the interests of the international community may differ from those of States.[816]

Examining the relationship between State consent and community interests, he termed State discretion to participate in certain global challenges as a 'recipe for global suicide'.[817] This situation was exacerbated, in his opinion, by the possibility that, even if States decided to participate in multilateral treaties addressing global challenges, such treaties might incorporate withdrawal clauses.[818] In this case, the treaty in question could be reminiscent of 'a marriage contract with a protocol for divorce'.[819]

This discussion concerning the notion of community interests inspired the theory and practice of international law.[820] In 1997, Weeramantry expressed the view – in his separate opinion to the *Gabcikovo-Nagymaros* decision – that 'we have entered an era' in which international law 'subserves not only the interests of individual States, but looks beyond them and their parochial concerns to the greater interests of humanity and planetary welfare'.[821]

Attempting to identify such greater interests, Trindade proposed that a new *jus gentium*, i.e. an international law for humankind, was emerging.[822] He argued that the 'growing consciousness of the need to bear in mind common values in pursuance of common interests has brought about a fundamental change in the outlook of international law in the last decade'.[823]

Feichtner proposed a novel conceptualisation of community interests by drawing a distinction between the objectives of community interests, on the one hand, and community interest norms, on the other.[824] According to her

---

815 Simma (n 803) para 12.

816 ibid para 6.

817 ibid para 88.

818 ibid.

819 Simma quoted after A. Chayes, T. Ehrlich and A. F. Lowenfeld, *International Legal Process. Materials for an Introductory Course* (Boston, Little, Brown and Company, Vol. II, 1969) 999.

820 For instance, see Ulrich Fastenrath and others, *From Bilateralism to Community Interest: Essays in Honour of Bruno Simma* (Oxford University Press 2011).

821 *Case Concerning Gabcikovo-Nagymaros Project (Hungary/Slovakia)* Judgment [1997] ICJ Rep. 7, Separate opinion of Vice-President Weeramantry.

822 His first book was based on the General Course on Public International Law which he delivered at the Hague Academy of International Law. He published the first version of his study of the corpus juris in 2005, which he revised in the new editions in 2010, 2013 and 2020. See Cançado Trindade (n 19).

823 ibid.

824 Feichtner (n 796).

typology, community interests have four distinguishable objectives: the protection and creation of common goods; the protection of common values; the internationalisation of common spaces; and redistributive and intergenerational justice.[825] Community interest norms, on the other hand, are specific sub-set of rules of international law that protect and pursue the objectives of community interests.[826]

Expounding on her categories, the examples she provided for common goods[827] include world peace and security,[828] the earth's atmosphere[829] and climate,[830] and common markets created under regional trade agreements.[831] Common values include special treaty regimes that aim to protect (e.g. refugees,[832] human rights[833] and biological diversity[834]) or to combat (e.g. desertification,[835] disaster risk[836] and the proliferation of nuclear weapons[837]) in relation to a matter of international concern. The internationalisation of common spaces generally refers to the extinguishing of all national claims and the establishment of a more universal regime of administration for spaces, such as outer space,[838] the deep

825 ibid.

826 ibid. Also see Christian J Tams, 'Individual States as Guardians of Community Interests' in Ulrich Fastenrath and others, *From Bilateralism to Community Interest: Essays in Honour of Bruno Simma* (Oxford University Press 2011) 380; Besson (n 814).

827 For an interesting discussion on the origins and definition of common goods, see Joshua Paine, 'International Adjudication as a Global Public Good?' [2019] EJIL.

828 Charter of the United Nations (adopted 24 October 1945) 1 UNTS XVI.

829 For instance, see Montreal Protocol on Substances that Deplete the Ozone Layer (adopted 26 August 187, entered into force 26 August 1989).

830 UNFCCC (n 248).

831 Some examples include the European Union, the European Economic Area, the Caribbean Community, the African Union, and the South Common Market (MERCOSUR). For an interesting discussion on why countries form regional trade agreements, see Teresa L. Cyrus, 'Why Do Countries Form Regional Trade Agreements? A Discrete-Time Survival Analysis' [2020] Open Economies Review.

832 Refugee Convention (n 70); Global Compact on Refugees (n 9).

833 For instance, UDHR (n 397).

834 Convention on Biological Diversity (adopted 5 June 1992, entered into force 29 December 1993) 1760 UNTS 69 (CBD).

835 UNCCD (n 250).

836 Sendai Framework (n 496).

837 Treaty on the Non-Proliferation of Nuclear Weapons (adopted 1 July 1968, entered into force 5 March 1970) 729 UNTS 161; Treaty on the Prohibition of Nuclear Weapons (adopted 7 July 2017, entered into force 26 October 2020) 729 UNTS 168.

838 Treaty on Principles Governing Activities of States in the Exploration and Use of Outer Space, Including the Moon and Other Celestial Bodies (adopted 27 January 1967, entered into force 10 October 1967) 610 UNTS 205.

seabed,[839] the high seas[840] and, to some extent, Antarctica.[841] Finally, Feichtner argued that the objective of redistributive and intergenerational justice bloomed, particularly as a result of the demands of the New International Economic Order.[842] Community interest norms, such as CBDR, financial assistance, economic assistance, technology transfer, technical assistance and sustainable development can be supported on the grounds of redistributive and intergenerational justice, according to Feichtner.[843]

With the aim of discussing the protection of general interests in the international community, Gaja examined several treaty regimes, as well as principles and rules of general international law.[844] He concluded that there is 'clearly scope for expanding the category of general interests that international law protects'.[845] The major concern, however, is political in nature, according to Gaja.[846] In practice, States and international organisations 'do not act adequately' for the purpose of protecting general interests in the international community, and thus, Gaja concluded that, 'only the pressure of public opinion and of some non-governmental organisations may succeed in prompting certain States, even when no specific interest of their own is at stake, to respond to violations by other States of obligations towards the international community'.[847]

Benedek, de Feyter, Kettemann and Voigt investigated common interests in international law and discussed 'how international law and human rights in particular, is progressively moving away from a system based on territorial sovereignty to a system based on shared responsibilities among States and other

839 United Nations Convention on the Law of the Sea (adopted 10 December 1982, entered into force 16 November 1994) 1833 UNTS 396.

840 ibid.

841 The Antarctic Treaty 'froze' territorial claims in Antarctica, therefore some interpret the treaty as establishing a *res communis omnium*. See Wolfrum (n 800). For an interesting discussion on territorial claims in Antarctica and the drafting history of the Antarctic Treaty, see Shirley V. Scott, 'Ingenious and innocuous? Article IV of the Antarctic Treaty as imperialism' [2011] The Polar Journal.

842 See Nils Gilman, 'The New International Economic Order: A Reintroduction' [2015] 6 Humanity (Philadelphia, Pa.) 1.

843 Feichtner (n 796).

844 Gaja's book was based on his general course lecture at The Hague Academy of International Law in 2011. See Gaja (n 794) 1.

845 ibid 182.

846 ibid.

847 ibid 182.

actors'.[848] They put forward three different approaches to the designation of common interests.[849] One option is to ground common interests in common values, thus perceiving international law as a legal system underpinned by strong moral values.[850] Another option is to take 'the measure of support' as a criterion and to search for 'a communal legal spirit', i.e. the *opinio iuris communis*, which can include soft law instruments, as well as the positions taken at international fora by a plethora of actors, even if these actors are not recognised as international legal persons.[851] The final option is to view common interests as those interests that can only be safeguarded through common action.[852] These are the interests that must be protected in the interest of humanity as a whole, through an international agreement that pays attention to the sharing of burdens and benefits, in light of the capabilities and capacities of States.[853]

Building on this literature, Benvenisti and Nolte proposed a conceptual framework for undertaking a legal enquiry framed in terms of the notion of community interests.[854] According to them, this is an exercise exploring 'the extent to which contemporary international law expects States, when forming and implementing their policies, negotiating agreements, and in general conducting their relations with other States, to take into account the interests of others, namely third States or their citizens'.[855] This approach embraces all sources of international law, including treaties, customary international law, general principles of law and, additionally, soft law instruments, as indicators of such a duty to take into account.[856]

---

848 The authors used the phrase 'common interests', however, in this book, common interests and community interests are used interchangeably. Wolfgang Benedek and others (eds), *The Common Interest in International Law* (Intersentia 2014).

849 Wolfgang Benedek, Koen de Feyter, Matthias C. Kettemann and Christina Voigt, 'The Common Interest in International Law – Perspectives for an Undervalued Concept' in Wolfgang Benedek and others (eds), *The Common Interest in International Law* (Intersentia 2014).

850 ibid 219.

851 ibid.

852 ibid.

853 As an example, the authors comment that 'although free migration can only be safeguarded through common action, it has not so far been recognised as a global common interest'. ibid 220.

854 Benvenisti and Nolte (n 20) 3.

855 ibid.

856 Rudiger Wolfrum, *Solidarity and Community Interests: Driving Forces for the Interpretation and Development of International Law* (General Course at the Hague Academy of International Law 2020).

Furthermore, according to Benvenisti and Nolte, multilateral and international courts and tribunals, as well as charter-based and treaty-based human rights bodies[857] have a significant role to play in the construction of community interests.[858] Through treaty interpretation techniques, such as systemic interpretation, and, more rarely, through the identification of customary international law and general principles of law, these actors can contribute to the identification and protection of community interests.[859] Although this is not 'utopian', the rules of procedure, such as standing and jurisdiction, as well as the mandate of the actors rendering decisions determine how far their role can go.[860] The increasing role played by non-State actors and the multilateral and international adjudication process provides insight into the 'rising world of other actors', which in some clear instances demonstrate a push toward 'more and thicker' community interests.[861]

To conclude, the notion of community interests devotes attention to the general interests of humanity and planetary welfare, transcending the interests

---

857 An example of a charter-based body is the UNHRC. These bodies derive their establishment from the provisions of the UN Charter. Treaty-based bodies, on the other hand, derive their existence from provisions contained in a specific legal instrument. For instance, the UNHRCom was established to monitor the implementation of the ICCPR and its optional protocols. For more information, see UN, 'UN Documentation: Human Rights' official webpage (2020) <https://research.un.org/en/docs/humanrights/charter> accessed 6 April 2022.

858 Benvenisti and Nolte refer to the chapter written by Klabbers in his contribution to the edited volume. In his chapter, Klabbers argues that IOs can promote, and even embody community interests, through at least three ways: merely by existing and serving as a platform for the formulation of that interest; developing ideas and consensus by way of adopting documents to maintain and enhance the community interest; and rarely, through the coercion of States. See Jan Klabbers, 'What Role for International Organizations in the Promotion of Community Interests? Reflections on the Ideology of Functionalism' in Eyal Benvenisti, Georg Nolte and Keren Yalin-mor (eds), *Community Interests across International Law* (Oxford University Press 2018) 86–92.

859 Besson (n 814).

860 Politics of the day have impacts on the work of dispute settlement bodies. A recent example is the 'break down' of the 25-year-old Appellate Body of the WTO on 10 December 2019, when new members could not appointed and too few arbiters were left to rule. See WTO, 'Farewell speech of Appellate Body Member Peter van den Bossche' (28 May 2019) <https://www.wto.org/english/tratop_e/dispu_e/farwellspeech_peter_van_den_bossche_e.htm> accessed 6 April 2022; Chad P. Bown and Soumaya Keynes, 'Why Trump Shot the Sheriffs: The End of WTO Dispute Settlement 1.0' [2020] Peterson Institute for International Economics Working Paper No. 20–4.

861 Georg Nolte, 'The International Law Commission and Community Interests' in Eyal Benvenisti, Georg Nolte and Keren Yalin-mor (eds), *Community Interests across International Law* (Oxford University Press 2018) 117.

of a single State. Although the objectives and norms of community interests may be alluded to, it may be less easy to define community interests a priori, and a better approach may be to formulate community interests in the process of exploring concrete problems.[862] As international law has no central law-making authority that could legislate in the community interest, the actors that take part in the construction of community interests are generally understood to include States and non-State actors, as well as the international and multilateral adjudication processes. Similarly, the protection of community interests foresees the participation of State and non-State actors, including, for instance, non-governmental organisations, which can induce pressure from public opinion to prompt States to act. This reinforces the idea that the principal duty bearers for the protection of community interests may be identified as States.[863]

1.2 *Legal Effects: Obligations Erga Omnes as a Reflection of Community Interests*

Two expectations flow from the identification of community interests.[864] First, it would be expected that a community interest norm would be created, which posits a specific rule that protects and pursues the objectives of community interests.[865] Second, it would be expected that an institutional structure providing for the promotion, as well as the protection, of this specific community interest norm would be established.[866] However, in order to address situations of institutional shortcomings, general international law developed several concepts and mechanisms 'as a sort of compensation'.[867] The concept of obligations *erga omnes* is a widely acknowledged example, which has 'raised high hopes' in relation to the protection of fundamental interests shared by the 'international community as a whole'.[868] Simply put, the concept of *erga omnes* facilitates the integration of community interests into international

862 Besson (n 814).

863 It must be noted that the responsibility of IOs have been codified by the UN ILC in its draft articles on the responsibility of international organisations (ARIO). According to Art 43 of ARIO, IOs have standing to invoke obligations *erga omnes*. ILC, 'Draft articles on the Responsibility of International Organisations' (2011) (ARIO), art 43.

864 Simma (n 790) para 89.

865 ibid. Also see S Villalpado, 'The Legal Dimension of the International Community: How Community Interests are Protected in International Law' [2010] 21 EJIL 2, 387–419.

866 Simma (n 790) para 89.

867 ibid para 45.

868 See Tams (n 801) preface xv.

law.[869] This section begins by analysing the *obiter dictum* in the ICJ's *Barcelona Traction* case, where obligations *erga omnes* prominently appeared.[870] Then, it distinguishes between different types of *erga omnes* effects in international law and international relations.[871] Finally, it concludes with an examination of the enforcement of obligations *erga omnes*.

Paragraphs 33 and 34 of the *Barcelona Traction* case represent one of the most famous judicial pronouncements in the ICJ's history.[872] This 'stray dictum'[873] referred to obligations *erga omnes* and deserves to be quoted in full:

> 33. When a State admits into its territory foreign investments or foreign nationals, whether natural or juristic persons, it is bound to extend to them the protection of the law and assumes obligations concerning the treatment to be afforded them. These obligations, however, are neither absolute nor unqualified. In particular, an essential distinction should be drawn between the obligations of a State towards the international community as a whole, and those arising vis-à-vis another State in the field of diplomatic protection. By their very nature the former are the concern of all States. In view of the importance of the rights involved, all States can be held to have a legal interest in their protection; they are obligations *erga omnes*.
>
> 34. Such obligations derive, for example, in contemporary international law, from the outlawing of acts of aggression, and of genocide, as also from the principles and rules concerning the basic rights of the human person, including protection from slavery and racial discrimination. Some of the corresponding rights of protection have entered into the body of general international law (*Reservations to the Convention on the Prevention and Punishment of the Crime of Genocide, Advisory Opinion, I.C.J. Reports 1951, p. 23*); others are conferred by international instruments of a universal or quasi-universal character.[874]

---

869 Craig Eggett and Sarah Thin, 'Clarification and Conflation: Obligations Erga Omnes in the Chagos Opinion) (21 May 2019, EJIL:Talk!) <https://www.ejiltalk.org/clarification-and-conflation-obligations-erga-omnes-in-the-chagos-opinion/> accessed 6 April 2022.

870 *Case Concerning the Barcelona Traction* (n 793).

871 Tams (n 801) 101.

872 *Case Concerning the Barcelona Traction* (n 793).

873 James Crawford, 'Foreword' in Tams (n 801) xiii-xiv.

874 It should be noted that the authoritative language in the *Barcelona Traction* case is French.

The starting assertion of the ICJ is that there is an 'essential distinction' between the obligations of a State towards the international community as a whole, and the obligations of a State vis-à-vis another State in the field of diplomatic protection.[875] Obligations of the latter kind are owed to one State in particular, whereas obligations in the former sense – even though the Court did not elaborate upon the legal basis for their existence – are owed to the 'international community as a whole'.[876]

Defining the 'international community as a whole' has proven to be problematic, not least because interpreting it as a collective entity, rather than individual States, would mean that the 'party' to which the obligation is owed lacks a capacity to act.[877] The ILC's approach to this conundrum was to address a variety of primary obligations, which 'may be owed to another State, to several States, or to the international community as a whole'.[878] However, the ILC deferred the debate about the identification of such primary obligations.[879]

The ICJ further explained that there is a 'legal interest' in the protection of the rights involved in obligations *erga omnes*. The designation of the interest as 'legal' may be interpreted as providing the ground to invoke the legal responsibility of a State for the breach of an obligation *erga omnes*.[880] This was articulated by the ILC by drawing a distinction between an 'injured State' and 'any State other than an injured State', while permitting both categories to 'protect the community or collective interest at stake'.[881]

875 See Rosalyn Higgins, 'Aspects of the Case Concerning the Barcelona Traction, Light and Power Company, Ltd'. [1970] 11 Virginia Journal of International Law, 327–343.

876 Erika de Wet, 'Invoking Obligations Erga Omnes in the Twenty-First Century: Progressive Developments Since Barcelone Traction' [2013]37 SAYIL, 1–20.; Erika de Wet, 'Jus Cogens and Obligations Erga Omnes' in Dinah Shelton (ed), *The Oxford Handbook on Human Rights* (OUP 2013).

877 James Crawford, *Chance, Order, Change: The Course of International Law* (2014) 365 Recueil des Cours de l'Académie de Droit International, 340; Weil (n 806) 432.

878 ILC codified and progressively developed the law on a State's right to invoke the responsibility of a breaching State in ARSIWA. See ILC, 'Articles on the Responsibility of States' (2001) UN Doc A/56/49(Vol.1)/Corr.4, art 33(1) (ARSIWA).

879 Robert Rosenstock, 'The ILC and State Responsibility Symposium: The ILC's Responsibility Articles' [2002] 96 AJIL 4, 792; James Crawford, 'The ILC's Articles on Responsibility of States for Internationally Wrongful Acts: A Retrospect' [2002] 96 AJIL 4, 874–980.

880 Tams (n 801) 95.

881 Under Article 42 of the ARSIWA, an 'injured State', either individually, or as a part of a group of States or the international community as a whole, is entitled to invoke the responsibility of the breaching State. Under Article 48 of the ARSIWA, 'any State other than an injured Stated' is entitled to invoke the responsibility of a breaching State if, (i) the obligation beached is owed to a group of States including that State, and is established for the protection of a collective interest of the group; or (ii) the obligation breached is owed to the international community as whole. See ARSIWA (n 878) arts 42 and 48.

As for the identification of obligations *erga omnes*, the ICJ indicated, rather elusively, that 'by their very nature' and 'in view of the importance of the rights involved', these obligations are the 'concern of all States'.[882] In other words, obligations acquire the status of *erga omnes* because of their 'heightened importance'.[883] In the author's view, that heightened importance does not depend on functional criteria (such as the effect of the breach or whether that right is actually protected under a treaty).[884] As for the required threshold of importance, the ICJ does not provide a clear test. Presumably, the non-exhaustive list of examples of obligations *erga omnes* given by the Court pass this threshold.[885] These examples are: the outlawing of acts of aggression, the outlawing of genocide and obligations deriving from 'the principles and rules concerning the basic rights of the human person' (such as the protection from slavery, and the protection from racial discrimination).[886] In the *Chagos* Advisory Opinion, the obligation *erga omnes* to respect the right to self-determination has also been clearly articulated.[887]

---

882 Stemming from this, Tanaka argues, for instance, that there is a two-tier test to the identification of obligations *erga omnes*: the non-reciprocal nature of the obligations, and the common interests of the international community as a whole. See Yoshumi Tanaka, 'Legal Consequences of Obligations *Erga Omnes* in International Law' [2021] Netherlands International Law Review.

883 Some commentators specify the 'non-reciprocal' or 'non-bilateralisable' character of obligations *erga omnes*, which, in the author's view, is contrary to the jurisprudence that highlights the importance of safeguarding the essential values of the international community. See François Voeffray, *L'actio popularis ou la défense collectif devant des juridictions internationals* (Paris Presses Universitaires de France 2004) 243; Gaetano Arangio Ruiz, 'Fourth Rerport on State Responsibility', Yearbook of International Law Commission 1992 Vol II, 34 para 92.

884 This can be contrasted with Okowa, who argues that the seriousness of breaches would be relevant, and Oellers-Frahm, who states that only gross violations on a widespread scale clearly qualify as *erga omnes* breaches. See Phoebe Okowa, State Responsibility for Transboundary Air Pollution in International Law (Oxford University Press 2000) 215–216; Karin Oellers-Frahm, 'Third States and Sanctions in Public International Law' [1992] 30 Archiv des Völkerrechts 1, 35. Also see Tams (n 801) 137.

885 See, in general, Maurizio Ragazzi, *Concept of International Obligations Erga Omnes* (Oxford University Press 2000).

886 ibid.

887 Previously, it has been used as 'rights erga omnes' of peoples to self-determination in East Timor. The Chagos Advisory Opinion clarified the term as an 'obligation erga omnes'. See *Legal Consequences of the Separation of the Chagos Archipelago from Mauritius* (Advisory Opinion) [2019] ICJ 169; Besfort T Rrecaj, 'Case Notes: Legal Consequences of The Separation of the Chagos Archipelago from Mauritius in 1965' 35 Utrecht Journal of International and European Law 1, 50–55; Eggett and Thin (n 869).

The appearance of the concept of obligations *erga omnes* in the obiter dictum of the *Barcelona Traction* case gave rise to a lively debate. Comments have ranged from disqualifying it as an 'isolated dictum' to welcoming it as a paradigm shift towards a value-oriented constitutional order.[888] Pragmatic approaches present a more balanced view: the ICJ drew on a variety of antecedents to move beyond treaty law, laying the basis for 'a more systematic approach' to the protection of the fundamental general interests of the international community.[889] It must be noted, however, that the 'more systematic approach' being offered is not devoid of 'teething problems'.[890]

The first problem with respect to the concept of *erga omnes* is that its different types of effects create confusion.[891] In the *Barcelona Traction* case, the ICJ only dealt with one type of *erga omnes* effect: the right of standing to invoke obligations *erga omnes*.[892] Previously, the concept *erga omnes* was used to refer to modifications of the scope (*ratione personae*) of a primary rule of international law, thereby broadening the circle of States bound by the rule.[893] Shortly after its pronouncement in the *Barcelona Traction* case, the Court brought back this 'traditional' usage of the concept of *erga omnes*, thus acknowledging its effects beyond the secondary rules governing the invocation of responsibility.[894]

888 For instance, Judge de Castro stated that the dictum in the Barcelona Traction should be taken 'cum grano salis'. See *Nuclear Tests, New Zealand v France* [1974] ICJ Rep 457 (Judge de Castro, Dissenting Opinion). Also see *Nuclear Tests, New Zealand v France* [1974] ICJ Rep 457 (Judge Onyeama, Dissenting Opinion), (Judge Dillard, Dissenting Opinion), (Judge Jimenez de Arechaa, Dissenting Opinion).

889 Ragazzi, for instance, stated that: '[F]or a long time before the International Court's dictum in the Barcelona Traction case, efforts had been made to regulate by treaty the common interests of States in such a way that rights and obligations might potentially be valid erga omnes, or at least for a wider circle of States than the parties to the treaty in question'. See Ragazzi (n 885).

890 Tams (n 801) 54.

891 ibid.

892 ibid.

893 The ICJ itself mentioned in its *South West Africa* judgment in 1966 that a court decision could bring about a 'general judicial settlement', with an 'effect *erga omnes*'. See *South West Africa, Ethiopia v South Africa* [1961] ICJ Rep 319, [70]. Another example is Waldock's proposal for the inclusion of the concept of 'objective regimes' in ARSIWA, which would lead to obligations and rights valid *erga omnes*. See ILC, Yearbook 1966, Vol II 231, para 4. For a discussion of the ILC members on this topic, see ILC Yearbook 1964, Vol. I., 83, paras 29–33. An earlier example is found in the *Island of Palmas* arbitration decision, in which Max Huber observed that the title to territory 'is valid *erga omnes*'. Island of Palmas (or Miangas), United States v Netherlands (Award) [1928] II RIAA 829.

894 See *The Legal Consequences for States of the Continued Presence of South Africa in Namibia* (Advisory Opinion) [1971] ICJ; *Nuclear Tests, New Zealand v France* (n 888) (Judge Bedjaoui).

A new facet was possibly added in the *Genocide* case, in which, after recognising the 'rights and obligations enshrined by the [Genocide] Convention are rights and obligations *erga omnes*', the Court ruled that 'the obligation each State thus has to prevent and to punish the crime of genocide is not territorially limited by the Convention'.[895] In this instance, instead of modifying the scope of a primary rule, or the right of standing according to secondary rules, the Court modified the content of the obligation in question: an *erga omnes* obligation could not be territorially restricted.[896]

Another problem of the concept of *erga omnes* is with respect to its enforcement.[897] Two main means of enforcing obligations *erga omnes* have received particular attention: international adjudication and countermeasures.[898] There are serious limitations to the enforcement of obligations *erga omnes* through an international court or tribunal.[899] For instance, obligations *erga omnes* do not affect procedural rules regarding jurisdiction.[900] With respect to

895 *Case Concerning Application of the Convention on the Prevention and Punishment of the Crime of Genocide* (*Croatia v. Serbia*) [1996] ICJ Rep 616.

896 Tams refers to this as modifying the 'depth' of the primary rule. See Tams (n 801) 111–112.

897 For instance, in the Advisory Opinion on Reservations to the Convention on the Prevention and Punishment of the Crime of Genocide, the ICJ stated that: 'In such a convention the contracting States do not have an interest of their own; they merely have, one and all, a common interest, namely the accomplishment of those high purposes which are the raison d'être of the convention. Consequently, in a convention of this type, one cannot speak of individual advantages or disadvantages to States, or of the maintenance of a perfect contractual balance between the rights and duties'. This pronouncement has been found confusing, and it is generally interpreted to mean that individual contracting States have the right to request the fulfilment of the commitments of other contracting States. See Antoni Pigrau, 'Reflections on the effectiveness of peremptory norms and erga omnesobligations before international tribunals, regarding the request for an advisory opinion from the International Court of Justice on the Chagos Islands' [2018] QIL Zoom-out 55, 131–146; Jan Wouters and Sten Verhoeven, 'The Prohibition of Genocide as a Norm of Ius Cogens and Its Implications for the Enforcement of the Law of Genocide' [2005] 5 International Criminal Law Review 3, 401–416.

898 Tams (n 801) 180; Alexander Stremitzer, 'Erga Omnes Norms and the Enforcement of International Law' [2009] 165 Journal of Institutional and Theoretical Economics 1, 29–34.

899 Tanaka (n 882).

900 The ICJ clearly pronounced in the *East Timor* case that 'the *erga omnes* character of a norm and the rule of consent to jurisdiction are two different things' and denied jurisdiction on the ground that Indonesia was an 'indispensable party' to the proceedings but had not accepted its jurisdiction. Whether there is a shift from this approach is currently being discussed by analysing the ICJ's decision on provisional measures in *Gambia v Myanmar*, according to which the Gambia had *prima facie* standing. Myanmar argued that it had made a reservation to exclude the application of the provision of the Genocide Convention which permitted the Court to render a decision. Thus, Myanmar argued, by conferring locus standi to The Gambia, the Court vitiated the requirement of

countermeasures that are taken by States which are not directly injured, the current state of positive international law remains uncertain.[901]

Another important aspect to consider is the relationship between peremptory norms of general international law (*jus cogens*) and obligations *erga omnes*.[902] Peremptory norms of international law give rise to obligations owed to the international community as a whole, and they are therefore accepted as obligations *erga omnes*.[903] However, it is widely considered that not all obligations *erga omnes* arise from peremptory norms of general international law.[904] This is particularly important in light of the legal effects of peremptory norms, which do not allow for any derogation.[905] Thus, peremptory norms could be seen as non-derogable obligations *erga omnes*, which the 'international community as a whole' has a legal interest in protecting.[906]

Under Article 41 of ARSIWA, serious breaches of peremptory norms have specific legal consequences.[907] Although the ICJ has not explicitly made a

---

Myanmar's consent to jurisdiction. See *Application of the Convention on the Prevention and Punishment of the Crime of Genocide* (*The Gambia v. Myanmar*) (Provisional Measures) [2020] ICJ (Separate Opinion of Vice-President Xue).

901 See Tanaka (n 882).

902 The UN ILC has been studying the peremptory norms of general international law (*jus cogens*) since 2015. The Special Rapporteur for the topic, Mr. Dire Tladi, has produced four reports. Draft conclusions were adopted by the Drafting Committee on first reading in 2019 and transmitted to Governments for comments and observations through the UN Secretary-General. Governments, international organisations and others have until 30 june 2021 to submit comments and observations about the draft conclusions. For draft conclusions, see ILC, 'Peremptory norms of general international law (*jus cogens*) Text of the draft conclusions and draft annex provisionally adopted by the Drafting Committee on first reading' (29 May 2019) UN Doc A/CN.4/L.936. Also see ILC, 'First report on *jus cogens* by Dire Tladi, Special Rapporteur' (8 March 2016) A/CN.4/693; ILC 'Second report on *jus cogens* by Dire Tladi, Special Rapporteur' (16 March 2017) UN Doc A/CN.4/706; ILC 'Third report on peremptory norms of general international law (*jus cogens*) by Dire Tladi, Special Rapporteur' (12 February 2018) UN Doc A/CN.4/714; ILC, 'Fourth report on peremptory norms of general international law (*jus cogens*) by Dire Tladi, Special Rapporteur' (31 January 2019) UN Doc 1/CN.4/727.

903 ILC, 'Peremptory norms of general international law (*jus cogens*) Text of the draft conclusions and draft annex provisionally adopted by the Drafting Committee on first reading' (29 May 2019) UN Doc A/CN.4/L.936, Draft Conclusion 17.

904 ibid draft Conclusion 17 Commentary.

905 Ibid. Also see Christian Tomuschat, 'Reconceptualising the debate on *jus cogens* and obligations *erga omnes*: concluding observations' in Christian Tomuschat and Jean-Marc Thouvenin (eds), *The Fundamental Rules of the International Legal Order: Jus Cogens and Obligations Erga Omnes* (Brill 2006).

906 ILC, 'Peremptory norms of general international law' (n 903).

907 See ARSIWA (n 878) art 41.

pronouncement on the link between peremptory norms and obligations *erga omnes*, it has applied Article 41 of ARSIWA to breaches of obligations that it has pronounced as *erga omnes*.[908] For instance, in its recent *Chagos* Advisory Opinion, it stated that the breach of an obligation *erga omnes* generated a binding obligation on all States to cooperate towards the realisation of the right in question (in this instance, the right to self-determination).[909] However, under Article 41 (1) of ARSIWA, States are obliged to cooperate to bring to an end through lawful means any serious breach of a peremptory norm.[910] In the author's view, this confusion could have been avoided if the ICJ explicitly pronounced the right to self-determination as a peremptory norm or articulated that obligations *erga omnes* also result in a duty to cooperate.[911]

Regardless of the confusion surrounding the *erga omnes* concept, the ICJ affirmed the existence of obligations *erga omnes* both by reference to the object and purpose of multilateral treaties, as well as in customary international law.[912] Commentators are proposing new candidates for obligations *erga omnes*, including in the fields of international human rights, international development and international environmental law.[913] The obligation *erga omnes* to mitigate and manage climate change has also been proposed to argue that States should grant international protection to 'forced climate migrants'.[914]

---

908 *Legal Consequences of the Separation of the Chagos Archipelago from Mauritius* (n 887) para 180; *Legal Consequences of the Construction of a Wall in the Occupied Palestinian Territory* (Advisory Opinion) [2003] ICJ, para 159.

909 *Legal Consequences of the Separation of the Chagos Archipelago from Mauritius* (n 887) para 180. Also see Eggett and Thin (n 869).

910 ARSIWA (n 878). Also see de Wet (n 876) 543.

911 Also see separate opinion of Judge Cançado Trindade, *Legal Consequences of the Separation of the Chagos Archipelago from Mauritius* (n 887), [169], [191] and [200].

912 For instance, the Genocide Convention expresses the prohibition of genocide, whereas the right to self-determination derives from customary international law. See *Legal Consequences of the Separation of the Chagos Archipelago from Mauritius* (n 887).

913 For instance, see Nicholas A. Robinson, 'Environmental Law: Is an Obligation Erga Omnes Emerging?' (*IUCN* 2018) <https://www.iucn.org/sites/dev/files/content/documents/2018/environmental_law_is_an_obligation_erga_omnes_emerging_interamcthradvisoryopinionjune2018.pdf> accessed 6 April 2022; Samantha Besson, 'The Erga Omnes Effect of Judgments of the European Court of Human Rights: What's in a Name?' (La Cour européenne des droits de l'homme après le Protocole 14, 2011) <https://hal.archives-ouvertes.fr/hal-02557350/document> accessed 6 April 2022; Patricia Wouters and A. Dan Tarlock, 'The Third Wave of Normativity in Global Water Law: The Duty to Cooperate in the Peaceful Management of the World's Water Resources: An Emerging Obligation Erga Omnes?' [2013] 23 Journal of Water Law, 51.

914 Giovanni Sciaccaluga, *International Law and the Protection of 'Climate Refugees'* (Palgrave 2020).

This raises the interconnected questions of whether the international protection of PMDCC can be framed as a community interest and whether it can enforced as an obligation *erga omnes*. These issues are addressed in the next section.

2 The Application of a Community Interest Approach: Towards an Obligation *Erga Omnes* to Protect Persons Mobile in the Context of Disasters and Climate Change

This section makes the argument that it is realistic, not optimistic, to identify the international protection of PMDCC as an obligation *erga omnes*, and to seek accountability. The starting point is the identification of the international protection of PMDCC as an obligation *erga omnes*. Noting that there is no conclusive test for identifying obligations *erga omnes* in general international law,[915] the author argues as follows: if (i) the international protection of PMDCC derives from the principles and rules concerning the basic rights of the human person[916] and if (ii) it is a community interest,[917] it follows that (iii) the international protection of PMDCC is an obligation *erga omnes* and all States can be held to have a legal interest in its performance. This chapter then discusses the enforcement of the international protection of PMDCC as an obligation *erga omnes*. It attempts to shed light on two pathways:[918] using the existing procedural aspects of international law and using the follow-up and review mechanisms of the Global Compact for Migration and the Global Compact on Refugees.

915 See, in general, Tomuschat and Thouvenin (eds) (n 905).

916 The ICJ pronounced this view in the following decisions: *Case Concerning the Barcelona Traction* (n 793) para 34; *Legal Consequences of the Construction of a Wall* (n 908) para 155; *Application of the Convention on the Prevention and Punishment of the Crime of Genocide (Bosnia and Herzegovina v Serbia and Montenegro)* (Judgment) [2007] ICJ <http://www.icj-cij.org/icjwww/idocket.htm> accessed 6 April 2022 [147]. However, whether all human rights qualify as obligations *erga omnes* is debatable. See Michael Byers, 'Conceptualising the Relationship Between Jus Cogens and Erga Omnes' [1997] 66 Nordic Journal of International Law 2-3, 211–239.

917 For a discussion on the reference by the ICJ to community interests, see Benedek and others (eds) (n 849).

918 The two commonly discussed methods of enforcing obligations *erga omnes* are judicial enforcement (particularly by instituting ICJ proceedings) and taking countermeasures. The analyses undertaken in this book are without prejudice to these options.

2.1 *Identification*

According to the UDHR, 'everyone is entitled to a social and international order in which rights and freedoms [...] can be fully realized'.[919] The kind of social and international order of which the framers of the UDHR dreamt is being disrupted by the effects of disasters and climate change.[920] The recognition of the international protection of PMDCC as an obligation *erga omnes* can contribute to preventing, minimising and addressing the impact of disasters and climate change on people's well-being and living conditions. In order to facilitate the identification of this obligation, this section argues that the international protection of PMDCC derives from the principles and rules concerning the basic rights of the human person and that it is a community interest.[921]

By its very nature, the international protection of PMDCC concerns the effective enjoyment of a range of basic human rights.[922] There is extensive evidence that disasters and climate change adversely affect a number of rights: the right to life; the right to freedom from cruel, inhuman or degrading treatment or punishment; the right to food; the right to water; and the right to a healthy environment.[923] These basic rights are inextricably linked to the fulfilment of other rights, and refer to a body of internationally agreed norms that have raised basic needs (such as to food, shelter and water) to the level of entitlements for all.[924]

Climate change multiplies threats and has long-term adverse implications for human security, human health and sustainable development.[925] Due

919 UDHR (n 397) preamble.

920 See International Bar Association, 'Achieving Justice and Human Rights in an Era of Climate Disruption: Climate Change Justice and Human Rights Task Force Report' (IBA 2014).

921 As Tams notes, 'Erga omnes outside jus cogens is likely to remain uncharted territory until States begin to invoke the concept more frequently in formalised proceedings'. See Tams (n 801) 157.

922 See Chapter 1.1.2 and Chapter 2.1.6 of this book for discussions on the relationship between HMDCC and international human rights.

923 See Note by Secretary-General, 'Human Rights of Internally Displaced Persons' (2020) UN Doc A/75/207; Report of the Special Rapporteur on the Impacts of Climate Change on the Right to Food (2019) UN Doc A/70/287; Report of the Special Rapporteur on the Right to Food in the Context of Natural Disasters (2018) UN Doc A/HRC/37/61.

924 Stephen Humphreys (ed), *Human Rights and Climate Change* (Cambridge University Press 2010) 9.

925 Here, human security can be understood very broadly 'as a condition that exists when the vital core of human lives is protected, and when people have the freedom and capacity to live with dignity'. See Adger and others, 'Human Security' in IPCC, *Climate Change 2014: Impacts, Adaptation and Vulnerability* (Cambridge University Press 2014), 759. See also, Ferris and Weerasinghe (n 654). In its resolution 68/4 on the Declaration of the High-level Dialogue on International Migration and Development, the UNGA recognised that

to its long-term effects, the climate crisis has been labelled as a 'child rights crisis'.[926] At least 155 States have now recognised in law the human right to a safe, clean, healthy and sustainable environment.[927] Internationally, States have been cooperating under different treaty regimes (such as the TFD of the UNFCCC), as well as establishing new initiatives (such as the PDD) which are instrumental to developing an international legal framework for the protection of PMDCC.[928] Focusing on the nexus of climate change, sustainable development, peace and security, human rights, and humanitarian issues, the UN has also been addressing displacement and migration, notably as a part of its 'system strategic approach on climate change action'.[929] In a landmark UN resolution, the UNHRC recognised for the first time in 2021 that having a clean, healthy and sustainable environment is a fundamental right and appointed Ian Fry as the new Special Rapporteur on the Protection of Human Rights in the Context of Climate Change.[930]

The international protection of PMDCC entails novel challenges too. As the implications of sea-level rise demonstrate, statehood and the right to self-determination are impacted by climate change and disasters.[931] More than seventy States are or are likely to be directly affected by sea-level rise.[932] In Paragraph 14 of the 2030 Agenda, the UNGA recognised that 'the survival of many societies, and of the biological support system of the planet, is at risk' and that sea level rise is 'seriously affecting coastal areas and low-lying coastal countries, including many least developed countries and small island developing States'.[933] The UN Security Council has held open debates and Arria Formula meetings on the issue of climate change, international peace and

human mobility is a key factor for sustainable development. See UNGA Res 68/4 (2014) GAOR 68th Session.

926 UNICEF, 'The climate crisis is a child rights crisis' (UNICEF, 6 December 2019) <https://www.unicef.org/press-releases/fact-sheet-climate-crisis-child-rights-crisis> accessed 6 April 2022.

927 Note by the Secretary-General, 'Human rights obligations relating to the enjoyment of a safe, clean, healthy and sustainable environment' (2019) UN Doc A/74/161, para 43.

928 See Chapter 2 of this book for a detailed analysis of relevant international treaty regimes, and cooperative initiatives.

929 UN CEB, 'United Nations System Strategic Approach on Climate Change Action' <https://unsceb.org/united-nations-system-strategic-approach-climate-change-action> accessed 6 April 2022.

930 UNHRC (n 10).

931 Oral (n 523) 3.

932 ILC (n 168) 326. Also see ILA (n 168).

933 2030 Sustainable Development Agenda (n 236) para 14.

security since 2007.[934] Although a resolution has not been adopted yet, the Security Council has expressed its 'concern that possible security implications of loss of territory of some States caused by sea-level-rise may arise, in particular in small low-lying island States'.[935] In the case of low-lying island countries, sea-level rise might cause significant loss of territory, perhaps eventually submerging their entire territory.[936] Before being completely submerged, sea-level rise, combined with other stressors, might render low-lying islands uninhabitable, by causing saltwater intrusion into already vulnerable groundwater sources and into arable land, severely undermining water and food security.[937]

This leads to the question of how the international protection of PMDCC concerns the core human rights principles of equality and non-discrimination.[938] As the OHCHR observed, 'by disproportionally affecting already marginalised groups, including children, older persons, persons with disabilities, women at risk, migrant workers, indigenous peoples, minorities and the poor, climate change threatens State commitments related to non-discrimination and equality'.[939] On an international scale, climate justice frames the disproportionate impacts of climate change and disasters.[940] Climate justice is based on the reality that those that have contributed the least to climate change suffer from it the most.[941] Perhaps the greatest hurdle is 'the failure to understand climate change as a phenomenon of historical and systemic inequality as well as a geopolitical one [...]. Because of its causes and effects, and the deeply

934 For instance, see UNSC UN Doc SC/900 (17 April 2007); UNSC UN Doc SC/10332 (20 July 2011); UNSC UN Doc SC/11991 (30 July 2015).

935 UNSC, 'Sea-level rise and implications for international peace and security – UN Security Council Arria-formula meeting' (18 October 2021) <https://media.un.org/en/asset/k1i/k1im1x4i6t> accessed 6 April 2022.

936 Soons (n 534); Lean (n 534); Powers and Stucko (n 534).

937 Storlazzi and others (n 533); Bird and Prescott (n 533); Bowett (n 533).

938 OHCHR, 'OHCHR's Key Messages on Human Rights, Climate Change and Migration' <https://environmentalmigration.iom.int/sites/default/files/Key%20Messages%20HR_CC_Migration.pdf> accessed 6 April 2022; OHCHRC, 'The rights of those disproportionately impacted by climate change' (Discussion Paper, 30 September 2016) <https://www.ohchr.org/Documents/Issues/ClimateChange/EM2016/DisproportionateImpacts.pdf> accessed 6 April 2022.

939 ibid.

940 Henry Shue, *Climate Justice: Vulnerability and Protection* (OUP 2014); Stephen M. Gardiner, 'Climate Justice' in John S Dryzek, Richard B. Norgaard and David Schlosberg, *The Oxford Handbook of Climate Change and Society* (Oxford University Press 2011) 309–322.

941 David Schlosberg and Lisette B. Collins, 'From Environmental to Climate Justice: Climate Change and the Discourse of Environmental Justice' [2014] 5 WIREs Climate Change 3.

lopsided nature of them, "climate change" is a political term as well as a scientific one'.[942]

Human mobility lies at the heart of this dialogue: if people are forced to move, then the protection needs of individuals will be increased.[943] Thus, action must be taken to reduce the impacts of environmental changes on communities and persons, by way of, for instance, adopting rigorous climate change action and better preparing for disasters.[944] By contrast, if migration with dignity is facilitated, through laws and policies on planned relocation and on the facilitation of the movement of persons, amongst other things, specific human rights protection needs can be addressed.[945] The international protection of PMDCC therefore derives from the principles and rules concerning the basic rights of the human person.

It is increasingly urgent to address the international protection of PMDCC as a matter that concerns the international community as a whole. States have been deviating from a purely consent-based conception of the norms relating to HMDCC and conveying commitments towards the common protection of PMDCC.[946] Most notably, under the Global Compact on Refugees and the Global Compact for Migration, States have made important commitments to mitigating the impact of disasters, climate change and environmental degradation on human movement, and specifically commitments to facilitate safe, orderly and regular migration.[947] Countries have been implementing their

942 Maxine Burkett, 'Justice and Climate Migration. The Importance of Nomenclature in the Discourse on Twenty-First-Century Mobility' in Simon Berhman and Avidan Kent (eds), *'Climate Refugees' Beyond the Legal Impasse?* (Routledge 2018) 84.

943 Fornalé (n 329).

944 For instance, a recent policy brief urged the Australian government to create more temporary and long-term visa opportunities to provide a 'release valve' for Pacific islanders at risk of displacement due to climate change and disasters. Jane McAdam and Jonathan Pryke, 'Policy Brief 10 - Climate Change, Disasters and Mobility: A Roadmap for Australian Action | Kaldor Centre' [2020] UNSW Kaldor Centre for International Refugee Law.

945 Elisa Fornalé, Jeremie Guélat and Etienne Piguet, 'Framing Labour Mobility Options in Small Island States Affected by Environmental Changes' in Robert McLeman, Jeanette Schade, Thomas Faist (eds), *Environmental Migration and Social Inequality* (Springer 2015) 167–187.

946 Scott (n 14); Dina Ionesco, Daria Mokhnacheva, and François Gemenne, *The Atlas of Environmental Migration* (Routledge 2017); Susanna Schwan and Xiaohua Yu, 'Social Protection as a Strategy to Adress Climate-induced Migration' [2017] 10 International Journal of Climate Change Strategies and Management 1.

947 See Chapter 1.3 of this book.

commitments under the compacts in multiple ways.[948] Measures include incorporating climate change considerations into national migration policies, cooperating with other States to 'develop solutions such as human rights–based disaster displacement and relocation guidelines', and commissioning research 'to better understand the links between migration and climate change and to build evidence of drivers and effective responses'.[949]

The claims that the international protection of PMDCC derives from the principles and rules concerning the basic rights of the human person and that there is an undeniable community interest in its protection provide the basis for its identification as an obligation *erga omnes*. Going beyond reciprocal relations among States based on consent, this recognition can ensure that international law continues to address the pressing concerns of the international community as a whole, both old and new.

2.2 *Pathways to Using the Existing Procedural Aspects of International Law*

Although the relationship between obligations *erga omnes* and treaty enforcement rights 'depend[s] less on abstract principles than on a detailed examination of specific conflicts', a few general observations can still be made.[950] First, it is open to interpretation whether the breach of an obligation *erga omnes* as the result of the conclusion of a treaty may render that treaty void.[951] Second, there is no clear incompatibility between international treaty law and multilateral treaties protecting community interests.[952] In fact, treaty regimes aiming to protect a specific obligation *erga omnes* have come to be termed *erga*

948 UNEC, 'Regional Review of the Global Compact for Safe, Orderly and Regular Migration' (Summary Report, 12–13 November 2020) <https://migrationnetwork.un.org/country-regional-network/europe-north-america> accessed 6 April 2022.

949 Report of the Secretary-General, 'Global Compact for Safe, Orderly and Regular Migration' (2020) GAOR 75th Session UN Doc A/75/542; UK Government, 'The Global Compact for Migration European Regional Review' <https://migrationnetwork.un.org/sites/default/files/docs/uk_submission_-_gcm_european_regional_review_. pdf> accessed 6 April 2022; German Government, 'Global Compact for Safe, Orderly and Regular Migration' <https://migrationnetwork.un.org/sites/default/files/docs/germany.pdf> accessed 6 April 2022.

950 Tams (n 801) 255.

951 This can be compared with the conclusion of treaties conflicting with a peremptory norm, which becomes void and terminates. Vienna Convention on the Law of Treaties (adopted 22 May 1969, entered into force 27 January 1980) 1155 UNTS 331 (VCLT), arts 53. See also, ILC, 'Fourth report on peremptory norms of general international law (*jus cogens*) by Dire Tladi, Special Rapporteur' (31 January 2019) UN Doc 1/CN.4/727.

952 See Besson (n 814) 58.

omnes partes.[953] Third, obligations *erga omnes* may be taken into account in treaty interpretation through different channels, depending on the case.[954] Fourth, whether States are actually interested in requesting the performance of an obligation *erga omnes* by invoking the responsibility of another State in vindication of a breach under treaty enforcement mechanisms is usually perceived as a political decision, and States have often been called 'reluctant' to act.[955]

Based on these general observations, this section proposes pathways to using the existing procedural aspects of international law to enforce the international protection of PMDCC as an obligation *erga omnes*.[956] The pathways discussed here present an alternative both to bringing a claim before the ICJ and to countermeasures.[957] Furthermore, they foresee that the construction and protection of rights *erga omnes* includes the participation of a variety of actors, including non-State actors.[958] With this aim, four legal areas will be examined: the international human rights regime, the international climate change regime, the international labour regime and the international trade regime (with an emphasis on the WTO).

Under international human rights law, the core UN human rights conventions provide for the establishment of independent bodies, known as committees, to monitor the implementation of the respective treaty by the State Parties.[959] The terms of reference of the treaty bodies differ according to the convention, and hence the means at the disposal of the committees to monitor

953 Pok Yin Stephenson Chow, 'On Obligations Erga Omnes Partes' [2020] 52 Georgetown Journal of International Law 2, 469–504.

954 Besson identifies three channels for the incorporation of community interests in treaty interpretation: first, systemic interpretation according to Art 31(3)(c) of the VCLT, second, evolutive interpretation of a community interest norm according to Art 31(3)(b) of the VCLT, and third, teleological interpretation according to Art 31(1) VCLT. See Besson (n 814) 59–65.

955 Gaja (n 794); Simma (n 790).

956 These relevant treaty regimes have been discussed in Chapter 1 of this book.

957 They also present an alternative to acquiring an advisory opinion from the ICJ. See Harry Gould, *The Legacy of Punishment in International Law* (Palgrave Macmillan 2010) 65–79. Also see BIICL, 'Rising Sea Levels: A Matter for the ICJ?' (Webinar, 11 March 2021) <https://www.biicl.org/events/11468/webinar-series-rising-sea-levels-promoting-climate-justice-through-international-law?cookiesset=1&ts=1619444541> accessed 6 April 2022.

958 Klabbers, for instance, argues that 'the notion of community interests do not exist in isolation from particular projects, it always and by definition assumes someone pouring meaning to it'. See Klabbers (n 858).

959 Human rights are also monitored at the universal level also through the mechanisms established by UN resolutions, such as the system of country or thematic special rapporteurs and the OHCHR. See UNGA Res 48/141 (1994). See Cassese (n 22) 386–393.

compliance are not uniform.[960] Nonetheless, individual communication procedures, which allows victims of alleged human rights violations or their representatives to initiate formal procedures against the violating State before the respective committee, exist for all core UN human rights treaties.[961]

As indicated by the *Teitiota* decision of the UNHRCom, along with the *Sac chi et al.* decision of the UNCRCom, the treaty bodies are already receiving communications in relation to climate change from victims of alleged human rights violations.[962] Amongst other things, this provides the opportunity to interpret the respective human rights treaties by taking into account 'any relevant rules of international law applicable in the relations between the parties'.[963] Also referred to as 'systemic interpretation', this method acts as a 'master-key' to enable us to take into account the international protection of PMDCC as an obligation *erga omnes*.[964] Admittedly, 'systematic interpretation cannot necessarily resolve conflicts with community interest norms or

---

960 These 'treaty bodies', as they are often called, are Committees composed of independent experts elected by States parties to the relevant treaty. For a full list, see OHCHR, 'Human Rights Treaty Bodies – Individual Communications' <https://www.ohchr.org/EN/HRBodies/TBPetitions/Pages/IndividualCommunications.aspx#overviewprocedure> accessed 6 April 2022. Also see Kälin and Künzli (n 22) 210–220.

961 A complaint under one of the eight treaties may be brought against a State that satisfies two conditions. First, it must be a party (through ratification or accession) to the treaty that provides for the rights which have allegedly been violated. Second, the State party must have recognized the competence of the committee monitoring that treaty to receive and consider complaints from individuals. Currently, only the complaint mechanism for the ICMW has not yet entered into force. See OHCHR, 'Human Rights Treaty Bodies – Individual Communications' <https://www.ohchr.org/EN/HRBodies/TBPetitions/Pages/IndividualCommunications .aspx#overviewprocedure> accessed 6 April 2022.

962 The Teitiota decision is discussed in more detail in Chapter 2.2.1. of this book. For the *Teitiota* decision, see *Ioane Teitiota* (n 83). The *Sacchi et al.* decision is discussed in more detail in Chapter 2.1.6. of this book. For the Sacchi et al. decision, see CRCom (n 10).

963 This is by virtue of Article 31(3)(c) of the VCLT. As a matter of treaty law, the VCLT applies only to the States Parties to the relevant human rights convention and to the VCLT. However, there is also agreement that most of the rules of the VCLT are now part of customary international law. As Schlütter points out, the UN treaty bodies 'generally' follow the rules of interpretation articulated in the VCLT. However, 'treaty interpretation in general, and human rights interpretation in particular, is a complex matter, and any attempt to delineate the rules of interpretation as applied by the major UN human rights treaty bodies is almost impossible …'. Birgit Schlütter, 'Aspects of Human Rights Interpretation by the UN Treaty Bodies' in Helen Keller and Geir Ulfstein, *UN Human Rights Treaty Bodies: Law and Legitimacy* (Cambridge University Press 2012) 273.

964 On systemic interpretation, see Study Group on the Fragmentation of International Law (n 166); Campbell McLachlan, 'The Principle of Systemic Integration and Article 31(3)(c) of the Vienna Convention' [2005] 54 ICLQ 279, 281.

guarantee that community interest norms are respected in priority thereafter'.[965] However, assuming that the complaint is admissible, and that the complainant includes reference to the international protection of PMDCC as an obligation *erga omnes*, the committee may be in a position to take into account this reference.[966]

Furthermore, another possible route for non-State actors to observe this obligation is by contributing to the UPR process. The UPR was established by the UNGA in 2006 to create a cooperative mechanism to assess the human rights performance of all UN Member States.[967] It is 'based on an interactive dialogue, with the full involvement of the country concerned and with consideration given to its capacity building needs'.[968] It aims to complement the work of other human rights monitoring mechanisms, mainly the treaty bodies and the special procedures.[969] The UPR is essentially a peer review in which the diplomatic delegates of UN Member States evaluate each other's performance based on three background documents: the national report, the compilation of UN information and the summary of stakeholders' information.[970] The process has been hailed as success for voluntarily bringing all UN Member

965 See Besson (n 814) 60.

966 One of the grounds of admissibility is the exhaustion of domestic remedies. However, UN treaty bodies only require complainants to exhaust remedies that are 'available and effective'. Relying on this, sixteen children filed a complaint to the UNCRCom without exhausting domestic remedies in 5 nations (Argentina, Brazil, France, Germany, and Turkey), as such action may have been 'unreasonably prolonged or unlikely to bring effective relief'. See UNHRCom, Vicente et al. v. Colombia, Communication 612/1995, Views of 29 July 1997, UN Doc CCPR/C/60/D/612/1995, [5.2] <http://hrlibrary.umn.edu/undocs/612-1995.html> accessed 6 April 2022.

967 UNGA Res GA Res 60/251 (2006) GAOR 60th Session, Agenda Items 46 and 120.

968 ibid.

969 Treaty bodies are committees of independent experts that monitor the implementation of the core international human rights treaties. Special procedures, on the other hand, are individual independent human rights experts or groups of such experts that report on human rights issues. See OHCHR, 'Human rights treaty bodies' <https://www.ohchr.org/EN/HRBodies/Pages/TreatyBodies.aspx> accessed 6 April 2022. Also see International Justice Resource Center, 'Special Procedures of the UN Human Rights Council' <https://ijrcenter.org/un-special-procedures/> accessed 6 April 2022.

970 UNHRC, 'Basic Facts about the UPR' (2019) <https:// www.ohchr.org/EN/HRBodies/UPR/Pages/BasicFacts.aspx> accessed 6 April 2022; UPR info, 'The Civil Society Compendium: Comprehensive guide for Civil Society Organisations engaging in the Universal Periodic Review, Geneva' (UPR Info, 2017) <https://www.upr-info.org/sites/default/files/general-document/pdf/upr_info_cso_compendium_en.pdf> accessed 6 April 2022.

States to subject their human rights record to international scrutiny.[971] The outcome report of the UPR can be either 'accepted' or 'noted', but the possibility of rejection is not envisaged.[972]

Measures taken to observe the international protection of PMDCC as an obligation *erga omnes* can be included in the UPR process, through the national reports, as well as the stakeholders' information. This would not be a radical inclusion. States have already been reporting on the measures they have taken with respect to HMDCC. For instance, the national submissions of Vanuatu and Fiji to the UPR mechanism included references to their planned relocation policies in the context of disasters and climate change.[973] This can play a pivotal role in promoting and seeking to ensure full respect for the international protection of PMDCC.

It must also be restated that, in 2021, the UNHRC recognised for the first time that having a clean, healthy and sustainable environment is a fundamental right and created a new Special Rapporteur on the Protection of Human Rights in the Context of Climate Change.[974] This creates an opportunity for the further engagement and deliberation on the international protection of PMDCC as an obligation *erga omnes*.

Turning to international climate change law, the NDCs of countries submitted under the Paris Agreement may include measures to protect PMDCC at the international level, especially by preventing future GHG emissions.[975] NDCs are determined 'bottom-up', meaning that their content will be based on domestic politics, which provides non-State actors with the opportunity

971 Elvira Dominguez-Redondo, 'The Universal Periodic Review – Is There Life Beyond Naming and Shaming in Human Rights Implementation?' [2012] 4 New Zealand Law Review, 673–706.

972 UNHRC Res 60/25 (2007) 50th Session, UN Doc A/HRC/RES/5/1.

973 See Chapter 3.3 of this book for a discussion on the planned relocation policies of Fiji and Vanuatu. Also see UNHRC, 'National Report Submitted in Accordance with Paragraph 5 of the Annex to Human Rights Council Resolution 16/21' (2018) UN Doc A/HRC/WG.6/34/FJI/1; UNHRC, 'Report of the Working Group on the Universal Periodic Review' (2019) UN Doc A/HRC/43/8; UNHRC, 'National Report Submitted in Accordance with Paragraph5 of the Annex to Human Rights Council Resolution 16/21' (2018) UN Doc A/HRC/WG.6/32/VUT/1.

974 UNHRC (n 10). Also see UNHRC (n 80).

975 Currently, under the Paris Agreement and the 'Paris Rulebook', the content of the NDCs are subject to 'weak accountability'. Other than the progression requirement, their content is decided bottom-up. See Christina Voigt and Gao Xiang, 'Accountability in the Paris Agreement: The Interplay Between Transparency and Compliance' [2020] 1 Nordic Environmental Law Journal, 31–57.

to participate in the process of determining national climate ambition.[976] Another possibility is participating in the ongoing work of the TFD.[977] In 2015, the UNFCCC WIM was mandated to create the TFD with the aim of developing recommendations to 'avert, minimize and address displacement related to the adverse impacts of climate change'.[978] Comprising fourteen members, the Task Force represented perspectives from the fields of development, adaptation, human mobility, humanitarian, civil society, least-developed countries, and loss and damage.[979] Their recommendations were delivered in 2018 during the COP 24, which was 'welcomed' by COP.[980] As it is currently undertaking its second phase, the TFD's plan of action fosters deeper engagement with policy and legal considerations to implement its recommendations.[981] The TFD's work envisages an inclusive approach, engaging and collaborating with relevant stakeholders, including civil society, which provides an opportunity to build momentum on the international protection of PMDCC.[982]

Turning to international labour law, it provides a sophisticated avenue to take into account the international protection of PMDCC thanks to the tripartite structure of the ILO, consisting of governments, workers' organisations and employers' organisations in its governing organs.[983] Its conventions are

---

976 For instance, Torstad, Selen and Boyum argue that a country's level of democracy and vulnerability to climate change have positive effects on NDC ambition, while coal rent and GDP have negative effects. See Vegard Torstad, Hakon Sele and Live Standal Boyum, 'The Domestic Politics of International Climate Commitments: Which Factors Explain Cross-Country Variation in NDC ambition?' [2020] 15 Environmental Research Letters 2. Swiss referendum 2021.

977 See Chapter 2.1.2 of this book for a discussion on TFD.

978 Conference of the Parties to the United Nations Framework Convention on Climate Change, *Report of the Conference of the Parties on its Twenty-First Session*, 21st sess, (29 January 2016) UN Doc FCCC/CP/2015/10/Add. 1 <https://www.un.org/en/development/desa/population/migration/generalassembly/docs/globalcompact/FCCC_CP_2015_10_Add.1.pdf> accessed 6 April 2022.

979 Task Force on Displacement (n 1); UNFCCC, 'Task Force on Displacement – Membership' <https://unfccc.int/process/bodies/constituted-bodies/WIMExCom/TFD/membership> accessed 6 April 2022.

980 UNFCCC (n 15).

981 UNFCCC, 'Task Force on Displacement Plan of Action 2019–2021' <https://unfccc.int/sites/default/files/resource/TFD%20PoA%202nd%20phase.pdf> accessed 6 April 2022. Also see Odeyemi (n 229).

982 Especially through the UNFCCC NGO Constituency Group 'Youth NGOs', and the Advisory Group on Climate Change and Human Mobility. See Harriet Thew, Lucie Middlemiss and Jouni Paavola, 'Does youth participation increase the democratic legitimacy of UNFCCC-orchestrated global climate change governance?' [2021] Environmental Politics.

983 The ILO itself is participating in international efforts on HMDCC. It is a member of the TFD, and contributes to PDD. Furthermore, it has signed an MOU with UNCCD to combat

similarly premised on the right to participation of all constituents.[984] The rights of workers, including migrant workers, to establish their own independent organisations and to bargain collectively must be respected in order to foster the democratic decision-making dealing with the working conditions of PMDCC.[985] The tripartite structure can particularly be used by all relevant parties to guarantee the incorporation of HMDCC when applying the ILS.[986] The Governing Body settles the agenda for all meetings of the ILO Conference, which provides its constituent members with the opportunity to discuss the relationship between the ILS and the obligation *erga omnes* to provide international protection the PMDCC.

Finally, under WTO GATS Mode 4, Member States have made binding commitments to the movement of natural persons to supply services.[987] Services mobility facilitates safe, orderly and regular migration, and it plays a critical role in promoting migration as an adaptation strategy to the impacts of disasters and climate change.[988] One way of enforcing the international protection of PMDCC as an obligation *erga omnes* is by giving attention to the Trade Policy Review Mechanism (TPRM).[989] All WTO Members are subject to review under the TPRM with different review cycles.[990] Reviews are conducted by the Trade

---

desertification and migration related challenges. See ILO, 'Climate change, displacement and labour migration' <https://www.ilo.org/global/topics/labour-migration/climate-change/green-jobs/lang--en/index.htm> accessed 6 April 2022.

984 See ILO Convention No 144 on Tripartite Consultation (1976).

985 UNECE's Aarhus Convention recognises the importance of public participation in decision-making and access to justice in environmental matters. See Aarhus Convention (adopted 25 June 1998, entered into force 30 October 2001) 2161 UNTS 447.

986 Jean-Michel Servais, *International Labour Law* (Wolters Kluwer 2020) para 73–110.; Lene Olsen and Dorit Kemter, 'The International Labour Organization and the Environment: The Way to a Socially Just Transition for Workers' in Nora Räthzel and David Uzzell (eds), Trade Unions in the Green Economy (Routledge 2013) 41–57; Maria Nillson and Tord Kjellstrom, 'Climate change impacts on working people: how to develop prevention policies' [2010] 3 Global Health Action 3; Katherine H. Regan, 'The Case for Enhancing Climate Change Negotiations with a Labor Rights Perspective' [2010] 35 Columbia Journal of Environmental Law 249.

987 See Chapter 2.1.5 of this book for a discussion in more detail.

988 Fornalé (n 329); Jonathan Barnett and Michael Webber, 'Migration as Adaptation: Opportunities and Limits' in Jane McAdam (ed), *Climate Change and Displacement: Multidisciplinary Perspectives* (Hart Publishing 2010).

989 Marrakesh Agreement Establishing the World Trade Organization (adopted 15 April 1994, entered into force 1 January 1995) 1867 UNTS Annex 3.

990 The WTO rules mandate that the four Members with the largest shares of world trade (currently the European Union, the United States, Japan and China) be reviewed each two years, the next sixteen be reviewed each four years, and others be reviewed each six years. A longer period may be fixed for least-developed country members. As a result of an

Policy Review Body of the WTO, based on the policy statement by the Member State under review, and a report is prepared by economists in the Trade Policy Review Division of the WTO Secretariat.[991] Unlike the UPR in the human rights regime, the TPRM of the WTO does not allow non-State actors to contribute to the review process. Nonetheless, Member States might be encouraged to include in their policy statements measures to address the international protection of PMDCC by revising their commitments under GATS Mode 4.[992]

This would not be a radical inclusion. For instance, the relationship between the environment and trade has been increasingly studied.[993] There has been a push towards a circular economy as a sustainability paradigm, which has raised questions about the role of the WTO.[994] One study demonstrates that governments have realised the need for national-level circular-economy policies, such as adopting re-use in order to reduce the over-reliance on other manufacturing countries for essential goods, the further development of bio-based material research to promote bio-economy and devising legal frameworks to promote green logistics and waste management to incentivise local production and manufacturing.[995] States' notifications to the WTO reflect this realisation: as of 2018, 16% of all notifications to the WTO contained an environment-related measure, compared with only 8% in 1997.[996] More specifically, there were some 370 measures which referred to the activities related to the circular economy in WTO notifications between 2009 and 2017.[997] One commentator

amendment to Annex 3 in 2017, these review cycles are three, five and seven years respectively since 1 January 2019. See WTO, 'Amendment of the Trade Policy Review Mechanism' (27 July 2017) WT/L/1014.

991 Sam Laird and Raymundo Valdes, 'The Trade Policy Review Mechanism' in Martin Daunton, Amrita Narlikar and Robert M. Stern (eds), *The Oxford Handbook on the World Trade Organization* (Oxford University Press 2012).

992 On the limits of GATS Mode 4, see Dawson (n 343) 1–23.

993 Ryan Abman, Clark Lundberg and Michele Ruta, 'The Effectiveness of Environmental Provisions in Regional Trade Agreements' (Policy Research Working Paper No 9601, World Bank, 2021) <https://openknowledge.worldbank.org/handle/10986/35354> accessed 6 April 2022.

994 Shunta Yamaguchi, 'International Trade and Circular Economy – Policy Alignment' (OECD Trade and Environment Working Papers 2021/02).

995 T Ibn-Mohamed et al., 'A critical analysis of the impacts of COVID-19 on the global economy and ecosystems and opportunities for circular economy strategies' [2021] 164 Resources, Conservation and Recycling.

996 WTO, 'Role of trade in promoting circular economy' (Official Webpage) <https://www.wto.org/english/news_e/news19_e/envir_03dec19_e.htm> accessed 6 April 2022.

997 A.H. Lim and others, 'Trade and environment: what can we learn from trade policy reviews?' (WTO Staff Working Papers No. ERSD-2020-06, 2020). The analysis is based on notifications containing one or more of the following keywords (and close variations): eco-design, reuse, repair, refurbishment, remanufacturing, recycling,

argues that, in order for the WTO to make a positive contribution to the circular economy, the members need to: improve their collective understanding of trade-circular economy interactions; build trust and confidence to engage in mutually beneficial activities related to this topic; open and facilitate trade in key areas of the circular economy; and support related efforts in developing countries.[998] Similarly, with the identification of the international protection of PMDCC as an obligation *erga omnes*, and the relevant activism and scholarly work, WTO Member States can include their measures to increase services mobility, in order to facilitate safe, orderly and regular migration.

This section has discussed four areas of international law and how their procedural aspects can be used to promote the international protection of PMDCC as an obligation *erga omnes*. It has shown that the procedural aspects of international human rights law, international climate change law, international labour law and WTO law provide mechanisms for taking into account the international protection of PMDCC. These pathways entail the participation of State, as well as non-State actors, and might not always lead to the creation of binding obligations upon relevant State parties. Yet, recourse may be had to these pathways, in order to reinforce the view that international law can be understood as a values-based system, in which universal values and the rights of individual persons are protected.[999]

2.3 *Pathways to Using the Follow-up and Review Mechanisms of the Global Compact for Migration and the Global Compact on Refugees*

The golden threads of the Global Compact for Migration and the Global Compact on Refugees are the concrete frameworks for action to which States can be held to account, at least politically.[1000] Since both compacts explicitly refer to the impact of climate change, natural disasters and environmental

---

biodegradable, compostable and waste-to-energy. The analysis does not distinguish between measures that are aligned with the goals of the circular economy and measures that are not.

998 Karsten Steinfatt, 'Trade Policies for a circular economy: What can we learn from WTO experience?' (WTO Staff Working Paper, 2020).

999 For a discussion on international law as a value-based system, see Heike Krieger and Georg Nolte, 'The International Rule of Law – Rise or Decline? – Approaching Current Foundational Challenges' in Heike Krieger, Georg Nolte and Andreas Zimmermann, *The International Rule of Law: Rise or Decline?* (Oxford University Press 2019) 3–33.

1000 For instance, Guild and Wieland argue that the Global Compact for Migration 'comes with a host of non-legal implementation mechanisms. These "design elements" form an implementation framework that use non-binding norms based on technical and professional know-how to find the optimal mode of implementation'. See Elspeth Guild and Raoul Wieland, 'The UN Global Compact for Safe, Orderly and Regular Migration: What does it

degradation as drivers of human movement, the implementation of these commitments may induce the development of dedicated policy and legal responses.[1001] This section focuses on the follow-up and review mechanisms of the compacts to make the argument that the international protection of PMDCC as an obligation *erga omnes* can be enforced by means of these oversight mechanisms.

The Global Compact for Migration has three important pillars for implementation: the UN Network on Migration, a capacity-building mechanism and the International Migration Review Forum.[1002] These mechanisms can be perceived as creating a 'partial or limited hybrid forum, in which experts and laypersons contribute to the debate'.[1003] The UN Network on Migration aims to support the implementation, follow-up and review of the Global Compact for Migration.[1004] The network is the successor to the Global Migration Group, which was established by the UN in 2006 as an inter-agency group bringing together fourteen UN agencies to address global migration.[1005] The IOM serves as the coordinator and secretariat of the network, which consists of the members of the UN system that wish to be a part of it and for whom migration is of relevance to their mandates.[1006] As of December 2018, there are 38 UN entities in the UN Network on Migration.[1007]

The capacity-building mechanism aims to support the implementation efforts of Member States.[1008] It consists of a connection hub, a start-up fund, and a global knowledge platform as an online open data source.[1009] The start-up fund, called 'The Migration Multi-Partner Trust Fund', was launched in

---

mean in International Law?' [2020] 10 Global Community: Yearbook of International Law and Jurisprudence, 8.

1001 See Chapter 1.3 of this book for a discussion on the Global Compact for Migration and the Global Compact on Refugees.

1002 Global Compact for Migration (n 9) para 40–54.

1003 Scott D. Watson and Corey Robinson, 'Knowledge Controversies of Global Migration Governance: Understanding the Controversy Surrounding the Global Compact' in Catherine Dauvergne (ed), Research Handbook on the Law and Politics of Migration (Edgar Elgar 2021) 323–339.

1004 ibid.

1005 OHCHR, 'Global Migration Group' <https://www.ohchr.org/EN/Issues/Migration/Pages/Global MigrationGroupIndex.aspx> accessed 6 April 2022. Also see Antoine Pécoud, 'Narrating an ideal migration world ? An analysis of the Global Compact for Safe, Orderly and Regular Migration' [2020] 42 Third World Quarterly 1.

1006 Global Compact for Migration (n 9) para 45.

1007 UN Network on Migration, 'Migration Network Hub' <https://migrationnetwork.un.org/hub> accessed 6 April 2022.

1008 Global Compact for Migration (n 9) para 43.

1009 ibid.

May 2019; as of April 2021, it has raised over USD 15 million.[1010] The connection hub and the global knowledge platform have been launched under the title 'Migration Network Hub', and core working groups and thematic working groups have been established.[1011]

The International Review Forum serves as the primary intergovernmental global platform for Member States to discuss and share progress on their implementation.[1012] The forum is the successor to the High-Level Dialogue on International Migration and Development.[1013] It is intended to take place every four years beginning in 2022.[1014] Each forum will result in a Progress Declaration, which may be taken into consideration by the high-level political forum on sustainable development.[1015] The modalities for the forum were agreed in 2019.[1016] It shall be convened under the UNGA, chaired by the UNGA President, last for four days and take place during the first semester of 2022.[1017] An informal interactive multi-stakeholder hearing prior to each forum will be organised and presided by the UNGA President.[1018]

These efforts are designed to be supported by regional and sub-regional dialogues, national action plans, as well as through the efforts of other stakeholders, such as migrants, the private sector, civil society, academia, local

1010 Although it must be noted that its funding target for 2020 was initially set at USD 25 million. See IOM, 'United Nations Launches Multi-Partner Trust Fund Office to Support Cooperation on Safe, Orderly and Regular Migration' (17 July 2019); UNDP, 'Multi-Partner Trust Fund Office' <http://mptf.undp.org/factsheet/fund/MIG00> accessed 6 April 2022.

1011 These groups are as follows: Core working group 1.2 migration network hub, core working group 2.1 stronger UN system for implementation, core working group 2.2 GCM national implementation plans, thematic working group 1 data, thematic working group 2 alternatives to detention, thematic working group 3 regular pathways for migrants in vulnerable situations, thematic working group 4 bilateral labour migration agreements, thematic working group 5 return and reintegration, thematic working group 6 access to services. See UN Network on Migration, 'Migration Network Hub' <https://migrationnetwork.un.org/hub/working_groups?text=&gcm_objectives=All&cross_cutting_theme=All&region=All&country=All> accessed 6 April 2022.

1012 Global Compact for Migration (n 9) para 49.

1013 See Lena Kainz and Alexander Betts, 'Power and Proliferation: Explaining the Fragmentation of Global Migration Governance' [2020] Migration Studies, 1–25.

1014 Global Compact for Migration (n 9) para 49.

1015 ibid.

1016 UNGA, 'Format and organizational aspects of the international migration review forums' (Final draft, 12 July 2019) <https://www.un.org/pga/73/wp-content/uploads/sites/53/2019/07/IMFR-silence-procedure.pdf> accessed 6 April 2022.

1017 ibid.

1018 ibid.

authorities and the media.[1019] The compact refers to these as 'concerted efforts' at the global, regional, national and sub-national levels.[1020]

The current multi-stakeholder architecture for discussing the implementation of the Global Compact for Migration provides several opportunities to explicitly mention and enforce the international protection of PMDCC.[1021] The UN Network on Migration developed the guidance and the booklet, which provide further indications.[1022] According to the booklet, environmental factors are incorporated into the implementation of three objectives of the compact: Objective 1 (collect and utilise accurate and disaggregated data as the basis for evidence-based policies), Objective 2 (minimise the adverse drivers and structural factors that compel people to leave their country of origin) and Objective 5 (enhance availability and flexibility of pathways for regular migration).[1023] In addition, the implementation of Objective 16 (empower migrants

1019 Global Compact for Migration (n 9) para 40–44.

1020 Allinson and Weatherhead interpret this as a 'direction-normalisation-amplification' approach. Direction is the way that the Global Compact for Migration will be taken both individually and collectively. According to the authors, the direction should be more than the prioritisation of certain elements, and focus on holding the compact together to progress it. This can help to avoid national governments pursuing certain target areas in line with policy interests, such as controlling borders or emphasising return of irregular migrants. Normalisation refers to incorporating the compact into everyday work. The cooperative framework structured in the compact brings together key actors and provides a blueprint for strategic planning. The recommendations of the authors range from coming up with indicators to assess implementation to making references to the compact in reports, policies, and other mechanisms, such as the Universal Periodic Review and the Sustainable Development Goals. Finally, amplification refers to creating and maintaining momentum to ensure that there are positive impacts for migrants. The authors stated that the opportunity must be seized to engage a range of stakeholders, especially academics who have a role to clarify and scrutinise the content and implementation. See Kathryn Allinson and Katharine T. Weatherhead, 'The Global Compact for Migration is more than just its objectives' (RLI, 26 September 2019) <https://rli.blogs.sas.ac.uk/2019/09/26/the-global-compact-for-migration-is-more-than-just-its-objectives/> accessed 6 April 2022.

1021 McAdam, 'The Global Compacts on Refugees and Migration: A New Era for International Protection?' [2018] 30 IJRL 4, 571–574; Sciaccaluga (n 914) 151–156.

1022 Since the Global Compact for Migration does not have an indicator framework for implementation, the guidance and the booklet aim to fill this gap. See UN Network on Migration, 'Implementing the Global Compact for Safe, Orderly and Regular Migration: Guidance for governments and all relevant stakeholders' (Advanced Draft, 15 October 2020) <https://migrationnetwork.un.org/sites/default/files/docs/gcm_implementation_guide_finalized_revised_15_october.pdf> accessed 6 April 2022; UN Network on Migration, 'Booklet' <https://migrationnetwork.un.org/sites/default/files/docs/gcm_booklet_finalized_revised_15_october_002.pdf> accessed 6 April 2022.

1023 UN Network on Migration, 'Booklet' <https://migrationnetwork.un.org/sites/default/files/docs/gcm_booklet_finalized_revised_15_october_002.pdf> accessed 6 April 2022.

and societies to realise full inclusion and social cohesion) and Objective 23 (strengthen international cooperation and global partnerships for safe, orderly and regular migration) incorporate climate change, while Objective 22 (establish mechanisms for the portability of social security entitlements and earned benefits) incorporates disasters.[1024]

There are concrete examples of implementation by different stakeholders.[1025] For instance, IOs have been launching new initiatives, such as the International Data Alliance for Children on the Move, and the Migrant Union's commissioned report on digitalisation and displacement.[1026] National implementation examples demonstrate that human mobility has been integrated into national climate change and disaster policies.[1027] In some cases, countries have chosen to adopt new measures.[1028] For instance, the Intergovernmental

1024 ibid.

1025 However, for a critical evaluation, see Christina Oelgemöller and Kathryn Allinson, 'The Responsible Migrant, Reading the Global Compact on Migration' [2020] 31 Law and Critique, 183–207.

1026 In March 2020, UNICEF, IOM, UNHCR and OECD launched the International Data Alliance for Children on the Move, which aims to support evidence-based policymaking on migrant and displaced children, in partnership with State and non-State actors. The Migrant Union, which is an ongoing initiative to advance approaches to enabling the growing numbers of displaced people accessing sustainable livelihoods and enabling capabilities, rights and resources, has commissioned a report to explore the nexus between the changing nature of work, particularly driven by digitalisation, and livelihood opportunities for displaced people.

1027 For instance, the first report of the UN Secretary-General on the implementation of the Global Compact for Migration mentions the 2019 revision of the Guetamala National Plan of Action on Climate Change integrates a section on human mobility with concrete commitments. Belize is integrating human mobility and planned relocation into its climate strategy. Peru is developing a specific national plan of action to address climate-related climate-related drivers of migration. However, it must be noted that there are concrete examples of States incorporating human mobility considerations into their national climate policies before the adoption of the compact. See Report of the Secretary-General, 'Global Compact for Safe, Orderly and Regular Migration' (2020) GAOR 75th Session UN Doc A/75/542; UK Government, 'The Global Compact for Migration European Regional Review' <https://migrationnetwork.un.org/sites/default/files/docs/uk_submission__gcm_european_regional_review_.pdf> accessed 6 April 2022. Also see IOM, 'Mapping Human Mobility and Climate Change in Relevant National Policies and Institutional Frameworks' (UNFCCC WIM TFD, 2018) <https://unfccc.int/sites/default/files/resource/20180917%20WIM%20TFD%20I.1%20 Output%20final.pdfY> accessed 6 April 2022.

1028 The second report of the UN Secretary-General on the implementation of the Global Compact for Migration dedicates a subsection to the implementation of the commitments with respect to environmental and disaster mobility. According to the report, several countries, such as Nepal and Vanuatu, drafted policies focused on human mobility stemming from environmental factors. Germany convened an independent commission to develop recommendations on root causes of displacement. The Global Mayors Task

Authority on Development (IGAD) Ministers on Foreign Affairs adopted the Protocol on the Free Movement of Persons, which includes provisions allowing people affected by disasters to enter and stay in IGAD member states.[1029] Furthermore, the US Task Force to the President on the Climate Crisis and Global Migration recommended to the government, amongst others, options for the 'protection and resettlement of individuals displaced directly or indirectly from climate change'.[1030] It must be noted, however, that such measures do not fully respect the international protection of PMDCC as an obligation *erga omnes*. The multi-stakeholder approach to implementing the compact must be used to deal with the issue more rigorously, with the aim of going beyond the current implementation measures under the Global Compact for Migration.[1031]

Turning to the Global Compact on Refugees, the arrangements for the follow-up and review of the Global Compact on Refugees are designed to be primarily conducted through the Global Refugee Forum, high-level officials' meetings, and the annual reporting of the UNHCR to the UNGA.[1032] Furthermore, in order to support its implementation, an indicator framework was developed

Force on Climate and Migration was launched in 2021 to address the impacts of the climate crisis on migration in cities and to accelerate global responses. See UN Secretary-General, 'Global Compact for Safe, Orderly and Regular Migration Report to the Secretary-General' UN Doc A/76/642 (2022).

1029 IGAD Communiqué of the Sectorial Ministerial Meeting on the Protocol on Free Movement of Persons in the IGAD Region (26 February 2020, Khartoum, Republic of Sudan) <https://igad.int/attachments/article/2373/Communique%20on%20Endorsement%20of%20the%20Protocol%20of%20Free%20Movement%20of%20Persons.pdf> accessed 6 April 2022. Also see ILO, 'UN Agencies and IGAD Secretariat launch a regional initiative to address mitigation and climate change in East Africa' (ILO 2021) <https://www.ilo.org/global/docs/WCMS_794443/lang--en/index.htm> accessed 6 April 2022.

1030 Task Force to the President on the Climate Crisis and Global Migration, 'A Pathway to Protection for People on the Move' (Refugees International 2021).

1031 Ideally, regional migration and asylum policies must be in line with this vision. For a critical evaluation of regional approaches, see Geoff Gilbert, 'The New Pact on Migration and Asylum and the Global Compact on Refugees and Solutions' in Serio Carrera and Andrew Geddes, *The EU Pact on Migration and Asylum in light of the United Nations Global Compact on Refugees* (EUI 2021); Pauline Melin, 'Two Years After the Adoption of the Global Compact for Migration: Some Thoughts on the Role Played by the EU' in Wybe Doume and others, The Evolving Nature of EU External Relations Law (TMC Asser Press 2021); Fatima Khan and Cecile Sackeyfio, 'Situating the Global Compact on Refugees in Africa: Will it make a difference to the lives of refugees "languishing in camps"?' [2021] 65 Journal of African Law, 35–57.

1032 Global Compact on Refugees (n 9).

and published in July 2019.[1033] However, the indicator framework focuses on the four main objectives of the compact (easing pressures on host countries, enhancing refugee self-reliance, expanding access to third country solutions and supporting conditions in countries of origin for return in safety and dignity) and does not address HMDCC.[1034]

The Global Refugee Forum is scheduled to take place every four years, bringing together States and non-State actors to share good practices and to galvanise pledges and contributions, which can take different forms, including financial, material and technical assistance, places of resettlement, and complementary pathways for admission to third countries.[1035] The first Global Refugee Forum took place in December 2019 in Geneva and was dedicated to receiving formal pledges and contributions.[1036] It generated some 1,400 pledges.[1037] There were several commitments to support sustainable energy and environmental conservation.[1038] For instance, the Clean Energy Challenge was launched to provide access to affordable, reliable, sustainable and modern energy to all refugee settlements and nearby host communities by 2030.[1039] The challenge can be situated within the broader frame of addressing the accommodation and environmental impacts of large numbers of refugees, and facilitates access to appropriate accommodation for refugees and host communities.[1040] Other

1033 UNHCR, 'Global Compact on Refugees: Indicator Framework' (2019) <https://www.unhcr.org/5cf907854> accessed 6 April 2022.

1034 Global Compact on Refugees (n 9).

1035 ibid para 18. Also see UNHCR, 'What are pledges?' (15 June 2020) <https://globalcompactrefugees.org/article/what-are-pledges> accessed 6 April 2022.

1036 Global Refugee Forum Outcome Document (2019) <https://www.unhcr.org/5ecd458c4.pdf> accessed 6 April 2022.

1037 Ten outcomes were aimed: Progress in broadening the base of support for comprehensive refugee responses; support for the development of more inclusive national policies in host countries; launch of support platforms; additional funding and the effective and efficient use of resources; dedicated support to expand access to secondary, tertiary and higher education for refugees; financial, technical and material contributions in support of sustainable green energy and environmental conservation; private sector announcements in the form of investments, employment, innovation, advocacy and philanthropy; contributions towards solutions, including the 3-year resettlement and complementary pathways strategy; launch of the Asylum Capacity Support Group; and launch of the Global Academic Interdisciplinary Network. See Global Refugee Forum Outcome Document (2019) <https://www.unhcr.org/5ecd458c4.pdf> accessed 6 April 2022.

1038 Global Refugee Forum Outcome Document (2019) <https://www.unhcr.org/5ecd458c4.pdf> accessed 6 April 2022.

1039 ibid.

1040 UNHCR, 'Global Refugee Forum Guidance Note: Pledges and Contributions and Good Practices' (17–18 December 2019) <https://globalcompactrefugees.org/sites/default/files/2020-07/GRF%202019%20Guidance%20Note%20on%20Pledges%20and%20Contributions%20and%20Good%20Practices.pdf> accessed 6 April 2022.

examples include: planning for environmentally conscious land use in refugee-hosting areas; facilitating the inclusion of refugees in climate change resilience and adaptation programming; and including refugees in disaster risk reduction strategies related to infrastructure for essential services.[1041]

As with the Global Compact for Migration, there is a multi-stakeholder approach to the implementation of the Global Compact on Refugees.[1042] For instance, States committed to the establishment of 'a global academic network on refugee, other forced displacement, and statelessness issues', which was launched in 2019.[1043] The digital platform of the compact keeps count of pledges from multiple stakeholders, including the private sector, sports, faith-based and civil society organisations, as well as cities, municipalities and local authorities.[1044] Currently, some of the 1600 pledges registered in the digital platform demonstrate concrete measures for addressing HMDCC.[1045] Examples include: integrating suitable solutions for refugee responses into

1041 ibid.

1042 See Madeline Garlick and Claire Inder, 'Protection of refugees and migrants in the era of the global compacts' [2021] 23 International Journal of Postcolonial Studies 2, 207–226.

1043 UNHCR, 'About the Global Academic Interdisciplinary Network' (21 July 2020) <https://globalcompactrefugees.org/article/about-global-academic-interdisciplinary-network> accessed 6 April 2022.

1044 UNHCR, 'Pledges and Contributions' <https://globalcompactrefugees.org/channel/pledges-contributions> accessed 6 April 2022.

1045 For pledges about disasters, see: Kingdom of Lesotho Pledge ID 1047; Government of Nigeria Pledge ID 1205; National Commission for Refugees and IDPs Pledge ID 1282; Ministry of Foreign Affairs of the Republic of Korea Pledge ID 3050; Kaldor Centre for International Refugee Law UNSW Sydney Pledge ID 3055; Republic of Marshall Islands Pledge ID 3111; Agencia Española de Cooperación Internacional al Desarrollo Pledge ID 4022; Deltares (Stichting Deltares) Pledge ID 4033 and 4044; EU Pledge ID 4099 and 4105; Republic of Turkey, Ministry of Interior Disaster and Emergency Management Authority (AFAD) Pledge ID 4193; Save the Children Pledge ID 5032; INTERSOS Pledge ID 5043 and 5194; Compact for Young People in Humanitarian Action Pledge ID 5064; RET International Pledge ID 5081; UNICEF Pledge ID 5111; UNFPA Pledge ID 5118; RET International Pledge ID 5123 and 5184; Maya Vakfi Pledge ID 6056. For pledges about the climate and the environment, see: Government of South Sudan Pledge ID 1083; Government of Rwanda Pledge ID 1104; Permanent Mission of Mauritius Pledge ID 1241; Federal Democratic Republic of Ethiopia, Agency for Refugees and Returnees Affairs Pledge ID 1257; Republic of Zimbabwe Pledge ID 1279; Government of Rwanda Pledge ID 1352; Norwegian Ministry of Foreign Affairs Pledge ID 4008; Government of the Federal Republic of Germany Pledge ID 4012; Government of Ireland Pledge ID 4063; Denmark Ministry of Immigration and Integration Pledge ID 4107; Ministry of Foreign Affairs of Denmark Pledge ID 4289; Sweden Pledge ID 4320; Swedish International Development Cooperation Agency Pledge ID 4334, in UNHCR, 'All Pledges & Contributions' (2 March 2021) <https://globalcompactrefugees.org/channel/pledges-contributions> accessed 6 April 2022.

national disaster and climate change policies; establishing national authorities to enhance the coordination of actors in the management of disasters and human mobility; the relocation and reintegration of those displaced by disasters; and allocating budgets for disaster risk reduction resulting from climate change.[1046]

The preparation of new pledges for the 2023 Global Refugee Forum present a great opportunity to stress that the international protection of PMDCC is an obligation *erga omnes*. The implementation mechanisms of the Global Compact on Refugees engender intense efforts to create a new collaborative framework for an inclusive dialogue among the most relevant stakeholders. Even though the content of the compact does not explicitly mention the international protection of PMDCC,[1047] the references it contains to climate change, environmental degradation and natural disasters have opened up new horizons.[1048] The current pledges show that there are commitments to integrate different fields of law and policy in order to address HMDCC. These mechanisms can be employed to influence the outcomes of the international refugee regime in favour of responding to the protection needs of PMDCC.

This section has examined the follow-up and review mechanisms of the Global Compact for Migration and the Global Compact on Refugees in order to identify pathways to enforce the international protection of PMDCC as an obligation *erga omnes*. Although still in their 'embryo' stages, the mechanisms established to implement the compacts affirm the engagement of State and non-State actors to address HMDCC.[1049] However, the content of the relevant measures fall short of filling the protection needs of PMDCC and future involvement is needed to push for concerted efforts to prevent and address the adverse impact of disasters and climate change on people's well-being and living conditions.

1046 Kingdom of Lesotho Pledge ID 1047; Government of Nigeria Pledge ID 1205; National Commission for Refugees and IDPs Pledge ID 1282; Ministry of Foreign Affairs of the Republic of Korea Pledge ID 3050, in UNHCR, 'All Pledges & Contributions' (2 March 2021) <https://globalcompactrefugees.org/channel/pledges-contributions> accessed 6 April 2022.

1047 See Chapter 1.3.2 of this book for a detailed discussion.

1048 Although, it must be noted that these horizons are applicable to the countries that have adopted the Global Compact on Refugees. For a critical analysis, see Hilpold (n 96).

1049 Kainz and Betts (n 1013) 1–25.

3 Conclusion

This chapter has discussed the international protection of PMDCC as a matter of community interest. The discussion about the revival, content and legal effects of community interests demonstrated that the notion of community interests is invoked to refer to a transition from a bilateralist grounding of international law, towards an international legal order which protects and promotes the interests of humankind. Although community interests are difficult to identify a priori, scholarly works have been contributing to the identification of the objectives of community interests (i.e. the protection and creation of common goods, the protection of common values, the internationalisation of common spaces and redistributive and intergenerational justice) and community interest norms (i.e. the specific sub-set of rules of international law that protect and pursue these objectives).[1050] The recognition of rights and obligations *erga omnes* is one of the most significant achievements of the notion of community interests.[1051] Obligations *erga omnes* create obligations towards all and modify the right of standing to invoke the responsibility of a State.[1052] These norms of 'heightened importance' can be seen as an important 'enforcement tool', since all States have a legal interest in their protection.[1053]

By demonstrating that the international protection of PMDCC derives from the principles and rules concerning the basic rights of the human person, and that it is a community interest, this chapter has argued for a new right and obligation *erga omnes*. It has examined two pathways to enforcing this new obligation. First, it focused on the procedural aspects of four areas of international law, namely, international human rights law, international climate change law, international labour law and international trade law (with an emphasis on WTO law). This analysis has shown that each field has 'something to give': from the UPR to the TPRM, there are opportunities to take into account the international protection of PMDCC by paying attention to the procedural aspects.[1054] Second, the follow-up and review mechanisms established under the Global Compact for Migration and the Global Compact on Refugees were rigorously examined. It was shown that, although some of the concrete measures taken to implement the compacts address HMDCC, these measures do not adequately

1050 Feichtner (n 796).
1051 Simma (n 790).
1052 *Case Concerning the Barcelona Traction* (n 793).
1053 Tams (n 801) 51.
1054 For a similar discussion on procedural aspects, see Anthony J. Colangelo, 'Procedural Jus Cogens' [2021] 60 Columbia Journal of Transnational Law.

fill the 'lacuna' in international law with respect to the international protection of PMDCC. Thus, the chapter calls for future action to use the established multi-stakeholder mechanisms of the compacts to enforce the international protection of PMDCC as an obligation *erga omnes*.

CHAPTER 5

The International Protection of Persons Mobile in the Context of Disasters and Climate Change as a Common Concern of Humankind

This chapter proposes the creation of an international treaty to protect PMDCC, where the common concern of humankind provides the 'normative anchor'.[1055] Treaties have been used to shape international or neighbourly relations since ancient times – today, they are the principal instrument for ordering international relations.[1056] A common concern approach to treaty-making has the potential to govern the conduct of States to address shared and urgent problems which require the meaningful cooperation of everyone in response.[1057] Borrowing from Cottier and others, this chapter submits that there are two implications of a common concern approach: a novel duty to cooperate and a novel duty to act.[1058] Attached to the urgent, immediate and unavoidable need to provide international protection to PMDCC, common concern provides the basis and foundation for the crystallisation of more specific rights and obligations. In constructing its argument, this chapter first discusses the theory of common concern of humankind, before turning to its application in governing the matter of HMDCC.

1055 Jutta Brunnée, 'International Environmental Law and Community Interests: Procedural Aspects' in Eyal Benvenisti, Georg Nolte and Keren Yalin-mor (eds), *Community Interests across International Law* (Oxford University Press 2018), 166.

1056 Malgosia Fitzmaurice, 'Treaties' [2010] MPIL, para 5; Christian J. Tams, Antonios Tzanakopoulos and Andreas Zimmermann, 'Introduction' in Christian J. Tams, Antonios Tzanakopoulos and Andreas Zimmermann (eds), *Research Handbook on the Law of Treaties* (Edgar Elgar 2014) x; Crawford (n 864) 115–146.

1057 This book uses 'common concern of humankind' and 'common concern' interchangeably.

1058 Their work is the result of the research project titled 'Towards a Principle of Common Concern in Global Law: Foundations and Case Studies', which was funded by the Swiss National Science Foundation and undertaken at the World Trade Institute, University of Bern. The project was led by Professor Thomas Cottier and included four case studies by four authors: climate change (by Dr. Zaker Ahmad), violations of human rights (by Dr. Iryna Bogdanova), economic inequality (by Dr. Alexander Beyleveld), and monetary instability (by Dr. Lucia Satragno). See Cottier (ed) (n 21); Ahmad (n 27); Cottier and Shingal (n 332) 51–76.

DOI:10.1163/9789004522367_007

1 The Theory of the Common Concern of Humankind in International Law

The notion of the common concern of humankind does not have a settled or uniform definition in international law. Yet, as this section demonstrates, it has been a source of inspiration in international law-making. For instance, in 2018, States identified the 'predicament of refugees' as a common concern of humankind under the Global Compact on Refugees.[1059] More recently, in 2020, the 'protection of the atmosphere from atmospheric pollution and atmospheric degradation' was articulated as a common concern of humankind as a part of the ongoing work of the UN ILC.[1060] In order to frame the international protection of PMDCC as a common concern of humankind, the meaning, content and legal effects of the notion of common concern must be fleshed out. With this aim, this section first analyses the emergence and expressions of common concern, which is then followed by a doctrinal discussion of its possible legal effects.

1.1 *Emergence and Expressions*

The concept of common concern was developed from the 1980s onwards, as a part of the discussion about the environment and development.[1061] During this

1059 Global Compact on Refugees (n 9) para 1.

1060 Although this topic is explained in more depth later on in the Chapter, it can already be alluded to here that the Special Rapporteur Shinya Murase had actually framed the protection of the atmosphere as a common concern of humankind in 2015. This gave rise to a debate and as a result, the term 'pressing concern of humankind' was preferred at the time. However, upon the second reading in 2020, the language of 'common concern of humankind' was reintroduced. See Nolte (n 861) 113; Nilüfer Oral, 'The International Law Commission and the Progressive Development and Codification of Principles of International Environmental Law' [2019] 13 FIU L. Rev. 1075.

1061 It is important to note that the notion has been traced back to earlier treaties and arbitral awards addressing problems in shared jurisdiction and resources. For instance, Horn traces common concern back to a convention from 1949 between the USA and the Republic of Costa Rica declared tuna and other fish to be 'of common concern', expressing the need to maintain fish populations for the future. See Laura Horn, 'The Common Concern of Humankind and Legal Protection of the Global Environment' (PhD thesis University of Sydney 2000); Laura Horn, 'The Implications of the Concept of Common Concern of a Humankind on a Human Right to a Healthy Environment' [2004] Macquarie Journal of International and Comparative Environmental Law, 243; Laura Horn, 'Globalisation, Sustainable Development and the Common Concern of Humankind' [2007] Macquire Law Journal 7, 53–74. Inter-American Tropical Tuna Commission was set up for this purpose. The convention that established the commission has been ratified by twenty countries. See Convention between the USA and the Republic of Costa Rica for

period, common concern was recommended as 'a way out of the controversies' of the principle of common heritage of humankind.[1062] The common heritage approach aimed to establish the substance of the international administration of areas recognised as common goods based on the prohibition of national appropriation and the liberty of exploitation.[1063] Common concern, on the other hand, was devoid of proprietary connotations and focused on international cooperation in relation to protection.[1064] Opting for the latter approach, States referred to climate change and the loss of biological diversity as common concerns in 1992.[1065] Since then, common concern has been expressed in the preambles of several binding treaties as well as in non-binding UN instruments.[1066] This section discusses the emergence of common concern with reference to the principle of common heritage, followed by an examination of the expressions of common concern in international legal instruments.

In 1927, the Argentinian jurist and member of the League of Nations Committee of Experts for the Progressive Codification of International Law, José León Suárez, proposed that the living resources of the seas should be the 'heritage of mankind'.[1067] Forty years later, in 1967, the Maltese ambassador Arvid Pardo proposed the recognition of the governance of the seabed and

---

the establishment of an Inter-American Tropical Tuna Commission [adopted 31 May 1949, entered into force 3 March 1950] 80 UNTS 3.

1062 See 'Note from the UNEP Secretariat to the Meeting' in DJ Attard (ed), *The Meeting of the Group of Legal Experts to Examine the Concept of the Common Concern of Mankind in Relation to Global Environmental Issues* (Malta: University of Malta 1990) 38.

1063 The principle of common heritage of humankind was first developed under the name of common heritage of 'mankind'. This book uses common heritage, common heritage of humankind, and common heritage of mankind interchangeably. See generally, Kemal Baslar, *The Concept of the Common Heritage of Mankind in International Law* (Martinus Nijhoff Publishers 1998); Rüdiger Wolfrum, 'Common Heritage of Mankind' (Max Planck Encyclopedia 2009) <https://opil.ouplaw.com/view/10.1093/law:epil/9780199231690/law-9780199231690-e1149> accessed 6 April 2022.

1064 Zeynep Kivilcim, *Uluslararasi Kamu Hukukunda Insanligin Ortak Mirasi* (On Iki Levha Yayinlari 2010) 40–52.

1065 CBD (n 834); UNFCCC (n 248).

1066 International Treaty on Plant Genetic Resources for Food and Agriculture (adopted 3 November 2001, entered into force 29 June 2004) 2400 UNTS 303, preamble; United Nations Educational, Scientific and Cultural Organisation Convention for the Safeguarding of the Intangible Cultural Heritage (adopted 17 October 2003, entered into force 20 April 2006), preamble; Conference of the Parties, Adoption of the Paris Agreement (2016) UNFCCC Paris Agreement (Paris, 12 December 2015 and in force 4 November 2016), UN Doc. FCCC/CP/2015/L.9/Rev.1, 12 December 2015, preamble; Sendai Framework (n 496); Global Compact on Refugees (n 9) para 1.

1067 Tullio Scovazzi, 'The Seabed beyond the Limits of National Jurisdiction: General and Institutional Aspects' (Report submitted to the Fourth J. W. H. Verzijl Memorial

the ocean floor as a 'common heritage of mankind' within the framework of the UN.[1068] Observing the rapid development of technology to explore, occupy and exploit the world's seabed and ocean floor, Pardo stated that 'in accordance with historical precedent this capability will lead, indeed is already leading, to appropriation for national use of these areas, with consequences for all our countries that may be incalculable'.[1069] Some of the consequences he articulated included political tension, the risk of pollution and economic injustice, in light of which 'the strong would get stronger, the rich richer'.[1070] He advocated for the establishment of a universal regime of administration and control, governed under the common heritage principle.

Following Pardo's influential speech, the seabed and the ocean floor (along with its subsoil) lying beyond the limits of national jurisdiction (Area), as well as the resources of the Area were declared the common heritage of humankind in a UNGA Resolution in 1970.[1071] Shortly afterwards, two binding treaties – namely, the Moon Treaty of 1979 and UNCLOS of 1982 – adopted the common heritage principle.[1072] Furthermore, some commentators argue that the legal regimes for outer space, the high seas and – to a lesser

Symposium 'The legal regime of areas beyond national jurisdiction: current principles and frameworks and future direction', Utrecht, 21 November 2008).

1068 UNGA, Agenda item 92 (1967), 22nd Session, Annexes, 1. Also see *Note verbale* dated 17 August 1967, from the Permanent Mission of Malta to the UN Secretary General, Doc. No. A/6695.

1069 UNGA, 22nd Sess, Official Records, First Committee, 1515th meeting, New York, 1967, UN Doc A/C.1/PV.1515.

1070 Arvid Pardo, *The Common Heritage - Selected Papers on Oceans and World Order* (Malta University Press, 1975) 31.

1071 UNGA Res 2749 (1970) 'Declaration of Principles Governing the Seabed and the Ocean Floor and the Subsoil thereof beyond the limits of national jurisdiction XXV'.

1072 Art 11(1) of the Moon Treaty states that '[t]he moon and its natural resources are the common heritage of mankind'. Art 136 of UNCLOS states that '[t]he Area and its resources are the common heritage of mankind'. It must be noted that prior to these treaties, in 1967, the Treaty on Principles Governing the Activities of States in the Exploration and Use of Outer Space, including the Moon and Other Celestial Bodies (Outer Space Treaty) recognised in its preamble the 'common interest of all mankind' in the progress of the exploration and use of outer space for peaceful purposes. See Agreement Governing the Activities of States on the Moon and Other Celestial Bodies (adopted 18 December 1979, entered into force) 1363 UNTS (Moon Treaty); United Nations Convention on the Law of the Sea (adopted 10 December 1982, entered into force 16 November 1994) 1833 UNTS 396; Treaty on Principles Governing Activities of States in the Exploration and Use of Outer Space, Including the Moon and Other Celestial Bodies (adopted 27 January 1967, entered into force 10 October 1967) 610 UNTS 205.

extent – Antarctica are governed by common heritage.[1073] There were failed attempts to bring the management of other goods, such as cultural heritage and the human genome, under the common heritage regime.[1074]

The development of the common heritage regime occurred during the pressing demands for a New International Economic Order (NIEO). From the 1950s onwards, NIEO appeared as a movement in international law, which was majorly advocated by the newly created States of the Global South as a result of decolonisation.[1075] Their broader demands focused on correcting inequalities, ensuring steadily accelerating economic and social development, and peace and justice for present and future generations.[1076]

NIEO inspired the adoption of a UNGA Declaration and an Action Programme on the Establishment of a New International Economic Order, as well as the Charter of Economic Rights and Duties of States, all of which referred to the structural economic relations between developed and developing countries.[1077] In 1985, a study by UNITAR, at the request of the UNGA and presided over by Abi-Saab, identified the two cornerstones of NIEO demands: sovereign equality and the duty to co-operate closely with other States.[1078] Sovereign equality related to the right of States to choose their own economic system and the duty to co-operate called for preferential treatment of developing countries. In relation to natural resources governance, their demands emphasised the even and balanced development 'of all the peoples on Earth',[1079] leading

1073 Rüdiger Wolfrum argues this by examining the province of all humankind principle in Outer Space Treaty, Art 2 of the Geneva Convention on the High Seas and Article IV of the Antarctic Treaty. See Wolfrum (n 787). Also see Committee on the Role of International Law in Sustainable Natural Resources Management for Development '2020 ILA Guidelines on the Role of International Law in Sustainable Natural Resources Management for Development' in International Law Association Report of the Seventy-Ninth Conference (Kyoto 2020) 5.

1074 Kivilcim (n 1064) 12–17.

1075 Cassese (n 22) 42–45.

1076 See Philip Golub, 'From the New International Economic Order to the G20: how the global South is restructuring world capitalism from within' [2013] Third World Quarterly 34, 1004. For a critical reading of the NIEO, see Herbert G. Grubel, 'The Case Against the New International Economic Order' [1977] Weltwirtschaftliches Archiv, Bd 11.

1077 UNGA Res 3201 (S-VI) Declaration on the Establishment of a New International Economic Order (1974); UNGA Res 3281 (XXIX) Charter of Economic Rights and Duties (1974) UN Doc A/RES/29/3281.

1078 Report of the Secretary-General, 'Progressive Development of the Principles and Norms of International Law Relating to the New International Economic Order' (1984) UN Doc A/39/504/Add.1.

1079 Mohammed Bedjaoui, *Towards a New International Legal Order* (New York: Holmes & Meier 1979) 72.

to calls for stronger permanent sovereignty over resources in national jurisdictions and the development of a common heritage regime for resources in common goods, as a manifestation of the duty to co-operate.[1080]

However, the concept of common heritage was the target of significant criticism.[1081] In 1990, a group of experts were convened by UNEP to examine the concept of common concern, and they approached common heritage as generating 'controversies', while viewing common concern 'as a way out of these controversies'.[1082] These controversies can be summarised under three headings:

First, common heritage is applicable to common goods, which leads to free access and exploitation administered under an international regime.[1083] This was perceived as an unwanted outcome for natural resources within State jurisdiction, as States wanted to preserve their sovereign rights to exploit their resources according to domestic laws and policies.

Second, common heritage prescribes the liberty of exploitation, an element which 'appeared no longer satisfactory'.[1084] Some commentators approach common heritage as being 'locked' in an 'exploitation bias'.[1085] According to

---

1080 Umut Özsu, 'Neoliberalism and the New International Economic Order: A History of "Contemporary Legal Thought"' in Justin Desautels-Stein and Christopher Tomlins, *Searching for Contemporary Legal Thought* (CUP 2017); Nico J Schrijver, *The Evolution of Sustainable Development in International Law: Inception, Meaning and Status* (Pocketbooks of the Hague Academy of International Law Brill 2009) 47–56.

1081 On hindsight, whether common heritage delivered its initial promise to achieve a universal regime of administration and control in common goods can also be debated. Examining the Moon Treaty, it was ratified only by 18 States, and the international body that was supposed to administer the 'exploitation of the natural resources of the moon as such exploitation is about to become feasible', was never established. Examining the Area recognised as a common heritage under UNCLOS, one-third of the surface of the world ocean was allocated to thirty-five States in the form of an 'economic zone', which significantly shrank the areas where the common heritage principle would be applicable under UNCLOS. Furthermore, the international Enterprise that would conduct the exploitation operations was never established. However, the International Seabed Authority was created with a view to organising and controlling activities in the Area, especially with regards to the administration of resources.

1082 'Note from the UNEP Secretariat to the Meeting' in DJ Attard (ed), *The Meeting of the Group of Legal Experts to Examine the Concept of the Common Concern of Mankind in Relation to Global Environmental Issues* (Malta: University of Malta 1990) at page 38. The Group of Legal Experts also met in Malta 1990, Geneva 1991, Beijing 1991.

1083 Simon Bilderbeek, Ankie Wijgerde and Netty van Schaik (eds), *Biodiversity and International Law: The effectiveness of international environmental law* (IOS Press 1992) 87.

1084 Cançado Trindade (n 19) 295.

1085 See Isabel Feichtner and Surabhi Ranganathan, 'International Law And Economic Exploitation in The Global Commons: Introduction' [2019] 30 EJIL 2, 541–546.

this view, common heritage incorporates an 'economy of interests in which the rampant commercial exploitation of nature is justified with the satisfaction of societal needs' and underlies two competing interests: first, the participation in exploitation and revenue generation pursued by developing States and, second, access to raw materials pursued by industrialised States.[1086] During the Cold War era, this understanding justified the legal conditions for seizing both national and international jurisdiction.[1087]

Third, there was a growing consensus that the exploitation aspect of common heritage failed to deliver on the responsible conservation of natural resources in the interest of future generations.[1088] Most notably, the report of the World Commission on Environment and Development released in 1987 described the now-common term 'sustainable development' as development that 'meets the needs of the present without compromising the ability of future generations to meet their own needs'.[1089] It was in the aftermath of this report that common concern was conceived as showing 'universal interest and a shared responsibility in conservation and sustainable use'.[1090]

These criticisms highlight that there was, and still is, room for improvement with respect to the content and application of the common heritage

---

1086 Isabel Feichtner, 'Sharing the Riches of the Sea: the Redistributive and Fiscal Dimension of Deep Seabed Exploitation' in Symposium: International Law and Economic Exploitation In The Global Commons [2019] 30 EJIL 2, 601–633.

1087 Surabhi Ranganathan, 'Ocean Floor Grab: International Law and the Making of an Extractive Imaginary' in Symposium: International Law and Economic Exploitation In The Global Commons [2019] 30 EJIL 2, 573–600.

1088 See for instance, Alex Kiss and Dinah L. Shelton, *International Environmental Law* (Transnational Publishers, Ardsley-on-Hudson 1991) 380. Responses to these criticisms generally focus on the guidelines developed by the International Seabed Authority, which aim to contribute to the development of international environmental law and clarify what is meant by sustainable development with respect to the management of the resources in the Area. See Rüdiger Wolfrum, 'The Contribution of the Regulations of the International Seabed Authority to the Progressive Development of International Environmental Law' in Michael W. Lodge and Myron H. Nordquist (eds), *Peaceful Order in the World's Oceans Essays in Honor of Satya N. Nandan* (2014) 242.

1089 In 1983, on account of urgent problems over the environment, resources, development and people, the UNGA decided to establish the World Commission on Environment and Development to formulate 'a global agenda for change'. The Commission was led by Gro Harlem Brundtland, and released its report titled 'Our Common Future' in 1987. World Commission on Environment and Development, 'Our Common Future' (1987).

1090 Ahmed Yusuf, 'The UN Convention on Biological Diversity' in Najeeb Al-Nauimi and Richard Meese (eds) *International Legal Issues Arising under the United Nations Decade of International Law: Proceedings of the Qatar International Law Conference* (Springer Netherland 1994) 1171.

principle.[1091] Common concern emerged as a means to address these criticisms. In 1988, the UNGA recognised that climate change is a common concern.[1092] In 1992, common concern was acknowledged in the preambles of two binding international conventions, namely, the UNFCCC and the CBD.[1093]

Common concern has been adopted in different contexts since then. In 2001, the preamble of the International Treaty on Plant Genetic Resources termed plant genetic resources for food and agriculture as a common concern.[1094] Similarly, in 2003, the preamble of the UNESCO Convention for the Safeguarding of the Intangible Cultural Heritage included a reference to 'being aware of the universal will and the common concern to safeguard the intangible cultural heritage of humanity'.[1095] In 2015, the preamble of the Paris Agreement re-emphasised that climate change is a common concern.[1096] The same year, Sendai Framework for Disaster Risk Reduction similarly identified 'the reduction of disaster risk' as a 'common concern for all States'.[1097]

In 2018, the Global Compact on Refugees phrased 'the predicament of refugees' as a common concern.[1098] The wording 'common concern' was inserted into the text during the second round of consultations.[1099] The UNHCR's Assistant High Commissioner for Protection at the time, Dr Volker Türk, 'had the idea to include in the compact reference to the refugee issue as a common concern at the beginning, building upon one of the first UNGA Resolutions in 1946, which considered the refugee problem as a matter of international

1091 See Karin Mickelson, 'Common Heritage of Mankind as a Limit to Exploitation of the Global Commons' in Symposium: International Law And Economic Exploitation In The Global Commons [2019] 30 EJIL 2, 635–663.

1092 Based on a proposal by Malta, see UNGA Res 43/53 (1988).

1093 See Claire Shine and Palitha Kohona, 'The Convention on Biological Diversity: Bridging the Gap Between Conservation and Development' [1992] Review of European Community and International Environmental Law, 282. Furthermore, Kiss and Shelton note that Malta had initially proposed climate to be common heritage, which was rejected. See Kiss and Shelton (n 1088) 10.

1094 International Treaty on Plant Genetic Resources for Food and Agriculture (n 1066).

1095 United Nations Educational, Scientific and Cultural Organisation Convention for the Safeguarding of the Intangible Cultural Heritage (n 1066).

1096 Paris Agreement (n 1066).

1097 Sendai Framework (n 496).

1098 Global Compact on Refugees (n 9) para 1.

1099 See UNHCR, 'The global compact on refugees: Draft 1' (9 March 2018) <https://www.unhcr.org/events/conferences/5aa2b3287/official-version-draft-1-global-compact-refugees-9-march-2018.html> accessed 6 April 2022; UNHCR, 'The global compact on refugees: Draft 2' (30 April 2018) <https://www.unhcr.org/events/conferences/5ae758d07/official-version-draft-2-global-compact-refugees-30-april-2018.html> accessed 6 April 2022.

concern'.[1100] The inclusion of common concern in the text was welcomed and made it into the final adopted version.[1101]

Common concern continues to inspire international law-making. In 2020, the Draft Convention on the Right to Development acknowledged that 'the realisation of the right to development is a common concern of humankind'.[1102] Furthermore, the same year, the IUCN proposed a common concern approach to be included in the preamble of the treaty on marine biodiversity of areas beyond national jurisdiction (ABNJ).[1103] The negotiations for this treaty began following the decision of the UNGA in 2017 to convene an intergovernmental

---

1100 The first draft of the compact stated that the 'predicament of refugees is an important international concern'. In 1949 in a resolution, the UNGA had referred to the problem of refugees as international in scope and nature, and the necessary legal protection of refugees as a concern. Building on this, UNHCR's Assistant High Commissioner at the time, Dr. Volker Türk, had the idea to include in the Global Compact on Refugees a reference to the refugee issue as a common concern. Türk had already written in 2003 with Nicholson that the 1951 Refugee Convention and its 1967 Protocol set the core principles for the international protection of refugees, and reinforcing these global treaties as the foundation of the protection regime is a common concern. Reference to common concern was inserted in the second draft of the compact, and succeeded until the final adopted version. See UNGA Res 319, 'Refugees and stateless persons' (3 December 1949) UN Doc A/RES/319 <https://www.refworld.org/docid/3b00fied34.html> accessed 6 April 2022; Volker Türk and Frances Nicholson, 'Refugee Protection in International Law: An Overall Perspective' in Erika Feller, Volker Türk and Frances Nicholson, *Refugee Protection in International Law* (Cambridge University Press 2003).

1101 For instance, see the written contribution of the Business Fights Poverty to the UN Consultations on the Global Compact on Refugees. Business Fights Poverty, 'Written Contribution to the UN Consultations on the Global Compact on Refugees' <https://www.unhcr.org/events/conferences/5b3c8fba7/enabling-business-solutions-refugees-global-compact-refugees-mobilize-business.html> accessed 6 April 2022.

1102 UNHRC, 'Draft convention on the right to development' UN Doc A/HR/WG.2/21/2.

1103 IUCN proposed the following wording: 'Aware that the conservation of marine biodiversity is a common concern and the shared responsibility of all States and that States have the obligation to protect and preserve the marine environment in ABNJ and to assist other States to do the same'. See 'Textual proposals submitted by delegations by 20 February 2020, for consideration at the fourth session of the Intergovernmental conference on an international legally binding instrument under the United Nations Convention on the Law of the Sea on the conservation and sustainable use of marine biological biodiversity of areas beyond national jurisdiction (the Conference), in response to the invitation by the President of the Conference in her Note of 18 November 2019 (A/CONF.232/2020/3)' <https://www.un.org/bbnj/sites/ www.un.org.bbnj/files/textual_proposals_compilation_article-by-article_-_15_april_2020.pdf> accessed 6 April 2022, 5. Also see Pascale Ricard, 'Marine biodiversity beyond national jurisdiction: The launch of an intergovernmental conference for the adoption of a legally binding instrument under the UNCLOS' [2019] Maritime Safety and Security Law Journal.

conference to consider an international legally binding instrument under UNCLOS on the conservation and sustainable use of marine biological diversity of ABNJ.[1104] Oral is one of the proponents of the need to recognise the marine biodiversity of ABNJ as a common concern, and she interprets the ongoing negotiations as an opportunity to define the emerging principle.[1105] The fourth and final session of the intergovernmental conference has been postponed due to the COVID-19 pandemic, and it is to be seen whether the notion of common concern will prevail.

Another recent discussion on the use of common concern took place at the UN ILC. ILC Special Rapporteur Shinya Murase had proposed already in 2015 under the draft guidelines that '[t]he atmosphere is a natural resource essential for sustaining life on Earth, human health and welfare, and aquatic and terrestrial ecosystems, and hence the degradation of atmospheric conditions is a common concern of humankind'.[1106] This formulation gave rise to a 'controversial debate'.[1107] As a result, the ILC settled on the phrase 'pressing concern of the international community as a whole' at the time, which is the criterion it uses to select its own topics. According to ILC member Nolte, the ILC, '[b]eing a body which usually decides by way of consensus, no more emphatic or clearer articulation of the collective interest 'protection of the atmosphere' was possible at the moment'.[1108]

However, the conversation did not end there. States brought common concern back to the discussions on the protection of the atmosphere at the ILC. The EU suggested that the ILC use the wording 'common concern of humankind'

1104 UN, 'BBNJ', official webpage <https://www.un.org/bbnj/> accessed 6 April 2022; UNGA Res 72/249 (24 December 2017) UN Doc A/RES/72/249; UNGA Res 69/292 (6 July 2015) UN Doc A/RES/62/292.

1105 IUCN, 'ESIL Annual Conference: International Law, Global Public Goods, Global Commons and Fundamental Values' official webpage (11 September 2017) <https://www.iucn.org/news/world-commission-environmental-law/201709/esil-annual-conference-international-law-global-public-goods-global-commons-and-fundamental-values> accessed 6 April 2022.

1106 ILC, 'Second report on the protection of the atmosphere by Shinya Murase, Special Rapporteur' 67th sess (2 March 2015) UN Doc A/CN.4/681. Also see ILC, 'Third report on the protection of the atmosphere by Shinya Murase, Special Rapporteur' 68th sess (25 February 2016) UN Doc A/CN.4/692; ILC, 'Fourth report on the protection of the atmosphere by Shinya Murase, Special Rapporteur' 69th sess (31 January 2017) UN Doc A/CN.4/705; ILC, 'Fifth report on the protection of the atmosphere by Shinya Murase, Special Rapporteur' 70th sess (8 February 2018) UN Doc A/CN.4/711; ILC, 'Sixth report on the protection of the atmosphere by Shinya Murase, Special Rapporteur' 68th sess (11 February 2020) UN Doc A/CN.4/736.

1107 Nolte (n 861) 113.

1108 ibid 114. Also see, Oral (n 1060) 1075.

instead of the 'pressing concern of the international community'.[1109] Antigua and Barbuda, the Netherlands, Germany, Colombia, Iran, Japan, Sri Lanka and Viet Nam also supported the use of the expression 'common concern of humankind'.[1110]

The Nordic countries submitted that they would like to encourage the ILC to elaborate on the implications of the legal concept of common concern of humankind in the context of environmental law on the protection of the atmosphere.[1111]

Portugal argued that the protection of the atmosphere should be referred to as a common concern of humankind in accordance with international legally binding instruments of the UNFCCC, arguing that, for the progressive development of international law, a normative statement was preferable to a purely factual one.[1112]

In line with these comments, the Special Rapporteur proposed in his sixth report, which was distributed in February 2020, that 'recognising the protection of the atmosphere from atmospheric pollution and atmospheric degradation is a common concern of humankind'.[1113] The ILC is set to discuss the draft preamble and guidelines prepared by the Special Rapporteur and submit its final draft report to the UNGA, accompanied by a recommendation for further action.[1114]

In 2021, ILC Special Rapporteur Shinya Murase also prepared a report on epidemics and international law as a part of the Institut de Droit International in the capacity of Rapporteur, in which he has proposed that epidemics are matters of common concern of humankind.[1115]

To conclude, this section has demonstrated that common concern was developed as an alternative to the application of the common heritage principle. The fact that it is devoid of proprietary connotations, that it respects State sovereignty over relevant resources and that it calls for institutional cooperation in order to secure protection were the main reasons for its success in the climate change and biological diversity treaty negotiations. The notion of

1109 ILC, 'Sixth report on the protection of the atmosphere by Shinya Murase, Special Rapporteur' 68th sess (11 February 2020) UN Doc A/CN.4/736, para 24.

1110 ibid para 23–28.

1111 ibid para 65.

1112 ibid para 24.

1113 ibid para 33.

1114 ibid para 100–102.

1115 Institut de Droit International, 'Epidemics and International Law' 12éme Commission, Rapporteur: Shinya Murase (2021) <https://www.idi-iil.org/app/uploads/2021/05/Report-12th-commission-epidemics-vol-81-yearbook-online-session.pdf> accessed 6 April 2022.

common concern has undoubtedly expanded in scope since then, being used to address shared problems in other matters, such as disaster risk reduction and refugee protection. The ongoing negotiations for the treaty on marine biodiversity of ABNJ, and the draft guidelines for the protection of the atmosphere indicate that the concept of common concern continues to play a role in inspiring the development of international law.

1.2 *Legal Effects: Treaty Regimes as a Reflection of Common Concerns*

Common concern finds expression in several international legal instruments, but these fail to elaborate on its precise legal ramifications.[1116] Scholarly writings have attempted to fill this gap by fleshing out its material content and legal effects.[1117] Borrowing from Cottier and others, in the author's view, there should be two main normative effects of common concern: a novel duty to cooperate and a novel duty to act.[1118] This section analyses the doctrinal discussion to expound on the novel duties to cooperate and to act, with a focus on the climate change and refugee regimes where common concern has been adopted.

The starting point for discussing the legal effects of common concern is the articulation of its material content. The previous section has discussed the fact that common concern emerged as an alternative to the principle of common heritage. Unlike common heritage, common concern does not aim to suppress national claims in favour of creating a universal regime of administration and control, so that all States can exercise the liberty to exploit a natural resource.[1119]

1116 Zaker Ahmad, 'State Responsibility Aspects of a Common Concern Based Approach to Collective Action' in Samantha Besson (ed), *International Responsibility: Essays in Law, History and Philosophy* (Schulthess 2017) 97–116.

1117 Friedrich Soltau, 'Common Concern of Humankind' in Cinnamon Pinon Carlarne, Kevin R. Gray, Richard Tarasofsky (eds), The Oxford Handbook on International Climate Change Law (OUP 2016); Werner Scholtz, 'Human Rights and Climate Change: Extending the Extraterritorial Dimension via the Common Concern' in Wolfgang Benedek and others (eds), *The Common Interest in International Law* (Intersentia 2014) 134–135; Jimena Murillo, 'Common Concern of Humankind and its Implications in International Environmental Law' [2008] 5 Macquarie Journal of International and Comparative Environmental Law 133; Frank Biermann, '"Common Concern of Humankind": The Emergence of a New Concept of International Environmental Law' [1996] 34 Archiv des Völkerrechts 4, 426–481.

1118 Cottier (ed) (n 21).

1119 Jutte Brunnée, 'Common interests - Echoes from an Empty shell? Some thoughts on common interest and international environmental law' [1989] 49 ZaöRV, 791–808.

Instead, common concern is devoid of proprietary connotations and emphasises the element of protection.[1120] Building on these qualities, Trindade suggested that common concern: necessitates the engagement of all countries, societies and social segments within the countries; encompasses both the present and future generations; primarily gives attention to the causes of the problems (both for their prevention and for determing the responses to be given); and finally, applies equitable sharing of responsibility.[1121]

These constitutive elements of common concern are applied to issues of a specific character. First, these issues are 'common', meaning that they are shared or transboundary problems, transcending the boundaries of a single State.[1122] What makes them a 'concern' is the sense of urgency of the problem, which has a wide-ranging and long-term socio-economic impact.[1123] Second, the meaningful cooperation of everyone involved is necessary to address these shared problems.[1124] The contrary scenario might lead to the 'tragedy of the commons', which is a dilemma that occurs when multiple individuals act independently and according to their own self-interest, ultimately depleting a finite shared resource.[1125] Similarly, so-called beggar-thy-neighbour policies might be adopted, which attempt to remedy a problem by maximising one's own benefits at the expense of partners, neighbours and others that are impacted, thus worsening the situation for other parties involved.[1126]

To facilitate the identification of a transboundary problem as a common concern, Cottier and others proposed setting 'the potential and risk to threaten international stability, peace and welfare' as a threshold.[1127] They argue that

---

1120 Edith Brown Weiss, 'The Coming Water Crisis: A Common Concern of Humankind' [2012] 1 Transnational Environmental Law 1, 153–168.

1121 Cançado Trindade (n 19) 351.

1122 Dinah Shelton, 'Common Concern of Humanity' (Environmental Law and Policy 39/2, 2009).

1123 Christina Voigt, 'Delineating the Common Interest in International Law' in Wolfgang Benedek and others (eds), The Common Interest in International Law (Intersentia 2014) 19.

1124 Jutta Brunnée, 'Common Areas, Common Heritage, and Common Concern' in Daniel Bodansky, Jutta Brunnée and Ellen Hey (eds), *The Oxford Handbook of International Environmental Law* (OUP 2008).

1125 ibid. Also see Garrett Hardin, 'The Tragedy of the Commons' [1968] 162 Science 3859.

1126 ibid.

1127 Their work is the result of the research project titled 'Towards a Principle of Common Concern in Global Law: Foundations and Case Studies', which was funded by the Swiss National Science Foundation and undertaken at the World Trade Institute, University of Bern. The project was led by Professor Thomas Cottier and included four case studies by four authors: climate change (by Dr. Zaker Ahmad), violations of human rights (by Dr. Iryna Bogdanova), economic inequality (by Dr. Alexander Beyleveld), and monetary matters are deemed to be of common concern as the result of a 'process of claims and responses'.[1128] This refers to the initiatives, debates, approvals or rejections in the diplomatic and legal processes of law-making, and involves contributions from States and non-State actors.[1129] Scholarly works also hold a special place in this process, as these can be recognised in case law, international declarations and perhaps even in treaty law.[1130]

A closer look at the international climate regime and the international refugee regime, where common concern has been adopted, expounds on the legal ramifications of common concern. The adoption of the UNFCCC marks the beginning of an international legal process for ongoing exchange and negotiation on climate change, supported by treaty secretariats.[1131] In the preamble to the UNFCCC, climate change has been recognised as a common concern of humankind.[1132] This recognition was reiterated in the Paris Agreement in 2015.[1133]

In line with the notion of common concern, the regime's approach from the onset incorporated an understanding of 'minimised'[1134] interference with State sovereignty, calling instead for the 'widest possible cooperation by all countries and their participation in an effective and appropriate international response'.[1135] The setting out of common standards and commitments for further cooperation drives the regime.

One of its biggest challenges has been how to differentiate responsibilities to address climate change as a common concern.[1136] CBDR-RC was acknowledged in the UNFCCC as a key structural principle.[1137] Translated into

instability (by Dr. Lucia Satragno). Cottier (ed) (n 21); Beyleveld (n 21); Satragno (n 21); Bogdanova (n 21); Ahmad (n 27).

1128 Cottier (ed) (n 21).

1129 ibid.

1130 ibid.

1131 Bodansky (n 219); Stephen D. Krasner, 'Structural Causes and Consequences: Regimes as Intervening Variables' in John J. Kirton (ed), *International Organization* [1982] 36 Spring 2.

1132 UNFCCC (n 248), preamble.

1133 Paris Agreement (n 1066).

1134 Soltau (n 1117).

1135 UNFCCC (n 248), preamble.

1136 Margaretha Wewerinke-Singh, *State Responsibility, Climate Change and Human Rights under International Law* (Hart Publishing 2019) 41–69.

1137 Rio Declaration on Environment and Development (Rio de Janeiro, 3–14 June 1992) A/CONF.151/26, vol.I, principle 7; Lavanya Rajamani, *Differential Treatment in International Environmental Law* (Oxford Scholarship Online 2006) 134; Sonja Klinsky and Harald Winkler, 'Equity, sustainable development and climate policy' [2014] 14 Climate Policy 1, 1–7.

responsibilities, it first landed on a stark South-North differentiation under the 1997 Kyoto Protocol, in which only Annex I countries were obliged to reduce or limit their GHG emissions.[1138] A 'more nuanced and dynamic differentiation' was achieved with the invention of NDCs for a number of reasons.[1139] First, the distinction between Annex I and non-Annex I country groupings effectively disregarded the emissions of emerging economies such as China and India.[1140] Second, the US never ratified the Kyoto Protocol, Canada withdrew from it, and Japan and Russia had no binding targets in its second commitment period.[1141] Third, the measures for the Annex I countries mostly related to mitigation, and the need to include adaptation and finance was increasingly stressed.[1142] Thus, the NDCs were adopted under the Paris Agreement to address the delicate balance between equitable burden sharing, on the one hand, and the need to hold all States to sufficiently high standards of responsibility, on the other.[1143]

However, it is difficult to argue that the common concern approach to climate change has been successful. The attempt to limit the global temperature rise to well below 2 degrees Celsius above pre-industrial levels – with a view to pursuing further efforts to limit it to 1.5 degrees Celsius – is failing. The world

1138 Annex I countries included the industrialised countries that were members of the OECD in 1992, and countries with economies in transition. The Doha Amendment to the Kyoto Protocol was adopted for a second commitment period, starting in 2013 and lasting until 2020. UNFCCC, Doha Amendment to the Kyoto Protocol <https://unfccc.int/files/kyoto_protocol/application/pdf/kp_doha_amendment_english.pdf> accessed 6 April 2022 See Nada Maamoun, 'The Kyoto Protocol: Empirical evidence of a hidden success' [2019] 95 Journal of Environmental Economics and Management, 227–256; Roger Guesnerie, 'A Future for the Kyoto Protocol?' in Ajit Sinha and Siddhartha Mitra, *Economic Development, Climate Change, and the Environment* (Routledge 2006).

1139 It must be noted that when the first commitment period of the Kyoto Protocol expired in 2012, the global emissions were approximately 50% higher than they were in 1990. Bang, Hovi and Skodvin explain this by at least four forms of free riding. See Guri Bang, Jon Hovi and Tora Skodvin, 'The Paris Agreement: Short-Term and Long-Term Effectiveness 2016. Also see Brunnée (n 1034) 165.

1140 Karoliina Hurri, 'Rethinking climate leadership: Annex I countries' expectations for China's leadership role in the post-Paris UN climate negotiations' [2020] 35 Environmental Development.

1141 Christian Almer and Ralph Winkler, 'Analyzing the effectiveness of international environmental policies: The case of the Kyoto Protocol' [2017] 81 Journal of Environmental Economics and Management, 125–151.

1142 Dale Jamieson, 'Adaptation, Mitigation, and Justice' [2015] 5 Perspectives on Climate Change, Science, Economics, Politics, Ethics, 217–248.

1143 Peter Pauw et al., 'Beyond headline mitigation numbers: we need more transparent and comparable NDCs to achieve the Paris Agreement on climate change' [2017] 147 Climatic Change, 23–29.

is on track to see global warming of around 3 degrees Celsius by the end of this century, even if countries live up to their current commitments.[1144]

At least two features of the international climate change regime can explain this. First, the Paris Agreement creates obligations of conduct, instead of obligations of result.[1145] Essentially, the Paris Agreement leaves the target to unilateral commitments by States.[1146] Party States are to prepare, communicate and maintain successive NDCs, and 'pursue domestic mitigation measures, with the aim of achieving the objectives of such contributions'.[1147] Each State is expected to set its own priorities and ambitions 'bottom-up', which stimulates countries' self-differentiation of responsibilities and capabilities.[1148] So far, the level of ambition for reducing emissions is very weak: the NDC submissions up to 31 December 2020 show that there would be less than –1% change in the total emissions in 2030 as compared to 2010.[1149] By contrast, the IPCC has indicated that, in order to meet the 1.5°C temperature goal, emissions reduction should be around –45% in 2030 as compared to 2010.[1150] More recent studies unfortunately do not show positive progress. In its sixth assessment report published in August 2021, the IPCC confirmed that in the near term (2021–2040) 1.2°C global warming is happening.[1151] Furthermore, prior to COP26 to the UNFCCC, the UNFCCC Secretariat published a report in October 2021 which showed that the communicated NDCs may lead to a temperature rise of about 2.7°C by the end of this century.[1152]

1144 UNEP, 'Emissions Gap Report 2020' (2020).

1145 Jutta Brunnée, *Procedure and Substance in International Environmental Law* (The Hague Academy of International Law, Brill 2021).

1146 See Pieter Pauw and others, 'Conditionally national determined contributions in the Paris Agreement: foothold for equity or Achilles heel?' [2020] 20 Climate Policy 4; Benoit Mayer, 'International Law Obligations Arising in Relation to Nationally Determined Contributions' [2018] 7 Cambridge Core 2; Lavanya Rajamani, 'Ambition and Differentiation in the 2015 Paris Agreement: Interpretative Possibilities and Underlying Politics' [2016] 65 ICLQ 493.

1147 Paris Agreement (n 1066) art 4(2).

1148 Amita Punj, 'Common but Differentiated Responsibility' in Koen de Feyter, Gamze E. Türkelli and Stéphanie de Moerloose, *Encylopedia of Law and Development* (Edgar Elgar 2021).

1149 UNFCCC, 'Nationally Determined Contributions Synthesis Report' (26 February 2021) FCCC/PA/CMA/2021/2.

1150 IPCCC, 'Special Report on Global Warming of 1.5°C' (2018).

1151 IPCC (n 26) 14.

1152 UNFCCC Secretariat, 'Nationally determined contributions under the Paris Agreement. Revised Note by the Secretariat' UN Doc FCCC/PA/CMA/2021/8/Rev.1 (2021).

Second, the Achilles' heel of the Paris Agreement is compliance.[1153] Compliance, in a legal sense, applies to legally binding obligations, and under the Paris Agreement, the legally binding obligations relate to procedural obligations.[1154] For instance, States Parties must communicate their NDCs every five years.[1155] However, substantive issues such as the content of the NDCs (other than the procedural requirement of submitting an NDC that represents a 'progression') or the mobilisation of climate finance cannot be subject to noncompliance measures.[1156] In fact, States even reserve the right to withdraw from the treaty, as exemplified by the US, which had a short sojourn (totalling 107 days) outside the Paris Agreement.[1157]

1153 See Anna Huggins, 'The Paris Agreement's Compliance Mechanism: An Incomplete Compliance Strategy' in Alexander Zahar and Benoit Mayer (eds), *Debating Climate Change* (CUP 2021); Zerrin Savasan, *Paris Climate Agreement: a deal for better compliance?* (Springer 2019); Alexander Zahar, 'A Bottom-Up Compliance Mechanism for the Paris Agreement' [2017] Chinese Journal of International Law 69–98.

1154 Some of these procedural aspects – those relating to the carbon market mechanisms under Article 6 – are brought together under the 'Paris Rulebook' which has been finalised during COP26. Beyond the submission of NDCs, there are also procedural requirements relating to reporting and global stocktaking. Furthermore, there is a standing committee on implementation and compliance to monitor progress. See UK Government, 'COP26: The Negotiations Explained' (*UK Government* 2021) <https://ukcop26.org/wp-content/uploads/2021/11/COP26-Negotiations-Explained.pdf> accessed 6 April 2022; UNFCCC, 'Paris Agreement Implementation and Compliance Committee Meets to Assess Challenges' (*UN News* 2022) <https://unfccc.int/news/paris-agreement-implementation-and-compliance-committee-meets-to-assess-challenges> accessed 6 April 2022; Joanna Depledge, Miguel Saldivia and Cristina Penasco, 'Glass half full or glass half empty? The 2021 Glasgow Climate Conference' [2022] 22 Climate Policy 2, 147–157.

1155 See UNFCCC, 'Nationally determined contributions' (UNFCCC 2022) <https://unfccc.int/process-and-meetings/the-paris-agreement/nationally-determined-contributions-ndcs/nationally-determined-contributions-ndcs> accessed 6 April 2022.

1156 UNFCCC, 'COP26 Outcomes: Finance for Climate Adaptation' (*UNFCCC* 2022) <https://unfccc.int/process-and-meetings/the-paris-agreement/the-glasgow-climate-pact/cop26-outcomes-finance-for-climate-adaptation> accessed 6 April 2022. Also see Zahar (n 1127); Lavanya Rajamani, 'The 2015 Paris Agreement: Interplay Between Hard, Soft and Non-Obligations' [2016] 28 Journal of Environmental Law 2; Christina Voigt, 'The Compliance and Implementation Mechanism of the Paris Agreement' [2016] 25 Review of European, Comparative & International Environmental Law 2; Daniel Bodansky, 'The Legal Character of the Paris Agreement' [2016] 25 Review of European, Comparative & Environmental Law 2.

1157 The US withdrew from the Paris Agreement on 4 November 2020 under President Trump, and rejoined the agreement on 19 February 2021 under President Biden. See White House, 'Fact Sheet: President Biden sets 2030 Greenhouse Gas Pollution Reduction Target aimed at Creating Good-Paying Union Jobs and Securing U.S. Leadership on Clean Energy

In contrast with the climate change regime, the refugee regime did not adopt a common concern approach from the outset.[1158] States recognised the 'predicament' of refugees as a common concern under the Global Compact on Refugees in 2018.[1159] In the author's view, the common concern framing of the predicament of refugees has two implications for the international refugee regime: first, it politically reinforces the predicament approach to refugees and, second, it calls for the widest possible cooperation to address burden- and responsibility-sharing whilst respecting State sovereignty.

The so-called predicament approach in refugee law looks at the potential refugee's predicament, focusing on the link between the risk of persecution and whether this risk is due to one of the five Refugee Convention grounds.[1160] The predicament approach does not require a persecutor's intent to cause serious harm; it also does not require that the harm be the direct consequence of discrimination or that the harm and discrimination experienced come from the same source.[1161] In other words, '[t]here is no need for the persecutor to have a punitive intent to establish the causal link. The focus is on the reasons for the applicant's feared predicament within the overall context of the case, and how he or she would experience the harm rather than on the mind-set of the perpetrator'.[1162] By clearly identifying refugees' predicament as a common concern under the Global Compact on Refugees, States Parties have now

Technologies' (Statements and Releases, 22 April 2021) <https://www.whitehouse.gov/briefing-room/statements-releases/2021/04/22/fact-sheet-president-biden-sets-2030-greenhouse-gas-pollution-reduction-target-aimed-at-creating-good-paying-union-jobs-and-securing-u-s-leadership-on-clean-energy-technologies/> accessed 6 April 2022; US Department of State, 'On the U.S. Withdrawal from the Paris Agreement' Press Statement by Michael R. Pompeo, Secretary of State (4 November 2019) <https://www.state.gov/on-the-u-s-withdrawal-from-the-paris-agreement/> accessed 6 April 2022; Hai-Bin Zhang and others, 'U.S. withdrawal from the Paris Agreement: Reasons, impacts, and China's Response' [2017] 8 Advances in Climate Change Research 4.

1158 Although 'the problem of refugees' was recognised as 'international in scope and nature' in 1949. See UNGA Res 319, 'Refugees and stateless persons' (3 December 1949) UN Doc A/RES/319 <https://www.refworld.org/docid/3b00f1ed34.html> accessed 6 April 2022.

1159 Global Compact on Refugees (n 9) para 1.

1160 For its possible application to climate change, see Lauren Nishimura, 'Climate change and international refugee law: A predicament approach' (RefLax, 19 October 2018). For its possible application to children, see James C Hathaway and Michelle Foster, *The Law of Refugee Status* (Cambridge University Press 2014) 192–193.

1161 Nishimura (n 1160).

1162 UNHCR, 'Guidelines for International Protection No. 9: Claims to Refugee Status Based on Sexual Orientation and/or Gender Identity within the Context of Article 1A(2) of the 1951 Convention and/or Its 1967 Protocol Relating to the Status of Refugees' (2012) HCR/GIP/12/09 para 39 <https://perma.cc/9QDS-8MQU> accessed 6 April 2022.

committed to conducting refugee status determination procedures in accordance with this interpretation.[1163]

International cooperation in burden- and responsibility-sharing is an important pillar for the realisation of the predicament of refugees as a common concern.[1164] Although the Refugee Convention acknowledged that without international cooperation, the granting of asylum may place unduly heavy burdens on certain countries, it failed to clearly establish the content of the duty to cooperate.[1165] Commentators have been examining practical cooperation for burden- and responsibility-sharing for refugees, especially at the regional level, and pointing out that 'the contributions and political and moral support for the displaced waver and formal obligations are elusive'.[1166] The numbers speak volumes: as of mid-2020, 86% of the world's refugees and Venezuelans displaced abroad are hosted in developing countries.[1167] Sutherland characterised this as 'responsibility by proximity', according to which refugees are expected to stay in the first country they enter.[1168]

It was in this context that the Common Refugee Response Framework (CRRF) was developed.[1169] CRRF specifically relates to large refugee situations,

1163 Also see Scott (n 14).

1164 Volker Türk and Madeline Garlick, 'From Burdens and Responsibilities to Opportunities: The Comprehensive Refugee Response Framework and a Global Compact on Refugees' [2016] 28 IRJL 4, 656–678. See also, Volker Türk, 'Prospects for Responsibility Sharing in the Refugee Context' [2018] Journal on Migration and Human Security.

1165 UNHCR Executive Committee Conclusion No 89 (LI) (2000); UNHCR Executive Committee Conclusion No 100 (LV) (2004). Also see Alexander Betts and Paul Collier, *Refuge: Transforming a Broken Refugee System* (Penguin 2017).

1166 Goodwin-Gill and McAdam (n 56) 504.

1167 Turkey hosts the largest number of refugees, with 3.6 million people. Colombia is second with 1.8 million, including Venezuelans displaced abroad. Pakistan and Uganda are third, each hosting 1.4 million refugees. See UNHCR, 'Figures at a Glance' <https://www.unhcr.org/en-us/figures-at-a-glance.html> accessed 6 April 2022.

1168 UN News, 'Interview: "Refugees are the responsibility of the world … Proximity doesn't define responsibility – Peter Sutherland' (2 October 2015) <https://news.un.org/en/story/2015/10/511282-interview-refugees-are-responsibility-world-proximity-doesnt-define> accessed 6 April 2022.

1169 Volker Türk's proposal for a framework for burden- and responsibility-sharing served as a key inspiration for the CRRF. He argued that a more predictable, systematic and equitable responsibility sharing has at least three advantages: it can help alleviate tensions between States, mitigate against potential negative consequences for refugees, and ensure that States are able to respond to refugees more effectively. His responsibility-sharing arrangement includes triggering mechanisms and proportional contributions in line with State capacity, which would be agreed upon in advance of large-scale movements of people. For the new system to work, States must find new ways to uphold their obligations to refugees, for instance, through new forms of group refugee status determinations to ensure

including in protracted situations (as an integral and distinct part of an overall humanitarian response, where it exists).[1170] It was annexed to the New York Declaration in 2016 and incorporated into the Global Compact on Refugees under Part II.[1171]

Before being adopted, it was piloted in fifteen countries.[1172] These applications show that, once the UNHCR – in close coordination with relevant States and other relevant UN entities – initiates the CRRF, a multi-stakeholder approach to addressing the large refugee situations is triggered.[1173] In that case, there is international support for refugees, as well as for host countries and communities.[1174] The response provided also envisages durable solutions, to 'help refugees thrive, not just survive'.[1175] Overall, areas that find support range from reception and admission, meeting needs and supporting communities, to solutions such as resettlement, complementary pathways for admission to third countries and local integration.[1176]

An important shortcoming of the CRRF is the fact that the host countries can choose to withdraw from it (Tanzania is a case in point).[1177] Furthermore, the support coming from other States is mostly decided on the basis of their 'pledges' which are put forward in the Global Refugee Forum.[1178] The other

that the protection needs of individuals and persons in a targeted group are addressed. See Türk and Garlick (n 1164) 656–678; Türk (n 1164).

1170 See Randall Hansen, 'The Comprehensive Refugee Response Framework: A Commentary' [2018] 31 Journal of Refugee Studies 2, 131–151.

1171 New York Declaration (n 119), Annex 1 'Comprehensive Refugee Response Framework'; Global Compact on Refugees (n 9) Part II 'Comprehensive Refugee Response Framework'.

1172 UNHCR, 'Bringing the New York Declaration to Life: Applying the Comprehensive Refugee Response Framework' (UNHCR, January 2018) <https://www.unhcr.org/593e5ce27> accessed 6 April 2022.

1173 Garlick and Inder (n 1021) 207–226.

1174 UNHCR, 'Global Update on the Comprehensive Refugee Response Framework' (UNHCR, September 2018) <https://www.unhcr.org/events/conferences/5bd041e33/global-update-comprehensive-refugee-response-framework.html> accessed 6 April 2022.

1175 UNHCR, 'Comprehensive Refugee Response Framework' <https://www.unhcr.org/comprehensive-refugee-response-framework-crrf.html#:~:text=The%20New%20York%20Decla ration%20lays,the%20countries%20that%20host%20them.> accessed 6 April 2022.

1176 Global Compact on Refugees (n 9) Part II 'Comprehensive Refugee Response Framework'.

1177 Mans Fellesson, 'From Roll-Out to Reverse: Understanding Tanzania's Withdrawal from the Comprehensive Refugee Response Framework (CRRF)' [2019] Journal of Refugee Studies.

1178 In the author's view, this is conceptually akin to the NDCs under the Paris Agreement. There is the notion of self-differentiation of responsibilities, in a sense. On how the compacts can shift the dominance of 'self-serving' migration and refugee policies, see Nicholas Maple, Susan Reardon-Smith and Richard Black, 'Immobility and the containment of

arrangements for burden- and responsibility-sharing, as well as the arrangements for follow-up and review, are devised to create further incentives for participation.[1179] However, whether and how much each State is willing to participate in burden- and responsibility-sharing remains entirely a political decision, with no legal ramifications in relation to compliance or enforcement.

In this sense, the recognition of the predicament of refugees as a common concern under the Global Compact on Refugees supports the view that the duty to cooperate is firmly grounded in State sovereignty. Although the precise modalities in which international cooperation should take place in large refugee situations has been given more clarity, the responsibilities of individual States with respect to their capacities and capabilities have not been clearly articulated.[1180]

In the author's view, for the progressive development of international law, common concern should be employed as a normative statement rather than a factual one.[1181] The examination of the international climate and refugee regimes demonstrates that common concern is employed in connection to an international cooperation mechanism, with modalities for responsibility-sharing and implementation.[1182] However, there are significant shortcomings in both regimes. Common concerns cannot be addressed by all States, if constraints on State sovereignty are not adequately and effectively established.[1183]

A normative concept of common concern thus needs to address these shortcomings and introduce a novel duty to cooperate and a novel duty to act.[1184] The minimum content of the novel duty to cooperate should consist

solutions: Reflections on the Global Compacts, Mixed Migration and the Transformation of Protection' [2020] 23 International Journal of Postcolonial Studies 2, 326–347.

1179 For instance, see Inter-Agency, 'Revised Uganda Country Refugee Response Plan' (July 2020 – December 2021) <https://data2.unhcr.org/en/documents/details/84715> accessed 6 April 2022; UNHCR, 'South Sudan Regional Refugee Response Plan' (January 2020 – December 2021) <https://data2.unhcr.org/en/documents/details/79194> accessed 6 April 2022; UNHCR, 'The Democratic Republic of the Congo Regional Refugee Response Plan' (January 2020 – December 2021) <https://data2.unhcr.org/en/documents/details/74403> accessed 6 April 2022; UNHCR, 'Burundi Regional Refugee Response Plan' (January – December 2021) <https://data2.unhcr.org/en/documents/details/84923> accessed 6 April 2022.

1180 McAdam and Wood (n 16) 191–206.

1181 Thomas Cottier and Rosa Losada, 'Migration as a Common Concern of Humankind' in Thomas Cottier (ed), *The Prospects of Common Concern of Humankind in International Law* (Cambridge University Press 2021) 292–345.

1182 ibid.

1183 ibid.

1184 ibid.

of transparency, a duty to consult and negotiate, burden-sharing and differentiated responsibility, and cooperation in implementation and compliance.[1185] According to the normative framework established by Cottier and others, transparency involves the obligation to publish laws, regulations and precedents, akin to the multilateral trading system of the WTO.[1186] The duty to consult and negotiate implies seeking agreement and, if an agreement fails, stating the reasons.[1187] Burden-sharing and differentiated responsibility is commensurate with the economic performance, and levels of social and economic development of States.[1188] Cooperation in implementation and compliance involve transposing the international commitments into domestic law and policy, as well as mutual assistance by administrative bodies and judicial assistance by legal authorities.[1189] A novel duty to act goes beyond a right to act, and should aim to avoid free-riding and offset lack of reciprocity.[1190] This entails the domestic implementation of international obligations, as well as measures to secure compliance.[1191]

Formulated under these two novel duties, common concern has the potential to deploy legal effects.[1192] A more rigorous engagement with transboundary problems calls for reviewing the principle of State sovereignty supported by more stringent international obligations. The application of the novel duties to cooperate and act can provide a basis and foundation for the crystallisation of more specific rights and obligations.

This section has discussed the legal effects of the concept of common concern of humankind, which has never been fully defined. As the analyses of the climate change and the refugee regimes have demonstrated, common concern relates to the creation of a cooperative mechanism to address the matter

1185 Cottier (ed) (n 21).
1186 ibid.
1187 ibid.
1188 ibid.
1189 ibid.
1190 ibid.
1191 According to the normative framework established by Cottier and others, domestic measures can have extraterritorial effects, although, a 'careful balance' must be sought. The balance will be assessed as to 'whether the measure and action is able to support the attainment of a Common Concern as defined by the international community'. Measures to secure compliance, on the other hand, call for seriously reviewing the existing rules and moving towards majority decisions in areas other than the use of force. Economic measures on behalf of the international community is one recommendation by the authors. Another is arguing that common concern entails obligations *erga omnes* and can be invoked by all States under Art. 48 of ARSIWA. Cottier (ed) (n 21).
1192 ibid.

identified as a shared problem, generally (but not exclusively) by establishing a treaty regime which identifies modalities for responsibility-sharing. An important feature of common concern is that national sovereignty over the shared problem remains strong. Some scholarly attention has been paid to the potential ramifications of constraining State sovereignty to address common concerns. The proposal by Cottier and others fleshes out a novel duty to cooperate and a novel duty to act to deploy legal effects, both of which will be explored in more depth in the next section.

2 The Application of a Common Concern Approach: Towards a New Treaty Regime

One way of applying the concept of common concern to a shared problem is the creation of a treaty regime that prescribes a novel duty to cooperate and a novel duty to act. In contrast to the treaty proposals on this topic in scholarship, the main goal here is to operationalise the international protection of PMDCC as a common concern of humankind.[1193] As explained earlier, the international protection of PMDCC aims to: (i) provide protection against return to the country of origin; (ii) prevent future displacement; (iii) facilitate safe, orderly and regular migration in the context of disasters and climate change.[1194] The common concern approach offers a normative framework which gives rise to specific obligations. The 'success' of such a treaty would depend on whether it is on the 'rise': it would need to gather more and more ratifications, its law-making and compliance systems need to start to work and it must represent the most widely shared approach to the problem of HMDCC.[1195] By placing a novel duty to cooperate and a novel duty to act at the heart of its 'success',

1193 For instance, Prieur and others from the University of Limoges developed an international convention to recognise and protect the status of environmentally-displaced persons. See Michel Prieur, 'Draft Convention on the International Status of Environmentally-Displaced Persons' <https://unfccc.int/files/adaptation/groups_committees/loss_and_damage_executive_committee/application/pdf/prieur-convention_on_the_international_status_of_environmentally.pdf> accessed 6 April 2022. Docherty and Giannini proposed a convention on climate change refugees, which would theoretically become a protocol to the 1951 Refugee Convention or the UNFCCC. See Bonnie Docherty and Tyler Giannini, 'Confronting A Rising Tide: A Proposal For A Convention on Climate Change Refugees' [2009] 33 Harvard Environmental Law Review 2, 349.

1194 See Chapter 1.2.2 of this book for a detailed discussion.

1195 Georg Nolte, 'Treaties and Their Practice – Symptoms of Their Rise and Decline' (218) 329 Recueil des Cours de l'Académie de Droit International, 167.

this section discusses the international protection of the PMDCC as a common concern of humankind under a treaty regime.

2.1 *A Novel Duty to Cooperate*

So far, the 'facilitation' of human mobility has been the focus of international and multilateral cooperation on human movement.[1196] The conversation on the facilitation of human mobility takes place in the context of, on the one hand, freedom of movement – a fundamental, 'incomplete' human right – and, on the other hand, migration control and management – 'indispensable' exercises of State sovereignty.[1197] Aiming to harmonise these aspirations, the facilitation of human mobility refers to making migration easier by lowering barriers to mobility and does not mean absolute free movement or open borders.[1198] A common concern approach to the international protection of PMDCC would build on these cooperative initiatives by calling for the introduction of a rule-based system that can address and prevent the impact of disasters and climate change on people's livelihoods. This section fleshes out

---

1196 François Crépeau, 'Towards a Mobile and Diverse World: "Facilitating Mobility" as a Central Objective of the Global Compact on Migration' [2018] 30 IJRL 3, 650–656; Annick Pijnenburg, Thomas Gammeltoft-Hansen and Conny Rijken, 'Controlling migration through international cooperation' [2018] 20 European Journal of Migration and Law 4, 365–371.

1197 Freedom of movement is a fundamental human right with a long history, and it came to be embodied in, most notably, the UDHR and the ICCPR. Article 13 of the UDHR formulates the freedom of movement as follows: '1. Everyone has the right to freedom of movement and residence within the borders of each State. 2. Everyone has the right to leave any country, including his own, and to return to his country'. Article 12 of the ICCPR states as follows: '1. Everyone lawfully within the territory of a State shall, within that territory, have the right to liberty of movement and freedom to choose his residence. 2. Everyone shall be free to leave any country, including his own. 3. The above-mentioned rights shall not be subject to any restrictions except those which are provided by law, are necessary to protect national security, public order (ordre public), public health or morals or the rights and freedoms of others, and are consistent with the other rights recognized in the present Covenant. 4. No one shall be arbitrarily deprived of the right to enter his own country'. See CCPR General Comment No. 27: Article 12 (Freedom of Movement) (OHCHR, 2 November 1999) UN Doc CCPR/C/21/Rev.1/Add.9; Jane McAdam, 'An Intellectual History of Freedom of Movement: The Right to Leave as a Personal Liberty' in Mary Crock (ed), *Refugees and Rights* (Routledge 2015).

1198 François Crépeau, 'Foreword' in Helmut Kury and Slawomir Redo (eds), *Refugees and Migrants in Law and Policy Challenges and Opportunities for Global Civic Education* (Springer 2018). For an interesting conversation on free movement and open borders, see François Gemenne, '10 Reasons Why Borders Should be Opened' (TedX 2016) <https://www.youtube.com/watch?v=RRcZUzZwZIw> accessed 6 April 2022. Also see Satvinder S Juss, 'Free Movement and the World Order' [2004] 16 IJRL 3, 289–335.

a 'thicker' form of international cooperation, first, by examining the international and multilateral initiatives concerning the facilitation of human mobility and, second, by proposing fundamental principles under the common concern approach.

The Berne Initiative, which was launched by the government of Switzerland in 2001, represents one of the earliest State-led consultative processes on international migration.[1199] It enabled governments from all over the world to engage in a process that would led to the creation of 'an informal international reference system or framework of guiding principles to facilitate the management of migration'.[1200] In 2005, as a result of several consultations and meetings of experts in Berne, along with regional consultations in Africa, Europe and Central Asia, Asia and the Pacific, and the Americas and the Caribbean, the International Agenda for Migration Management (IAMM) was developed.[1201] The IAMM was designed to be an 'open exchange of information and experience' and consisted of common understandings and effective practices on a wide-range of issues.[1202] Importantly, it dedicated a section to migration and the environment, acknowledging that 'natural disasters, man-made catastrophes and ecological degradation are causes of population displacement'.[1203] Noting that States 'more and more recognize the increasing significance of ecological issues and interdependence of disaster reduction, protection of national resources, and environmental management', it called for 'an intensification of international cooperation and efforts to protect and improve the

1199 Michele Klein Solomon, 'Berne Initiative' [2013] The Encyclopaedia of Global Human Migration.

1200 The discourse on international migration management has generally been aiming to maximise the benefits and minimise the costs of migration. Bimal Ghosh was one of the earliest to address this concept in 1993, at the request of the UN Commission on Global Governance and the government of Sweden. Critical accounts see the notion of migration management as aiming to 'discipline' migration by 'introducing a specific rationality to what may otherwise turn out to be a disruptive process' which 'implies the transformation of a complex, multifaceted, sometimes unlawful and always challenging process into "predictable", "sound", "manageable", "orderly" and rule-obeying dynamics'. See Antoine Pécoud, 'Introduction: Disciplining the Transnational Mobility of People' in Martin Geiger and Antoine Pécoud (eds), *Disciplining the Transnational Mobility of People* (Springer 2012); Bimal Ghosh, 'Managing Migration: Whither the Missing Regime? How Relevant is Trade Law to Such a Regime?' [2007] 101 American Society of International Law, 303–306. Alexander Betts. 2012. Introduction: Global Migration Governance, in Global Migration Governance, edited by A Betts. Oxford: Oxford University Press, page 4.

1201 The Berne Initiative, 'International Agenda for Migration Management' (IOM and FOM 2005) <https://publications.iom.int/system/files/pdf/iamm.pdf> accessed 6 April 2022.

1202 ibid.

1203 ibid 64.

environment'.[1204] IAMM has been widely disseminated among governments to serve as a reference document for enhancing migration policies at the regional, national and international levels.[1205] In particular, its emphasis on 'safe, orderly and humane migration' resonates well with the initiatives following the IAMM, including the Global Compact for Migration.[1206]

Also in 2001, the IOM launched the International Dialogue on Migration (IDM), which has been brought together 'all migration stakeholders' at the global level to discuss an annual theme related to the opportunities and challenges of migration, in order to 'strengthen cooperation on migration issues between governments and with other actors'.[1207] For instance, the theme for the IDM session in 2020 was 'COVID-19 Crisis: Reimagining the Role of Migrants and Human Mobility for the Achievement of the Sustainable Development Goals'.[1208] Importantly, the 2011 session specifically referred to climate change, environmental degradation and migration as a part of the grander theme of 'The Future of Migration: Building Capacities for Change'.[1209] The final report of this session called for developing strategies for 'a comprehensive approach to ensure effective protection and assistance to environmental migrants'.[1210]

In 2003, the then UN Secretary-General, Kofi Annan, established the first global panel addressing international migration, which was titled the Global Commission on International Migration (Global Commission).[1211] The Global

---

1204 ibid.

1205 Philip Martin, Susan Martin and Sarah Cross, 'High-Level Dialogue on Migration and Development' [2007] 45 International Migration 1, 7–25.

1206 Elspeth Guild, 'The UN Global Compact for Safe, Orderly and Regular Migration: to what extent are human rights and sustainable development mutually compatible in the field of migration?' [2020] 16 International Journal of Law in Context 3, 239–252.

1207 IOM, 'International Dialogue on Migration' <https://www.iom.int/international-dialogue-migration> accessed 6 April 2022.

1208 IOM, 'International Dialogue on Migration, COVID-19 Crisis: Reimagining the Role of Migrants and Human Mobility for the Achievement of the Sustainable Development Goals' (IOM 2021) <https://publications.iom.int/system/files/pdf/idm-30.pdf> accessed 6 April 2022.

1209 IOM, 'Climate Change, Environmental Degradation and Migration' (29–30 March 2011) <https://www.iom.int/idmclimatechange> accessed 6 April 2022.

1210 IOM, 'International Dialogue on Migration, Climate Change, Environmental Degradation and Migration' (IOM 2012) <https://publications.iom.int/system/files/pdf/rb18_eng_web.pdf> accessed 6 April 2022.

1211 The discourse on international migration management has been generally aiming to maximise the benefits and minimise the costs of migration. Bimal Ghosh was one of the earliest to address this concept in 1993, at the request of the UN Commission on Global Governance and the government of Sweden. Critical accounts see the notion of migration management as aiming to "discipline" migration by "introducing a specific rationality to what may otherwise turn out to be a disruptive process" which "implies

Commission was composed of 19 members from all regions of the world to develop a broader understanding of international migration and to promote a comprehensive debate.[1212] A year later, the Global Commission released its report, in which it reviewed government and other migration policy approaches and best practices, and explored interlinkages between migration and development, trade, human rights, human security, displacement and international cooperation, to mention only a few examples.[1213] The report emphasised the complexity of human mobility, and claimed that the Soviet Union epitomized this complexity by developing its own vocabulary for 'ecological migrants', which was defined as 'people who have been forced to move by environmental disasters'.[1214]

Following the surge of interest in migration issues, two important cooperative processes were established within the UN in 2006. The UNGA established the High-Level Dialogue on International Migration and Development (HLD) to 'identify appropriate ways' to 'maximise' the benefits of migration and 'minimise' its negative impacts.[1215] Furthermore, the UN Secretary-General established the Global Migration Group (GMG) as a UN interagency coordination mechanism, which was superseded by the UN Network on Migration with the adoption of the Global Compact for Migration.[1216]

In 2007, the Global Forum on Migration and Development (GFMD) initiated within the UN as a State-led, informal and non-binding process.[1217] The GFMD has been providing a commendable venue for governments, civil society, the private sector, the UN system and other relevant stakeholders to discuss the

---

the transformation of a complex, multifaceted, sometimes unlawful and always challenging process into 'predictable', 'sound', 'manageable', 'orderly' and rule-obeying dynamics". Pécoud (n 1200); Bimal Ghosh (ed), *Managing Migration: Time for a New International Regime?* (Oxford University Press 2001).

1212 Stephen Castles, 'International migration at a crossroad' [2014] 18 Citizenship Studies 2, 190–207.

1213 Global Commission on International Migration, 'Migration in an interconnected world: New directions for action' (2005) <https://www.iom.int/global-commission-international-migration> accessed 6 April 2022.

1214 ibid.

1215 UNGA Res 58/208 (23 December 2003); Kathleen Newland, 'The governance of international migration: mechanisms, processes and institutions' (Policy Paper, September 2005) <https://www.iom.int/sites/default/files/jahia/webdav/site/myjahiasite/shared/shared/mainsite/policy_and_research/gcim/tp/TS8b.pdf>.

1216 Global Migration Group, 'Background' <https://www.globalmigrationgroup.org/what-is-the-gmg> accessed 6 April 2022.

1217 Kathleen Newland, 'The GFMD and the Governance of International Migration' [2012] Global Perspectives on Migration and Development, 227–240.

multi-dimensional aspects of migration and development.[1218] Its 2021 summit was entitled 'The Future of Human Mobility: Innovative Partnerships for Sustainable Development', and it aimed to contribute to the implementation, follow-up and review of the Global Compact for Migration.[1219]

In 2013, during the second HLD, the UNGA recognised 'the need for international cooperation to address, in a holistic and comprehensive manner, the challenges of irregular migration to ensure safe, orderly and regular migration, with full respect for human rights'.[1220] The UNGA has also acknowledged 'the important contribution of migration in realizing the Millennium Development Goals, and recognize that human mobility is a key factor for sustainable development which should be adequately considered in the elaboration of the post-2015 development agenda'.[1221] This recognition translated to the 2030 Agenda. In SDG target 10.7, States committed to '[f]acilitate orderly, safe, regular and responsible migration and mobility of people, including through the implementation of planned and well-managed migration policies'.[1222] At least eight of the 169 SDG targets directly relate to migrants, thereby connecting the achievement of SDGs on poverty, health, education and gender equality to international migration.[1223]

1218 Stefan Rother, 'The Global Forum on Migration and Development as a venue of state socialization: a stepping stone for multi-level migration governance?' [2018] 45 Journal of Ethnic and Migration Studies 8, 1258–1274.

1219 GFMD, 'GFMD Working Group on Sustainable Development and International Migration: Terms of Reference' <https://gfmd.org/tors-wg-sustainable-development-and-international-migration> accessed 6 April 2022.

1220 UNGA Res A/68/4 'Declaration of the High-level Dialogue on International Migration and Development 2013' (3 October 2013).

1221 UNGA Res A/68/L.5, GAOR 68th Session, Agenda Item 21(e) (1 October 2013).

1222 Agenda for Sustainable Development (n 276). IOM defines 'orderly migration' as 'the movement of a person from his/her usual place of residence, in keeping with the laws and regulations governing exit of the country of origin and travel, transit and entry into the host country'. IOM defines regular migration as 'migration that occurs through recognized, legal channels'. See UN Department of Economics and Social Affairs, Population Division and IOM 'Development, validation and testing of a methodology for SDG indicator 10.7.2 on migration policies' (Technical Paper, 2019).

1223 In 2014, the UNGA recognised that 'human mobility is a key factor for sustainable development'. UNGA Res 68/4 (21 January 2014) UN Doc A/RES/68/4. See IOM 'Migration in the 2030 Agenda' (2017) <https://www.iom.int/sites/default/files/press_release/file/Migration%20in%20the%20 2030%20Agenda. pdf> accessed 6 April 2022. Also see Emily Wilkinson and others, 'Climate Change, Migration and the 2030 Agenda for Sustainable Development' (2016).

Aiming for a more concrete understanding of SDG target 10.7, the IOM developed the Migration Governance Framework (MiGOF) in 2015.[1224] MiGOF assembles the 'essential elements for facilitating orderly, safe, regular and responsible migration and mobility of people through planned and well-managed migration policies'.[1225] In order to assess the national policies according to MiGOF, Migration Governance Indicators (MGI) were developed. The MGI have six dimensions: migrant's rights, the whole of government approach, partnerships, the well-being of migrants, the mobility dimensions of crises and safe, orderly and dignified migration.[1226] Through the MGI assessment, the strengths and weaknesses of national migration policies are identified.[1227] The recent dataset comprising 49 countries with information collected between 2015 and 2019 demonstrates that 'silos remain' and that 'migration policies are often not in sync with other policy domains at national level'.[1228] The IOM stressed in its report that, '[t]here is a need to fully integrate human mobility considerations in other policy topics, such as human development, disaster management and climate change mitigation and adaptation, and not try to address them separately'.[1229]

In 2017, the Special Rapporteur on Human Rights of Migrants at the time, François Crépeau, proposed the development of a 2035 Agenda for Facilitating Human Mobility.[1230] Crépeau suggested that this agenda may be implemented

1224 IOM, 'Migration Governance Framework' <https://www.iom.int/sites/default/files/about-iom/migof_brochure_a4_en.pdf> accessed 6 April 2022.

1225 ibid.

1226 IOM, 'Migration Governance Indicators' <https://gmdac.iom.int/migration-governance-indicators> accessed 6 April 2022.

1227 ibid.

1228 Susanne Melde, 'Comprehensive approaches but in a silo: 3 findings from the Migration Governance Indicators' (Migration Data Portal, 30 January 2020) <https://migrationdataportal.org/blog/comprehensive-approaches-silo-3-findings-migration-governance-indicators-mgi> accessed 6 April 2022.

1229 ibid.

1230 UNGA Res A/72/173 (19 July 2017), GAOR 72nd Session, Item 73 (b) of the provisional agenda. Also see Report of the Special Rapporteur on the human rights of migrants to the United Nations General Assembly, 'Proposals for the development of the global compact on migration' (20 July 2016) UN Doc A/71/40767; Report of the Special Rapporteur on the human rights of migrants to the United Nations Human Rights Council, 'Bilateral and multilateral trade agreements and their impact on the human rights of migrants' (4 May 2016) UN Doc A/HRC/32/40; Report of the Special Rapporteur on the human rights of migrants to the United Nations General Assembly, 'Recruitment practices and the human rights of migrants' (11 August 2015) UN Doc A/70/310; Report of the Special Rapporteur on the human rights of migrants to the United Nations Human Rights Council, 'Banking on mobility over a generation: follow-up to the regional study on the management of the

in parallel to both the SDGs and the Global Compact for Migration. His agenda was inspired by the observation that, '[m]obility is key to development and prosperity, and with the proper vision we can make broader legal pathways for migration work for everyone'.[1231] According to the Special Rapporteur, practices such as the externalisation of national boundaries or stringent visa requirements do not respond to mobility needs, labour market shortages or the protection needs of the displaced and refugees.[1232] Therefore, Crépeau presented the solution as lying in the development of a long-term strategic vision for mobility policy.[1233] Although the content of the agenda remains to be determined, he recommended, amongst other things, multiplying the number of visa opportunities, reducing 'underground labour markets', opening access to permanent residence and citizenship, recognising visa-free travel programmes and developing refugee resettlement programmes.[1234] It is yet to be seen whether such an agenda will be followed up on and developed.

It is evident that international cooperation on human mobility has been growing more sophisticated, as epitomised by the recent adoption of the Global Compacts for Migration and on Refugees.[1235] The most conspicuous difference between international cooperation on human mobility and international cooperation on other matters (e.g. human rights, climate change, trade, the law of the sea and the use of force) consists in the fact that the overwhelming majority of the international norms relating to human mobility are legally non-binding.[1236] Only a handful of international treaties specifically address the treatment of certain categories of people on the move.[1237] Customary international law crystallises a few relevant rules, most notably the principle

---

external borders of the European Union and its impact on the human rights of migrants' (8 May 2015) UN Doc A/HRC/29/36.

1231 François Crépeau, 'A new agenda for facilitating human mobility after the UN Summits on refugees and migrants' (Open Democracy, 24 March 2017) <https://www.opendemocracy.net/en/beyond-trafficking-and-slavery/new-agenda-for-facilitating-human-mobility-after-un-summits-on-refuge/> accessed 6 April 2022.

1232 UNGA Res A/72/173 (19 July 2017), GAOR 72nd Session, Item 73 (b) of the provisional agenda.

1233 ibid.

1234 ibid.

1235 See Chapter 1.3 of this book for a discussion on the compacts.

1236 For instance, see Francesca Capone, 'The alleged tension between the Global Compact for Safe, Orderly and Regular Migration and state sovereignty: "Much Ado about Nothing?"' [2020] 33 Leiden Journal of International Law 3, 713–730.

1237 These include, the Refugee Convention and its Protocol, WTO GATS Mode 4, the ICRMW, and the ILO Conventions No 97 and No 143. See Chapter 2.1 of this book for a more detailed discussion.

of *non-refoulement*.[1238] Furthermore, international human rights law offers a non-discriminatory approach to rights protection, thereby providing a useful source for migrants to advocate their rights.[1239] However, the contours and content of the big issue, i.e. the facilitation of the movement of persons, still remains unaddressed under international law.[1240]

The starting point for framing the international protection of PMDCC under a common concern approach is addressing the shortcomings of international cooperation on international migration.[1241] A rule-based system created under a treaty, with binding obligations to cooperate, is well placed to offer a commendable solution.[1242] Thomas Cottier explains this effect of common concern as follows:

> As the principle of Common Concern seeks to prevent or remedy threats to international peace, security and welfare in a broader sense, the purpose is in line with the original goals of sovereignty enabling to maintain law and order, provide peace and welfare, and prosperity in society. The principle of Common Concern of Humankind thus complements the same goals aspired by self-determination and enters the stage where these very goals cannot be secured by States alone but depend upon international cooperation. Common Concern helps us to reshape and understand the proper functions of contemporary modern sovereignty. We can perceive it as a dialogue between the two concepts, influencing each other in shaping and coordinating their respective contours.[1243]

Transposed to the complex problem of HMDCC, the chief benefit of a common concern approach consists in the fact that it can justify limiting sovereignty over immigration matters in favour of international cooperation.[1244] A treaty-based system may 'fend off excessive domestic pressures and maintain peaceful relations with partner countries. It is wrong to assume that nations will lose

---

1238 Thomas Gammeltoft-Hansen and James Hathaway, 'Non-Refoulement in a World of Cooperative Deterrence' [2015] 53 Columbia Journal of Transnational Law 2, 235–284.

1239 Elspeth Guild, Stefanie Grant and C.A. Groenendjik, *Human Rights of Migrants in the 21st Century* (Routledge Focus 2017).

1240 Kainz and Betts (n 1013) 65–89.

1241 Alexander Betts (ed.), *Global Migration Governance* (Oxford: Oxford University Press 2011); Thomas Gammeltoft Hansen (n 97).

1242 Cottier and Losada (n 1181); Ghosh (n 1211) 303–306.

1243 Cottier (ed) (n 21) 54.

1244 This is especially important to rebut the presumptions about the pragmatic difficulties in the construction of a treaty solution. See McAdam (n 208).

sovereignty; in fact they will gain control in extending international cooperation in this complex field'.[1245]

Treaty negotiations to provide international protection to PMDCC would need to pay attention to balancing the interests of people living in their countries of origin as well as people on the move.[1246] 'Leaving no one behind' necessitates a better understanding of the impact of migration on income, wealth distribution, urbanisation and other related areas.[1247] People living in their countries of origin are concerned about the impact of migration on jobs, competition and levels of renumeration.[1248] Furthermore, the preventive aspect of the international protection of PMDCC requires people living in their countries of origin to mitigate the impact of climate change more rigorously, as a contribution to preventing future displacement.[1249] People on the move are generally concerned about the lack of an internationally binding framework that can help protect their rights.[1250] The existing mechanisms either appeal exclusively to specific categories of mobile persons or, in the case of the international human rights framework, lead to protection gaps.[1251] More specifically, PMDCC do not fall within the specific category of mobile persons that are internationally protected. A treaty can guarantee their fundamental rights, prevent their displacement, facilitate their movement, provide for a clear rule on their non-return to their country of origin, and hence produce lasting solutions.

The duty to cooperate must include due process transparency, the duty to consult and negotiate, burden-sharing and differentiated responsibility.[1252] According to the balance of interests, principles such as market access and non-discrimination may be envisaged.[1253] The duty to cooperate must also take into account cooperation for mutual assistance and capacity building.[1254]

1245 Cottier and Losada (n 1181).

1246 ibid. Also see Thomas Alexander Aleinikoff, 'International Legal Norms and Migration: A report' in Thomas Alexander Aleinikoff and Vincent Chetail (eds), *Migration and International Legal Norms* (TMC Asser Press 2003).

1247 For instance, see Athanassios Vozikis, Theodoros Fouskas and Symeo Sidiropoulos (eds), *No One Left Behind?: Migrant and Refugee Health in the COVID-19 Crisis in Greece* (IGI Global 2020).

1248 Cottier and Losada (n 1181) 333–336.

1249 Mayer (n 33) 16.

1250 Kritzman-Amir (n 433).

1251 See Chapter 2 of this book.

1252 Cottier and Losada (n 1181) 319–322.

1253 ibid.

1254 Chelsea Bowling, Elizabeth Pierson and Stephanie Ratte, 'Common Concern of Humankind: A Potential Framework for a New International Legally Binding Instrument on the Conservation and Sustainable Use of Marine Biological Diversity in the High Seas'

Furthermore, in order to empower the PMDCC to effectively defend their rights, a dispute settlement mechanism may be established.[1255]

Where the perspectives of diverse actors are glaringly different, prescribing a novel duty to cooperate under a treaty regime forms an essential pillar to providing effective protection for PMDCC. As this section has demonstrated, even though international cooperation for the facilitation of the movement of persons has mushroomed over the last thirty years, the content and contours of State obligations remain undefined. By incorporating principles such as the balance of interests, due process transparency, and burden-sharing and differentiated responsibility, a rule-based framework may be created under a treaty regime to provide international protection to PMDCC.

2.2 *A Novel Duty to Act*

It has been proposed that there are two dimensions of a novel duty to act under a common concern regime.[1256] First, States would be expected to transpose their obligations deriving from the treaty regime domestically, in other words, they would be obliged to 'do their homework'.[1257] Second, States would be expected to secure compliance and enforce the rules of the treaty.[1258] Expounding on these two dimensions, this section fleshes out a novel duty to act under a common concern approach to protect PMDCC at the international level.

The critical idea behind the duty to act is to build on the institution of international responsibility.[1259] This institution identifies international public goods for which States and any competent IOs ought to be assigned

---

[2018] <https://www.un.org/depts/los/biodiversity/prepcom_files/BowlingPiersonandRatte_Common_Concern.pdf> accessed 6 April 2022.

1255 See, in general, Duncan French, Matthew Saul and Nigel D White, *International Law and Dispute Settlement: New Problems and Techniques* (Hart Publishing 2010); Barbara Koremenos and Timm Betz, 'The Design of Dispute Settlement Procedures in International Agreements' in Jeffrey L. Dunoff and Mark A Pollack, *Interdisciplinary Perspectives on International Law and International Relations* (CUP 2013), 371–393.

1256 Cottier (ed) (n 21).

1257 Cottier and Losada (n 1181).

1258 Edith Brown Weiss, 'Rethinking compliance with international law' in Eyal Benvenisti and Moshe Hirsch, The Impact of International Law on International Cooperation: Theoretical Perspectives' (Cambridge University Press 2004), 134–165; Pierre-Marie Dupuy, 'International Law: Torn between Coexistence, Cooperation and Globalization. General Conclusions' [1998] 9 EJIL 2, 278–286; Menno T. Kamminga, *Inter-State Accountability for Violations of Human Rights* (Cloth 1992).

1259 See, in general, Katja Creutz, *State Responsibility in the International Legal Order: A Critical Appraisal* (Cambridge University Press 2020).

responsibilities.[1260] The ILC's Articles on State Responsibility is the most significant attempt to articulate the circumstances of when States have standing to protect against breaches of fundamental norms, and institute proceedings to vindicate their interests as a member of the international community.[1261] According to Article 48 of ARSIWA, if the obligation breached is owed to 'a group of States including that State, and is established for the protection of a collective interest of the group', any State other than an injured State is entitled to invoke the responsibility of another State.[1262] This category comprises what are often called obligations *erga omnes partes*, which purport to provide legal standing for States that are not directly injured, provided that these States are parties to the same treaty.[1263]

It is submitted that common concerns give rise to obligations *erga omnes partes*.[1264] The treaties protecting common concerns result from States having a vital interest in the creation and maintenance of certain rules and principles to address issues transcending their boundaries and for which international cooperation is required.[1265] A modification or breach of these rules and principles in any given case is likely to adversely affect all parties to the treaty, albeit not to the same degree. For instance, if a Party State breaches the obligation to reduce the impact of climate change, then other Party States vulnerable to the impact of climate change, especially those that are or likely to be adversely affected by sea-level rise, would be impacted by this breach to a greater degree. Nevertheless, obligations *erga omnes partes* provide for the injured State, as well as any State other than the injured State, to see the treaty provisions enforced.[1266]

1260 James Crawford and Jeremy Watkins, 'International Responsibility' in Samantha Besson and John Tasioulas (eds), *The Philosophy of International Law* (OUP 2010); Ruth W. Grant and Robert O. Keohane, 'Accountability and Abuses of Power in World Politics' [2005] 99 American Political Science Review 35.

1261 James Crawford, Alain Pellet and Simon Olleson (eds), *The Law of International Responsibility* (Oxford University Press, 2010).

1262 James Crawford, *The ILC's Articles on State Responsibility: Introduction, Text and Commentaries* (Cambridge University Press 2002); ARSIWA (n 878) art 33(1).

1263 Chow (n 953) 471.

1264 Cottier (ed) (n 21) 70–77; Shelton (n 1122); Thomas Cottier and others, 'The Principle of Common Concern and Climate Change' (WTI, Working Paper No 2014/18); Laura Horn, 'Climate Change and the Future Role of the Concept of Common Concern of Humankind' (2015) 11 Australian Journal of Environmental Law 33, 30.

1265 ibid.

1266 *Questions relating to the Obligation to Prosecute or Extradite (Belgium v Senegal)* Judgment, ICJ GL No 144, ICGJ 437 (ICJ 2012), 20th July 2012.

The novel duty to act aims to entrench two dimensions – doing 'homework' and securing compliance – in order to allow for the effective international protection of PMDCC as an obligation *erga omnes partes*.[1267] Doing 'homework' involves taking domestic measures at the local, subnational and national levels. Under the Global Compact for Migration, States committed to striving to 'create conducive conditions that enable all migrants to enrich our societies [...] and thus facilitate their contributions to sustainable development at the local, national, regional and global levels'.[1268] Similarly, the Sendai Framework calls for reducing disaster risk at 'local, national, regional and global levels by countries and other relevant stakeholders, leading to a decrease in mortality in the case of some hazards'.[1269] The Paris Agreement also recognises the 'local, subnational, national, regional and international dimensions' of climate change.[1270] As human mobility, disaster and climate change policies have become increasingly dispersed over various levels of government, local authorities have markedly developed different approaches.[1271] Further complicating the situation, States have also handed over significant powers to regional institutions, such as the EU, which might significantly limit Member States' policy discretion in the context of HMDCC.[1272] Whilst the common concern approach aims to prescribe the meaningful cooperation of everyone involved to address a shared problem, it also envisages autonomous domestic measures, which could go beyond the obligations of States to internationally protect the PMDCC under the treaty regime. The key test here would be whether the domestic measure or action is able to support the attainment of the common concern defined by the international community.[1273]

Securing compliance refers to the logical expectation that all States involved in a treaty regime would be able to offset free-riding and take measures of non-compliance.[1274] In international law, explanations of compliance often refer to a sense of legal obligation in the context of a decentralised system

1267 Cottier (ed) (n 21).
1268 Global Compact for Migration (n 9) para 18(d).
1269 Sendai Framework (n 496) para 3.
1270 Paris Agreement (n 1066) para 2.
1271 Elisa Fornalé, 'Environmental migration governance at regional level' in Tim Krieger, Diana Panke and Michael Pregernig (eds), *Environmental Conflicts, Migration and Governance* (Bristol University Press 2020) 136–156.
1272 Peter Scholten and Rinus Penninx, 'The Multilevel Governance of Migration and Integration' in Blanca Garcés-Mascarenas and Rinus Penninx (eds), *Integration Processes and Policies in Europe* (Springer 2016).
1273 Cottier (ed) (n 21).
1274 ibid.

of enforcement, the self-interest of States and perceptions of the distribution of power.[1275] Progressively developing these narratives, the theory of common concern prescribes a cooperative facilitation of compliance.[1276] It implies a positive obligation to act to correct the behaviour of non-compliant States.[1277] As Zaker Ahmad holds, 'the doctrine adds another layer of action, which is of due diligence nature, making sure that any outcome of cooperation is followed upon by the stakeholders with necessary implementation steps'.[1278] Applied to the international protection of PMDCC, it would call for setting up an institutional mechanism under the treaty regime to enforce compliance and, as a last resort, incorporate rules on taking unilateral countermeasures.[1279]

By emphasising the obligations to do homework and to secure compliance, a novel duty to act aims to influence rulemaking and provide the mainstay of a new treaty regime to internationally protect the PMDCC. As this section has specified, the international protection of PMDCC would entail obligations *erga omnes partes* under a common concern approach, and trigger responsibilities to take domestic action to implement and enforce treaty provisions.

3 Conclusion

This chapter has argued that the theory of common concern of humankind has the potential to inspire a treaty regime to protect PMDCC at the international level. In order to do so, it first discussed the emergence of common concern in international law and demonstrated that the theory was developed as a 'way out of the controversies' generated by the common heritage principle. Common heritage aims to establish the substance of the international administration of areas recognised as common goods based on the prohibition of national appropriation and the liberty of exploitation. Common concern, on the other hand, is devoid of proprietary connotations and focuses on international cooperation aimed at protection.

1275 Jutta Brunnée and Stephen Toope, *Legitimacy and Legality in International Law: An Interactional Account* (CUP 2010); Andrew Guzman, 'Reputation and International Law' [2006] 34 Georgia Journal of International and Comparative Law 2, 379–391; Harold Hongju Koh, 'Why do nations obey international law?' [1997] 106 The Yale Law Journal, 2598–2659; Louis Henkin, *How Nations Behave: Law and Foreign Policy* (Columbia University Press 1979).

1276 Ahmad (n 27).

1277 ibid 39.

1278 ibid.

1279 Cottier (ed) (n 21) 173.

Although common concern has found expression in several legal instruments, it is conceptually ambiguous, because its normative implications are not yet settled. Zooming in on two legal regimes that have adopted common concern, namely, the climate change regime and the refugee regime, this chapter has demonstrated that common concern implies international cooperation in burden- and responsibility-sharing. However, as the analyses of both regimes have shown, the voluntary and bottom-up commitments are not strong enough to generate sufficient action to address the particular common concerns in question. Constraints on State sovereignty must be adequately and effectively placed, in order to achieve specific end goals.

In the author's view, a convincing interpretation of common concern needs to deploy legal effects that can effectively address shared problems. Borrowing from the proposal by Cottier and others, this chapter has argued that common concern should invoke two legal implications: a novel duty to cooperate and a novel duty to act.[1280] Both dimensions call for the establishment of a rule-based framework, which can define the specific rights and obligations of States to address the common concern under a treaty regime. This chapter has demonstrated that a novel duty to cooperate would require States to accept principles such as the balance of interests, due process transparency, and burden-sharing and differentiated responsibility, under a binding treaty regime. The duty to act foresees that States will take domestic measures to transpose their obligations under the treaty, as well as to secure compliance to offset free-riding.

1280 ibid.

Conclusion

Summary and Outlook

Climate change and disaster-related migration, displacement and planned relocation are already a reality for many people around the world. There is a growing body of evidence suggesting that, as climate change continues to take its toll, the number of people affected will increase.[1281] Countries have acknowledged this reality, especially under the recently adopted Global Compact for Migration, and have been calling for the development of coherent approaches to address HMDCC.[1282]

In searching for coherency, the main goal of this book has been to propose an international minimum standard for the treatment of PMDCC. It did so by arguing for the international protection of PMDCC. In order to operationalise this proposal, the book discussed the theories of community interests and the common concern of humankind. The former theory laid the foundation for an obligation *erga omnes* to protect PMDCC at the international level, whereas the latter conceived a new treaty regime with novel duties to cooperate and to act. This conclusion conveys the principal findings of the book and identifies potential avenues for further research.

1 International Protection and Human Mobility in the Context of Disasters and Climate Change

Conceptualising HMDCC as a complex planetary and intergenerational problem is one of the novel contributions of this book to the literature. In doing so, the first chapter approached HMDCC as a problem situation which (i) emerges from the actions and interactions of multiple actors, (ii) has multiple, dynamic and interconnected variables, (iii) occurs in conditions of scientific uncertainty and evolving scientific knowledge, and (iv) is planetary in scope and intergenerational in impact.[1283]

1281 For an overview on estimations of 'environmental migrants', see Viviane Passos Gomes and Diana Viveiros, *Legal Protection for environmental migrants: current challenges and ways forward* (Punto Rojo Libros 2018) chapter 1.

1282 Global Compact for Migration (n 9) objective 2(l).

1283 For the definition of complex problems, see Brunnée (n 24) 211–232.

The first chapter also introduced the notion of international protection, based on the premise that, in order to effectively manage the complex problem of HMDCC, all countries must cooperate in promoting an international minimum standard. The author argued that the international protection of PMDCC should be that standard. The international protection of PMDCC serves as a golden thread woven throughout the book. It has three pillars: (i) granting protection against return to the country of origin (*non-refoulement*); (ii) preventing future displacement; (iii) facilitating safe, orderly, and regular migration in the context of disasters and climate change.

In order to demonstrate the relevance and importance of each pillar, the first chapter examined the relevant commitments made by States under the recently adopted Global Compact on Refugees and the Global Compact for Migration. The extensive legal stocktaking exercises in the second and third chapters supported this analysis. Overall, the book makes a number of key claims about the role of international protection in addressing HMDCC:

First, there can be no doubt about the immediate need of recognising the international protection of PMDCC. This has been made more evident with the increasing number of studies, projects and collaborations at the international level on the legal implications of HMDCC. In addition, the case study of the PIS demonstrated the urgency of formulating an international response.

Second, despite this rising awareness, there are major legal blind spots, since the current international legal infrastructure promotes fragmented and largely voluntary responses to addressing HMDCC. These legal gaps exacerbate the existing vulnerabilities and protection needs of PMDCC.

Third, effective and timely responses to HMDCC are not possible without specific measures to prevent future displacement. Focusing on the conditions that cause displacement in the context of disasters and climate change can avert future harm. This, in turn, calls for reconsidering the global commitments on climate change mitigation and disaster risk reduction.

Fourth, States must acknowledge the application of the prohibition of the *non-refoulement* of PMDCC (although States may establish criteria with a view to prohibiting the return of certain categories of PMDCC only). This recognition has an inseparable human rights aspect to it, which aims to provide international protection to all those who are unable to return home because of a serious threat to their life and physical integrity in the context of disasters and climate change.

Lastly, States must facilitate safe, orderly and regular migration in the context of disasters and climate change. Facilitating migration can enable *in situ* and *ex situ* adaptation. The former generally refers to internal relocation, while the latter refers to the search for temporary or permanent opportunities across borders. If conducted in line with the International Labour Standards, labour migration has the capacity to be an effective adaptive strategy to environmental changes. States have already emphasised the importance of this under the Global Compact for Migration, which must now be matched in practice.

2 Lessons Learnt about Community Interests and Common Concerns

Operationalising the international protection of PMDCC was both the greatest aspiration and the most difficult challenge of this book. The proposed formulations of the theories of community interests and of the common concern of humankind provided two different and non-contradictory pathways to operationalise the international protection of PMDCC.

The fourth chapter framed the international protection of PMDCC under the theory of community interests. The role of the theory of community interests in international law is to establish and protect multilateral rights and obligations in the interest of the 'international community as a whole'.[1284] Obligations *erga omnes* facilitate the integration of community interests into international law, by designating those obligations of a State towards 'the international community as a whole'.

The analysis of obligations *erga omnes* showed that these obligations modify: (i) the scope of a primary rule (by broadening the circle of States bound by the rule); (ii) the right of standing according to secondary rules (by permitting any State other than an injured State to protect the community interest at stake); (iii) the content of the obligation in question (for instance, in the *Genocide* case, the ICJ ruled that the obligation of each State to prevent and punish the crime of genocide is not territorially limited by the Genocide Convention).

It was also pointed out, however, that there is confusion surrounding obligations *erga omnes*, particularly in relation to their identification, types of effects, enforcement and relationship to obligations *jus cogens*.

Nonetheless, the concept *erga omnes* remains highly relevant, since the ICJ has affirmed the existence of obligations *erga omnes* with reference to multilateral treaties and in customary international law, while commentators continue to propose new candidates of obligations *erga omnes* in several legal fields. The concept *erga omnes* is also highly significant, because it ensures that

1284 See Chapter 4.1.2 of this book for a discussion on the meaning of 'international community as a whole'.

international law continues to address the old and emerging pressing concerns of 'the international community as a whole'.

To encourage the further development of *erga omnes*, the author proposed the identification of the international protection of PMDCC as an obligation *erga omnes*. The author structured her argument as follows: if (i) the international protection of PMDCC derives from the principles and rules concerning the basic rights of the human person and if (ii) it is a matter of community interest, it follows that (iii) the international protection of PMDCC is an obligation *erga omnes* and all States can be held to have a legal interest in its performance.

Next, the author provided a roadmap to promoting the performance of the international protection of PMDCC as an obligation *erga omnes*. This roadmap involves using the procedural aspects of the international human rights regime, the international climate change regime, the international labour regime and the international trade regime, more specifically: (i) the individual communication procedures under international human rights treaties; (ii) the Universal Periodic Review process; (iii) the formulation of the Nationally Determined Contributions; (iv) the work of the UNFCCC Task Force on Displacement; (v) the tripartite structure of the ILO; (vi) the Trade Policy Review Mechanism of the WTO.

The roadmap also encourages the utilisation of the follow-up and review mechanisms of the Global Compact for Migration, and the Global Compact on Refugees, more specifically: (i) the International Migration Review Forum, to be held in the first semester of 2022; (ii) the Migration Multi-Partner Trust Fund; (iii) the Migration Network Hub; (iv) the Global Refugee Forum, to be held in 2023; (v) the Global Academic Interdisciplinary Network.

Overall, relying on the theory of community interests has helped shape a legally binding obligation imposed on all States to provide international protection the PMDCC. This solution is especially useful for inducing the cooperation of States that would otherwise prefer to remain free from legal fetters.

However, the fact remains that 'the best instrument to produce legal change' in international law is the treaty.[1285] Treaties have the advantage of creating written law with which contracting States formally undertake to comply.

In order to ground a treaty solution, the fifth chapter discussed the international protection of PMDCC as a common concern of humankind. The extensive research on the theory of common concern of humankind has demonstrated

1285 See Antonio Cassese (ed), *Realizing Utopia: The Future of International Law* (Oxford University Press 2012) 657–658.

that common concern: (i) was conceptually developed 1980s onwards 'as a way out of the controversies' resulting from the concept of the common heritage of humankind; (ii) gives emphasis to international cooperation and equitable burden-sharing to address transboundary problems; (iii) is devoid of proprietary connotations; (iv) takes into account both present and future generations; (v) has been adopted in several international instruments.

Even though common concern continues to inspire international law-making, its content and legal effects are not yet settled. In order to further clarify the concept, two international instruments were examined: the Paris Agreement, which reiterates climate change as a common concern, and the Global Compact on Refugees, which recognises the predicament of refugees as a common concern.

The analysis has shown that, under both instruments, States remain largely free to decide on their own contributions to addressing the relevant common concern. This leads to ineffective problem solving. For instance, developing countries continue to host an overwhelming majority (86% as of 2021) of the world's refugees, while in the case of climate change, we are heading for a global temperature rise of 3 degrees Celsius, even if countries meet commitments made under the Paris Agreement.

Hence, in order to facilitate genuine problem solving, the author proposed employing common concern as a normative statement rather than a factual one. Common concerns cannot be addressed by all States, if constraints on State sovereignty are not adequately and effectively established.

Borrowing from the normative conceptualisation of common concern articulated by Cottier and others, the author also argued that the international protection of PMDCC as a common concern should involve a treaty regime which incorporates a novel duty to cooperate and a novel duty to act.[1286]

The novel duty to cooperate justifies limiting sovereignty over immigration matters in favour of the international protection of PMDCC. Furthermore, it incorporates: (i) the interests of the people living in their countries of origin, as well as of people on the move; (ii) due process transparency; (iii) a duty to consult and negotiate; (iv) modalities on burden-sharing and differentiated responsibility.[1287]

The novel duty to act envisages that States: (i) 'do their homework', in other words, transpose the obligations deriving from the treaty domestically, and (ii) secure compliance and enforce the rules of the treaty.

1286 Cottier (ed) (n 21).

1287 Cottier and Losada (n 1181).

The possibility of establishing a rule-based framework to protect PMDCC at the international level is the chief advantage of the proposed common concern approach. It also ensures the trickle-down effect of the international minimum standard on the treatment of PMDCC into domestic legal orders.

In conclusion, in order to operationalise the international protection of PMDCC, the author searched for theories that supplied conceptions of international law which do not merely rest on the self-interests of States. The theories of community interests and the common concern of humankind transcend self-interests by taking into account 'the international community as a whole', including the present and future generations. In the author's view, these theories are far from being utopian. In fact, they represent the function of international law more realistically. International law is (and should be) well equipped to address complex planetary and intergenerational problems, such as HMDCC.

3 Outlook

Looking forward, the research carried out here can be taken further in at least three respects. First, the notion of international protection in international law could be fleshed out in more detail. International criminal law and private international law, in particular, might provide valuable insights for this purpose. Second, the complex problem of HMDCC could be understood better. Primary research focusing on the local, national and regional impacts of climate change and disasters is particularly important for informing future legislation and policy-making. Third, the theories of community interests and common concern of humankind can be taken further. The proposed formulations of these theories can be applied to other problematic situations that humanity is facing.

In the event that the reader was convinced by the arguments presented in this book, they can look for ways to implement its proposals. There is much work that needs to be done in order to achieve the recognition of the international protection of PMDCC as an obligation *erga omnes* and/or a common concern of humankind. The good news is that there is space for everyone to get involved.

Bibliography

Monographs and Books

Ahmad, Z, *WTO Law and Trade Policy Reform for Low-Carbon Technology Diffusion* (Brill 2021).

Alcock, AE, *History of the International Labour Organisation* (Palgrave Macmillan 1971).

Armiero, M and Tucker, R (eds), *Environmental History of Modern Migrations* (Routledge 2017).

Barnes, GN, *History of International Labour Office* (Willians and Norgate Limited 1926).

Baslar, Kemal, *The Concept of the Common Heritage of Mankind in International Law* (Martinus Nijhoff Publishers 1998).

Bedjaoui, M, *Towards a New International Legal Order* (New York: Holmes & Meier 1979).

Benvenisti, E, Nolte, G and Yalin-mor, K (eds), *Community Interests across International Law* (Oxford University Press 2018).

Beyleveld, AD, *Taking a Common Concern Approach to Economic Inequality* (Brill 2022).

Bilderbeek, S, Wijgerde, A and Van Schaik, N (eds), *Biodiversity and International Law: The effectiveness of international environmental law* (IOS Press 1992).

Bogdanova, I, *Unilateral Sanctions in International Law and the Enforcement of Human Rights* (Brill 2022).

Brunnée, J, *Procedure and Substance in International Environmental Law* (The Hague Academy of International Law, Brill 2021).

Cançado Trindade, AA, *International Law for Humankind: Towards a New Jus Gentium* (2nd edn, Martinus Nijhoff Publishers 2013).

Cassese, A, *International Law* (2nd edn, Oxford University Press 2005).

Choudry, A, *Just Work?: Migrant Workers' Struggles Today* (Pluto Press 2016).

Cottier, T (ed), *The Challenge of WTO Law: Collected Essays* (The Blissett Group 2007).

Cottier, T (ed), *The Prospects of Common Concern of Humankind in International Law* (Cambridge University Press 2021).

Crawford, J, *Brownlie's Principles of Public International Law* (9th edn, Oxford University Press 2019).

Crawford, J, *Chance, Order, Change: The Course of International Law* (365 Recueil des Cours de l'Académie de Droit International 2014).

Crawford, J, *Multilateral Rights and Obligations in International Law* (319 Recueil des cours de l'Académie de Droit International, Leiden: Nijhoff 2006).

Crawford, J, Pellet, A and Olleson, S (eds), *The Law of International Responsibility* (Oxford University Press, 2010).

Criddle, EJ and Fox-Decent, E, *Fiduciaries of Humanity* (Oxford University Press 2016).

Fastenrath, U and others, *From Bilateralism to Community Interest: Essays in Honour of Bruno Simma* (Oxford University Press 2011).

Ferris, EG and Donato, KM, *Refugees, Migration and Global Governance* (Routledge 2020).

Fitzmaurice, M, *International Protection of the Environment* (Volume 293, Collected Courses of the Hague Academy of International Law 2001).

French, D, Saul, M and White, NG, *International Law and Dispute Settlement: New Problems and Techniques* (Hart Publishing 2010).

Frimston, R and others (eds), *International Protection of Adults* (Oxford University Press 2015).

Fry, G and Tarte, S, *The New Pacific Diplomacy* (Australian National University Press 2015).

Gaja, G, *The Protection of General Interests in the International Community* (364 Recueil des cours de l'Académie de Droit International, Leiden: Nijhoff 2011).

Gemenne, F, *Environmental Changes and Migration Flows: Normative Frameworks and Policy Responses* (PhD thesis, Institut d'Etudes Politiques de Paris and Université de Liége 2009).

Goodwin-Gill, GS and McAdam, J, *The Refugee in International Law* (3rd edn, Oxford University Press 2007).

Hathaway, J, *The Law of Refugee Status* (Butterworths 1991).

Hughes, S and Haworth, N, *The International Labour Organisation: Coming in from the Cold* (Routledge 2011).

Humphreys, S (ed), *Human Rights and Climate Change* (Cambridge University Press 2010).

Huntington, E, *The Pulse of Asia: A Journey in Central Asia Illustrating the Geographic Basis of History* (Mifflin and Co 1907).

Ionesco, D, Mokhnacheva, D and Gemenne, F, *The Atlas of Environmental Migration* (Routledge 2017).

Khor, HE, Kronenberg, RP and Tumbarello, P (eds), *Resilience and Growth in the Small States of the Pacific* (IMF 2016).

Kiss, A and Shelton, DL, *International Environmental Law* (Transnational Publishers, Ardsley-on-Hudson 1991).

Kivilcim, Z, *Uluslararasi Kamu Hukukunda Insanligin Ortak Mirasi* (On Iki Levha Yayinlari 2010).

Krieger, T, Panke, D and Pregernig, M (eds), *Environmental Conflicts, Migration and Governance* (Bristol University Press 2020).

Kälin, W and Künzli, J, *The Law of International Human Rights Protection* (2nd edn, Oxford University Press 2019).

Levine, S, *Pacific Ways: Government and Politics in the Pacific Islands* (Victoria University Press 2016).

Lowenfeld, A, *International Economic Law* (2nd edn, Oxford University Press 2002).

Matthews, G, *The Other Side of Slave Revolts* (The Society for Caribbean Studies, East Yorkshire 2000).

Maul, D, *The International Labour Organization: 100 Years of Global Social Policy* (De Gruyter and the ILO 2019).

Mayer, B and Crépeau, F (eds), *Research Handbook on Climate Change, Migration and the Law* (Edward Elgar 2017).

Mayer, B, *The Concept of Climate Migration* (Edward Elgar Publishing, 2016).

McAdam, J, *Climate Change, Forced Migration and International Law* (Oxford University Press 2012).

Murray, J, Webb, T and Wheatley, S, *Complexity Theory and Law: Mapping An Emergent Jurisprudence* (Routledge 2019).

Myers, N and Kent, J (ed), *The New Atlas of Planet Management* (University of California Press 2005).

Naser, MM, *The Emerging Global Consensus on Climate Change and Human Mobility* (Routledge 2021).

Oels, A, *From Securitization of Climate Change to Climatization of the Security Field* (Springer 2012).

Okowa, P, *State Responsibility for Transboundary Air Pollution in International Law* (Oxford University Press 2000).

Opeskin, B, Perruchoud, R, Redpath-Cross, J, *Foundations of International Migration Law* (Cambridge University Press 2012).

Pardo, A, *The Common Heritage - Selected Papers on Oceans and World Order* (Malta University Press, 1975).

Parker, G, *Global Crisis: War, Climate Change and Catastrophe in the Seventeenth Century* (Yale University Press 2013).

Piguet, E, Pecoud, A and de Guchteneire, P (eds), *Migration and Climate Change* (Cambridge University Press and UNESCO Publishing 2011).

Pincock, K and Betts, A, *The Global Governed? Refugees as Providers of Protection and Assistance* (Cambridge Univeristy Press 2020).

Polanco, R, *The Return of Home State to Investor-State Disputes* (Cambridge University Press 2018).

Puggioni, R, *Rethinking International Protection: The Sovereign, the State, the Refugee* (Palgrave Macmillan 2016).

Ragazzi, M, *Concept of International Obligations Erga Omnes* (Oxford Univeristy Press 2000).

Roth, A, *The Minimum Standard of International Law Applied to Aliens* (Sijthoff, Leiden 1949).

Satragno, L, *Monetary Stability as a Common Concern in International Law* (Brill 2022).

Schrijver, NJ, *The Evolution of Sustainable Development in International Law: Inception, Meaning and Status* (Pocketbooks of the Hague Academy of International Law Brill 2009).

Sciaccaluga, G, *International Law and the Protection of 'Climate Refugees'* (Palgrave 2020).

Scott, M, *Climate Change, Disasters and the Refugee Convention* (Cambridge University Press 2020).

Servais, JM, *International Labour Law* (Wolters Kluwer 2020).

Shue, H, *Climate Justice: Vulnerability and Protection* (Oxford University Press 2014).

Simma, B, *From Bilateralism to Community Interest in International Law* (250 Recueil des cours de l'Académie de Droit International, Leiden: Nijhoff 1994).

Thürer, D, *International Humanitarian Law: Theory, Practice, Context* (Hague Academy of International Law 2011).

Tomuschat, C and Thouvenin, JM (eds), *The Fundamental Rules of the International Legal Order: Jus Cogens and Obligations Erga Omnes* (Brill 2006).

Trachtman, JP, *The International Law of Economic Migration: Toward the Fourth Freedom* (WE Upjohn Institute for Employment Research 2009).

Turabi, OA, *Protection from Slavery in the International Legal Order* (Doctoral thesis, University of Bern 2006).

Van den Bossche, P and Zdouc, W, *The Law and Policy of the World Trade Organization* (4th edn, Cambridge University Press 2017).

Van Liempt, I and Bilger, V (eds), *The Ethics of Migration Research Methodology: Dealing with Vulnerable Immigrants* (Sussex Academy Press 2009).

Vargas-Silva, C (ed), *Handbook of Research Methods in Migration* (Edward Elgar 2012).

Vincent, C, *International Migration Law* (Oxford University Press 2019).

Voeffray, F, *L'actio popularis ou la défense collectif devant des juridictions internationals* (Paris Presses Universitaires de France 2004).

Wang, A, *The Interpretation and Application of the Most-Favoured-Nation Clause in Investment Arbitration* (Brill 2022).

Weissbrodt, D, *The Human Right to Citizenship* (University of Pennsylvania Press 2015).

Wolfrum, R, *Solidarity and Community Interests: Driving Forces for the Interpretation and Development of International Law* (General Course at the Hague Academy of International Law 2020).

Yildirim, AB, *Value Chains and WTO Disputes: Compliance at the dispute settlement mechanism* (Palgrave Macmillan 2020).

Articles, Contributions to Compilations, Working Papers and Reports (All Online Materials Last Accessed 6 April 2022)

Abi-Saab, G, 'Whither the International Community?' [1998] 9 European Journal of International Law 2.

Adger, WN and others, 'Human Security' in IPCC, *Climate Change 2014: Impacts, Adaptation and Vulnerability* (Cambridge University Press 2014).

Agius, MF, 'Treaty Regimes in International Law' in Maria Fogdestam Agius, *Interaction and Delimitation of International Legal Orders* (Brill 2015) 28–55.

Ahmad, Z, 'State Responsibility Aspects of a Common Concern Based Approach to Collective Action' in Samantha Besson (ed), *International Responsibility: Essays in Law, History and Philosophy* (Schulthess 2017) 97–116.

Alston, P, 'Core labour standards and the transformation of the international labour rights regime' [2004] 15 European Journal of International Law 3, 457–521.

Allain, J, 'The jus cogens nature of non-refoulement' [2001] 13 International Journal of Refugee Law 4, 533–558.

Allan, C and O'Donnell, T, 'A Call to Alms? Natural Disasters, R2P, Duties of Cooperation and Unchartered Consequences' [2012] 17 Journal of Conflict and Security Law 3.

Aleinikoff, TA, 'The Unfinished Work of the Global Compact on Refugees' [2018] 30 International Journal of Refugee Law, 611–617.

Anderson, A, Foster, M, Lambert, H and McAdam, J, 'Imminence in refugee and human rights law: a misplaced notion for international protection' [2019] 68 ICLQ 1, 111–140.

Andrew, NL and others, 'Coastal proximity of populations in 22 Pacific Island Countries and Territories' [2019] 14 Plos One 9.

Asian Development Bank, 'An Existential Threat: How Climate Change is Impacting the Atoll Countries' (9 December 2019) <https://www.adb.org/news/videos/existential-threat-how-climate-change-impacting-atoll-countries>.

Asia-Pacific Network for Global Change Research (APN), 'Community Relocation as an Option for Adaptation to the Effects of Climate Change and Climate Variability in Pacific Island Countries' (Suva, APN, 2005) <https://www.sprep.org/att/irc/ecopies/pacific_region/643.pdf>.

Atapattu, S, 'Climate change and displacement: protecting "climate refugees" within a framework of justice and human rights' [2020] 11 Journal of Human Rights and the Environment 1, 86–113.

Badell, D, 'The EU, migration and contestation: the UN Global Compact for migration, from consensus to dissensus' [2021] Global Affairs.

Baldwin, A and Fornalé, E, 'Adaptive Migration: Pluralising the debate on climate change and migration' [2017] 183:4 The Geographical Journal, 323.

Baldwin, A, Fröhlich, C and Rothe, D, 'From climate migration to anthropocene mobilities: Shifting the debate' [2018] 14 Mobilities 3, 289–297.

Barnett, J and McMichael, C, 'The effects of climate change on the geography and timing of human mobility' 39 Population and Environment, 339–356.

Barnett, J and Webber, M, 'Migration as Adaptation: Opportunities and Limits' in Jane McAdam (ed), *Climate Change and Displacement: Multidisciplinary Perspectives* (Hart Publishing 2010).

Barnett, J, 'Adapting to Climate Change in Pacific Island Countries: The Problem of Uncertainty' [2001] 29 World Development 6, 977–993.

Bast, J, 'Commentary on the Annex on Movement of Natural Persons Supplying Services Under the Agreement' in Rüdiger Wolfrum, Peter Tobias Stoll and Clemens Feinäugle (eds), *WTO – Trade in Services* (Martinus Nijhoff 2008) 573–595.

Bartolini, G, 'A Universal Treaty for Disasters: Remarks on International Law Commission's Draft Articles on the Protection of Persons in the Event of Disasters' [2019] 99 International Review of the Red Cross 906, 1103–1138.

Bates, D, 'Environmental Refugees? Classifying Human Migrations Caused by Environmental Change' [2002] 23 Population and Environment 5, 465–477.

Behrman, S and Kent, A, 'The Teitiota case and the limitations of the human rights framework' [2020] 75 QIL, 25–39.

Benjamin, L, Thomas, A, Haynes, R, 'An 'Islands' COP'? Loss and Damage at COP23' [2018] 27 Review of European, Comparative and International Environmental Law 3, 332–340.

Bellinkx, V and others, 'Addressing Climate Change through International Human Rights Law: From (Extra)Territoriality to Common Concern of Humankind' [2021] 11 Transnational Environmental Law 1, 69–93.

Benedek, W, de Feyter, K, Kettemann, MC and Voigt, C, 'The Common Interest in International Law – Perspectives for an Undervalued Concept' in Wolfgang Benedek and others (eds), *The Common Interest in International Law* (Intersentia 2014).

Bennett, WL, 'Communicating global activism' [2003] 6 Information, Communication and Society 2, 143–168.

Bergeron, C, 'Temporary Protected Status after 25 Years: Addressing the Challenge of Long-Term Temporary Residents and Strengthening a Centerpiece of US Humanitarian Protection' [2018] 2 Journal on Migration and Human Security 1, 22–43.

Bertana, A, 'The role of power in community participation: Relocation as climate change adaptation in Fiji' [2020] 38 Environment and Planning: Politics and Space 5, 902–919.

Bertana, AR, 'Environmentally induced migration in Fiji' (PhD thesis, University of Utah, May 2018) <https://www.proquest.com/docview/2306288585?pq-origsite=gscholar&fromopenview=true>.

Besson, S, 'Community Interests in International Law: Whose Interests Are They and How Should We Best Identify Them?' in Eyal Benvenisti, Georg Nolte and Keren Yalin-mor (eds), *Community Interests across International Law* (Oxford University Press 2018) 47–49.

Bettini, G, 'Climate migration as an adaptation strategy: de-securitizing climate-induced migration or making the unruly governable?' [2014] 2 Critical Studies on Security 2, 180–195.

Bettini, G, 'Climate Barbarians at the Gate? A critique of apocalyptic narratives on climate refugees' [2013] 45 Geoforum, 63–72.

Betts, A, 'Survival Migration: A New Protection Framework' in Alynna Lyon and others (eds), Global Governance: A Review of Multilateralism and International Organizations (Brill Nijhoff 2020).

Betts, A, 'The Global Compact on Refugees: Towards a Theory of Change?' 30 IJRL 4, 623–626.

Betts, A, 'The Refugee Regime Complex' [2010] 29 Refugee Survey Quarterly 1, 12–37.

Biermann, F, '"Common Concern of Humankind": The Emergence of a New Concept of International Environmental Law' [1996] 34 Archiv des Völkerrechts 4, 426–481.

Biermann, F and Boas, I, 'Preparing for a Warmer World: Towards a Global Governance System to Protect Climate Refugees' [2010] 10 Global Environmental Politics 1, 60–88.

Biermann, F and Boas, I, 'Protecting Climate Refugees: The Case for a Global Protocol' [2008] 50 Environment: Science and Policy for Sustainable Development 6, 8–17.

Bilak, A, and Shai, A, 'Internal Displacement Beyond 2018: The Road Ahead' [2018] 59 Forced Migration Review, 49–52.

Bird, E, and Prescott, V, 'Rising global sea levels and national maritime claims' [1989] 1 Marine Policy Reports 3, 1–20.

Blowfield, M and Frynas, JG, 'Setting New Agendas: Critical Perspectives on Corporate Social Responsibility in the Developing World' [2005] 81 International Affairs 3, 499–513.

Blowfield, M, 'Corporate Social Responsibility: Reinventing the Meaning of Development?' [2005] 81 International Affairs 3, 515–524.

Boas, I and others, 'Climate migration myths' [2019] 9 Nature Climate Change, 901–903.

Bodansky, D, 'The History of the Global Climate Change Regime' in Urs Luterbacher and Detlef F. Sprinz, *International Relations and Global Climate Change* (Massachusetts Institute of Technology 2001) 23–40.

Bodansky, D, 'The Role of the International Court of Justice in Addressing Climate Change: Some Preliminary Reflections' [2017] 49 Arizona State Law Journal 689–712.

Bogner, A, Littig, B and Menz, W, 'Introduction: Expert Interviews – An Introduction to a New Methodological Debate' in Alexander Bogner, Beate Littig and Wolfgang Menz (eds), *Interviewing Experts* (Palgrave Macmillan 2009).

Bogner, A, and Manz, W, 'The Theory-Generating Expert Interview: Epistemological Interest, Forms of Knowledge, Interaction' in Alexander Bogner, Beate Littig and Wolfgang Menz (eds), *Interviewing Experts* (Palgrave Macmillan 2009).

Boiral, O and others, 'Sustainability rating and moral fictionalism: opening the black box of nonfinancial agencies' [2021] 34 Accounting, Auditing and Accountability Journal 8, 1740–1768.

Borchert, I and others, 'The Evolution of Services Trade Policy Since the Great Recession' (World Bank Group, Policy Research Working Paper 9265, June 2020).

Bowett, DW, 'The legal regime of islands in international law' [1979] Oceana Publications.

Bowling, C, Pierson, E and Ratte, S, 'Common Concern of Humankind: A Potential Framework for a New International Legally Binding Instrument on the Conservation and Sustainable Use of Marine Biological Diversity in the High Seas' [2018] <https://www.un.org/depts/los/biodiversity/prepcom_files/BowlingPiersonandRatte_Common_Concern.pdf>.

Bredford, R, Bredford, C, Wall, J and Young, M, 'Managed Temporary Labour Migration of Pacific Islanders to Australia and New Zealand in the Early Twenty-first Century' [2017] 48 Australian Geographer 1, 37–57.

Broude, T, 'Most-Favoured Nation Principle, Equal Protection, and Migration Policy' [2010] 24 Georgetown Immigration Law Journal 3, 553–564.

Brown, LR, McGrath, P and Stokes, B, 'Twenty Two Dimensions of the Population Problem' [1976] Worldwatch Institute, 7–82.

Bronen, R, 'Climate-induced Community Relocations: Creating an Adaptive Governance Framework Based in Human Rights Doctrine' [2011] 35 New York University Review of Law & Social Change 2, 394–395.

Brzoska, M, 'Climate Change as a Driver of Security Policy' in Jürgen Scheffran and others, *Climate Change, Human Security and Violent Conflict* (Springer 2012).

Burkett, M, 'Justice and Climate Migration. The Importance of Nomenclature in the Discourse on Twenty-First-Century Mobility' in Simon Berhman and Avidan Kent (eds), *'Climate Refugees' Beyond the Legal Impasse?* (Routledge 2018) 84.

Buchanan, K, 'New Zealand: 'Climate change refugee' case overview' [2013] Global Legal Research Center: The Law Library of Congress.

Brunnée, J, 'Common Areas, Common Heritage, and Common Concern' in Daniel Bodansky, Jutta Brunnée and Ellen Hey (eds), *The Oxford Handbook of International Environmental Law* (OUP 2008).

Brunnée, J, 'Common interests – Echoes from an Empty shell? Some thoughts on common interest and international environmental law' [1989] 49 ZaöRV, 791–808.

Brunnée, J, 'International Environmental Law and Community Interests: Procedural Aspects' in Eyal Benvenisti, Georg Nolte and Keren Yalin-mor (eds), *Community Interests across International Law* (Oxford University Press 2018).

Brunnée, J, 'The Rule of International (Environmental) Law and Complex Problems' in Heike Krieger, Georg Nolte and Andreas Zimmermann, *The International Rule of Law: Rise or Decline?* (Oxford University Press 2019) 211–232.

Byrne, M and Leighton, M, 'Organizational Perspectives from the ILO', in Benoit Mayer and Francois Crépeau(eds), *Research Handbook on Climate Change, Migration and the Law* (Edward Elgar 2017).

Byers, M, 'Conceptualising the Relationship Between Jus Cogens and Erga Omnes' [1997] 66 Nordic Journal of International Law 2-3, 211–239.

Cain, TN, 'The Renaissance of the Melanesian Spearhead Group' in Greg Fry and Sandra Tarte, The New Pacific Diplomacy (Australian National University Press 2016) 151–160.

Cali, B, Costello, C and Cunningham, S, 'Hard Protection through Soft Courts? Non-refoulement before the United Nations Treaty Bodies' [2020] 21 German Law Journal 3, 355–384.

Carnaziga, A, 'A Warmer Welcome? Access of Natural Persons under PTAs' in J Marchetti and M Roy (eds), *Opening Markets for Trade in Services: Countries and Sectors in Bilateral and WTO Negotiations* (Cambridge University Press 2008).

Carrera, S, 'What does free movement mean in theory and practice in an enlarged EU?' [2005] 11 European Law Journal 6, 699–721.

Carraro, V, 'Promoting Compliance with Human Rights: The Performance of the United Nations' Universal Periodic Review and Treaty Bodies' [2019] 63 International Studies Quarterly 4, 1079–1093.

Carter, G, 'Pacific Island States and 30 Years of Global Climate Change Negotiations' in Carola Klöck and others (eds), *Coalitions in the Climate Change Negotiations* (Routledge 2021).

Caskey, C, 'Non-Refoulement and Environmental Degradation: Examining the Entry Points and Improving Access to Protection' (Global Migration Research Paper No 26, 2020) Global Migration Centre, Graduate Institute of International and Development Studies.

Carzaniga, A, 'The GATS, Mode 4, and Pattern of Commitments' in Aaditya Mattoo and Antonia Carzaniga (eds), *Moving People to Deliver Services* (The World Bank/Oxford University Press 2003).

Chanda, R, 'Mobility of Less-Skilled Workers under Bilateral Agreements: Lessons for the GATS' [2009] 43 Journal of World Trade 3, 479–506.

Chanda, R, 'Movement of Natural Persons and the GATS' [2001] 24 The World Economy 5, 631–654.

Chakraborty, I and Prasenjit, A, 'COVID-19 outbreak: Migration, effects on society, global environment and prevention' [2020] 728 Science of the Total Environment 138882, 1–7.

Charan, D, Kaur, M and Singh, P, 'Customary Land and Climate Change Induced Relocation – A Case Study of Vunidogoloa Village, Vanua Levu, Fiji' in Leal Filho (ed), *Climate Change Adaptation in Pacific Countries* (Springer 2017) 19–33.

Charnovitz, S, 'Trade Law Norms on International Migration' in T Alexander Aleinikoff and Vincent Chetail (eds), *Migration and International Legal Norms* (TMC Asser Press 2003) 252.

Chetail, V, 'The Transnational Movement of Persons under General International Law – Mapping the Customary Law Foundations of International Migration Law' in

Vincent Chetail and Céline Bauloz (eds), *Research Handbook on International Law and Migration* (2014) 1–72.

Chetail, V, 'Are Refugee Rights Human Rights? An Unorthodox Questioning on the Relations between International Refugee law and International Human Rights Law' in R Rubio-Marin (ed), *Human Rights and Immigration* (Collected Courses of the Academy of European Law, Oxford University Press 2014) 36–37.

Cholewinski, R, 'International Labour Migration' in Brian Opeskin and others (eds), *Foundations of International Migration Law* (Cambridge University Press 2012).

Chow, PYS, 'On Obligations Erga Omnes Partes' [2020] 52 Georgetown Journal of International Law 2, 469–504.

Cohen, R, 'Nowhere to Run, No Place to Hide' [2002] 58 Bulletin of the Atomic Scientists 6, 36–45.

Cottier, T, 'Preparing for Structural Reform in the WTO' [2007] 10 Journal of International Economic Law 3, 497–508.

Cottier, T and Shingal, A, 'Migration, Trade and Investment: Towards a New Common Concern' [2021] 55 Journal of World Trade 1, 51–76.

Crawford, J, 'The ILC's Articles on Responsibility of States for Internationally Wrongful Acts: A Retrospect' [2002] 96 AJIL 4, 874–980.

Crépeau, F, 'Towards a Mobile and Diverse World: "Facilitating Mobility" as a Central Objective of the Global Compact on Migration' [2018] 30 IJRL 3, 650–656.

Cristani, F, Fornalé, E and Lavenex, S, 'Environmental Migration Governance at the Regional Level' in Tim Krieger, Diana Panke and Michael Pregernig (eds), *Environmental Conflicts, Migration and Governance* (Bristol University Press 2020).

Crisp, J, 'Mobilizing political will for refugee protection and solutions: A framework for analysis and action' (World Refugee Council Research Paper 1, 2018).

Connell, J and Coelho, S, 'Planned relocation in Asia and the Pacific' [2018] 59 Forced Migration Review, 46–49.

Dawson, LR, 'Labour Mobility and the WTO: The Limits of GATS Mode 4' [2012] 51 International Migration 1, 1–23.

De Wet, E, 'Invoking Obligations Erga Omnes in the Twenty-First Century: Progressive Developments Since Barcelone Traction' [2013] 37 SAYIL, 1–20.

De Wet, E, 'Jus Cogens and Obligations Erga Omnes' in Dinah Shelton (ed), *The Oxford Handbook on Human Rights* (Oxford University Press 2013).

Dema, B, 'Sea level Rise and the Freely Associated States: Addressing Environmental Migration under the Compacts of Free Association' [2012] 37 Columbia Journal of Environmental Law, 177–204.

Deng, F and Adeola, R, 'The Normative Influence of the UN Guiding Principles on the Kampala Convention in the Protection of Internally Displaced Persons in Africa' [2021] 65 Journal of African Law, 59–72.

Dominguez-Redondo, E, 'The Universal Periodic Review – Is There Life Beyond Naming and Shaming in Human Rights Implementation?' [2012] 4 New Zealand Law Review, 673–706.

Drake, WJ and Nicolaidis, K, 'Ideas, Interests and Institutionalisation: Trade in Services and the Uruguay Round' [1992] 46 International Organisation 1, 37–100.

Dreher, T and others, 'Climate Refugees or Migrants? Contesting Media Frames on Climate Justice in the Pacific' [2014] 9 Environmental Communication 1, 1–19.

Edelenbos, C, 'Committee on Migrant Workers and implementation of the ICRMW' in Ryszard Cholewinski, Paul de Guchteneire and Antoine Pécoud (UNESCO 2009) 100–122.

Edwards, A, 'Temporary Protection, Derogation and the 1951 Refugee Convention' [2012] 13 Melbourne Journal of International Law, 1–40.

El Hinnawi, E, 'Environmental Refugees' [1985] 2 UNEP, 1–41.

Elmadmad, K, 'Asylum in Islam and Modern Refugee Law' [2008] 27 Refugee Survey Quarterly 2, 51–63.

Faber, D and others, 'Give me Shelter from the Storm: Framing the Climate Refugee Crisis in the Context of Neoliberal Capitalism' [2017] 28 Capitalism Nature Socialism 3, 1–17.

Falstrom, DZ, 'Stemming the Flow of Environmental Displacement: Creating a Convention to Protect Persons and Preserve the Environment' [2001] 1 Colorado Journal of International Environmental Law and Policy, 1–19.

Farbotko, C and others, 'Relocation planning must address voluntary immobility' (Nature, 13 July 2020) <https://www.nature.com/articles/s41558-020-0829-6>.

Ferris, E and Weerasinghe, S, 'Promoting Human Security: Planned Relocation as a Protection Tool in a Time of Climate Change' [2020] 8 Journal on Migration and Human Security 2, 134–149.

Ferris, EE and Martin, SF, 'The Global Compacts on Refugees and for Safe, Orderly and Regular Migration: An Introduction to the Special Issue' [2019] 57 International Migration 6, 5–18.

Fisher, D, 'Legal Implementation of Human Rights Obligations to Prevent Displacement Due to Natural Disasters' [2010] 41 Studies in Transnational Legal Policy, 551–590.

Fornalé, E, 'A l'envers: Setting the Stage for a Protective Environment to Deal with "Climate Refugees"' [2020] 22 European Journal for Migration Law 4, 518–540.

Fornalé, E and Yildiz, A, 'GCM Indicators: Objective 2: Minimize the adverse drivers and structural factors that compel people to leave their country of origin' (Refugee Law Initiative, 8 August 2019).

Fornalé, E and Yildiz, A, 'GCM Indicators: Objective 18: Invest in skills development and facilitate mutual recognition of skills, qualifications and competences' (Refugee Law Initiative, 14 May 2019).

Fornalé, E, 'The Future Role of Labor Mobility Mechanisms in the Context of Environmental Degradation: Building or Crumbling Adaptation Strategies?' in Elisa Fornalé and Sophia Kagan, 'Climate Change and Human Mobility in the Pacific Region: Plans, Policies and Lessons Learned' (KNOMAD Working Paper 31, 2017).

Fornalé, E, 'Regional migration governance and social protection of migrant workers' in Oreste Foppiani, Oana Scarlatescu, Family, Separation, and Migration: An Evolution-Involution of the Global Refugee Crisis. Population, Family and Society (Peter Lang 2018) 107–120.

Fornalé, E, Guélat, J and Piguet, E, 'Framing Labour Mobility Options in Small Island States Affected by Environmental Changes' in Robert McLeman, Jeanette Schade, Thomas Faist (eds), *Environmental Migration and Social Inequality* (Springer 2015) 167–187.

Fornalé, E, Yildiz, A and Cristani, F, 'Objective 18: Invest in skills development and facilitate mutual recognition of skills, qualifications and competences' in Elspeth Guild and Tugba Basaran (eds), The UN's Global Compact for Safe, Orderly and Regular Migration [2018] Refugee Law Initiative, 51–52.

Fornalé, E, 'Floating Rights in Times of Environmental Challenges' in Cataldi and others (eds), *Migration and Fundamental Rights: The Way Forward* (Napoli: Editoriale Scientifica 2019).

Francioni, F, 'Public and Private in the International Protection of Global Cultural Goods' [2012] 23 European Journal of International Law 3, 719–730.

Francis, A, 'Free Movement Agreements & Climate-Induced Migration: A Caribbean Case Study' [2019] 1 Columbia Law School, 1–28.

Gardiner, SM, 'Climate Justice' in John S Dryzek, Richard B. Norgaard and David Schlosberg, *The Oxford Handbook of Climate Change and Society* (Oxford University Press 2011) 309–322.

Garlick, M and Inder, C, 'Protection of refugees and migrants in the era of the global compacts' [2021] 23 International Journal of Postcolonial Studies 2, 207–226.

Gammeltoft Hansen, T, 'The Normative Impact of the Global Compact on Safe, Orderly and Regular Migration' in Marion Panizzon, Elspeth Guild, Isobel Roele and Violeta Moreno-Lax (eds), *What is a Compact? Migrants' Rights and State Responsibilities Regarding the Design of the UN Global Compact for Safe, Orderly and Regular Migration* (Raoul Wallenberg Institute of Human Rights and Humanitarian Law 2017).

Geiger, M, 'Migration governance at the global level: Intergovernmental organizations and environmental change-induced migration' in Tim Krieger, Diana Panke and Michael Prepernig, *Environmental Conflicts, Migration and Governance* (Bristol University Press 2020).

Gemenne, F and Brücker, P, 'From the Guiding Principles on Internal Displacement to the Nansen Initiative: What the Governance of Environmental Migration Can Learn

From the Governance of Internal Displacement' [2015] 27 International Journal of Refugee Law 2, 245–263.

Gemenne, F and Blocher, J, 'How can migration support adaptation? Different options to test the migration-adaptation nexus' (IOM Working Paper Series No.1/2016) <https://publications.iom.int/system/files/pdf/working_paper_series_1.pdf>.

German Cooperation GIZ and PIK, 'Home Lands: Island and Archipelagic States' Policymaking for Human Mobility in the Context of Climate Change' (GIZ 2020).

Georgetown University, United Nations High Commissioner for Refugees (UNHCR) and International Organisation for Migration (IOM), 'A Toolbox: Planning Relocations to Protect People from Disasters and Environmental Change' (2017) <https://www.refworld.org/pdfid/596f15774.pdf>.

Ghosh, B, 'Managing Migration: Whither the Missing Regime? How Relevant is Trade Law to Such a Regime?' [2007] 101 American Society of International Law, 303–306.

Gilbert, G, 'The New Pact on Migration and Asylum and the Global Compact on Refugees and Solutions' in Serio Carrera and Andrew Geddes, *The EU Pact on Migration and Asylum in light of the United Nations Global Compact on Refugees* (EUI 2021).

Gilman, N, 'The New International Economic Order: A Reintroduction' [2015] 6 Humanity (Philadelphia, Pa.) 1.

Global Protection Cluster Working Group, 'Handbook for the Protection of Internally Displaced Persons' (31 March 2010).

Global Camp Coordination and Camp Management Cluster, 'The MEND Guide: Comprehensive Guide for Planning Mass Evacuations in Natural Disasters' (31 December 2014).

Global Protection Cluster Working Group, 'Handbook for the Protection of Internally Displaced Persons' (31 March 2010) <https://www.unhcr.org/protection/idps/4c2355229/handbook-protection-internally-displaced-persons.html?query=internally%20displaced%20persons>.

Global Protection Cluster, 'Protection in a Climate of Change: Strategic Framework 2020–2024' (2020) <https://www.globalprotectioncluster.org/wp-content/uploads/GPC-Strategic-Framework_digital_version-1.pdf>.

Global Protection Cluster, 'Consultation event report, Climate Preparedness and Community-based Protection' <https://www.globalprotectioncluster.org/wp-content/uploads/PHAP_Climate-preparedness-and-community-based-protection-Consultation-event-report-1.pdf>.

Global Protection Cluster, 'GP20 Plan of Action for Advancing Prevention, Protection and Solutions for Internally Displaced People' <https://www.globalprotectioncluster.org/_assets/files/unhcr-gp20-plan_of_action-a5-scren.pdf>.

Guild, E and Grant, S, 'Migration Governance in the UN: What is the Global Compact and What does it mean?' (2017) Queen Mary School of Law Legal Studies Research Paper No. 252/2017, 15.

Guild, E, 'The UN Global Compact for Safe, Orderly and Regular Migration: to what extent are human rights and sustainable development mutually compatible in the field of migration?' [2020] 16 International Journal of Law in Context 3, 239–252.

Gutmann, M and others, 'Two Population-Environment Regimes in the Great Plains of the United States, 1930–1990' [2006] 27 Population and Environment 2, 191–225.

Hathaway, J, 'Food Deprivation: A Basis for Refugee Status?' [2014] 81 Soc Res 327.

Hardin, G, 'The Tragedy of the Commons' [1968] 162 Science 3859.

Hasenau, M, 'Part I: The Genesis of the Convention: ILO Standards on Migrant Workers: The Fundamentals of the UN Convention and Their Genesis' [1991] 25 International Migration Review 4, 687–697.

Hayden, SS, 'The International Protection of Wild Life: An Examination of Treaties and Other Agreements for the Preservation of Birds and Mammals' (Columbia University Press 2020).

Hennebry, JL and Petrozziello, AJ, 'Closing the Gap? Gender and the Global Compacts for Migration and Refugees' [2019] 57 IOM 6, 115–138.

Helbling, M, 'Attitudes towards climate change migrants' [2020] 160 Climatic Change, 89–102.

Higgins, R, 'Aspects of the Case Concerning the Barcelona Traction, Light and Power Company, Ltd'. [1970] 11 Virginia Journal of International Law, 327–343.

Hilpold, P, 'Opening up a new chapter of law-making in international law: The Global Compacts on Migration and for Refugees of 2018' [2021] 26 European Law Journal 3-4, 226–244.

Hinck, J, 'The Republic of Palau and the United States: Self-Determination Becomes the Price of Free Association' [1990] 78 California Law Review, 915–972.

Hodgkinson, D and others, '"The Hour When The Ship Comes In": A Convention for Persons Displaced by Climate Change' [2010] 36 Monash University Law Review 1, 69–120.

Homer-Dixon, T, 'On the Threshold: Environmental Changes as Causes of Acute Conflict' [1991] 16 International Security 2, 76–116.

Horn, L, 'Globalisation, Sustainable Development and the Common Concern of Humankind' [2007] 7 Macquire Law Journal , 53–74.

Horn, L, 'The Common Concern of Humankind and Legal Protection of the Global Environment' (PhD thesis University of Sydney 2000).

Horn, L, 'The Implications of the Concept of Common Concern of a Humankind on a Human Right to a Healthy Environment' [2004] 1 Macquarie Journal of International and Comparative Environmental Law 2 , 233–257.

Høeg, E and Tulloch, CD, 'Sinking strangers: Media representations of climate refugees on the BBC and Al Jazeera' [2013] 43 Journal of Communication Inquiry 3, 225–248.

Hughes, S and Wilkinson, R, 'The Global Compact: Promoting Corporate Responsibility?' [2001] 10 Environmental Politics 1, 155–159.

Hugo, G and Bardsley, DK, 'Migration and Environmental Change in Asia' in Etienne Piguet and Frank Laczko, *People on the Move in a Changing Climate* (Springer 2014).

International Bar Association, 'Achieving Justice and Human Rights in an Era of Climate Disruption: Climate Change Justice and Human Rights Task Force Report' (IBA 2014).

International Labour Organisation, 'Global Estimates on International Migrant Workers – Results and Methodology' (ILO 2015).

International Labour Organisation, 'Multilateral framework on labour migration: Non-binding principles and guidelines for a rights-based approach to labour migration' (ILO 2008).

International Labour Organisation, 'Working on a warmer planet: The effect of heat stress on productivity and decent work' (ILO 2009).

Interagency Standing Committee, 'Guidance Note on Using the Cluster Approach to Strengthen Humanitarian Response' (24 November 2006).

Interagency Standing Committee, 'IASC Operational Guidelines on the Protection of Persons in Situations of Natural Disasters' (The Brookings – Bern Project on Internal Displacement, January 2011) <https://interagencystandingcommittee.org/system/files/legacy_files/Operational_guidelines_nd.pdf>.

Internal Displacement Monitoring Centre, 'Global Report on Internal Displacement 2021' (IDMC 2021).

Internal Displacement Monitoring Centre, 'No matter of choice: displacement in a changing climate' (Thematic Series, IDMC, 2018).

Internal Displacement Monitoring Centre, 'The Invisible Majority: The Displacement Continuum' (IDMC Thematic Series, November 2017) <https://www.internal-displacement.org/sites/default/files/inline-files/20171113-idmc-intro-cross-border-thematic-series_1.pdf> accessed 29 May 2021.

International Labour Organisation, "Decent work for sustainable development – the challenge of climate change' (Governing Body Working Party on the Social Dimension of Globalization, 2007).

International Labour Organisation, 'Working in a changing climate: The Green Initiative: Report of the Director General to the International Labour Conference', 106th Session (ILO, 2017).

International Labour Organisation, 'Guidelines for a Just Transition Towards Environmentally Sustainable Economies and Societies for All' (ILO, 2015).

International Labour Organisation, 'The Global Crisis: Causes, Responses and Challenges' (ILO, 2011).

International Law Association Committee on Baselines under the International Law of the Sea, Final Report (2012), Sofia Conference, 30, <http://ilareporter.org.au/wpcontent/uploads/2015/07/Source-1-Baselines-Final-Report-Sofia-2012.pdf>.

Intergovernmental Panel on Climate Change, 'Annex I: Glossary. Global Warming of 1.5°C. An IPCC Special Report on the impacts of global warming of 1.5°C above pre-industrial levels and related global greenhouse gas emission pathways, in the context of strengthening the global response to the threat of climate change, sustainable development, and efforts to eradicate poverty' (2018).

Intergovernmental Panel on Climate Change, 'Climate Change 2021: The Physical Science Basis. Contribution of Working Group I to the Report of the Intergovernmental Panel on Climate Change' (Cambridge University Press 2021).

Intergovernmental Panel on Climate Change, 'First Assessment Report' (WMO 1990).

Intergovernmental Panel on Climate Change, 'Policymakers' summary of the potential impacts of climate change. Report from Working Group II to IPCC' (1990) 20.

International Organisation for Migration, 'Global Compact for Migration' (IOM) <https://www.iom.int/global-compact-migration> accessed 8 April 2021.

International Organisation for Migration, 'International Dialogue on Migration 2017: Strengthening International Cooperation and Governance of Migration' (18–19 April 2017).

International Organisation for Migration, 'United Nations Launches Multi-Partner Trust Fund Office to Support Cooperation on Safe, Orderly and Regular Migration' (17 July 2019).

International Organisation for Migration and United Nations Convention on Combatting Desertification, 'Addressing the Land Degradation – Migration Nexus: the Role of the UNCCD' (1 August 2019).

Jacobson, J, 'Environmental Refugees: A Yardstick of Habitability' [1988] Worldwatch Paper No: 86.

Jacobsson, J, 'GATS Mode 4 and Labour Mobility: The Significance of Employment Market Access' in Marion Panizzon, Gottfried Zürcher and Elisa Fornalé (eds), *The Palgrave Handbook of International Labour Migration: Law and Policy Perspectives* (Palgrave 2015) 61–95.

Jacobsson, J, 'Liberalisation of Service Mobility in the EU's International Trade Agreements: As External as it Gets' [2013] 15 European Journal of Migration and Law 3, 245–261.

Jamero, ML, 'In-situ adaptation against climate change can enable relocation of impoverished small islands' [2019] 108 Marine Policy 103614, 1–28.

Johnston, P, Everard, M, Santillo, D and Robert, KH, 'Reclaiming the definition of sustainability' [2007] 14 Environmental Science and Pollution Research International 1, 60–66.

Johnson, PM, Mayrand, K and Paquin, M, 'The United Nations Convention to Combat Desertification in Global Sustainable Development Governance' in Pierre March Johnson, Karel Mayrand and Marc Paquin (eds), *Governing Global Desertification: Linking Environmental Degradation, Poverty and Participation* (Routledge 2016) 1–10.

Kainz, L and Betts, A, 'Power and Proliferation: Explaining the Fragmentation of Global Migration Governance' [2020] Migration Studies, 1–25.

Kagan, S, Byrne, M, and Leighton, M, 'Organizational Perspectives from the ILO', in Benoit Mayer and Francois Crépeau (eds), *Research Handbook on Climate Change, Migration and the Law* (Edward Elgar 2017).

Karatani, R, 'How history separated refugee and migrant regimes: In search of their institutional origins' [2005] 17 International Journal of Refugee Law 3, 517–541.

Kautoke-Holani, A, 'Labour Mobility in the PACER Plus' [2018] 5 Asia and the Pacific Policy Studies 1, 90–101.

Khan, F and Sackeyfio, C, 'Situating the Global Compact on Refugees in Africa: Will it make a difference to the lives of refugees "languishing in camps"?' [2021] 65 Journal of African Law, 35–57.

Keane, D, 'Environmental causes and consequences of migration: A search for the meaning of "environmental refugees"' [2004] 16 Georgetown Environmental Law Review, 209–223.

Keene, E, 'Resources for Relocation: In Search of a Coherent Federal Policy on Resettling Climate-Vulnerable Communities' [2018] 48 Texas Environmental Law Journal 1, 119–142.

Kell, G, '12 Years Later: Reflections on the Growth of the UN Global Compact' [2012] 52 Business and Society 1, 31–52.

Kell, G and Levin, D, 'The Global Compact Network: An historic experiment in learning and action' [2003] 108 Business and Society Review 2, 151–181.

Kempf, W, 'A sea of environmental refugees? Oceania in an age of climate change' in E. Hermann, K. Klenke and M. Dickhardt (eds), *Form, Macht, Differenz: Motive und Felder ethnologischen Forschens* (Göttingen: Göttingen University Press 2009).

Keohane, RO and Victor, DG, 'The Regime Complex for Climate Change' [2011] 9 Perspectives on Politics 1, 7–23.

Kirsch, S, 'Lost Worlds: Environmental Disaster, "Culture Loss, and the Law"' [2001] 42 Current Anthropology 2, 167–198.

Knox, J, 'Horizontal Human Rights Law' [2008] 102 American Journal of International Law 1, 1–47.

Knox, J, 'Linking Human Rights and Climate Change at the United Nations' [2009] 33 Harvard Environmental Law Review 2, 477–495.

Kolmannskog, V and Trebbi, L, 'Climate change, natural disasters and displacement: a multi-track approach to filling the protection gap' [2010] 92 ICRC 879, 713–730.

Kolmannskog, V, 'Climate Change, Environmental Displacement and International Law' [2012] 24 J Int Dev 1071.

Komai, M, 'Fiji's Foreign Policy and the New Pacific Diplomacy' in Greg Fry and Sandra Tarte, *The New Pacific Diplomacy* (Australian National University Press 2015) 111–124.

Kopf, A, Fink, M and Weber, E, 'Gender Vulnerability to Climate Change and Natural Hazards: The Case of Tropical Cyclone Winston, Fiji' in Sara N. Amin, Danielle Watson, and Christian Girard, *Mapping Security in the Pacific: A Focus on Context, Gender and Organisational Culture* (Routledge 2020).

Kälin, W, 'The Migration Compact on Migration: A Ray of Hope for Disaster-Displaced Persons' [2018] 30 IJRL 4, 664–667.

Kälin, W, 'The Guiding Principles on Internal Displacement as international minimum standard and protection tool' [2005] 24 Refugee Survey Quarterly 3, 27–36.

Kälin, W and Schrepfer, N, 'Protecting People Crossing Borders in the Context of Climate Change Normative Gaps and Possible Approaches' (UNHCR Legal Protection and Policy Research Series, 2012).

Kälin, W and McAdam, J, 'Environmental displacement' in Yann Aguila and Jorge E. Vinuales (eds), A Global Pact for Environment (C-EENRG 2019) 159–166.

Klabbers, J, 'What Role for International Organizations in the Promotion of Community Interests? Reflections on the Ideology of Functionalism' in Eyal Benvenisti, Georg Nolte and Keren Yalin-mor (eds), *Community Interests across International Law* (Oxford University Press 2018).

Koremenos, B, and Betz, T, 'The Design of Dispute Settlement Procedures in International Agreements' in Jeffrey L. Dunoff and Mark A Pollack, *Interdisciplinary Perspectives on International Law and International Relations* (Cambridge University Press 2013), 371–393.

Koser, K, 'Internally Displaced Persons' in Alexander Betts (ed), *Global Migration Governance* (Oxford University Press 2011).

Kott, S, 'ILO: Social Justice in a Global World? A History in Tension' [2019] 11 International Development Policy, 21–39.

Kowlowski, R, 'International Travel Security and the Global Compacts on Refugees and Migration' [2019] 57 IOM 6.

Krieger, H and Nolte, G, 'The International Rule of Law – Rise or Decline? – Approaching Current Foundational Challenges' in Heike Krieger, Georg Nolte and Andreas Zimmermann, *The International Rule of Law: Rise or Decline?* (Oxford Univeristy Press 2019).

Kritzman-Amir, T, 'Community Interests in Migration and Refugee Law' in Eyal Benvenisti, Georg Nolte and Keren Yalin-mor (eds), *Community Interests across International Law* (Oxford University Press 2018) 351.

Laczko, F and Piguet, E, 'Regional Perspectives on Migration, the Environment and Climate Change' in Etienne Piguet and Frank Laczko (eds), *People on the Move in a*

Changing Climate: Global Migration Issues (Global Migration Issues, Vol. 2, Springer 2014) 16.

Laird, S and Valdes, R, 'The Trade Policy Review Mechanism' in Martin Daunton, Amrita Narlikar and Robert M. Stern (eds), *The Oxford Handbook on the World Trade Organization* (Oxford University Press 2012).

Lauterpacht, E and Bethlehem, D, 'The Scope and Content of the Principle of Non-Refoulement' in Erika Feller, Volker Türk and Frances Nicholson (eds), *Refugee Protection in International Law: UNHCR's Global Consultations on International Protection* (CUP 2003) 252.

Lavenex, S, 'Regional migration governence – building block of global initiatives?' [2019] 45 Journal of Ethnic and Migration Studies 8, 1275–1293.

Lean, G, 'Disappearing World: Global Warming Claims Tropical Island' (Independent, 24 December 2006).

Leighton, M, 'Desertification and Migration' in in Pierre March Johnson, Karel Mayrand and Marc Paquin (eds), *Governing Global Desertification: Linking Environmental Degradation, Poverty and Participation* (Routledge 2016) 43–58.

Lesniewska, F and Siegele, L, 'The Talanoa Dialogue: A Crucible to Spur Ambitious Global Climate Action to Stay Within the 1.5°C Limit' [2018] 12 Carbon and Climate Law Review 1, 41–49.

Lewicka, M, 'Place attachment: How far have we come in the last 40 years?' [2011] 31:3 Journal of Environmental Psychology.

Liu, C, 'Disaster Displacement in Humanitarian and Development Contexts' in Veronica Fynn Bruey and Steven W. Bender, *Deadly Voyages: Migrant Journeys across the Globe* (The Rowman and Littlefield Publishing Group Inc 2020).

Limon, M, 'Human Rights and Climate Change: Constructing a Case for Political Action' [2009] 33 Harvard Environmental Law Review 2, 439–476.

Luetz, J and Hausia Havea, P, 'We're not Refugees, We'll Stay Here Until We Die! Climate Change Adaptation and Migration Experiences Gather From the Tulun and Nissan Atolls of Bougainville, Papua New Guinea' in Leal Filho (ed), *Climate Change Impacts and Adaptation Strategies for Coastal Communities: Climate Change Management* (Springer 2018).

Lyster, R, 'The idea of (Climate) Justice, neoliberalism and the Talanoa Dialogue' [2019] Journal of Human Rights and the Environment, 35–61.

MacNaughton, G and Frey, DF, 'Decent Work, Human Rights and the Sustainable Development Goals' [2016] 47 Georgetown Journal of International Law, 607–664.

Martin, P, 'Low-Skilled Labour Migration and Free Trade Agreements' in Marion Panizzon, Gottfried Zürcher and Elisa Fornalé (eds), *The Palgrave Handbook of International Labour Migration: Law and Policy Perspectives* (Palgrave 2015) 205–230.

Mawi, L, 'Fiji's Emerging Brand of Pacific Diplomacy: A Fiji government perspective' in Greg Fry and Sandra Tarte, The New Pacific Diplomacy (Australian National University Press 2015) 101–110.

Mayer, B, 'Migration in the UNFCCC workstream on loss and damage: an assessment of alternative framings and conceivable responses' [2017] 6 Transnational Environmental Law 1, 107–129.

Mayer, B, and Crépeau, F, 'Introduction' in Benoit Mayer and François Crépeau (eds), *Research Handbook on Climate Change, Migration and the Law* (Edward Elgar 2017).

Mazzeschi, RP, 'The Relationship Between Human Rights and the Rights of Aliens and Immigrants' in Ulrich Fastenrath and others (eds), *From Bilateralism to Community Interest: Essays in Honour of Bruno Simma* (Oxford University Press 2011).

McAdam, J and others, 'International Law and Sea-Level Rise: Forced Migration and Human Rights' (FNI Report 1/2016).

McAdam, J and Pryke, J, 'Policy Brief 10 - Climate Change, Disasters and Mobility: A Roadmap for Australian Action | Kaldor Centre' [2020] UNSW Kaldor Centre for International Refugee Law.

McAdam, J and Wood, T, 'The Concept of "International Protection" in the Global Compacts on Refugees and Migration' [2021] 23 International Journal of Postcolonial Studies 2, 191–206.

McAdam, J, 'Refusing "refugee" in the Pacific: (de)constructing climate-induced displacement in international law' in Etienne Piguet, Antoine Pecoud and Paul de Guchteneire (eds), *Migration and Climate Change* (Cambridge University Press and UNESCO Publishing 2011).

McAdam, J, 'Displacement in the Context of Climate Change and Disasters' in Cathryn Costello, Michelle Foster and Jane McAdam, *The Oxford Handbook of International Refugee Law* (Oxford University Press 2021).

McAdam, J, 'From the Nansen Initiative to the Platform on Disaster Displacement: Shaping International Approaches to Climate Change, Disasters and Displacement' [2016] 39 University of New South Wales Law Journal 4, 1518–1546.

McAdam, J, 'Historical Cross-Border Relocations in the Pacific: Lessons for Planned Relocations in the Context of Climate Change' [2014] 49 Journal of Pacific History, 301.

McAdam, J, 'Protecting People Displaced by the Impacts of Climate Change: The UN Human Rights Committee and the Principle of non-refoulement' [2020] 114 AJIL 718.

McAdam, J, 'Relocation and resettlement from colonisation to climate change: the perennial solution to danger zones' [2015] 3 London Review of International Law 1.

McAdam, J, 'Swimming Against the Tide: Why a Climate Change Displacement Treaty is Not the Answer' in Mary Crock (ed), *Refugees and Rights* (Routledge 2015).

McAdam, J, 'The Emerging New Zealand Jurisprudence on Climate Change, Disasters and Displacement' [2015] 3(1) Migration Studies 131.

McMichael, C, Farbotko, C and McNamara, KE, 'Climate-Migration Responses in the Pacific Region' in Cecilia Menjivar, Marie Ruiz, and Immanuel Ness (eds), *The Oxford Handbook of Migration Crises* (Oxford University Press 2019) 297–314.

McNamara, K and Des Comboes, HJ, 'Planning for Community Relocations Due to Climate Change in Fiji' [2015] 6 International Journal of Disaster Risk Science.

McLachlan, C, 'The Principle of Systemic Integration and Article 31(3)(c) of the Vienna Convention' [2005] 54 International and Comparative Law Quarterly 279.

Melanie, P, 'Planned Relocation from the Impacts of Climate Change in Small Island Developing States: the Intersection Between Adaptation and Loss and Damage' in Walter Leal Filho, *Managing Climate Change Adaptation in the Pacific Region* (Springer, 2020) 129–150.

Melde, S, Laczko, F and Gemenne, F (eds), 'Making mobility work for adaptation to environmental changes: Results from the MECLEP global research' (IOM 2017).

Melin, P, 'Two Years After the Adoption of the Global Compact for Migration: Some Thoughts on the Role Played by the EU' in Wybe Doume and others, *The Evolving Nature of EU External Relations Law* (TMC Asser Press 2021).

Mobjörk, M and others, 'Climate-related security risks: towards an integrated approach' (Stockholm International Peace Research Institute, Stockholm, 2016).

Montoute, A, Mohammed D, and Francis, J, 'Prospects and Challenges for Civil Society and Climate Change Engagement in the Caribbean: The Case of Trinidad and Tobago' 47 Caribbean Studies 2.

Morris, K, 'Navigating the Compact of Free Association: Three Decades of Supervised Self-Governance' [2019] 41 University of Hawaii Law Review 2, 388–440.

Mundaca, L and others, 'The global expansion of climate mitigation policy interventions, the Talanoa Dialogue and the role of behavioural insights' [2019] 1 Environmental Research Communications 6.

Munoz, SM, 'Environmental Mobility in a Polarized World: Questioning the Pertinence of the "Climate Refugee" Label for Pacific Islanders' [2021] Journal of International Migration and Integration.

Myers, N and Kent, J, 'Environmental Exodus: An Emergent Crisis in the Global Arena' [1995] Climate Institute.

Newman, B, 'Sunk Coast Fallacy: How Island Nations Should Approach Climate Diplomacy' (Council on Foreign Relations, 7 August 2019).

Newmark, RL, 'Non-Refoulement Run Afoul: The Questionable Legality of Extraterritorial Repatriation Programs' [1993] 71 Washington University Law Review 3.

Nillson, M and Kjellstrom, T, 'Climate change impacts on working people: how to develop prevention policies' [2010] 3 Global Health Action 3.

Nita, S, 'Free Movement of People within Regional Integration Processes: A Comparative View' in Sonja Nita and others, *Migration, Free Movement and Regional Integration*

(UNESCO Publishing and UNU Institute on Comparative Regional Integration Studies 2017).

Nolte, G, 'Treaties and Their Practice – Symptoms of Their Rise and Decline' (218) 329 Recueil des Cours de l'Académie de Droit International, 167.

Norman Forbes, B, 'AOSIS v The World: A Blueprint for the First International Multi-Party Climate Change Case' [2021] 8 Groningen Journal of International Law 2.

'Note from the UNEP Secretariat to the Meeting' in DJ Attard (ed), *The Meeting of the Group of Legal Experts to Examine the Concept of the Common Concern of Mankind in Relation to Global Environmental Issues* (Malta: University of Malta 1990).

Nzeyimana, V and Ahouga, Y, 'The Global Compact for Migration: One Year Later' (Foraus, 13 December 2019) <https://www.foraus.ch/posts/the-global-compact-for-migration-one-year-later/>.

Obergassel, W and others, 'The calm before the storm: an assessment of the 23rd Climate Change Conference (COP 23) in Bonn' [2018] 30 Environmental Law and Management, 104–113.

Odeyemi, C, 'UNFCCC's posture on displacement riskification: Conceptual suggestions' [2021] 10 Progress in Disaster Science.

OECD, World Bank and IOM, 'A Quick Guide to the GATS and Mode 4' (Geneva, Palais des nations, 12–14 November 2003) <https://www.iom.int/sites/default/files/jahia/webdav/site/myjahiasite/shared/shared/mainsite/microsites/IDM/workshops/Trade_2004_04051004/related%20docs/quick_guide.pdf>.

Oellers-Frahm, K, 'Third States and Sanctions in Public International Law' [1992] 30 Archiv des Völkerrechts 1.

Office of the High Commissioner for Human Rights and Inter-Parliamentary Union, 'Handbook for Parliamentarians' (OHCHR and Inter-Parliamentary Union 2016) 31–38.

Olsen, L and Kemter, D, 'The International Labour Organization and the Environment: The Way to a Socially Just Transition for Workers' in Nora Räthzel and David Uzzell (eds), *Trade Unions in the Green Economy* (Routledge 2013).

Oral, N, 'The International Law Commission and the Progressive Development and Codification of Principles of International Environmental Law' [2019] 13 FIU L. Rev. 1075.

Oral, N, 'International Law as an Adaptation Measure to Sea-level Rise and Its Impacts on Islands and Offshore Features' [2009] 34 The International Journal of Marine and Coastal Law 3.

O'Donnell, T, 'Vulnerability and the International Law Commission's Draft Articles on the Protection of Persons in the Event of Disasters' [2019] 68:3 ICLQ 573.

Özsu, U, 'Neoliberalism and the New International Economic Order: A History of "Contemporary Legal Thought"' in Justin Desautels-Stein and Christopher Tomlins, *Searching for Contemporary Legal Thought* (Cambridge Univeristy Press 2017).

Paine, J, 'International Adjudication as a Global Public Good?' (EJIL 2019).

Panizzon, M, Zürcher, G and Fornalé, E, 'Introduction: Conceptualising a Pluralist Framework for Labour Migration' in Marion Panizzon, Gottfried Zürcher and Elisa Fornalé (eds), *The Palgrave Handbook of International Labour Migration: Law and Policy Perspectives* (Palgrave 2015) 1–14.

Panizzon, M, 'A Ménage à Trois? GATS Mode 4, EPAs, and Bilateral Migration Agreements' [2010] 44 Journal of World Trade 6, 1207–1252.

Panizzon, M, 'The Global Migration Compact and the Limits of 'Package Deals' for Migration Law and Policy' in in Marion Panizzon, Elspeth Guild, Isobel Roele and Violeta Moreno-Lax (eds), *What is a Compact? Migrants' Rights and State Responsibilities Regarding the Design of the UN Global Compact for Safe, Orderly and Regular Migration* (Raoul Wallenberg Institute of Human Rights and Humanitarian Law 2017).

Parsons, L and Ostergaard Nielsen, J, 'The Subjective Climate Migrant: Climate Perceptions, Their Determinants, and Relationship to Migration in Cambodia' [2020] 111 Annals of the American Association of Geographers, 971–988.

Perry, RW and Lindell, MK, 'Principles for Managing Community Relocation as a Hazard Mitigation Measure' [1997] 5 Journal of Contingencies and Crisis Management 1, 49–59.

Pécoud, A, 'Narrating an ideal migration world? An analysis of the Global Compact for Safe, Orderly and Regular Migration' [2020] 42 Third World Quarterly 1.

Piggott-McKellar, AE and others, 'Moving People in a Changing Climate: Lessons from Two Case Studies in Fiji' [2019] 8 Social Sciences 5.

Pigrau, A, 'Reflections on the effectiveness of peremptory norms and erga omnesobligations before international tribunals, regarding the request for an advisory opinion from the International Court of Justice on the Chagos Islands' [2018] QIL Zoom-out 55, 131–146.

Piguet, E, "From Primitive Migration" to "Climate Refugees": The Curious Fate of the Natural Environment in Migration Studies' [2012] 103 Annals of the Association of American Geographers 1.

Piguet, E, 'Linking climate change, environmental degradation, and migration: a methodological overview' [2010] WIREs Climate Change, 517–524.

Podesta, J, 'The Climate crisis, Migration and Refugees' (Report Brooklings, 25 July 2019) <https://www.brookings.edu/research/the-climate-crisis-migration-and-refugees/>.

Powers, A and Stucko, C, 'Introducing the Law of the Sea and the Legal Implications of Rising Sea Levels' in Michael B. Gerrard and Gregory E. Wannier, *Threatened Island Nations: Legal Implications of Rising Seas and a Changing Climate* (Cambrigde University Press 2013).

Rush, N, 'Avoiding the quicksand of the Global Compact on Refugees' [2018] Center for Immigration Studies.

Randall Lesaffer, 'Peace Treaties and the Formation of International Law' in Bardo Fassbender and Anne Peters (eds), *The Oxford Handbook of the History of International Law* (Oxford University Press 2012) 71–94.

Ranganathan, S, 'Ocean Floor Grab: International Law and the Making of an Extractive Imaginary' in Symposium: International Law and Economic Exploitation In The Global Commons [2019] 30 EJIL 2, 573–600.

Rantanen, J, Muchiri, F, and Lehtinen, S, 'Decent Work, ILO's Response to the Globalization of Working Life: Basic Concepts and Global Implementation with Special Reference to Occupational Health' [2020] International Journal of Environmental Research and Public Health.

Ravenstein, EG, 'The Laws of Migration' [1889] 52 Journal of the Royal Statistical Society 2.

Rechkemmer, A, 'Societal Impacts of Desertification: Migration and Environmental Refugees?' in Hans Günter Brauch and others (eds), *Facing Global Environmental Change* (Springer 2009) 151–158.

Regan, KH, 'The Case for Enhancing Climate Change Negotiations with a Labor Rights Perspective' [2010] 35 Columbia Journal of Environmental Law 249.

Rigaud, K and others, 'Groundswell: Preparing for Internal Climate Migration' (World Bank 2018) <https://www.worldbank.org/en/news/infographic/2018/03/19/groundswell---preparing-for-internal-climate-migration>.

Roele, I, 'What are the Forms of UN International Agreements/Understandings and What is Their Legal Effect?' in Marion Panizzon, Elspeth Guild, Isobel Roele and Violeta Moreno-Lax (eds), *What is a Compact? Migrants' Rights and State Responsibilities Regarding the Design of the UN Global Compact for Safe, Orderly and Regular Migration* (Raoul Wallenberg Institute of Human Rights and Humanitarian Law 2017).

Ronneberg, E, 'Small Islands and the Big Issue: Climate Change and the Role of the Alliance of Small Island States' in Cinnamon Pinon Carlarne, Kevin R. Gray and Richard Tarasofsky (eds), *The Oxford Handbook of International Climate Change Law* (Oxford University Press 2016) 761–790.

Rosenstock, R, 'The ILC and State Responsibility Symposium: The ILC's Responsibility Articles' [2002] 96 American Journal of International Law 4.

Rrecaj, BT 'Case Notes: Legal Consequences of The Separation of the Chagos Archipelago from Mauritius in 1965' 35 Utrecht Journal of International and European Law 1, 50–55.

Salvati, L, 'Economic Causes and Consequences of Desertification' [2021] Oxford Research Encyclopedia of Environmental Science.

Schade, J, 'Climate Change and Planned Relocation: Risks and a Proposal for Safeguards' in Thomas Faist and Jeanette Schade (eds), *Disentangling Migration and Climate Change: Methodologies, Political Discourses and Human Rights* (Netherlands, Springer 2013).

Scheffran, J, Marmer, E and Sow, P, 'Migration as a contribution to resilience and innovation in climate adaptation: Social networks and co-development in Northwest Africa' [2012] 33 Applied Geography 119.

Scheffran, J, Marmer, E and Sow, P, 'Migration as a contribution to resilience and innovation in climate adaptation: Social networks and co-development in Northwest Africa' [2012] 33 Applied Geography 119.

Schlosberg, D and Collins, LB, 'From Environmental to Climate Justice: Climate Change and the Discourse of Environmental Justice' [2014] 5 WIREs Climate Change 3.

Schlütter, B, 'Aspects of Human Rights Interpretation by the UN Treaty Bodies' in Helen Keller and Geir Ulfstein, UN Human Rights Treaty Bodies: Law and Legitimacy (Cambridge University Press 2012).

Scholtz, W, 'Human Rights and Climate Change: Extending the Extraterritorial Dimension via the Common Concern' in Wolfgang Benedek and others (eds), The Common Interest in International Law (Intersentia 2014) 134–135.

Schwan, S and Yu, X, 'Social Protection as a Strategy to Adress Climate-induced Migration' [2017] 10 International Journal of Climate Change Strategies and Management 1.

Scovazzi, T, 'The Seabed beyond the Limits of National Jurisdiction: General and Institutional Aspects' (Report submitted to the Fourth J. W. H. Verzijl Memorial Symposium 'The legal regime of areas beyond national jurisdiction: current principles and frameworks and future direction', Utrecht, 21 November 2008).

Sealey-Huggins, L, '1.5°C to stay alive': climate change, imperialism and justice for the Caribbean' [2017] 38 Third World Quarterly 11, 2444–2463.

Secretariat of the Pacific Regional Environment Programme, 'Atoll nations make a collective stand for their right to remain in their islands in the face of climate change' (12 December 2019) <https://reliefweb.int/report/kiribati/atoll-nations-make-collective-stand-their-right-remain-their-islands-face-climate>.

Shuster, DR, 'The Republic of Palau and its Compacts, 1995–2009' [2009] 44 The Journal of Pacific History 3, 325–332.

Sicakkan, HG, 'A Comparative Research Framework for Studying the Global Refugee Compact's Impact on International Protection' (University of Bergen 2021).

Silva, V, 'The ILO and the future of work: The politics of global labour policy' [2021] Global Social Policy.

Simperingham, E, 'State responsibility to prevent climate displacement: The importance of housing, land and property rights' in Dimitra Manou and others, *Climate*

Change, Migration and Human Rights: Law and Policy Perspectives (Routledge 2017) 86–98.

Smith, R and McNamara, KE, 'Future migrations from Tuvalu and Kiribati: exploring government, civil society and donor perceptions' [2015] 7 Climate and Development 1, 47–59.

Smith, R, 'Should they stay or should they go? A discourse analysis of factors influencing relocation decisions among the outer islands of Tuvalu and Kiribati' [2013] 1 Journal of New Zealand and Pacific Studies 1, 23–39.

Solomon, MK, 'Berne Initiative' [2013] The Encyclopaedia of Global Human Migration.

Soltau, F, 'Common Concern of Humankind' in Cinnamon Pinon Carlarne, Kevin R. Gray, Richard Tarasofsky (eds), *The Oxford Handbook on International Climate Change Law* (Oxford University Press 2016).

Soons, A, 'The Effects of a Rising Sea Level on Maritime Limits and Boundaries' [1990] 37 Netherlands International LR 207.

Steiner, A, 'Foreword' in UNEP, Columbia University Sabin Center for Climate Change Law, 'Climate Change and Human Rights' (2015) <https://wedocs.unep.org/bitstream/handle/20.500.11822/9934/Climate-Change-Human-Rights.pdf?sequence=1&isAllowed=y>.

Steinfatt, K, 'Trade Policies for a circular economy: What can we learn from WTO experience?' (WTO Staff Working Paper, 2020).

Storlazzi, C and others, 'Most atolls will be uninhabitable by the mid-21st century because of sea-level rise exacerbating wave-driven flooding' [2018] 4 Science Advances 4.

Stremitzer, A, 'Erga Omnes Norms and the Enforcement of International Law' [2009] 165 Journal of Institutional and Theoretical Economics 1, 29–34.

Sudmeier-Rieux, K and others, 'Introduction: Exploring Linkages Between Disaster Risk Reduction, Climate Change Adaptation, Migration and Sustainable Development' in Karen Sudmeier-Rieux and Others (eds), *Identifying Emerging Issues in Disaster Risk Reduction, Migration, Climate Change and Sustainable Development* (Springer 2017).

Suhrke, A, and Vinsentin, A, 'The Environmental Refugee: A New Approach' [1991].

Swain, A, 'Environmental Migration and Conflict Dynamics: Focus on Developing Regions' [1996] 17 Third World Quarterly 5.

Tams, CJ and Asteriti, A, 'Erga Omnes, Jus Cogens and Their Impact on the Law of State Responsibility' in Malcolm D. Evans and Panos Koutrakos (eds), *The International Responsibility of the European Union* (Cambridge University Press 2013).

Tams, CJ, Tzanakopoulos, A and Zimmermann, A, 'Introduction' in Christian J. Tams, Antonios Tzanakopoulos and Andreas Zimmermann (eds), *Research Handbook on the Law of Treaties* (Edgar Elgar 2014).

Tanaka, Y, 'Legal Consequences of Obligations Erga Omnes in International Law' [2021] Netherlands International Law Review.

Task Force on Displacement, 'Report of the Task Force on Displacement' (17 September 2018) <https://unfccc.int/sites/default/files/resource/2018_TFD_report_17_Sep.pdf>.

Thew, H, Middlemiss, L and Paavola, J, 'Does youth participation increase the democratic legitimacy of UNFCCC-orchestrated global climate change governance?' [2021] Environmental Politics.

Thomas, A, 'The International Labour Organization: Its Origins, Development and Future' [1921] 1 International Labour Review.

Tladi, D, 'The International Law Commission's Draft Articles on the Protection of Persons in the Event of Disasters: Codification, Progressive Development or Creation of Law from Thin Air?' [2017] 16:3 Chinese Journal of International Law 425.

Tronquet, C, 'From Vunidogoloa to Kenani: An Insight into Successful Relocation' [2015] The State of Environmental Migration Review.

Türk, V and Garlick, M, 'From Burdens and Responsibilities to Opportunities: The Comprehensive Refugee Response Framework and a Global Compact on Refugees' [2016] 28 IRJL 4.

Toscano, J, 'Climate Change Displacement and Forced Migration: An International Crisis' [2015] 6 Arizona Journal of Environmental Law and Policy 1, 460–487.

Türk, V, 'Prospects for Responsibility Sharing in the Refugee Context' [2018] Journal on Migration and Human Security.

Türk, V and Nicholson, F, 'Refugee Protection in International Law: An Overall Perspective' in Erika Feller, Volker Türk and Frances Nicholson, Refugee Protection in International Law (Cambridge University Press 2003).

UK Government Office for Science, 'Foresight: Migration and Global Environmental Change' (2011) Final Project Report, London.

UK Climate Change and Migration Coalition, 'Climate Outreach and Information Network. Migration as Adaptation: exploring mobility as a coping strategy for climate change' <http://climatemigration.org.uk/wp-content/uploads/2014/02/migration_adaptation_climate.pdf>.

Underhill-Sem, Y and Marsters, E, 'Labour Mobility in the Pacific: A Systematic Literature Review of Development Impacts' [2017] New Zealand Institute for Pacific Research.

Underwood, RA, 'The amended U.S. Compacts of Free Association with the Federates States of Micronesia and the Republic of the Marshall Islands: less free, more compact' (East-West Center Working Papers, September 2003).

United Nations Chief Executive Boards Coordination, 'United Nations System Strategic Approach on Climate Change Action' <https://unsceb.org/united-nations-system-strategic-approach-climate-change-action>.

United Nations Economic and Social Commission for Asia and the Pacific (UNESCAP) and International Labour Organisation, 'Climate Change and Migration Issues in the Pacific' (ILO 2014); ILO, 'The employment impact of climate change adaptation: Input Document for the G20 Climate Sustainability Working Group' (ILO 2018).

United Nations Environment Programme, Columbia University Sabin Center for Climate Change Law, 'Climate Change and Human Rights' (2015) <https://wedocs.unep.org/bitstream/handle/20.500.11822/9934/Climate-Change-Human-Rights.pdf?sequence=1&isAllowed=y>.

United Nations Framework Convention on Climate Change Warsaw International Mechanism Task Force on Displacement and International Organisation for Migration, 'Mapping Human Mobility and Climate Change in Relevant National Policies and Institutional Frameworks' (Activity I.1, 2018).

United Nations Framework Convention on Climate Change, 'Report of the Executive Committee of the Warsaw International Mechanism for Loss and Damage associated with Climate Change Impacts' Decision -/CP.24 <https://unfccc.int/sites/default/files/resource/cp24_auv_ec%20wim.pdf>.

United Nations Framework Convention on Climate Change, 'Plan of Action' <https://unfccc.int/process-and-meetings/bodies/constituted-bodies/executive-committee-of-the-warsaw-international-mechanism-for-loss-and-damage-wim-excom/task-force-on-displacem ent/documents#eq-2>.

United Nations Framework Convention on Climate Change, 'Integrating human rights at the UNFCCC' <https://www.ohchr.org/EN/Issues/HRAndClimateChange/Pages/UNFCCC.aspx>.

United Nations Framework Convention on Climate Change, 'Report of the Executive Committee of the Warsaw International Mechanism for Loss and Damage associated with Climate Change Impacts' Decision -/CP.24 <https://unfccc.int/sites/default/files/resource/cp24_auv_ec%20wim.pdf>.

United Nations Framework Convention on Climate Change, 'Task Force on Displacement Plan of Action 2019–2021' <https://unfccc.int/sites/default/files/resource/TFD%20PoA%202nd%20phase.pdf>.

United Nations High Commissioner for Refugees Antonio Guterres, 'Migration, Displacement and Planned Relocation' (31 December 2012) <https://www.unhcr.org/news/editorial/2012/12/55535d6a9/migration-displacement-planned-relocation.html?query=2050>.

United Nations High Commisioner for Refugees, 'Climate change and disaster displacement' <https://www.unhcr.org/climate-change-and-disasters.html>.

United Nations High Commisioner for Refugees, 'A Special Report: Ending Statelessness Within 10 Years' <https://www.unhcr.org/protection/statelessness/546217229/special-report-ending-statelessness-10-years.html>.

United Nations High Commisioner for Refugees, 'The Global Compact on Refugees' (UNHCR) <https://www.unhcr.org/the-global-compact-on-refugees.html>.

United Nations Office for the Coordination of Humanitarian Affairs (UNOCHA), Fiji: Building resilience in the face of climate change, Geneva, UNOCHA, 2014 <https://www.unocha.org/story/fiji-building-resilience-face-climate-change>.

United Nations Office of the High Representative for the Least Developed Countries, Landlocked Developing States and Small Island Developing States (UN-OHRLLS), About SIDS-UN-OHRLLS, Geneva, UN-OHRLLS, 2019 <http://unohrlls.org/about-sids/>.

United Nations Global Compact, '2020 Annual Management Report' (2020) <https://ungc-communications-assets.s3.amazonaws.com/docs/publications/2020-Annual-Management-Report.pdf>.

United Nations Global Compact, '2017 United Nations Global Compact Progress Report: Business Solutions to Sustainable Development' (2017) <https://d306pr3pise04h.cloudfront.net/docs/publications%2FUN+Impact+Brochure_Concept-FINAL.pdf>.

United Nations Global Compact, 'Activity Report 2015' (2014) <https://d306pr3pise04h.cloudfront.net/docs/publications%2FUNGC_2015_Activity_Report.pdf>.

United Nations, 'Climate Change and Migration Issues in the Pacific' (2014) <https://www.unescap.org/sites/default/files/Climate-Change-and-Migration-Issues-in-the-Pacific.pdf>.

United Nations International Children's Emergency Fund (UNICEF) United Kingdom, 'No Place to Call Home: Protecting Children's Rights When the Changing Climate Forces Them to Flee' (UNICEF United Kingdom 2017).

United Nations University Institute for Environment and Human Security, 'Factsheet: Climate Change and migration in the Pacific: Links, attitudes and future scenarios in Nauru, Tuvalu and Kiribati' <http://i.unu.edu/media/ehs.unu.edu/news/11747/RZ_Pacific_EHS_ESCAP_151201.pdf>.

Van Daele, J, 'The International Labour Organization in Past and Present Research' [2008] 53 International Review of Social History 3.

Vandenhole, W, 'Obligations and responsibility in a plural and diverse duty-bearer human rights regime' in Wouter Vandenhole (ed), *Challenging Territoriality in Human Rights Law* (Routledge 2015).

Vermeer-Künzli, A, 'As If: The Legal Fiction in Diplomatic Protection' [2007] 18 European Journal of International Law 1.

Vidas, D, Freestone, D and McAdam, J, 'International Law and Sea Level Rise: The New ILA Committee' [2019] Brill Research Perspectives in International Law.

Vidas, D, 'Sea-level Rise and International Law: At the Convergence of Two Epochs' [2014] 4 Climate Law 1, 70–84.

Villalpado, S, 'The Legal Dimension of the International Community: How Community Interests are Protected in International Law' [2010] 21 European Journal of International Law 2, 387–419.

Voigt, C and Xiang, G, 'Accountability in the Paris Agreement: The Interplay Between Transparency and Compliance' [2020] 1 Nordic Environmental Law Journal, 31–57.

Voigt, C, 'Delineating the Common Interest in International Law' in Wolfgang Benedek and others (eds), The Common Interest in International Law (Intersentia 2014) 19.

Voigt-Graf, C and Kagan, S, 'Migration and labour mobility from Kiribati' (Australian National University, Development Policy Centre Discussion Paper 56, Marc 2017).

Walenta, J, 'Climate risk assessments and science-based targets: A review of emerging private sector climate action tools' [2019] 11 WIREs Climate Change 2.

Ward, N, 'Facilitating temporary movement' in Rahel Kunz, Sandra Lavenex and Marion Panizzon, *Multilayered Migration Governance: The Promise of Partnership* (Routledge 2012).

Warner, K, 'Global environmental change and migration: Governance challenges' [2010] 20 Global Environmental Change 3.

Warner, K, 'Human Migration and Displacement in the Context of Adaptation to Climate Change: the Cancun Adaptation Framework and Potential for Future Action' [2012] 30 Government and Policy 6, 1066.

Watson, SD and Robinson, C, 'Knowledge Controversies of Global Migration Governance: Understanding the Controversy Surrounding the Global Compact' in Catherine Dauvergne (ed), *Research Handbook on the Law and Politics of Migration* (Edgar Elgar 2021) 323–339.

Webb, J, 'Law, Ethics and Complexity: Complexity Theory & the Normative Reconstruction of Law' [2005] 52 Cleveland State Law Review 227.

Weber, E, 'Envisioning South-South relations in the fields of environmental change and migration in the Pacific Islands – past, present and futures' [2015] 2 Bandung: Journal of the Global South 6.

Weerasinghe, S, 'In Harm's Way: International protection in the context of nexus dynamics between conflict or violence and disaster or climate change' (UNHCR 2018) <https://www.unhcr.org/5c1ba88d4.pdf> accessed 11 November 2020.

Weil, P, 'Towards Relative Normativity in International Law?' [1983] American Journal of International Law 77.

Weiss, EB, 'The Coming Water Crisis: A Common Concern of Humankind' [2012] 1 Transnational Environmental Law 1, 153–168.

Westing, A, 'The Environmental Component of Comprehensive Security' (Sage 1989).

Wewerinke-Singh, M and Van Geelen, T, 'Protection of Climate Displaced Persons under International Law: A Case Study from Mataso Island, Vanuatu' [2018] 19 Melbourne Journal of International Law 1, 18.

Wickramasekara, P, 'Globalisation, International Labour Migration and Rights of Migrant Workers' [2009] 29 Third World Quarterly 7, 1247–1264.

Williams, OF, 'UN Global Compact: The Challenge and the Promise' [2004] 14 Business Ethics Quarterly 4, 755–774.

Wilkinson, E and others, 'Climate-induced migration and displacement: closing the policy gap' (ODI 2016).

Wilmsen, B and Webber, M, 'What can we learn from the practice of development-force displacement and resettlement for organised resettlements in response to climate change?' [2015] 58 Geoforum 1, 76–85.

Winters, LA, 'The Temporary Movement of Workers to Provide Services' in Aaditya Mattoo and Antonia Carzaniga (eds), *Moving People to Deliver Services* (The World Bank/Oxford University Press 2003) 480–540.

Wolfrum, R, 'Identifying Community Interests in International Law: Common Spaces and Beyond' in Eyal Benvenisti, Georg Nolte and Keren Yalin-mor (eds), *Community Interests across International Law* (Oxford University Press 2018).

World Bank Group, 'Pacific Possible. Long-term Economic Opportunities and Challenges for Pacific Island Countries' (2017) <https://documents1.worldbank.org/curated/en/168951503668157320/pdf/ACS22308-PUBLIC-P154324-ADD-SERIES-PPFullReportFINALscreen.pdf>.

World Commission on Environment and Development, 'Our Common Future' (1987).

Wouters, J and Verhoeven, S, 'The Prohibition of Genocide as a Norm of Ius Cogens and Its Implications for the Enforcement of the Law of Genocide' [2005] 5 International Criminal Law Review 3, 401–416.

Wouters, C, 'International Refugee and Human Rights Law: Partners in Ensuring International Protection and Asylum' in Scott Sheeran and Nigel Rodley (eds), *Routledge Handbook of International Human Rights Law* (Routledge 2013) 231–243.

Yamaguchi, S, 'International Trade and Circular Economy – Policy Alignment' (OECD Trade and Environment Working Papers 2021/02).

Yusuf, A, 'The UN Convention on Biological Diversity' in Najeeb Al-Nauimi and Richard Meese (eds) *International Legal Issues Arising under the United Nations Decade of International Law: Proceedings of the Qatar International Law Conference* (Springer Netherland 1994) 1171.

Zaidi, KR, 'Harmonizing Trade Liberalization and Migration Policy through Shared Responsibility: A Comparison of the Impact of Bilateral Trade Agreements and the GATS in Germany and Canada' [2010] 37 Syracuse Journal of International Law 267.

Zemanek, K, 'New Trends in the Enforcement of Erga Omnes Obligations' [2000] Max Planck Yearbook of United Nations Law.

Zickgraf, C, 'Climate change, slow onset events and human mobility: reviewing the evidence' [2021] 50 Current Opinion in Environmental Sustainability, 21–30.

Zickgraf, C, 'Keeping people in place: political factors of (im)mobility and climate change' [2019] 8 Social Sciences 8.

All Other Websites Cited in this Monograph (All Online Materials Last Accessed 6 April 2022)

An Open Letter by Global Civil Society and Indigenous Peoples for the Establishment of a new UN Special Rapporteur on Human Rights and Climate Change, To the States Members and Observers of the United Nations Human Rights Council' (2021) <https://franciscansinternational.org/fileadmin/media/2021/UN_Sessions/HRC47/Open_Letter_SRCC_HRC47.pdf>.

Besson, S, 'The Erga Omnes Effect of Judgments of the European Court of Human Rights: What's in a Name?' (La Cour européenne des droits de l'homme après le Protocole 14, 2011) <https://hal.archives-ouvertes.fr/hal-02557350/document>.

Bruno, K and Karliner, J, 'Tangled up in blue' (Corpwatch, 1 September 2000) <https://corpwatch.org/article/tangled-blue>.

Cecilia Jimenez-Damary, 'Open letter from the Special Rapporteur on the Human Rights of Internally Displaced Persons on the inclusion of IDPs in the Global Compact on Safe, Regular and Orderly Migration, in line with the New York Declaration on Refugees and Migrants' (UN Human Rights Special Procedures, 12 March 2018) <OpenLetterInclusion12March2018.pdf (ohchr.org)>.

Cerulus, L and Schaart, E, 'How the UN migration pact got trolled' (Politico, 3 January 2019) <politico.eu/article/united-nations-migration-pact-how-got-trolled/>.

Climate Action Pacific Partnership, 'Background to the Climate Action Pacific Partnership' (2017) <https://cop23.com.fj/wp-content/uploads/2019/03/CAPP_III_CAPP_backgroud.pdf>.

'Climate Change Recognized as "Threat Multiplier", UN Security Council Debates Its Impacts on Peace', UN News (25 January 2019) <https://news.un.org/en/story/2019/01/1031322>.

Climate Vulnerable Forum, 'Climate Change and Human Rights' (Joint Statement, 46th Session of the Human Rights Council, 09 March 2021) <https://thecvf.org/our-voice/statements/chair/46th-hrc-session-joint-statement-on-climate-change-and-human-rights/>.

'Coal Addiction "Must Be Overcome" to Ease Climate Change, UN Chief Says in Bangkok' (UN News, 2 November 2019).

Currie, K, 'Explanation of vote in a meeting of the third committee on a UNHCR omnibus resolution' (US Mission to the United Nations, 13 November 2018) <https://usun.usmission.gov/explanation-of-vote-in-a-meeting-of-the-third-committee-on-a-unhcr-omnibus-resolution/>.

Curtain, R and Howes, S, 'Governance of the Seasonal Worker Programme in Australia and sending countries' (Development Policy Centre, 8 December 2020) <https://apo.org.au/sites/default/files/resource-files/2020-12/apo-nid309985.pdf>.

Curtain, R, 'Is PLMAM fit for purpose?' (Development Policy Blog, 21 October 2019) <https://devpolicy.org/is-plmam-fit-for-purpose-20191021>.

Delval, E, 'From the UN Human Rights Committee to European Courts: Which protection for climate-induced displaced persons under European Law?' (EU Migration and Asylum Law and Policy Blog, 8 April 2020) <https://eumigrationlawblog.eu/from-the-u-n-human-rights-committee-to-european-courts-which-protection-for-climate-induced-displaced-persons-under-european-law/>.

Dickerson, H, 'Minimum standards' (Max Planck Encyclopedia 2010) <https://opil.ouplaw.com/view/10.1093/law:epil/9780199231690/law-9780199231690-e845?prd=EPIL>.

Eggett, C and Thin, S, 'Clarification and Conflation: Obligations Erga Omnes in the Chagos Opinion' (EJIL: Talk!, 2009) <https://www.ejiltalk.org/clarification-and-conflation-obligations-erga-omnes-in-the-chagos-opinion/>.

Eggett, C and Thin, S, 'Clarification and Conflation: Obligations Erga Omnes in the Chagos Opinion' (EJIL:Talk! 2019) <https://www.ejiltalk.org/clarification-and-conflation-obligations-erga-omnes-in-the-chagos-opinion/>.

Espinoza, MV, Hadj-Abdou, L and Brumat, L, 'Global Compact for Migration_ what is it and why are countries opposing it?' (The Conversation, 7 December 2018) <https://theconversation.com/global-compact-for-migration-what-is-it-and-why-are-countries-opposing-it-106654>.

Feichtner, I, 'Community Interest' (Max Planck Encyclopedia 2007) <https://opil.ouplaw.com/view/10.1093/law:epil/9780199231690/law-9780199231690-e1677?prd=EPIL>.

Fitzmaurice, M, 'Treaties' (Max Planck Encyclopedia 2010) <https://opil.ouplaw.com/view/10.1093/law:epil/9780199231690/law-9780199231690-e1481?prd=EPIL>.

Grant, H, Randerson, J and Vidal, J, 'UK Should Open Borders to Climate Refugees, Says Bangladeshi Minister' (The Guardian, 4 December 2009) <http://www.guardian.co.uk/environment/ 2009/nov/30/rich-west-climate-change/print>.

Gupta, S, 'Pacific swallowing remote island Chain' (CNN, 2007) <CNN.http://edition.cnn.com/CNN/Programs/anderson.cooper.360/blog/2007/07/pacific-swallowing-remote-island-chain.html.Accessed May 15, 2017>.

International Institute for Sustainable Development, 'CCD COP-7 Highlights' (Earth Negotiations Bulletin, Vol 4 No 183, 25 October 2005) <https://enb.iisd.org/fr/node/5682>.

International Labour Organisation, 'Ratifications of CO97 – Migration for Employment Convention (Revised), 1949 <https://www.ilo.org/dyn/normlex/en/f?p=NORMLEXPUB:11300:0::NO::P11300_INSTRUMENT_ID:312242>.

International Labour Organisation, 'Ratifications of C143 – Migrant Workers (Supplementary Provisions) Convention' <https://www.ilo.org/dyn/normlex/en/f?p=NORMLEXPUB:11300:0::NO:11300:P11300_INSTRUMENT_ID:312288:NO>.

International Union for Conservation of Nature, 'ESIL Annual Conference: International Law, Global Public Goods, Global Commons and Fundamental Values' official webpage (11 September 2017) <https://www.iucn.org/news/world-commission-environmental-law/201709/esil-annual-conference-international-law-global-public-goods-global-commons-and-fundamental-values>.

Ionesco, D, 'Let's Talk About Climate Migrants, Not Climate Refugees' (UN Sustainable Development Goals Blog 2019) <https://www.un.org/sustainabledevelopment/blog/2019/06/lets-talk-about-climate-migrants-not-climate-refugees/> accessed 27 May 2021.

Kagan, S, 'Making the case for preferential access to labour markets for Kiribati and Tuvalu migrants' (Development Policy Blog, 20 January 2015) <https://devpolicy.org/making-the-case-for-preferential-access-to-labour-markets-for-kiribati-and-tuvalu-migrants-20140120/>.

Kugalmann, D, 'Refugees' (Max Planck Encyclopedia 2010) <https://opil.ouplaw.com/view/10.1093/law:epil/9780199231690/law-9780199231690-e866>.

Narsey, W, 'PICTA, PACER and EPAs: weaknesses in Pacific island countries' trade policies' (Pacific Economic Bulletin, 19 (3), 2004, Asia Pacific Press) <https://openresearch-repository.anu.edu.au/bitstream/1885/157729/1/193_picta.pdf>.

Nishimura, L, 'Climate change and international refugee law: A predicament approach' (RefLax, 19 October 2018) <https://reflaw.org/climate-change-and-international-refugee-law/>.

Robinson, NA, 'Environmental Law: Is an Obligation Erga Omnes Emerging?' (IUCN 2018) <https://www.iucn.org/sites/dev/files/content/documents/2018/environmental_law_is_an_obligation_erga_omnes_emerging_interamcthradvisoryopinion-june2018.pdf>.

Saphore, S, 'Why Canada needs to think about accepting climate change refugees' (CBC, 21 May 2021) <https://www.cbc.ca/news/science/what-on-earth-trees-climate-refugees-1.6034396> accessed 22 May 2021.

Schachter, CB and Mingrone, F, 'A UN Special Rapporteur on Human Rights & Climate Change? Regional Perspectives' (Centre for International Environmental Law, January 2021) <https://www.ciel.org/wp-content/uploads/2021/02/UNSR-Report_English_2-5.pdf>.

Stickles, N and Jiang, H, 'Haitian migrants, homeless from Hurricane Dorian, could now be deported from the Bahamas' (Business Insider, 21 October 2019) <https://www.businessinsider.com/haitian-hurricane-dorian-evacuees-pushed-out-of-bahamas-2019-10?r=US&IR=T>.

Swiss Federal Council (Press Release, 3 February 2021) <https://www.admin.ch/gov/en/start/documentation/media-releases/media-releases-federal-council.msg-id-82217.html>.

United Nations Committee on Economic, Social and Cultural Rights, 'General Comment No 24' (10 August 2017) UN Doc E/C.12/GC/24.

United Nations Commission on Human Rights, 'Migrants in Vulnerable Situations: UNHCR's Perspective' (UNHCR 2017) <https://www.refworld.org/docid/596787174.html>.

United Nations Commission on Human Rights, 'The legal implications of disappearance of States and otherterritories for environmental reasons, including the implications for the human rights of their residents, with particular reference to the rights of indigenous peoples' (Report on the 61st session, 14 March–22 April 2005) E/CN.4/DEC/2005/112.

United Nations Disaster Risk Reduction, 'Disaster' (UNDRR 2022) <https://www.undrr.org/terminology/disaster>.

United Nations High Commissioner for Refugees, 'Legal Considerations on Refugee Protection for People Fleeing Conflict and Famine Affected Countries' (UNHCR 2017).

United Nations High Commissioner for Refugees, 'Legal considerations regarding claims for international protection made in the context of the adverse effects of climate change and disasters' (1 October 2020) <https://www.refworld.org/pdfid/5f75f2734.pdf>.

United Nations High Commissioner for Refugees Executive Committee, 'Report of the Working Group on Solutions and Protection to the Forty-second Session of the Executive Committee of the High Commissioner's Programme' (12 August 1991) UN Doc EC/SCP/64.

United Nations High Commissioner for Refugees, 'New York Declaration FAQs' (UNHCR, February 2018) <https://www.unhcr.org/584689257>.

United Nations Office of the High Representative for the Least Developed Countries, Landlocked Developing Countries and Small Island Developing States (OHRLLS), 'SIDS Accelarated Modalities of Action Pathway' <http://prdrse4all.spc.int/sites/default/files/samoa-pathway.pdf>.

United Nations Secretary-General, 'Secretary-General's remarks on Climate Change [as delivered]' (UN News 10 September 2018) <https://www.un.org/sg/en/content/sg/statement/2018-09-10/secretary-generals-remarks-climate-change-delivered>.

United Nations, 'Consultation in Asia concludes with recommendations on disaster displacement for UN High-Level Panel' (19 November 2020) <https://www.un.org/internal-displacement-panel/content/consultation-asia-concludes-recommendations-disaster-displacement-un-high-level-panel>.

United Nations, 'General Assembly Endorses First-Ever Global Compact on Migration, Urging Cooperation among Member States in Protecting Migrants' (UN News, 19 December 2018) <https://www.un.org/press/en/2018/ga12113.doc.htm> accessed 2 August 2021.

United Nations, 'Terms of Reference: High-Level Panel on Internal Displacement' <https://www.un.org/internal-displacement-panel/sites/www.un.org.internal-displacement-panel/files/tor_of_the_panel.pdf>.

United Nations, 'Pacific governments call for urgent action on disaster displacement in light of the climate crisis' (11 February 2011).

United Nations, 'UN affirms "historic" global compact to support world's refugees' (UN News 17 December 2018) <https://news.un.org/en/story/2018/12/1028791>.

United Nations, 'UN Secretary-General's Statement announcing the establishment of a High-Level Panel on Internal Displacement' (23 October 2019, New York) <https://www.un.org/internal-displacement-panel/news/23-october-2019-secretary-generals-statement-announcing-establishment-high-level-panel-internal>.

US Mission to the UN, 'National Statement of the United States of America on the Adoption of the Global Compact on Safe, Orderly and Regular Migration' (7 December 2018) <https://usun.usmission.gov/national-statement-of-the-united-states-of-america-on-the-adoption-of-the-global-compact-for-safe-orderly-and-regular-migration/>.

Voigt-Graf, C, 'Melanesians on the Move' (Development Policy Centre, 2 February 2015) <http://devpolicy.org/wp-content/uploads/wp-post-to-pdf-enhanced-cache/1/melanesians-on-the-move-20150202.pdf>.

Wolfrum, R, 'Common Heritage of Mankind' (Max Planck Encyclopedia 2009) <https://opil.ouplaw.com/view/10.1093/law:epil/9780199231690/law-9780199231690-e1149>.

Wolfrum, R, 'International Law of Cooperation' (Max Planck Encyclopedia 2010) <https://opil.ouplaw.com/view/10.1093/law:epil/9780199231690/law-9780199231690-e1427?prd=EPIL>.

World Bank, 'Services, value added (% of GDP)' <https://data.worldbank.org/indicator/NV.SRV.TOTL.ZS>.

World Bank, 'Trade in services (% of GDP) – European Union' <https://data.worldbank.org/indicator/BG.GSR.NFSV.GD.ZS?locations=EU>.

World Trade Organisation, 'Farewell speech of Appellate Body Member Peter van den Bossche' (28 May 2019) <https://www.wto.org/english/tratop_e/dispu_e/farwellspeech_peter_van_den_bossche_e. htm>.

Yardley, W, 'Alaskan Town Seeks Lifeline amid Climate Change', The New York Times (2007) <https://www.nytimes.com/2007/05/27/world/americas/27iht-27alaska.5880856.html>.

Index

www.ingramcontent.com/pod-product-compliance
Lightning Source LLC
Chambersburg PA
CBHW071324230926
51849CB00002B/307
* 9 7 8 9 0 0 4 5 2 2 2 6 8 *